Haila Manteghi is a lecturer at the University of Münster and recently completed her second PhD, on the Persian Alexandrian tradition, at the University of Exeter. Her first PhD, on the *Shāhnāma* of Firdawsī, was completed at the University of Alicante, and she has published in peer-reviewed journals and edited collections.

'Though Alexander's conquest of Persia and assumption of the Persian throne is a historical fact, the transmission of his legendary story from the Greek original, via the fifth-century CE Syriac translation, to Persian literature has until now eluded explanation. Haila Manteghi's masterly exploration of the question shows for the first time what had been suspected but never demonstrated, that Pahlavi oral tradition played an important part in the centuries between the end of the Achaemenid Empire and the beginning of the epic tradition with Firdawsī: echoes of the Parthian Khudāynāmag can be found in Arabic and Persian writers even before Firdawsī. The question of the existence (or not) of a full Pahlavi translation of the Syriac is treated authoritatively.'

Richard Stoneman,
University of Exeter

'*Alexander the Great in the Persian Tradition* will no doubt remain for decades the key work on the *Alexander Romance*'s influence on later Persian literature and poetry.'

Leonard Lewisohn,
Senior Lecturer in Persian, Institute of Arab and Islamic Studies, University of Exeter

'A wonderful piece of scholarship which contributes to the discussion of Helleno-Iranica, in both history and literature.'

Touraj Daryaee,
Maseeh Chair in Persian Studies and Culture and Director of the Dr Samuel M. Jordan Center for Persian Studies and Culture, University of California, Irvine

ALEXANDER THE GREAT IN THE PERSIAN TRADITION

History, Myth and Legend in Medieval Iran

Haila Manteghi

I.B. TAURIS
LONDON · NEW YORK

Published in 2018 by
I.B.Tauris & Co. Ltd
London • New York
www.ibtauris.com

Library of Medieval Studies 8

ISBN: 978 1 78831 030 7
eISBN: 978 1 78672 366 6
ePDF: 978 1 78673 366 5

A full CIP record for this book is available from the British Library
A full CIP record is available from the Library of Congress

Library of Congress Catalog Card Number: available

Typeset in Garamond Three by OKS Prepress Services, Chennai, India
Printed and bound by CPI Group (UK) Ltd, Croydon, CR0 4YY

FSC www.fsc.org
MIX
Paper from responsible sources
FSC® C013604

To Richard Stoneman, the raison d'être of this book

CONTENTS

List of Tables ix
List of Plates x
Foreword xii
Acknowledgements xiv

Introduction 1
A Review of Key Secondary Sources on the *Alexander Romance* 5

1. Greek and Syriac Versions of the *Alexander Romance* and their Development in the East 10
The Greek Background 10
Syriac Sources Relevant to this Study 13
The Development of the *Alexander Romance* in the East 17

2. Alexander the Great and the Legacy of Sasanian Historiography 21
Introduction 21
Arabic Sources and Historical Tradition in Pre-Islamic Iran 24
The *Khudāynāmag*: Content and Sources 25
Alexander the Great in the *Khudāynāmag* 41
Conclusion: The Origin and Development of the *Alexander Romance* in the Arabo-Persian Tradition 43

3. **Alexander the Great in the *Shāhnāma* of Firdawsī** 46
Sources and Content of the *Shāhnāma* 47
Summary of the *Alexander Romance* in the *Shāhnāma* 48
Distinguishing Characteristics and Motifs of Firdawsī's *Alexander Romance* 52
Syriac Materials in the *Shāhnāma* 62
Conclusion: Firdawsī's Sources and his Portrayal of Alexander 70

4. **Alexander in the *Iskandarnāma* of Niẓāmī Ganjavī (1141–1209)** 71
Literary and Historical Contexts of Alexander's Personality in Niẓāmī's *Sharafnāma* 72
Alexander's Birth and Early Years in Niẓāmī's *Sharafnāma* 90
Of Banquets and Battles (*bazm u razm*): Alexander as a Warrior 95
The Further Adventures of Alexander: Journeys to China, Russia, India and the Land of Darkness 111
Conclusion 125

5. **Alexander in the *Iqbālnāma* of Niẓāmī Ganjavī** 128
Introduction 128
Alexander in Wisdom Literature 131
Alexander in the Dhū'l-Qarnayn Tradition 137
Mirabilia: Alexander and the Marvels of the World 141
Conclusion 154

Conclusion 158
The Genesis of the Persian *Alexander Romance* 159
The *Shāhnāma* of Firdawsī 164
The *Iskandarnāma* of Niẓāmī Ganjavī 165

Appendix Summary of the Syriac Alexander Romance 167
Notes 175
Bibliography 232
Index 251

LIST OF TABLES

Table 1.1 Variants of motifs in later versions of the *Alexander Romance* 12

Table 2.1 Motifs of the *Alexander Romance* in Arabic and Persian Sources 39

Table 4.1 Sixteen Motifs of the *Alexander Romance* found both in Firdawsī's *Shāhnāma* and Niẓāmī's *Sharafnāma* 89

LIST OF PLATES

Plate 1 Alexander the Great Mourns the Dying Darius. By Muḥammad Mīrak ibn Mīr Muḥammad al-Ḥusaynī al-Ustādī, most probably in Herat in 1028/1618–19. Illustration from Firdawsī's *Book of Kings* (*Shāhnāma*). Courtesy of the Walters Museum Collection, Ms. W.602, folio 423 verso.

Plate 2 Alexander and his Men Watch Naked Girls Swim in the Black Sea. By Muḥammad Mūsā al-Mudhahhib in Safavid Iran in 924/1518. Illustration of the *Iskandar-nāma* from a *Khamsa* (Quintet) by Niẓāmī. Courtesy of the Walters Museum Collection, Ms. W.606, folio 354 verso.

Plate 3 Battle of Alexander the Great with the Ethiopians. By Yādkār the Calligrapher (al-Kātib) in 935/1529, Iran. Illustration of the *Iskandar-nāma* from a *Khamsa* (Quintet) by Niẓāmī. Courtesy of the Walters Museum Collection, Ms. W.607, folio 193 verso.

Plate 4 Alexander the Great Admires his Portrait Commissioned by Queen Nūshāba. Copied by Yādkār the Calligrapher (al-Kātib) in 935/1529, Iran. Illustration of the *Iskandar-nāma* from a *Khamsa* (Quintet) by Niẓāmī. Courtesy of the Walters Museum Collection, Ms. W.607, folio 223 verso.

Plate 5 Alexander the Great at the Fountain of Life with the Prophets Khiḍr and Ilyās (Elias). Copied by Yādkār the Calligrapher (al-Kātib) in 935/1529, Iran. Illustration of the *Iskandar-nāma* from a *Khamsa*

(Quintet) by Niẓāmī. Courtesy of the Walters Museum Collection, Ms. W.607, folio 258 verso.

Plate 6 The Talking Tree. Illustration from *Ajā'ib al-'ālam* (Marvels of the World) by Zakariyā' al-Qazwīnī, copied in Herat in 1022/1613 in the library of the governor of Khurāsān, Ḥusayn Khān Shāmlū-yi Bīklirbīkī (Beglerbegi). Courtesy of the Walters Museum Collection, Ms. W.652, folio 137 verso.

Plate 7 Birth of Alexander the Great. Anonymous, executed in Safavid Iran, dated to the middle of the tenth century AH/sixteenth century CE. Illustration of the *Iskandar-nāma* from a *Khamsa* (Quintet) by Niẓāmī. Courtesy of the Walters Museum Collection, Ms. W.610, folio 249 recto.

Plate 8 Invention of the Mirror in the Presence of Alexander the Great. By the royal scribe 'Abd al-Raḥīm 'Ambarīn Qalam in the fortieth year of Akbar's reign (1004/1595), probably in Lahore. Illustration of the *Iskandar-nāma* from a *Khamsa* (Quintet) by Niẓāmī. Courtesy of the Walters Museum Collection, Ms. W.613, folio 16 verso.

Plate 9 The Invention of the Mirror. By the royal scribe 'Abd al-Raḥīm 'Ambarīn Qalam in the fortieth year of Akbar's reign (*circa* 1004/1595), probably in Lahore. Illustration of the *Iskandar-nāma* from a *Khamsa* (Quintet) by Niẓāmī. Courtesy of the Walters Museum Collection, Ms. W.613. folio 17 recto.

Plate 10 Kay Khusraw Crosses Lake Zarah in Pursuit of Afrāsiyāb. By Muḥammad Mīrak ibn Mīr Muḥammad al-Ḥusaynī al-Ustādī, most probably in Herat in 1028/1618–19. Illustration from Firdawsī's *Book of Kings (Shāhnāma)*. Courtesy of the Walters Museum Collection, Ms. W.602, folio 319 recto.

Plate 11 Alexander and the Seven Philosophers. Anon., executed in Safavid Iran and dated to the middle of the tenth century AH / sixteenth CE. Illustration of the *Iskandar-nāma* from a *Khamsa* (Quintet) by Niẓāmī. Courtesy of the Walters Museum Collection, Ms. W.610, fol. 345 recto.

FOREWORD

The conquests of Alexander the Great (356–323 BC) changed the political shape of the world from the Mediterranean to the Himalayas. Every people with whom he came into contact turned him into a figure of legend: he had explored the ends of the earth, the oceans and the heavens, had fought with monstrous beasts, giants and pygmies, had left an enduring legacy of wise sayings, and – being a pupil of the great philosopher Aristotle – had even written treatises on astrology and magic. These legends were told in a variety of narrative texts, all of which trace their beginnings to one Greek book, which began to be assembled in Egypt within two generations of the conqueror's death: the *Alexander Romance* of Pseudo-Callisthenes.

Apart from its penetration of every language of medieval Europe, the *Alexander Romance* has its widest and deepest impact in the Persian language and in the Persianate world of medieval Central Asia. The earliest surviving texts are the *Shāhnāma* of Firdawsī and the *Dārābnāma* of Abū Ṭāhir Tarsūsī, but Alexander's story became the sole subject of works such as Niẓāmī's *Iskandarnāma*, Jāmī's *Khiradnāma-yi Iskandarī*, the *Mirror of Alexander* of Amīr Khusraw of Delhi (1253–1325) and the *Wall of Alexander* of the Chagatay poet Alī-Shīr Navā'ī (Alisher Navoi), now the national poet of Uzbekistan (1441–1501). He is also a point of reference in the classical lyric poetry of Persia, of Ḥāfiẓ and others.

Though Alexander's conquest of Persia and assumption of the Persian throne is a historical fact, the transmission of his legendary story from the Greek original, via the fifth century AD Syriac translation, to Persian literature has until now eluded explanation. Haila Manteghi's masterly exploration of the question shows for the first time what has been suspected but never demonstrated: that Pahlavi oral tradition played an important part in the centuries between the end of the Achaemenid Empire and the beginning of the epic tradition with Firdawsī – echoes of the Parthian *Khudāynāmag* can be found in Arabic and Persian writers even before Firdawsī. The question of the existence (or not) of a full Pahlavi translation of the Syriac is treated authoritatively.

In addition, Alexander was a significant figure in Arabic literature following his appearance in Sura 18 of the Qur'ān; his multifarious appearances in Arabic, especially in wisdom literature, also had an impact on Persian writing. Manteghi explores Alexander's importance for this wisdom literature and the *mirabilia* tradition. In addition, she provides a subtle analysis of the portrayal of the hero in the two great epic poems of Firdawsī and Niẓāmī, raising along the way such intriguing questions as whether Niẓāmī knew Greek.

This is by no means the end of the story, and the reverberations of the conqueror and prophet, sage and Sufi explorer and philosopher, continue through later Persian literature and constitute a major subject in medieval Persian painting. There is more to be said on all these matters, but all future research and criticism will build on what Dr Manteghi has demonstrated about the beginnings of the Persian Alexander.

Professor Richard Stoneman
University of Exeter

ACKNOWLEDGEMENTS

Firstly, I would like to express my sincere gratitude to Professor Lynette Mitchell and Dr Leonard Lewisohn for their continuous support, patience, motivation and insightful comments on this book, which encouraged me to widen the scope of my research from various perspectives. I am especially indebted to Dr Lewisohn for the fine translation of verses that I have used in the study.

My greatest debt belongs to Professor Richard Stoneman, who is the main reason and the fount of inspiration for this study. He encouraged me to apply for doctoral study at the University of Exeter and supported my application. He kindly read the complete draft of this study and gave me invaluable comments and timely encouragement.

I would like to thank Professor Dr Norbert Hintersteiner at the University of Münster (Germany), where I currently work, for giving me the opportunity of being part of his academic team and allowing me the time to make the final touches to this book.

Last but not least, I would like to thank my family for supporting me all these years. Their guidance and comments have illuminated my path during this time. I owe them all so much that there are no words to thank them enough. Without them, I would not have reached where I am.

INTRODUCTION

حدیث آن که سکندر کجا رسید و چه کرد
ز بس شـــنیدن گـشته است خلق را از بر

The *dicta* and *exempla* of Alexander,
The tale of his exploits and of where he went
Have so much been heard by men wide and far,
His story now is known to all by heart.

Farrukhī Sīstānī (eleventh century)[1]

Although many of the great works of Greek literature remained unknown to the Muslims, some forms of Greek literature persisted and re-emerged in Arabic (and Persian) guise.[2] One of the most influential works of the literature of late Greek antiquity, the *Alexander Romance*, attributed to the so-called Pseudo-Callisthenes, had a deep impact on the Persian world. This impact is mainly attested by popular romances, epic literature, heroic cycles and historical sources of the Islamic era. As indicated by the verses quoted above from the Persian court poet Farrukhī Sīstānī,[3] by the eleventh century AD Alexander's story was so famous that it was known intimately and recited from memory. To give an example of the popularity of Alexander's story in the Persian tradition, it is worth mentioning that in Khāqānī's twelfth-century *Dīvān*s and Farrukhī's and 'Unṣurī's eleventh-century *Dīvān*s alone, Alexander and his deeds are mentioned more than 30 times.[4]

Alexander as a literary figure is one of the most popular figures in Persian literature, and many books are dedicated to his stories. Unfortunately, all known versions of the legend of this great Greek hero were written down in the Islamic period in Arabic or Persian, as a result of which most are highly Islamised. However, it is still possible to detect and trace some of the pre-Islamic Persian stories about Alexander in these sources.

Because of the lack of pre-Islamic Persian sources, it is difficult to tell the extent to which these versions of the *Alexander Romance* actually reflect pre-Islamic traditions and history, or articulate later Islamic hagiographical biases. Almost all extant Pahlavi texts represent Alexander as a cursed figure who set fire to the holy scriptures of the Persians, razed their fire temples and generally destroyed the entire country; they thus view him as one of the greatest enemies of historical Iran. This negative vision further complicates the study of the Alexander legend in the classical Persian tradition. However, it should be recalled that the Persian kings dominated a vast territory that was home to many different ethnic and religious groups, each with their own languages and traditions, so this negative vision of Alexander in the Pahlavi sources, which primarily reflects the Zoroastrian tradition, is not always uniform. The heroic and historical traditions, which mainly present Alexander as a Persian king or hero, are reflected in later Arabic and Persian sources.

While the Greek and Latin literatures of the Roman Empire – the Persians' main rival – were substantially preserved by later generations according to their own peculiar historical circumstances, Persian literature of the same period is almost completely lost. Middle Persian was displaced by Arabic after the Arab conquest, and for the next two centuries Arabic superseded written Iranian languages almost entirely. However, despite the lack of pre-Islamic literature in Middle Persian, some scholars have proven that a number of Greek books were first translated into Middle Persian during the Sasanian period and then translated from Middle Persian into Arabic during the early 'Abbāsid period (from the second half of the eighth century AD to the early ninth century AD).[5] Nearly all of the original Middle Persian versions have been lost along with most of that language's literature, but some survive in Arabic translation or in New Persian. Their survival in Arabic is, in fact, the only reason we know of the Middle Persian stage. In our search for texts in Middle Persian, these

Arabic texts suffice to prove that some form of Middle Persian literature on Alexander existed.

Within this framework, the Persian Alexander tradition is an important but little-discussed component of the Persian literary tradition. Although the Alexander literature in Persian is part of a very widespread Arabic tradition, the latter itself belongs to a tradition developed in the Middle East and Central Asia, and consists of several branches. A great number of these branches are based on Syriac and Middle Persian sources. Therefore, the content of these different Arabic and Persian sources lies at a crossroads of two areas of investigation: that of the Syriac sources and that of Middle Persian literature, reflected in Arabic and Persian literature. The Syriac traditions on Alexander the Great played a fundamental role in the development of his legend in the Islamic world. For this reason, this book focuses on Syriac sources as well as the better-known Arabic and Persian texts.

Almost all Arabic and Persian sources that mention Alexander are based on the Pseudo-Callisthenes tradition. The first chapter of this book investigates the different hypotheses that have been proposed to explain the historical origins and different versions of the Pseudo-Callisthenes in Greek. The chapter also endeavours to set out the development of the *Alexander Romance* in Syriac sources to investigate which elements, from the various areas within the Alexander literary corpus, were influential in the Persian tradition.

Chapter 2 deals with Arabic historical sources that are supposed to be influenced by the *Khudāynāmag* (*Book of Sovereigns*) tradition. It explores evidence on the pre-Islamic Persian *Alexander Romance* and on traditions that point to the transmission of the work into Middle Persian, thus showing different hypotheses regarding the development of the *Alexander Romance* in the East. It is vital to establish each component part of this *Alexander Romance* that historians incorporated into their universal histories from the *Khudāynāmag* or from other Persian legends concerning Alexander the Great. There is no doubt that among the Arabic Alexander traditions there was an important Persian line of transmission of the seventh-century text, which was in circulation in territories that had belonged to the Sasanians before the Arab conquest. This book rebuilds the components of this Persian line of transmission by highlighting the similarities shared by the *Romance* with various Arabic histories – written by historians who were generally Iranian in origin or lived in eastern Iran, especially in Khurāsān – and juxtaposing these with accounts found in the Persian *Shāhnāma* of Firdawsī (from the tenth to eleventh centuries). All these sources treated the story of Alexander as a part of 'Persian history', an issue that is thoroughly explored in the second and third chapters. In this process, the story of Alexander in the *Shāhnāma* is a very important clue because it represents certain characteristics that have not survived in any other source, as we will see in the third chapter. Therefore, the *Shāhnāma*, as a representative of the *Khudāynāmag* tradition, will shed light on the development of the *Romance* in the pre-Islamic Persian tradition.

Chapters 4 and 5 are dedicated to the study of the first and second parts of the twelfth-century *Iskandarnāma* (*Book of Alexander*) of Niẓāmī Ganjavī, the *Sharafnāma* (*Book of Honour*) and the *Iqbālnāma* (*Book of Fortune*) respectively. In the *Iskandarnāma*, Niẓāmī compiled a large number of stories on Alexander from the Sasanian period. The poet of Ganja had already shown his knowledge of Sasanian literature in two other works: the *Khusraw u Shīrīn* (*Khusraw and Shīrīn*) and the *Haft Paykar* (*The Seven Beauties*), which deal with the adventures of two Sasanian kings, Khusraw II (r. 590–628) and Bahrām V Gōr (r. 420–38). The *Iskandarnāma* is thus a valuable work in the pre-Islamic Persian tradition on Alexander. Since there is almost no comprehensible translation of the *Iskandarnāma* in English, these chapters are inevitably descriptive. However, they are important because this is almost the first time that the *Iskandarnāma* has been studied deeply and in comparison with the Greek *Alexander Romance* in the English language. This study of the *Iskandarnāma* shows the great variety of fields and genres in which the *Alexander Romance* influenced the Persian tradition (*mirabilia*, wisdom literature and especially the 'mirror for princes' genre).

This book compares Greek, Syriac and Arabic sources with Persian sources in an attempt to establish the transmission line of the *Alexander Romance* from its earliest origins in Alexandria in the third century BC to its appearance in the Persian world in the tenth century AD (that is, in the *Shāhnāma* of Firdawsī). Apart from tracing the development of the *Alexander Romance* in the Persian tradition, this book reveals the *Romance*'s influence upon various genres of classical Persian literature (historiography, epic, romance and mirror for princes), in both verse and prose.

Various studies have been dedicated to delineating the different varieties of the *Alexander Romance* in Persian literature, but this book is novel in several ways. Firstly, it shows that the negative perspective on Alexander in the pre-Islamic Persian tradition was just one of many views. Secondly, it demonstrates that the *Alexander Romance* was included in the *Khudāynāmag*, and that this is why Arabic historical accounts (such as Ṭabarī and Dīnawarī) and Firdawsī represented Alexander in the Kayānid's cycle. Thirdly, this book makes use of the latest material in Persian (published over the past three decades) in terms of critical editions of historical texts, scholarly monographs, encyclopaedia articles and recent academic research published in various journals in Iran and the West. Most previous studies of the legend and romance of Alexander were undertaken at a time when critical editions of many of the Persian sources studied here were still unavailable, existing only in manuscript form and so largely unknown to scholars. The main sources used in this book are the *Shāhnāma* of Firdawsī, the *Sharafnāma* and the *Iqbālnāma* of Niẓāmī, and the *Dārābnāma* of Ṭarsūsī. All these books have been compared with the Greek *Alexander Romance*, as well as with important Syriac and Arabic sources.

A Review of Key Secondary Sources on the *Alexander Romance*

One of the most interesting aspects of the Persian sources on Alexander the Great is their particular 'Iranian' standpoint, which seems to reflect the view of a conquered people remembering their conqueror.[6] Most of the Persian sources were composed retrospectively many centuries later, and written down in the Islamic period. It is thus quite interesting to observe how, even after more than a thousand years, the memory of Alexander as a hero, conqueror and founder of a dynasty stubbornly persisted, being continuously retold and recast in the popular oral tradition, in historical chronicles and in literary accounts, both in prose and verse. The variety of Persian legends and stories about Alexander is proof of the great impact he had upon Persian culture. To understand this peculiar 'Iranian' image of Alexander found in Persian sources, it will first of all be helpful to provide an overview of the important recent scholarly research on the Persian versions of the *Alexander Romance*.

Recent studies on the Persian Alexander legends are almost as numerous as the various versions of the *Alexander Romance* (*Iskandarnāma*) themselves. The pioneer of studies of Persian accounts of the *Alexander Romance* in Iran was the late Īraj Afshār (d. 2013), who edited and published the anonymous *Iskandarnāma-yi manthūr* (*The Book of Alexander in Prose*),[7] which probably dates from the fifth/thirteenth century AD.[8] In the introduction to his edition of this text, Afshār explains the development of the *Alexander Romance* based on Nöldeke's theory of its transmission.[9] Minoo Southgate's translation of Afshār's edition of the *Iskandarnāma* constitutes one of the first studies of Persian sources on Alexander in English.[10] Southgate's work on the *Romance* also concentrates on the Iranian Islamic image of Alexander in the Persian tradition, providing a detailed analysis of the content, language and historical framework of this Persian *Alexander Romance*, briefly and succinctly comparing the portrayals of Alexander featured in various Persian accounts.[11]

Another Iranian scholar of similar calibre and importance to Afshār is the great literary historian Dhabīḥu'llāh Ṣafā, who edited the *Dārābnāma* of Abū Ṭāhir Ṭarsūsī (or Ṭarṭūsī). In his introduction to this text, Ṣafā briefly compares the content of Ṭarsūsī's *Dārābnāma* with the account of Dārā and Alexander given by Firdawsī in the *Shāhnāma* and, like Afshār, details the development of the *Romance* in the East based on Nöldeke's theory.[12] Ṣafā belongs to the camp of Iranian scholars who reject the possibility of the existence of any positive image of Alexander in pre-Islamic Persia, an opinion that he expresses in various works.[13] Ṣafā strongly advocates the view that Firdawsī's version of the *Alexander Romance* was not included in the Sasanian *Khudāynāmag* and was an independent work, incorporated into the *Shāhnāma* from an Arabic source; this is indeed the view of the majority of Iranian scholars.[14]

In the study of the development of the *Alexander Romance* in Persian tradition, the *Dārābnāma* of Ṭarsūsī occupies a very important place insofar as it preserves archaic, semi-mythological Iranian legends about Alexander that we cannot find in other sources because of the later Islamisation of Alexander's image. Furthermore, the text sheds valuable light on the process of reconstruction and the reception history of the Alexander legend in Persia.

The first scholar to detect these 'Iranian' characteristics in the *Dārābnāma* was William Hanaway. In his 1970 thesis on pre-Safavid romances, he contributed further to the study of this twelfth-century Persian prose romance.[15] In particular he included the *Dārābnāma* in a comparative study of five pre-Safavid prose romances, all of which he termed 'popular'. Concerning the *Dārābnāma*, this comparison mainly involved motifs relating to the Persianisation of Alexander in Persian literature. Hanaway's thesis was the first serious contribution towards the formulation of a basic knowledge of the contents of the *Dārābnāma*. He observed elsewhere that there was a relationship between Alexander and the goddess Anāhītā in the work.[16]

Three decades later, Marina Gaillard translated into French selections from the *Dārābnāma*, in the introduction to which she presented a valuable study of the development of the *Alexander Romance* in the Persian tradition. Gaillard posited that Alexander was introduced in the *Khudāynāmag*, although she did not analyse the possible portrayal of him presented in this Sasanian chronicle.[17]

Among other extensive studies on Alexander in Persian literature, the Persian monograph *Alexander and Persian Literature and his Religious Personality* (1985) by Ḥ. Ṣafavī deserves to be mentioned.[18] This study is divided into four principal chapters that explore different aspects of Alexander in Persian literature from historical, literary, mythological and religious points of view. Ṣafavī summarises and compares stories and legends concerning Alexander the Great based on Firdawsī's *Shāhnāma*, Niẓāmī's *Iskandarnāma* and Arabic historical accounts. The main focus of Ṣafavī's chapter on the religious aspect of Alexander concerns his role in the Qur'ān as the Bicornous/Two-Horned One and prophet (Dhū'l-Qarnayn).

Another two excellent studies by Majd al-Dīn Kayvānī on Alexander's place in Persian literature are worth mentioning.[19] Kayvānī examines the figure of Alexander as it appears in various versions of the *Romance* composed during the Islamic period. The novelty of his study lies in his analysis of the image of Alexander in Persian poetry, especially Sufi mystical poetry, and in the genre of the panegyric ode (*qaṣīda*). Kayvānī explores how different motifs from the *Alexander Romance* were used as similes and metaphors by various poets during their versification of the great deeds of a certain monarch, or while lamenting the transient nature of the world. His brief study on the different Persian *Iskandarnāma*s and their contents is also extremely useful.

The pioneer of the study of Persian versions of the *Alexander Romance* in Western languages was Yevgeni Edvardovich Bertels. In his *Roman ob Aleksandre*,[20] Bertels examined the development of the Persian legend of Iskandar, incorporating into his study a detailed discussion of the contents of the important poetic renditions of the *Romance* by Firdawsī, Niẓāmī, Amīr Khusraw, Jāmī and Alī Shīr Navā'ī. Unfortunately, he wrote his study before important works such as the *Dārābnāma* had been discovered. Not only does Bertels's study explore the different sources and versions of the legend of Iskandar in classical Persian poetry, it also offers a brief survey of different aspects of Alexander's image, such as his religious portrayal as Dhū'l-Qarnayn in the Qur'ān and his depiction in Persian *adab* literature.

Similarly, it is well worth mentioning the work of Faustina Doufikar-Aerts, who in *Alexander Magnus Arabicus* produced a valuable study of Alexander in Arabic literature and history.[21] She explores different aspects of the personality and legend of Alexander in the Arabic tradition, detecting four principal branches: the Pseudo-Callisthenes tradition, wisdom literature, portrayals of Alexander as Dhū'l-Qarnayn and the *Sīra* tradition (popular romances). *Alexander Magnus Arabicus* is a valuable contribution to the subject, covering the Alexander tradition through seven centuries. Nonetheless, such a study remains incomplete without considering the legacy of pre-Islamic Persian sources on Alexander in Arabic historical accounts of the ninth and tenth centuries of the Islamic era. Doufikar-Aerts regards possible texts derived from Pahlavi intermediaries as being outside the scope of her research, and affirms that 'Middle Persian influence appears to play no role in the romances of the Arabic Pseudo-Callisthenes tradition'.[22] However, this book will show that the study of the Persian Alexander tradition – especially that of the *Shāhnāma* of Firdawsī and the *Dārābnāma* of Ṭarsūsī – sheds light on the development of the *Alexander Romance* and indicates the legacy of pre-Islamic Persian sources in the Arabic tradition on Alexander.

This book demonstrates that there is indeed a Persian line of transmission in the Arabic Pseudo-Callisthenes tradition through Middle Persian sources. This line of transmission from Greek to Syriac, Arabic and Persian can be clarified and exposed by analysis of the *Shāhnāma* of Firdawsī, the *Dārābnāma* of Ṭarsūsī and the *Iskandarnāma* of Niẓāmī, besides taking into consideration the Middle Persian background of the Arabic materials. In this respect, examining the case of the so-called Pahlavi translation of the Pseudo-Callisthenes both complements and completes some of Doufikar-Aerts's conclusions. It is clear that Iranians displayed a particular interest in the life of Alexander and that this Pahlavi version must have influenced the compilation of the *Khudāynāmag.* This account influenced the early literary tradition in the Muslim world, and indirectly later on, Firdawsī's compilation of the *Shāhnāma.*

However, Jalāl Khaleghi-Motlagh believes that the Pahlavi translation of the Pseudo-Callisthenes is an independent work that was translated into Arabic in the Islamic period. He also believes that the legend of Alexander was not included in the Sasanian *Khudāynāmag* in the same form as it can be seen in the *Shāhnāma* of Firdawsī,[23] but he does not clarify what form Alexander's story might have taken in the pre-Islamic Persian sources. He affirms that the authors of the *Shāhnāma* of Abū Manṣūr added the story to the work through this Arabic version based on a Pahlavi translation of the Pseudo-Callisthenes, following Nöldeke's hypothesis, and that it was through this source that the legend of Iskandar entered the *Shāhnāma* of Firdawsī.[24] However, a study of the legend of Alexander in the *Shāhnāma* (see Chapter 3) will show the complex structure of Firdawsī's account, which is derived from various sources. This was a key account that received and transmitted much of the considerable pre-Islamic literary influence, in particular the influence of the Pseudo-Callisthenes tradition.

This book will discuss the possible Middle Persian source of Firdawsī, considering all the theories mentioned here. Until now, this subject has not been adequately explored, as little has been written on the Persian Alexander tradition, both in terms of content (stories, motifs, the profile of the hero and general concepts concealed in the narrative) and in terms of a failure to connect materials with the periods in which they were compiled. This book will address both of these areas, emphasising literary connections between the Greek Pseudo-Callisthenes tradition and the Persian versions, and analysing themes regarding the internal construction and folk elements of the Persian versions of the *Alexander Romance.*

CHAPTER 1

GREEK AND SYRIAC VERSIONS OF THE *ALEXANDER ROMANCE* AND THEIR DEVELOPMENT IN THE EAST

فسانه گشت و کهن شد حدیث اسکندر
سخن نو آر که نو را حلاوتیست دگر

The history of Alexander
Is all an ancient fable now.
– Go bring on what is novel, new,
For novelty's more savoury.

Farrukhī Sīstānī (d. 1037)[1]

The Greek Background

It seems that Persian and Arabic authors of the Islamic period had no access to so-called historical sources on Alexander the Great (that is, the apparently historical accounts of Arrian, Plutarch, Diodorus, Curtius and Justin – some of which are not historical, at least in a straightforward sense).[2] The Arabic and Persian sources that deal with Alexander's history are based on a Greek work of popular literature known as the *Alexander Romance*. It is also known as the Pseudo-Callisthenes because the work has erroneously been attributed to Callisthenes, the historian in Alexander's court, on the grounds of several fifteenth-century manuscripts.[3]

The formation of the *Alexander Romance* was a gradual process. The traditional view is that the composition of the work as a single entity did not take place until the third century AD, shortly before its translation from Greek into Latin by Julius Valerius.[4] The anonymous author of the *Romance* is believed to have been 'a competent speaker and writer of Greek' from Alexandria.[5]

The textual history of the Greek *Alexander Romance* is a very complicated one. The Greek work attributed to Pseudo-Callisthenes that appeared in the Middle Ages survives in three major versions known as 'recensions':[6]

(1) **The α-recension**: represented by a single manuscript[7] dated to the eleventh century AD.[8] It is the source of the Armenian version[9] (*c.* AD 500)[10] and the Latin version by Julius Valerius (*c.* AD 340).[11]

(2) **The β-recension**: the author of the β-recension wrote some time after the Latin translation of Julius Valerius (*c.* AD 340), but he was apparently unaware of the variants in the Greek source of the Armenian version.[12] The β-recension is represented by three 'sub-recensions':
   a. *Sub-recension* ε: (MS *Bodl. Barocc.* 17, thirteenth century AD): with a strong interest in Judaism (it contains the visit to Jerusalem).[13]
   b. *Sub-recension* λ: a variant of the β-recension, preserved in five manuscripts. The most substantial additions are in Book III.[14]
   c. *Sub-recension* γ: the longest of the Greek recensions. It follows the basic structure of α and β, but incorporates new material from ϵ.[15]
   d. Manuscript *L* (*Leidensis Vulcanianus 93*): a unique variant of β with more adventures, in particular the episodes of the diving bell and the flying machine (II, 38–41).[16]

(3) **The δ-recension**: not represented by any Greek manuscript. However, it is generally believed to be the source of oriental versions (in particular Syriac, Arabic, Persian and Ethiopian). It is also the source of the tenth-century Latin translation of Leo the Archpriest, known as *Historia de Proeliis.*[17]

The motifs in Table 1.1 are those that are only added to later versions of the *Romance*. The table shows which recension the later

Table 1.1 Variants of motifs in later versions of the *Alexander Romance*[18]

Motif/Recension	**α** (*c*.AD 338)	**β** (*c*.AD 550)	γ (**β** + ε) (9th c.)	ε (8th c.)	**λ** (8th c.)	**MS *L*** (composition 14th c.)
Olympic games in Olympia	✓	✓	In Rome	✓	✓	✓
Theban episode (end of Book I)	✓					
Debate in Athens	✓					
End of Book II (21–44)		✓	✓	✓	✓	✓
Sirens dancing around a lake			✓	✓		
Diving bell and flying machine					✓	✓
Campaign to conquer Rome				✓		
Alexander in Judaea and Egypt			✓			
Visit to Jerusalem			✓	✓		
Alexander's conversion to Judaism				✓		
Unclean Nations (from Pseudo-Methodius)[19]			✓	✓		
Palladius's *On the Life of Brahmans* (III, 7–16)[20]	✓		✓			

versions are based on. For instance, the twelfth-century Persian poet Niẓāmī is the only author who included the motif of mermaids dancing on the banks of a lake at night.[21] This leads us to conclude that his source was probably based on sub-recension ε or γ. Another example is the *Ā'īna-yi Iskandarī* (*Alexander's Mirror*) of Amīr Khusraw of Delhi (d. 1325), in which the motif of the diving bell appears.[22] Thus this implies that Amīr Khusraw had access to an ultimate source similar to manuscript *L* or sub-recension λ.

Syriac Sources Relevant to this Study

The most widespread Arabic and Persian traditions about Alexander are adaptations of three Syriac works – the *Romance*, the *Legend* and the *Poem* – which were translated at unknown but evidently early dates.[23] Another Syriac text, the *Laments of Philosophers at Alexander's Funeral* appears as an integrated part of the tale in Arabic and Persian versions of the *Alexander Romance*, although it was not included in the original version. A further Syriac text is the *Khuzistān Chronicle*, and while it is not related to the *Alexander Romance*, it demonstrates the Nestorian influence at the end of the Sasanian period, when the *Alexander Romance* was introduced into Persian literature. It is believed that all these textual traditions became commonplace in the Syriac context within Christian communities from the seventh century AD onward.[24]

The Syriac Alexander Romance (Tašʿītā d-'Aleksandrōs)

Without doubt, the Syriac version of the Pseudo-Callisthenes is the most influential of all oriental versions of the *Alexander Romance*, harking back to the seventh century AD.[25] Wallis Budge edited and translated it into English in 1889.[26] It consists of three sections that coincide with the Greek textual tradition of the Pseudo-Callisthenes. The source text was related to the Greek α-recension but differs so considerably that it has generally been reckoned to be evidence of a lost Greek recension known as the δ-recension, mentioned above. The first section contains 47 chapters, the second only 14, and the third has 24 chapters.[27]

There are two important aspects of this version relating to the Arabic and Persian sources. Firstly, the Syriac text offers a fairly complete and accurate account of Olympias's affair with the Egyptian pharaoh

Nectanebo, as related in the Greek version, which is not found in most Arabic and Persian sources. Secondly, it describes the expedition carried out by Alexander beyond the River Oxus in Central Asia and China,[28] including his visit to the Emperor of China and his adventures there (such as the dragon episode), which are also standard features of the Persian versions.[29]

The Syriac Alexander Legend

The *Exploits of Alexander* (*Neṣḥānā d-'Aleksandrōs*), translated into English by Budge as *A Christian Legend Concerning Alexander*, is a short appendix attached to Syriac manuscripts of the *Alexander Romance*.[30] It was probably composed by a Mesopotamian Christian in Amid or Edessa,[31] and was written down in AD 629–30 after the victory of Emperor Heraclius over the Sasanian king Khusraw II Parvīz.[32]

In this *Christian Legend*, Alexander becomes a Christian king who acts through God's will. The most important role of this text in the development of the *Alexander Romance* is the fact that the fusion of the motif of Alexander's barrier with the biblical tradition of the apocalyptic people, Gog and Magog, appears for the first time in this text.[33] The story of Gog and Magog and the Gates of Alexander became a very important component of Arabic and Persian sources.

The Syriac Alexander Poem*: A Metrical Discourse* (mēmrā) *on Alexander Attributed to Jacob of Serūgh (d. 521)*

The *Christian Legend* was the source for a metrical homily entitled 'Poem on the pious king Alexander and on the gate, which he built against Gog and Magog'.[34] The *Poem* was probably composed in around AD 630–40 by an anonymous Christian author[35] in northern Mesopotamia, probably in the neighbourhood of Amid.[36]

In this text, Alexander appears as a wise and pious king who is only God's instrument in his divine plan. This is said to be the text alluded to in the Qur'ān, which explains how a pagan conqueror managed to be praised in the Muslim holy book.[37]

The main content of the *Alexander Poem* deals with Alexander's travels to the Land of Darkness and his search for the Fountain of Life. Here Alexander starts his journey in Egypt and, after sailing for four months, he arrives in India, where the Fountain of Life is. Alexander's cook manages to bathe in the fountain when he goes to wash fish in it, but Alexander himself does not obtain immortality because he does not find the fountain. The other important element of the *Poem* is the 'brass and iron door' that Alexander builds to enclose Gog and Magog. Both motifs are important components of the Arabic and Persian versions of the *Alexander Romance.*

The Laments of the Philosophers over Alexander *in Syriac*

In the early Middle Ages, collections of sayings of various 'wise men' came to be attached to the story of Alexander's death, and in the course of time these gained enormous popularity both in the East, where they originated, and in the West, translated from Arabic.[38]

This text, which was originally an independent work, was subsequently incorporated into the *Alexander Romance* cycle. The Arabic texts of Ya'qūbī (d. 897),[39] Eutychius of Alexandria (d. 940),[40] and Mas'ūdī (d. 956),[41] and the Persian *Shāhnāma* of Firdawsī (completed in 1010)[42] contain the *Laments*. Furthermore, it is likely that the *Laments* were an integrated component of the *Alexander Romance* by the tenth century AD.

The Khuzistān Chronicle

In 1889 the Italian scholar Guidi edited an eastern Syrian chronicle that covers the late Sasanian and very early Islamic period. Four years later, Theodor Nöldeke translated the text into German, and dated it to the late seventh century AD, arguing that it was probably composed in around 652 or very soon afterwards, because the last reported event is the death of Yazdgird III, the last Sasanian king (AD 632–51). He also argued that its provenance was southern Iran.[43] Thus, the text is known as the *Khuzistān Chronicle*.[44] It fills 20 folios at the end of a manuscript (*Borg. Syr.* 82) of the *Synodicon Orientale*, a collection of the records of councils held by the Nestorian Church in Persia.

This single and very brief Syriac text is not related to the *Alexander Romance*. However, its contribution to knowledge of the present subject is considerable in two respects: firstly, it shows the position of extraordinary influence achieved by Yazdīn, Khusraw Parvīz's

(r. 590–628) Christian minister, which indicates the Christians' power in the Sasanian court in the seventh century AD;[45] secondly, it contains some brief information on Alexander that demonstrates what was known about Alexander the Great in Persia in the seventh century AD. The first passage is prefaced by a brief description of Merv[46] and a note about the conquests and death of its founder, Alexander the Great. The passage, according to Guidi's Latin translation,[47] is as follows:

> {Merv} was built by Alexander, son of Philip, and it was called Alexandria. Having defeated and subjugated many peoples of the East, he undertook to return to his country, but he was poisoned by his servants, {near} the Euphrates, at a place called Bāgniqyā in the Babylon area. He reigned twelve years and six months.[48]

The text also informs us that Alexander built Alexandria in Egypt on the advice of his tutor, Aristotle.[49] This kind of brief reference to Alexander's deeds and death can be found in the sources of the Islamic era too. He was particularly recorded as a founder of cities in Central Asia; for instance, the historian Ṭabarī also mentions the names of the cities that Alexander founded all around the conquered territories.[50]

The fact that Christians had influence in the court at the end of the Sasanian period is important because it shows that the *Alexander Romance* survived and was introduced into the Persian tradition thanks to the Nestorians. Some scholars[51] have doubted the existence of a Middle Persian version of the Pseudo-Callisthenes for ideological reasons. They base their theory on the Pahlavi literature, a faithful mirror of the political and religious ideology of the Sasanian era, which depicts Alexander as the 'cursed one' (*gujastak* in Pahlavi) and equivalent to the greatest enemies of Irānshar (that is, Ḍaḥḥāk and Afrāsīyāb).[52] Thus, they argue that the Sasanians would not have tolerated the translation of a text that represents one of the greatest enemies of Iran so positively. However, the presence of Christians and their influence in the Sasanian era[53] can shed new light on the development of the Pseudo-Callisthenes tradition in Persia before the Arab conquest. In addition, Byzantine and Arabic sources[54] bear witness to the existence of Greek works (in particular scientific and philosophical texts) that were translated into Middle Persian during the late Sasanian era, so it is virtually certain that they existed, though none of these works has come down to us.

Furthermore, the development of the *Alexander Romance* in the pre-Islamic Persian tradition needs to be studied by taking into account both historical elements besides the content of Arabic and Persian sources, which are based on Sasanian sources.

The Development of the *Alexander Romance* in the East

Theodor Nöldeke laid the foundations for research on the Eastern versions of the Pseudo-Callisthenes tradition. His most important contribution was his explanation, through a philological examination of the Syriac text, of what led to the development of the literary forms of the *Alexander Romance* found in Syriac, Arabic, Persian and Ethiopic literature. Nöldeke proposed the theory that a Pahlavi version must have preceded the Syriac version of the Pseudo-Callisthenes because the Syriac text contains some discrepancies with the Greek Pseudo-Callisthenes, and also a certain number of errors in the Syriac transliteration of Greek proper names.[55] He dated the lost Middle Persian intermediary to the late Sasanian era (*c.* sixth–seventh century AD).

Nöldeke's argument, which claims that the Syriac version must have been based on a lost intermediary Middle Persian translation of the original Greek, has been generally accepted ever since. However, Richard Frye[56] cast doubt on Nöldeke's theory by arguing that the Syriac version probably descends from a much older Syriac translation of the Greek Pseudo-Callisthenes. He based his theory mainly on three points. Firstly, the philological evidence does not reflect a Pahlavi source but might be the result of references to tales from folklore or oral tradition that were probably current throughout the Middle East and the Iranian world. Secondly, the Syriac version of the Pseudo-Callisthenes makes no mention of Alexander having Persian ancestry – this is mentioned by Ṭabarī and Firdawsī, and legitimates Alexander by making him the stepbrother of Darius III. Lastly, for ideological reasons a Middle Persian version of the Pseudo-Callisthenes could not have existed.

Nöldeke's theory has also been challenged by Claudia Ciancaglini, who believes that the Persian influence in the Syriac Pseudo-Callisthenes must be ascribed to Neo-Persian rather than Middle Persian. She argues that:

> Part of the history of the Syriac Pseudo-Callisthenes takes us back to northern Iraq, where we know that, at least before around 1500,

> the predominant language of culture was Persian. The Oriental Christians in this region addressed a public that was educated in Persian, not in Arabic: it is therefore highly likely that quite a large number of Persian elements, especially the glosses, entered the text long after the time of the first translation from the Greek.[57]

Kevin van Bladel does not accept Ciancaglini's arguments against Nöldeke on this issue.[58] He believes that 'the only explanation for the confusions in Greek names by the Syriac translator is to propose that there was a Middle Persian antecedent in Pahlavi script'.[59] In the same context, it is worth mentioning the argument of Monferrer-Sala, who also believes, for textual reasons, that 'the Syriac version cannot be considered a translation of any of the Greek PC [Pseudo-Callisthenes] texts'.[60]

Besides the different hypotheses on the translation of the Syriac Pseudo-Callisthenes, whether it came through a Middle Persian *Vorlage* or was based on a Greek original, we have to consider the analysis of another branch of *Alexander Romance* tradition. As very few texts of pre-Islamic Persian literature have survived, the only evidence we have for the existence of such a Middle Persian *Vorlage* is Arabic and Persian sources that mention different motifs from the Pseudo-Callisthenes tradition.

Here another problem arises: 'the Arabic PC [Pseudo-Callisthenes], if indeed it had ever existed, had been lost.'[61] However, it is believed that such an Arabic version did exist, because various elements from the Pseudo-Callisthenes tradition can be found in historical and geographical works in Arabic.[62] Furthermore, it is also important to point out the hypothesis regarding the development of the Pseudo-Callisthenes tradition in Arabic. According to Doufikar-Aerts, this hypothesis is generally accepted:

> It is now clear that three Syriac texts dating from the early seventh century were the sources for a great amount of Arabic material. In the seventh century, there was a Syriac translation of the Greek δ-recension of Pseudo-Callisthenes. The *Romance* was mediated by Middle Persian, according to Nöldeke, and it acquired a veneer of Iranian names during this stage. The two other texts were original compositions in Syriac, written between 628 and 640, and they

> reflect the political ideologies of their period. It is from these latter texts that the Arabic Alexander derives his character as a prophet. An Arabic translation, based on this Syriac Pseudo-Callisthenes, was probably made in the ninth century. Then, between the fourteenth and sixteenth centuries, an adaptation of this *Alexander Romance* was made in Ethiopic, based on an Arabic *Vorlage*. Because of the similarity between the Ethiopic Romance and the Syriac Pseudo-Callisthenes, the Arabic translation is generally believed to have been the intermediary between the Syriac and the Ethiopic Romance. This is just a hypothesis, since the Arabic translation has never been found and is thought to have been lost.[63]

This book will address two different areas of this debate. Firstly, the scholars mentioned above (Nöldeke, Ciancaglini, van Bladel and Monferrer-Sala) based their hypotheses on a philological examination of the Syriac Pseudo-Callisthenes. This causes some problems due to the date and origin of the Syriac manuscripts, the oldest of which dates only to 1709.[64] The influence of scribes, and the possible elements they might have added to the manuscripts, causes confusion when it comes to a textual and philological examination. In order to solve this problem, we should leave aside the philological examination of the Syriac text and instead explore its content in parallel with the Arabic and Persian texts. It is thus highly important to focus on the significance of the Sasanian legacy in these sources.

Secondly, an examination of the extensive Arabic tradition on Alexander shows two different branches: those versions that presented Alexander as a Persian king of the Kayānid dynasty, by naming him the half-brother of Darius III (Dārā), and the versions that did not. Doufikar-Aerts's excellent study on the different branches of the Arabic Alexander tradition missed an important element, namely the legacy of the Sasanian sources, especially in Arabic historiography. Due to this omission, she did not offer any solution to the problem of the 'lost Middle Persian *Vorlage*' in the transmission of the Pseudo-Callisthenes in the Arabic tradition. This book will examine the content of relevant Arabic and Persian sources in which it is possible to trace the Pseudo-Callisthenes tradition in a new light; this will show the influence of Sasanian sources on Arabic and Persian literature, especially in the field of historiography.

The Greek *Alexander Romance* originated in Alexandria (Egypt) in the third century AD and became the most influential source for the deeds and adventures of Alexander, especially in the East. It is therefore important to study its influence in the Persian versions of the tale. However, there is a huge gap between its composition in Alexandria in the third century AD and its appearance in the Persian tradition represented by the *Shāhnāma* of Firdawsī (completed in 1010), which is the first complete exemplar of the Pseudo-Callisthenes tradition. In order to fill this gap of seven centuries and provide a hypothesis regarding how this Greek work appeared in the Persian sources, we need to first consider the historical environment in which national Persian history was formed.

CHAPTER 2

ALEXANDER THE GREAT AND THE LEGACY OF SASANIAN HISTORIOGRAPHY

ما قصه ی سکندر و دارا نخوانده ایم
از ما به جز حکایت مهر و وفا مپرس

The yarn of Alexander and Darius is not
A tale I have read. Do not ask me to relate
Aught but romances of fidelity and love.

Ḥāfiz[1]

Introduction

In a verse concerning Alexander's search for the Water of Life, the Persian Sufi poet Farīd al-Dīn 'Aṭṭār (d. 1229) memorably complained:

> Howsoever in this wilderness shall I find the Water of Life,
> Since I'm lost like Alexander in the depths of darkness?

In the quest for what seems to be a Middle Persian *Vorlage* and the *Aqua Vitae* of historical certainty, we find ourselves similarly stranded in the wilderness and lost in darkness. We know that Arabic replaced Middle Persian after the Arab conquest (AD 636), and Sasanian literature came to be mainly rewritten in Arabic until the tenth century AD, when it began to be produced in Persian. In this situation practically all we can do is firstly examine the classical Arabic historiographical accounts written between the ninth and twelfth centuries in order to trace them back to their hypothetical origin, and secondly study Arabic sources that share motifs from the Pseudo-Callisthenes tradition with the extant Persian versions; here we should focus on the influence of Sasanian historiography on Arabic historical sources, the origin and contents of a lost Sasanian chronicle, and the place of Alexander in the pre-Islamic Persian tradition. Benighted as we are, by studying Arabic accounts dating from the ninth to eleventh centuries, we may hopefully trace our way out of this vale of darkness back to a 'Middle Persian' version of the *Alexander Romance*.

No complete Arabic version of the Pseudo-Callisthenes has ever been found. It is assumed that 'if indeed it had ever existed, it had been lost'. Instead, what we have in different historical and geographical accounts are only brief motifs from the Pseudo-Callisthenes tradition. Although Doufikar-Aerts's study of Arabic sources relating to Alexander did shed new light on this tradition, she rightly preferred to place the Middle Persian out of the scope of her study.

Although no version of the *Alexander Romance* from the pre-Islamic Persian tradition has survived, the evidence of the Arabic and Persian sources that include selections from this work leaves no doubt that the legends about Alexander did exist in written form, at least in the Sasanian period. The *Alexander Romance* is mainly reflected in the works of early Islamic historians and geographers and in Persian versions of the *Alexander Romance*, in particular in the *Shāhnāma* of Firdawsī. Some of the characteristics of these versions (such as proper names and Alexander's Persian ancestry) indicate a Middle Persian source. It is impossible to make stylistic judgements based on these details, but together they probably give an excellent idea of its content.

Early Arabic historical accounts of Alexander's life reflect a Middle Persian intermediary. In the works of the ninth to twelfth centuries, for example, the following common characteristics are visible:

(1) These sources deal with the history of Iran up to the Arab conquest, dividing it into four principal dynasties: the Pīshdādīyān (the first Persian kings), the Kayānīyān (Kayānids), the Ashkānīyān (Arsacids) and the Sasanians.

(2) Most of the authors of these sources are Iranian or of Iranian ancestry, which indicates that Persian sources were accessible to them.
(3) They all include Alexander in the Kayānid dynasty, making him the legitimate King of Iran and half-brother of Darius III (Dārā).
(4) The proper names mentioned in these sources indicate a Persian source and coincide with the equivalent names found in the Pahlavi texts (for instance Dārā for Darius III). They also contain certain Persian words or explanations based on the Persian meaning of a word, as will be discussed below.
(5) The oldest historical accounts do not apply the Islamic epithet Dhū'l-Qarnayn ('the Two-Horned One'), mentioned in the Qur'ān, to Alexander. This indicates that their source predated the identification of Dhū'l-Qarnayn with Alexander during the Islamic period.

The Arabic works with the above-mentioned characteristics are the historical accounts of Dīnawarī (d. 895),[2] Ṭabarī (d. 923),[3] the anonymous *Nihāya*[4] (possibly d. *c.*850)[5] and Tha'ālibī Nīshābūrī (d. 1038).[6] This list does not include of course, the *Shāhnāma* of Firdawsī, which is in Persian. In addition, Bīrūnī's (d. after 1050) brief mention of Alexander in the *Āthār al-bāqīya* (*Chronology of Ancient Nations*),[7] Ḥamza Iṣfahānī's (d. after 961) *On the Kings and Prophets*[8] and the geographical work *Kitāb al-Buldān* (*Book of Countries*) of Ibn al-Faqīh Hamadānī (d. *c.*903)[9] provide some evidence for the existence of a Middle Persian version of the *Alexander Romance.* The epithet Dhū'l-Qarnayn is not applied to Alexander by Dīnawarī, Ṭabarī or Firdawsī, which is very significant due to the identification of Alexander with this Qur'ānic figure in the Islamic period.[10]

In comparing these Arabic accounts in order to investigate and find any evidence for the existence of a Middle Persian version of the *Alexander Romance*, we will follow the methodology applied by Professor Yarshater in his chapter on 'Iranian National History' in the *Cambridge History of Iran*[11] and Professor Khaleghi-Motlagh's article 'From *Shāhnāma* to *Khudāynāma*: an inquiry into the direct and indirect sources of the *Shāhnāma*'.[12] In this way, the components of this lost version will be reconstructed by examining the common motifs mentioned by almost all of these Arabic works, as well as in the Persian *Shāhnāma* of Firdawsī.

Before analysing the content of Arabic accounts of Alexander, it is necessary to provide some background regarding the influence of Sasanian historiography in the Arabic tradition. In this respect, we need to address the following questions:

(1) Why do they have the same framework, dealing with Iranian history by dividing it into four principal dynasties?
(2) Why do they include Alexander among the Persian kings of the Kayānid cycle?
(3) Why do they use Persian proper names (such as Dārā for Darius)?

This chapter will attempt to give, or at least posit, probable answers to these questions, before discussing the development and sources of the *Alexander Romance* in the Arabo-Persian tradition.

Arabic Sources and Historical Tradition in Pre-Islamic Iran

Although no historical works survive from the pre-Islamic Persian tradition,[13] the existence of divergent texts is attested by later sources, which point to different versions of an official chronicle relating the history of Iran, from its mythological beginnings (the creation of the world and the first man/king) up to the time of its compilation during the Sasanian period. This chronicle is known by the standard designation *Khudāynāmag* (in Middle Persian *Xwadāy-nāmag*, meaning the *Book of Sovereigns*, equivalent to the term *Shāhnāma* in New Persian).[14] As to the date of this work, some scholars attribute its compilation to Khusraw I, Anūshīrvān (AD 531–79),[15] though others, like Shahbazi, maintain that the compilation of a national history was already well under way at the time of the Sasanian king Bahrām Gūr (AD 421–38), and had definitely taken a coherent form by the time of Khusraw I.[16] In any event, by the end of the sixth century AD, a national history of Iran existed in the royal archive at Ctesiphon, from which Agathias[17] derived his account of Sasanian history.[18]

None of the Middle Persian versions of this great Sasanian chronicle have survived, but it survives in Arabic derivatives and, notably, in the Persian *Shāhnāma* of Firdawsī.[19] An Arabic translation of this work is attested by later sources, which cite more than 20 versions of the chronicle,[20] called *Sayr al-mulūk* (*Lives of the Kings*) or *Tārīkh al-mulūk*

(*History of the Kings*).[21] Although all of these Arabic translations have also been lost, their content is known from the summaries of Arabic historiographers who based their histories of Iranians on this material. It is from this material in Arabic, and Persian adaptations of the ninth to eleventh centuries, as well as the remains of historical records, legends and myths in Avestan and Pahlavi texts, that a reconstruction of the contents of the lost *Khudāynāmag* has been undertaken.[22]

The *Khudāynāmag*: Content and Sources

The *Khudāynāmag* has been the subject of a great number of investigations,[23] as it represents a historical tradition that combined myth, legend and factual history. Its origins can be traced to oral traditions relating to Avestan figures in north-eastern Persia, which assumed a national character with the spread of Zoroastrianism, and continued to be orally transmitted until towards the end of the Sassanid period, when they were committed to writing.[24]

The compilers of the *Khudāynāmag* divided the Iranian past from the creation and appearance of the first man, into four dynastic periods, as has been attested by many Arabic historical accounts and the *Shāhnāma* of Firdawsī.[25] Among these four dynasties, the second (that of the Kayānids or Kayānīyān) is of most interest because it ends in Alexander's conquest. It is noteworthy that among these four dynasties there is no mention of the Achaemenids. The omission of the Medes and Achaemenids from the accounts of Persian history has given risen to certain theories among scholars.

Some decades ago, the great Iranian scholar Ehsan Yarshater published an article in which he discussed why the Medes and Achaemenids did not appear in the *Shāhnāma.*[26] He argued that the Sasanians were unaware of the Achaemenids and did not have any historical memory of them; and if the Sasanians were heirs to anyone, it was the Parthians (247 BC–AD 224).[27] Shahbazi argued that the early Sasanians did know about the Achaemenids, but for ideological reasons – especially during the time of Shāpūr II (AD 309–79) – they claimed to be the descendants of the kings in the *Avesta* (in particular the Kayānids) rather than the Achaemenids.[28] This debate has been recently revisited and re-examined by Touraj Daryaee, who explains the omission of the Achaemenids from the official history as being a consequence of the nature of Iranian historiography.[29] Daryaee rightly claims that the 'Sasanians did not forget, but must have ignored the Achaemenids purposefully to construct a sacred history which connected them not to the Achaemenids, but to the Kayanids. This meant a construction of the past which was sacred and removed from the Greco-Roman historiographical tradition.'[30] A similar pattern may be seen in the development of Christian Roman historiography, where Christianity became a focal point and a background to the history of the late Roman Empire.[31]

Therefore, in the history of Iran, the Achaemenid dynasty was replaced with the Kayānid dynastic cycle, into which the episode of Alexander was incorporated. It is worth briefly examining the origin of the Kayānid cycle of epic and Alexander's place within this dynasty. Boyce[32] and Tafaḍḍulī[33] both traced the Kayānid cycle back to Parthian times. Macuch also points out that:

> The central position of the *pahlawāns*, 'champions' or 'heroes' or 'Parthians' in the original sense of the word, and the outstanding features attributed to the House of Kārēn [one of the Parthian families] in the national epic indicate that members of important families, who claimed descent from the Arsacid house, had created a version[34] of the national history favourable towards themselves.[35]

Pourshariati has also studied the influence of Parthian families on the creation of an Iranian 'national history'.[36] She points out that the production of two of the most authoritative versions of the *Khudāynāmag*, namely the *Shāhnāma* of Abū Manṣūr (in prose) and the *Shāhnāma* of Firdawsī (completed in verse in 1010),[37] cannot be understood except in the context of their patronage by families of Parthian ancestry, or at least by families with pretensions to this ancestry, in the tenth century AD.[38]

Why, it may be asked, is the Parthian influence relevant to the appearance of Alexander in the Kayānid cycle? It is simply because the clue to understanding such a vast variety of legends on Alexander in the Persian tradition must be sought in the Parthian period. From the material culture, mainly the coinage, it appears that the Arsacids called themselves *Philhellenos* (φιλελληνος).[39] Their philhellenism is also brought to fore in the legends on their coins, which were usually in Greek.[40] In this context, it is worth pointing out that according to Tacitus (*Annals*, 6.31), the Arsacid king Ardawān II legitimised his claim over Roman territories by associating himself with Alexander and the Seleucids on the one hand, and with the Achaemenids on the other.[41]

In addition, in a recent study Daryaee points out the Arsacids' Irano-Hellenic cultural setting represented in a Middle Persian manuscript (MU29),[42] in which they are connected with Alexander and his legacy in Iran.[43] Thus, if we consider the possibility that Alexander's positive image in Persian literature has its origin in the Parthian period, the divergence between Alexander's negative image in the Zoroastrian tradition reflected in the Pahlavi texts[44] and his positive character in the national epic (that is, the *Khudāynāmag* tradition, as this book endeavours to prove) makes better sense. However, this is just a hypothesis because unfortunately no known Parthian-language literature survives in its original form,[45] since the Parthian tradition was an oral one, and being bardic in nature it was usually sung or recited with music by court minstrels called Gōsāns.[46] The discrepancies in the characterisation of Alexander between the Kayānid and Sasanian parts of the *Shāhnāma* of Firdawsī[47] may also be explained by the different sources (Parthian and Sasanian) of these two parts and the existence of more than one *Khudāynāmag* tradition.[48]

It has long been recognised that various *Khudāynāmag* traditions were incorporated into classical Arabic histories that were composed in the ninth and tenth centuries.[49] The *Khudāynāmag* chronicles played an important role in Arabic historiography, especially in the 'Abbāsid period.[50] These Arabic accounts will be examined below in order to reconstruct the content of Alexander's appearance in the *Khudāynāmag*; this will only include the extant Arabic histories of the first centuries of the Islamic era (the ninth to twelfth centuries), which, it can be deduced, used a derivation of the *Khudāynāmag* as their source. The majority of the authors of these Arabic histories were Persians who wrote in Arabic. The Sasanian sources were therefore available to them, though indirectly.

Beside these Arabic accounts – those of Dīnawarī, Ṭabarī, Bīrūnī and Iṣfahānī, as well as Tha'ālibī's *Ghurar akhbār* and the anonymous *Nihāya* – where needed, Firdawsī's *Shāhnāma* (in Persian) is also included here, as it is the most representative source for the *Khudāynāmag* tradition. However, since the passages on Alexander in the *Shāhnāma* of Firdawsī, being the first complete and most extensive representation of the Pseudo-Callisthenes tradition in the Islamic world, is worthy of an independent analysis, this will be studied in detail in the next chapter. The following sections examine different motifs in the *Alexander Romance* found in these Arabic histories from the Pseudo-Callisthenes tradition.

Alexander's Persian Ancestry and the Etymology of His Name

The first thing that Arabic historical accounts deal with is different traditions concerning Alexander's ancestry. In his *Kitāb al-Akhbār al-ṭawāl* (*Book of Extensive Histories*), Dīnawarī (d. 895) offers one of the fullest accounts of the *Alexander Romance* written during the Islamic era. Dīnawarī discusses at length the Persian variant of Alexander's ancestry.

He mentions that 'the people of Fārs' believe that Alexander was the son of Dārā and Philip's daughter. According to Dīnawarī, in a war between the Persian king Dārā, son of Bahman, and Philip [Fīlifūs], the latter was defeated. Philip agreed to pay an annual tribute of one hundred thousand golden eggs, and gave his daughter in marriage to Dārā. The Persian king detected an unpleasant odour on Philip's daughter, and had her cured with a herb called *sandar*. The night he was supposed to consummate the marriage with the Greek princess, he smelled the herb and cried out 'āl sandar', which means 'the *sandar* is strong' because, according to Dīnawarī, 'āl' in Persian means 'strong'.[51] Dārā thus eventually lost interest in her and sent her back to Rūm, unaware of her pregnancy. She gave birth to a boy and called him 'Ali[k] sandar' (*āl* + *sandar*).[52] The explanation given by Dīnawarī is very close to Alexander's name in Middle Persian: Aleksandar. This etymology of his name gradually became obsolete in later sources, where the herb was simply turned into 'iskandar', as we will see below.

This must have been at the heart of Alexander's legend in the *Khudāynāmag* tradition, for it is repeated in sources, with some variation. Ṭabarī's (d. 932) *Tārīkh al-rusul wa'l-mulūk* (*History of Prophets and Kings*) contains four different versions of Alexander's name and ancestry.[53] In the third version, Ṭabarī's account reports material from sources he claims are 'told by persons knowledgeable about the stories of the ancients'. He reports that Alexander and Dārā were brothers, and Alexander's mother was Philip's daughter Halāy.[54] She married the Persian king Dārā the Great

(*Dārā al-akbar*), son of Bahman, after Philip was defeated in a war. Ṭabarī's etymology of Alexander's name explains that he was named after the herb *sandarūs*, which cured his mother's bad breath. According to Ṭabarī, the origin of his name is 'Halāy-Sandarūs', which became Iskandarūs.[55]

The anonymous author of the *Nihāya*, in agreement with other historians whose source was a derivation of *Khudāynāmag*, places Alexander within the Kayānid dynasty. The passage on Alexander is handed down by the author in the name of Ibn al-Muqaffa', which indicates that he probably had access to the Arabic translation of the *Khudāynāmag* rendered by Ibn al-Muqaffa'.[56] It begins with a story about Alexander's Persian descent, although the author remarks that Arabs do not agree with Persians about Alexander's ancestry. The author adds that the people of Rūm believe that Alexander was the son of Fīlibūs (Philip). Here, the herb that cured Alexander's mother is simply called 'iskandar',[57] as it is in Firdawsī's account, where it burnt her palate.[58] Stoneman suggests that the word might be 'σκάνδιξ' (chervil, a relative of parsley),[59] while Grignaschi suggests sandal, the well-known fragrant wood, which in the Pahlavi script can be read as *sandar*.[60] Then again, Warner argues that the word derived either from the Greek σκόροδον (garlic) or the Latin *ascalonium* (shallot).[61] According to Dihkhudā, *sandar* or *sandarūs* is of Greek origin, from 'σανδαράκη', and is identified as the Arar tree, which produces a yellow resin.[62]

Abū Rayḥān Bīrūnī's *Āthār al-bāqīya* (*Chronology of Ancient Nations*), written in AD 1000, also contains the Persian descent variant mentioned above, although he claimed: 'That Alexander was the son of Philip is a fact too evident to be concealed.'[63]

In any case, through such creative elaborations in the Persian tradition, Alexander becomes the son of Dārā(b), son of Bahman Ardaxshīr, son of Isfandīyār. This invented Persian genealogy of Alexander links him firstly to the greatest Persian kings (such as Bahman Ardaxshīr/Artaxerxes I),[64] and secondly to Isfandīyār, the great hero of Iranian epic who, like Alexander, had a Greek mother and was the grandson of a 'Caesar of Rūm'.[65] This genealogy legitimised Alexander's kingship as a Persian of the Kayānid dynasty.

The legend of Alexander's birth contains certain symbols that show the double attitude of the Persian world towards the Macedonian king. In the Avestic tradition, bad odours (*gantāy*/*gaintī*) are related to Ahrīman,[66] with whom Alexander is associated in Pahlavi sources. Furthermore, the identification of the herb *sandar/iskandar* as garlic, 'which was so esteemed by the Iranians as a medicine and a means of warding off the evil eye and demonic power',[67] can be interpreted from the point of view that the bad breath of Alexander's mother is a sign of the *ahrīmanī* (demoniac) character of Alexander. According to Davis, since Alexander's mother is a Greek, the bad odour can also be linked with two Greek festivals (the Skirophoria and Thesmophoria),[68] which associated a ritual sexual abstinence with the stinking breath of the female partner.[69]

Davis also draws attention to historical data that may have influenced the invention of Alexander's Persian ancestry. In the fifth century BC, a Macedonian princess married a Persian. Her brother, who was the king of Macedonia at the time, was named Alexander.[70] Davis argues that it is possible that this story of Macedonian–Persian intermarriage involving a king of Macedonia named Alexander, was then combined with the patriotic stratagem of the Pseudo-Callisthenes to produce its own version of Alexander's paternity.[71]

In the above-mentioned Arabic accounts, the proper names are of Persian origin. Some of them also coincide with their equivalents in Pahlavi sources. For instance, Darius III is represented as Dārā-i Dārāyān (Dārā, son of Dārā). According to Firdawsī, Alexander's mother is named Nāhīd, which is the modern Persian form of the name of the goddess Ānāhītā.[72] Ṭabarī gives the name of Alexander's 'wondrous steed' as Būkefārasb,[73] which ends with the Persian *asb* (horse). In conclusion, the invented etymology of Alexander's name indicates a Persian source, although it is difficult to decipher the original Middle Persian origin of the name. This etymology, which makes him a legitimate king of a Persian dynasty by linking him to the greatest kings such as Artaxerxes I and Darius the Great, must have originated in the *Khudāynāmag* tradition represented in Arabic histories and the *Shāhnāma* of Firdawsī.

Iskandar Rūmī, *Alexander the Roman*

In Middle Persian Zoroastrian writings and in the Arabic accounts discussed here, Alexander the Great figures with the epithet *hrōmāyīg/rūmī* (Roman). According to Touraj Daryaee, it was the effects of Roman propaganda from the time of Caracalla to Alexander Severus that brought into existence an initial 'Alexander' story and memory, in which *imitatio Alexandri* played a central role and galvanised a Persian Alexander tradition, which lasted to the end of the Sasanian period.[74] The appearance of this epithet in historical Arabic accounts must have been due to the influence of Middle Persian writings too. It seems that the effects of the *imitatio Alexandri* of the Roman emperors in the second and third centuries AD on Middle Persian literature, also has a consequence for Arabo-Persian historical memory in the Islamic period. This explains the association of Alexander with the epithet rūmī in Arabic and Persian texts (*Hrōmīg* – Roman – in Middle Persian, that is, the Roman foe) as an influence of the Sasanian period.

The Tribute of Golden Eggs

According to Arabic histories and to Firdawsī as well, Philip paid his annual tribute to the Persian king Dārā(b) in the form of golden eggs. After Dārā(b)'s death, his son, named Dārā, ascended the throne and wrote a letter to Alexander, demanding the tribute that Philip used to pay. Alexander, who had succeeded his own father, refused to pay the tribute and replied that 'the hen that laid the golden eggs had died'. In fact, this sentence, which is repeated in all versions (and in particularly detailed accounts by Ṭabarī[75] and Firdawsī),[76] corresponds to the Syriac *Alexander Romance.*[77] Curiously, although there is no war between Philip and the Persian king mentioned in the Greek Pseudo-Callisthenes, the tribute of the golden eggs is mentioned there (I, 23). According to the Greek Pseudo-Callisthenes, when Alexander returned from Methone and went to visit his father, Philip, he saw Darius's ambassadors asking for the tribute of 'one hundred golden eggs, each weighing 20 pounds of solid gold'. According to the *Shāhnāma*, the golden eggs numbered 'one hundred thousand, each one weighing forty *mithqāl*' (roughly 6 oz or 170 g).[78] According to Arabic accounts and the *Shāhnāma*, Alexander's refusal to pay the tribute caused the war between Dārā and Alexander.[79]

Exchange of Symbolic Gifts

After the well-known sentence 'I have slain the hen that used to lay those eggs', some sources add a passage on the symbolic exchange of gifts between Dārā and Alexander. The origin of the motif of symbolic gifts is rather confusing (whether it was included in the *Khudāynāmag* or not) because it is absent from Dīnawarī's account and the *Shāhnāma* of Firdawsī, while Ṭabarī, the *Nihāya* and the *Ghurar* of Tha'ālibī contain it.[80] In the Greek Pseudo-Callisthenes (I, 36), Darius sends gifts – a whip, a ball and a chest of gold – along with a letter. However, the passage in Arabic accounts bears a great resemblance to the Syriac Pseudo-Callisthenes.[81] In the *Nihāya*, the author adds two more gifts: a golden coffin and a pure pearl.[82] The episode is seen in Ṭabarī's *History*[83] and in the Syriac Pseudo-Callisthenes too.[84]

The answer to the question as to why this passage is absent from the *Shāhnāma* and Dīnawarī's *Akhbār* can be found in Ṭabarī's account. As mentioned before, Ṭabarī includes four different variants on Alexander's history. The motif of symbolic gifts appears in a different version from the one in which the Persian descent variant is mentioned. The first variant is credited to 'a source other than Hishām',[85] while the second is based on 'some authorities on ancient history . . . those who say that Alexander was the brother of Dārā the Younger and the son of Dārā the Elder'.[86] Furthermore, it is likely that in the source in which Alexander is said to have possessed Persian ancestry, the motif of symbolic gifts does not appear, so it is also likely that this motif is not in the *Khudāynāmag*. It seems that this motif was incorporated into the version with the Persian ancestry afterwards, and thus it appears in Tha'ālibī's *Ghurar*, the *Nihāya*, the *Sharafnāma* of Niẓāmī and Bal'amī's *History*. This indicates that Firdawsī and Dīnawarī were working with an older source.[87] In Arabic accounts, the word 'whip', whatever it was in their original source, is translated as a 'polo mallet'. Ṭabarī used the word *ṣawlajān*, which is an Arabised form of *chawgān*, the Persian word for 'polo'.[88] It is worth mentioning that two recensions of the Hebrew *Alexander Romance*[89] translated from the same Arabic exemplar[90] used this Arabic word, adding the explanation that this is 'the stick with which young men engage in sport', implying that the Arabic exemplar had *al-ṣawlajān* here.[91] It is not clear how the 'whip' turned into a 'polo mallet', but once it was translated from Syriac, the word appears as the Arabised Persian word *chawgān* (polo), as it does in the Hebrew version. Due to the Persian origin of *chawgān*, and the fact that it fits very well in the context of 'playing', the Arabic intermediary may be based on a Middle Persian *Vorlage*.

The Battles between Alexander and Darius

While the Greek *Alexander Romance* only describes the actual battle at Gaugamela, the Arabic and Persian accounts give more details. The anonymous *Nihāya* and Ibn al-Faqīh Hamadānī report that in preparation for battle, Dārā lodged his family in the city of Hamadān, in what is now western Iran.[92] According to one of the traditions mentioned by Ṭabarī, the contenders met in the Jazīra,[93] and battled there for a year. Firdawsī mentions the bank of the Euphrates[94] as the first battlefield. According to Firdawsī and the *Nihāya*, there were three battles between Alexander and Dārā.[95] In the *Shāhnāma*, the poet's emphasis on historical information is remarkable. It seems very important for the poet to report where each detail happened. For example, the royal treasure was located in Jahrum,[96] the royal family resided in Iṣfahān and Alexander was crowned in Iṣṭakhr (with a *Kayānī* crown). There is no such interest in the Greek and Syriac versions.

Darius's Murderers

All the Arabic and Persian accounts, along with the Greek and Syriac version of the Pseudo-Callisthenes,[97] agree that Darius was murdered by his own men. Disagreement emerges, however, over whether his assassins were generals (*sarhang*), Zoroastrian priests (*mubad*),[98] chamberlains (*ḥājib*)[99] or ministers (*vazīr*, *dastūr*).[100] According to Ṭabarī and Dīnawarī, they were guards from Hamadān (Ecbatana).[101] Firdawsī mentions their names as Jānūspār (or Jānūshyār) and Māhyār.[102] Khaleghi-Motlagh identifies the name 'Jānūspār' as the Middle Persian *gyān-abespār*, which means 'bodyguard, soldier'.[103] Bīrūnī also affirms that Dārā was killed by his chief bodyguard, Nawjushānas, son of Ādharbakht.[104]

Firdawsī and the *Nihāya* affirm that Darius's murderers acted on their own in order to gain Alexander's favour and good grace, while Dīnawarī, Niẓāmī and Bal'amī report that Alexander agreed to make a compact with the murderers, but having arranged a deal with the generals to have Darius murdered, repented of the agreement and instead punished the traitors. Ṭabarī reports both versions.[105] In the *Nihāya*, Alexander tricks them into making themselves known, with the clever pretext that 'they will be elevated above the armies'. When Alexander wants to punish them, they protest. Alexander responds: 'I elevate you by hanging you.'[106]

Alexander Weeps at Dārā's Deathbed

A well-known motif from the Pseudo-Callisthenes is the scene in which Alexander finds the dying Darius, hears his last words and laments his death (II, 20).[107] Bīrūnī affirms that Alexander called Dārā 'brother'.[108] Many details of this passage in the Arabic and Persian versions stick closely to the version in the Greek *Romance.* For instance, Alexander's sentence begins in a similar way in the *Shāhnāma* of Firdawsī and in the Greek Pseudo-Callisthenes:

> The Greek *Romance*: 'Placing his hands on Darius's breast, he spoke these words, pregnant with pity: 'Stand up, King Darius. Rule your land and become master of yourself. Receive back your crown and rule your Persian people.'[109]
>
> The *Shāhnāma* of Firdawsī: 'Alexander places Darius's head on his knees ... and says: 'Stand up and sit on [your] golden throne ... I shall restore your kingdom to you.'[110]

Although this poignant scene is based on the Greek *Alexander Romance*, what is perhaps particularly interesting here is that the story hardly seems to have any motivation in the narrative of the Pseudo-Callisthenes; the incident (Alexander's pained reaction to the death of Darius) comes as a surprise. In contrast, in the Arabic and Persian accounts Alexander's reaction is given an elaborate motive: he is crying because of the death of his brother. Thus, although the Arabic versions and Firdawsī's *Shāhnāma* were composed in a far later historical period, the tale of Darius's death seems to be more fully integrated into these texts, while the tale of Alexander's sorrow is less so in the *Alexander Romance.*[111]

Dārā's Last Will

In the Greek *Romance* (II, 20), Darius asks Alexander to bury him with his own hands; he also commits his mother and wife to Alexander, and gives his daughter Roxana[112] to Alexander as a wife. To these personal deathbed gestures, the Arabic and Persian sources mentioned in this chapter add others that might seem to belong purely to a Persian version, since they make Alexander out to be the legitimate successor of the dying king. According to Ṭabarī, Dārā requests that Alexander 'should marry his daughter Rawshanak, and perpetuate Persian nobility and not to impose foreign rule upon the Persian nobility'.[113]

In the *Shāhnāma*, Dārā expresses the hope that a descendant of Alexander and Rawshanak will re-establish the glory of Zoroastrian feasts and customs. This passage shows Firdawsī's knowledge of the important Iranian feasts, and also mentions important figures in the Zoroastrian tradition, such as the great hero Isfandīyār and King Gushtāsp:

> Of her you might have a famous descendant who would revive the name of Isfandiyār, tend the fire of Zoroaster, gather up the *Zand-Avesta*, observe the presages and feast of Sada, also the glory of Nawrūz, of the fire temple and the feast of Mihrigān. He would wash his soul and face with the water of wisdom. He would revive the rites of Luhrāsp and follow the religion of Gushtāsp [Zoroastrianism].[114]

Alexander's Translations

According to Ṭabarī, Alexander destroyed Persian fire temples, killed Zoroastrian priests and burned their books.[115] He remarks: 'it is said that Alexander carried away the books of knowledge of the people of Persia, comprising their sciences, astronomy and philosophy after translating them into Syriac and the *rūmī* language'.[116]

The report about Alexander's acts of pillage and the translation of Persian books into Greek is derived from the late Sasanian period (in the early seventh century AD), recorded in various Middle Persian writings[117] and Arabic works. For instance, according to the *Book of Nativities* (*Kitāb al-Mawālīd*), 'when Alexander conquered the kingdom of Dārā the King, he had them all translated into the Greek language. Then he burnt the original copies which were kept in the treasure-houses of Dārā, and killed everyone whom he thought might be keeping away any of them.'[118] Another example of the transmission of the Zoroastrian sciences is presented by Abū Sahl ibn Nawbakht in his *Book of Nahmuṭān on the Nativities*:

> He [Alexander] had, however, copies made of whatever was collected in the archives and treasuries of Iṣṭakhr [Persepolis] and

> translated into Byzantine [Greek] and Coptic. After he was finished with copying whatever he needed from that [material], he burned what was written in Persian ... These books, along with the rest of the sciences, property, treasures, and learned men that he came upon, he sent to Egypt.[119]

Another variant of this tale is narrated by Ḥamza Iṣfahānī (d. after 961), according to which Alexander burned the Persian books after their translation into Greek because 'he envied the fact that [the Persians] had gathered together sciences the like of which no other nation had ever gathered'.[120]

According to these sources, any Greek book is by definition part of the Zoroastrian canon; and hence the translation and study of Greek works would mean recovering ancient Persian knowledge. As Daryaee rightly points out, 'these narratives suggest that there was probably a construction of an "Alexander plunder" story in the Sasanian period, elaborated and used by the Persians to justify the incorporation of "foreign" knowledge in the name of replacing the Persian heritage stolen or destroyed by Alexander'.[121]

King Frīdūn's Sons

Ṭabarī mentions a source in which Alexander speaks of 'close relations' between Dārā and himself. Ṭabarī adds: 'He meant, so this source maintained, the closeness between Salm and Īraj, the sons of Afrīdhūn.'[122] We come across this story in Middle Persian texts. It relates the division of the world by King Frīdūn among his three sons. He divided his kingdom (the world) between his sons, Salm, Tūr and Īraj. Īraj was given the best land (Irānshahr), while Salm ruled over the land of Rūm (Anatolia) and Tūr ruled the land of Turkistān (Central Asia).[123]

Thus, as Alexander rightly maintained, according to this story, the Persian kings and the kings of Rūm are indeed relatives, both descending from the same king (Frīdūn). Ṭabarī is the only historian who quotes this anecdote, which is very important in the epic tradition. Hence, according to Persian tradition, even if Alexander and Dārā were not brothers, they were still related, being descendants of King Frīdūn. In any case, Alexander's kingship was legitimised in the epic tradition of ancient Persia by a variety of sources.

Alexander's Speech on his Accession to the Throne of Persia

According to the *Shāhnāma*, when Alexander acceded to the throne of Persia, he gave a speech and wrote a letter to the Persian nobles.[124] The contents of his letter and speech legitimised his rule as a Persian king. According to Tafaḍḍulī, this type of speech on the occasion of accession to a throne is a stylistic characteristic of the *Khudāynāmag*.[125] Throughout the Arabic and Persian historical accounts there are examples of kings making speeches on ascending the throne, in particular the Sasanian kings.[126]

Alexander's Adventures

Some other motifs from the Pseudo-Callisthenes tradition appear in the Arabic accounts mentioned in this chapter, and will also be discussed in detail in later chapters. Dinawarī mentions Alexander's journey to India, the single combat between Alexander and Porus (the Indian king), the episode with Queen Candace (here called Qandāqa), Alexander's journeys to the Land of Darkness, to China and to the Land of Women (the Amazons), as well as his journey to Mecca.[127] Ṭabarī also cited a number of these motifs from the *Alexander Romance*. After the campaign in India, for instance, he relates Alexander's journeys to China and to the Land of Darkness in search of the Water of Life.[128]

The *Nihāya* also contains a passage on the Indian king Porus and his duel with Alexander, as well as an account of Alexander's journey to Mecca, an extensive episode concerning Queen Qandāfa (Candace), a Brahman story and the story of the Amazons. Some other motifs from the letter to Aristotle also appear in this book: tales of monsters, a talking tree and a version of the episode of the temple of Dionysus. The journey to China is also mentioned.[129]

Firdawsī's *Shāhnāma*, which contains the most extensive narrative on Alexander's adventures, will be examined in the next chapter. Firdawsī's work is a crucial source for casting light on whether these adventures were a part of the *Khudāynāmag* or added afterwards during the Islamic period.

Alexander, Founder of Cities

In Arabic and Persian sources, Alexander is recorded as the founder of many important cities, especially in Central Asia. According to the

Greek *Alexander Romance*, he founded 12 cities (III, 35). In the Syriac *Romance*, 13 are enumerated.[130] Dīnawarī reports the foundation of 12 cities, in agreement with the *Nihāya* and Ṭabarī. Ṭabarī also adds that each of them was named after Alexander (for instance, three in Khurāsān were Hirāt, Merv and Samarqand).

Tribal Kingdoms

According to Dīnawarī, Alexander feared that the nations whose kings he had killed would rebel when he died, and he therefore decided to slay the nobles of Iran. Following Aristotle's counsel, he divided Iran among the tribal princes.[131] This political division of the Persian Empire is attested by Middle Persian texts as the destruction of the unity of the Persian kingdom, with Alexander 'splintering it into a number of feudal orders' (*kadag-xwādāy*);[132] Arabic and Persian sources also describe 'the kings of the territorial divisions' (*mulūk al-ṭawā'if*).[133]

This frequently recorded tradition was the official Sasanian reckoning, and is attested by both Arabic historical accounts and the *Shāhnāma* of Firdawsī.[134]

Alexander's Death

In the Greek *Alexander Romance*, Alexander is said to have died in Babylon, poisoned, after having lived only 32 years (III, 35). In the Syriac *Alexander Romance*, he had lived only 32 years and seven months when he died in Babylon (III, XXIV).[135] According to Ṭabarī and Bīrūnī, Alexander died in a city near Babylon called Shahrazūr. This may be the city identified in the Syriac *Khuzistān Chronicle* as 'Bāgniqyā' in the Babylon area.[136] The Arabic and Persian sources both agree that Alexander died of an illness, but they disagree on his age when he died. Table 2.1 displays the main motifs presented in each source.

It is clear that certain motifs in the Middle Persian tradition acquired a specific form that distinguished them from other traditions. Taking Dīnawarī, the anonymous *Nihāya*, Firdawsī, Tha'ālibī and Ṭabarī as the main bases for this account, the contents of the *Alexander Romance* in the Middle Persian tradition will be summarised in the following section.

Table 2.1 Motifs of the *Alexander Romance* in Arabic and Persian Sources

Motif/source	Dīnawarī (9th c.)	*Nihāya* (11th c.)	Ṭabarī (10th c.)	Firdawsī (11th c.)	Tha‘ālibī (11th c.)	Syriac Pseudo-Callisthenes (7th c.)	Greek Pseudo-Callisthenes (3rd c.)
Tribute of golden eggs	✓	✓	✓	✓	✓	–	–
The herb	Sandar	Iskandar	Sandar	Iskandar	Iskandarūs	–	–
Alexander's mother	–	–	Halāy	Nāhīd	–	–	Olympias
Exchange of symbolic gifts	–	✓	✓	–	✓	✓	
The first battle	Euphrates	Euphrates	Jazīrah (Arbela)	Euphrates	Euphrates	River Strangas	Issus in Cilicia
Darius's murderers	✓	✓	✓	✓	✓	✓	✓
Alexander's translations	–	–	✓	–		–	–
King Porus	✓	✓	–	✓	✓	✓	✓
Brahmans			✓	✓	✓	✓	✓
Queen Candace	✓	✓	–	✓	✓	✓	✓
Alexander in China	✓	✓	✓	✓	✓	✓	–
Gog and Magog	✓	✓	✓	✓	✓	–	–
Land of Darkness/ Fountain of Life	✓	✓	✓	✓	✓	✓	✓
A half-human half-animal creature	–	–	–	✓	–	✓	✓

Table 2.1: *continued*

Motif/source	Dīnawarī (9th c.)	*Nihāya* (11th c.)	Ṭabarī (10th c.)	Firdawsī (11th c.)	Tha'ālibī (11th c.)	Syriac Pseudo-Callisthenes (7th c.)	Greek Pseudo-Callisthenes (3rd c.)
Place of Alexander's death	Jerusalem	Jerusalem	Shahrazūr near Babylon	Babylon	Shahrazūr near Babylon	Babylon	Babylon
Alexander's age when he dies	–	–	36	–	38	32 years and 7 months	32
The Laments	–	✓	–	✓	✓	–	–
Alexander's cities	12	12	12	10	–	13	12
Alexander's reign			14 years	14 years	14 years	12 years and 7 months	10 years
Tribal kingdoms after Alexander	✓	✓	✓	✓	✓	–	–
Dhū'l-Qarnayn	–	✓	–	–	✓	–	–

Alexander the Great in the *Khudāynāmag*

As we have seen in the first two sections of this chapter, early Islamic historiography, composed by authors of Iranian origin, not only was influenced by the Pseudo-Callisthenes tradition, but also contained various motifs (such as Alexander's Persian ancestry) that must have been based on a Middle Persian source. These motifs indicate that the legendary life of Alexander was adopted into the general body of the Iranian historical tradition.[137] The Iranian adaption of the *Romance* not only accepts the positive image of Alexander, but also links him to the last Kayānid kings by making the first Dārā his father and the second Dārā his half-brother, thus bestowing upon him the legitimacy of kingship. Judging from the common motifs discussed in this chapter, we can assume that the episode of Alexander's deeds and ancestry in the *Khudāynāmag* may have run as follows:

> Philip was defeated by the Persian king Dārā and accepted to pay an annual tribute in the form of golden eggs. He also gave his daughter in marriage to the Persian king. However, Dārā lost interest in her because she had bad breath. She was cured by a herb that in the Greek language was called *sandar* (or a similar word). She was sent back to Rūm without revealing that she was pregnant. There, she gave birth to a son whom she named after the herb that cured her bad breath. Philip accepted the child as his own and engaged Aristotle as his tutor. When Philip died, Alexander ascended the throne of Rūm.
>
> After sending back the Greek princess, Dārā had another son with another woman and gave him his own name, Dārā. The son then ascended the throne when his father, the first Dārā, died. He sent ambassadors to Alexander in order to claim the annual tribute. Alexander refused and said: 'The hen that used to lay the golden eggs has died, thus there is no tribute to pay.'
>
> This caused war between the two brothers. Alexander bribed two men of Hamadān who were Dārā's guards, and induced them to kill the Persian king. Thus, Dārā was killed by his own guards. Alexander found the dying king and heard his last words. Dārā asked him to marry his daughter Rawshanak, preserve the Iranian feasts and noble families, and punish his murderers.

Alexander buried Dārā according to Persian custom, punished the murderers and married Rawshanak. He sent a letter to the Persian nobles and made a speech on ascending the throne, which was the custom among the Persian kings. In his speech and letter, he legitimised his claim as the rightful King of Persia. Then he ordered the translation of Persian books into Greek and sent them to Rūm.

He built many cities, among which Samarqand, Merv and Bukhāra had a vivid memory of their founder. When he knew that his death was near, he wanted to kill the Persian nobles because he was afraid of their rebellion. But Aristotle advised him to separate the Persian Empire into local kingdoms, inaugurating the period known as *kadag-xwadāy* in Middle Persian.

Something like this summary of Alexander's deeds and ancestry must have been included in the *Khudāynāmag* because all the Arabic historical accounts mentioned in this chapter more or less repeat it.[138] However, the question as to whether other motifs from the Pseudo-Callisthenes tradition (such as the battle with the Indian king Porus and the search for the Water of Life) existed in the Sasanian *Khudāynāmag*, or whether they were incorporated into Arabic historical accounts after the Arab conquest, remains unanswered and is a matter of controversy among scholars. In this regard, there are two principal theories:

(1) Khaleghi-Motlagh, following Nöldeke's hypothesis, believes that the *Khudāynāmag* did not contain the account of Alexander (as reflected in the *Shāhnāma* of Firdawsī), but that it was an independent work translated from Middle Persian to Arabic by Ibn al-Muqaffa'.[139] He affirms that this Arabic translation was based on the Middle Persian version of the Pseudo-Callisthenes, as argued by Nöldeke.
(2) Tafaḍḍulī and Boyce both affirm that 'the compilers of the *Khudāynāmag* used written foreign sources ... notably a Syriac version of the *Alexander Romance*'.[140]

But Tafaḍḍulī and Boyce do not specify why and how they reached such a conclusion. If there had been a Middle Persian translation of the

Pseudo-Callisthenes, as Nöldeke argued, why would they need the Syriac translation?

Conclusion: The Origin and Development of the *Alexander Romance* in the Arabo-Persian Tradition

In this chapter, we have tried to clarify what the basic issues are in the study of the influence of Sasanian historiography on the Arabic historical sources of the *Alexander Romance*, based on the historical background of the translation movement in the Sasanian period. From this analysis, we can draw several conclusions.

Firstly, we may conclude that legends concerning Alexander the Great must have existed in the Iranian world from the Parthian period.[141] The era of Khusraw Anūshirvān (Chosroes I, r. 531–79) must be considered the time when these oral legends were amalgamated with the *Alexander Romance* and were written down by the authors of the *Khudāynāmag*, mainly because this is when Khusraw I accepted refugees from the Eastern Roman Empire when Justinian closed the Neoplatonist schools of Athens in 529.[142] There were also refugees from Alexandria in Egypt, where curiously the *Alexander Romance* originated. Khusraw I's welcome of these refugees could be the moment when the *Alexander Romance* entered the Persian tradition and completed a part of the history of Iran.[143] Stoneman and Daryaee also affirm that it is likely that the Greek tale became known to Persians as a result of the interest of this Sasanian king.[144] It is furthermore possible that the Syriac *Alexander Romance* was also translated under the patronage of Khusraw I. It is curious that Budge mentions that Syriac was not the translator's native language.[145]

In addition, there are other pieces of evidence for the possibility that the Syriac translation of the Pseudo-Callisthenes was undertaken in the Sasanian court. For one, every time we find the names of the Achaemenid kings they are referred to with the title Khusraw.[146] For instance, Xerxes is referred to in the Syriac version by the name of Khusraw, and Darius assumes titles that were used by Shābuhr II after the fourth century AD.[147] Nevertheless, it is likely that the Syriac and the Middle Persian versions were prepared almost at the same time and probably in the same court, but for different audiences and different purposes.[148] Furthermore, the Middle Persian version was modified and included in the *Khudāynāmag* in order to create a continuous history of Iran.

Secondly, the enormous variety of works on Alexander the Great in the Islamic world indicates that the Pseudo-Callisthenes tradition was translated into Arabic through two different channels:

(1) It is likely that the historical accounts (the *tārīkh* genre) that include Alexander among the Persian kings and claim that he was Dārā's brother, are based on the Middle Persian translation of the Pseudo-Callisthenes. This translation was included in the Sasanian chronicle *Khudāynāmag* (*The Book of Sovereigns*), and was then translated into Arabic as *Sayr al-Mulūk* in the eighth century AD, the most well known of which was the Ibn al-Muqaffaʿ translation. We can claim such a conclusion because the oldest representations of the *Alexander Romance* (those by Dīnawarī and Ṭabarī, and the *Nihāya*) include it as part of Persian history. Alexander's tale is always referenced with the Kayānids, and there is no independent version of this work until after the twelfth century AD.

(2) The Pseudo-Callisthenes account was also translated into Arabic directly from Syriac, possibly in the ninth century AD.[149] This was the source for the works (including the *Mujamal al-tavārīkh* and the Ethiopian version) that contained motifs such as the tale of Nectanebo and the foundation of Alexandria.

Thirdly, there is no doubt that the Arabic translation of the *Khudāynāmag* by Ibn al-Muqaffaʿ contained the Alexander episode – through which it became known to historians of the ninth and tenth centuries AD – because the *Nihāya* quotes Ibn al-Muqaffaʿ at the beginning of the passage on Alexander.[150] In addition, we have the testimony of the anonymous *Tārīkh-i Sīstān* (*The Sīstān Chronicle*),[151] which reports:

> Iskandar *Rūmī*, after Dārā's death and his marriage with Rawshanak, Dārā's daughter, decided to go to India. First he went to Sīstān and decided to build a castle, where there is another one built by Ardashīr Bābakān. Iskandar remained there for seven days ... but left Rawshanak in the castle until he returned from India. When he returned, the castle was finished. So he remained there one month and claimed: 'This castle must be named *ark.*' And *ark* in the *rūmī* language[152] means 'fort' and this is the reason why the castle of Sīstān is called 'Ark' [*Arg*]. This account is

> attested by various sources: one in *Akhbār-i Sīstān*, and another in Ibn al-Muqaffa''s *Sayr al-mulūk 'ajam.*[153]

The *Nihāya* and the *Tārīkh-i Sīstān* therefore prove that the Arabic translation of the *Khudāynāmag* of Ibn al-Muqaffa' contained accounts of Alexander.

The ensuing chapters of this book will help to clarify the complex development of the Pseudo-Callisthenes tradition in Persian literature. The next chapter in particular will discuss the various hypotheses mentioned above (by Boyce, Tafaḍḍulī and Khaleghi-Motlagh) regarding whether the Pseudo-Callisthenes was included in the *Khudāynāmag* and through which language (Syriac or Middle Persian). The *Shāhnāma* of Firdawsī features some characteristics of the *Alexander Romance* that did not survive in any other source and thus helps to clarify these questions. Furthermore, Firdawsī's grand poetic narrative of the history of ancient Persia, as we will see, is a valuable source in which it is possible to trace the 'missing link' between the appearance of the Pseudo-Callisthenes' version of the *Alexander Romance* in Alexandria in the third century AD and its reappearance in Khurāsān (in ancient Parthia) in the tenth century AD.

CHAPTER 3

ALEXANDER THE GREAT IN THE *SHĀHNĀMA* OF FIRDAWSĪ

کهن دولت به اقبال جوانان برنمی آیـد
قیاس از حال دارا و سکندر می توان کردن

Timeworn kingdoms don't cope well when juveniles
in the flush of fortune strut upon the scene.
One can conjecture and surmise this is the case
from Darius's and Alexander's circumstances.

Ṣā'ib Tabrīzī (d. 1676)[1]

Firdawsī's *Shāhnāma*, completed in 1010, though conceived as a historical work, is closer in mode to epic poetry.[2] Its register is highly sophisticated and bears comparison with Homeric language, particularly in the use of what has been called the 'Homeric simile'.[3] It reflects the pre-eminently Persian perception of history as focused on the deeds of the kings who ruled ancient Iran. Owing to its richness of detail, the *Shāhnāma* remains the most important source for the history, literature and culture of pre-Islamic Persia.[4]

The story of Alexander the Great in the *Shāhnāma* is also the first complete representative of the Pseudo-Callisthenes tradition in the Islamic world.[5] Like the sources that follow the *Khudāynāmag* tradition, as discussed in the previous chapter, the Alexander episode in the *Shāhnāma* covers three different reigns – including those of Dārā(b) and his sons Dārā and Alexander (Iskandar or

Sikandar) – and contains 2,458 verses in the Khaleghi-Motlagh edition.[6]

As Dick Davis points out, the Alexander story in the *Shāhnāma* is a bridge from legendary to quasi-historical material,[7] and thus deserves particular attention. This might be due to a change of perspective, which marked a turning point in the Persian conception of history. In order to analyse the Alexander episode in the *Shāhnāma*, we must first briefly look at the background of the poem's compilation and its possible sources, before we go on to examine its characteristics and motifs, especially those that distinguish Firdawsī's *Alexander Romance* from other versions. We can then focus on the Syriac materials that appear in the *Shāhnāma*, and what the presence of these materials tells us about the development of the *Alexander Romance* in the Persian tradition from the pre-Islamic to the Islamic period.

Sources and Content of the *Shāhnāma*

Firdawsī's *Shāhnāma* is based primarily on a Persian prose work compiled in 957/958 (completed in 1010 in Khurāsān, north-eastern Iran) by order of Abū Manṣūr ʿAbd al-Razzāq Ṭūsī, the governor of Ṭūs; however, the only part preserved is the glossary.[8] Derived ultimately from Sasanian sources, this prose work, which was also named *Shāhnāma* (*Book of Kings*), seems to have been independent of the Arabic translations and was probably based on Pahlavi material, since the names of the compilers are all Zoroastrian and they are also called *mubeds*, Mazdean priests.[9] This prose work incorporated not only the *Khudāynāmag* but also a number of historical fictions, popular tales and legends.[10]

Although some scholars have tried to demonstrate that Firdawsī's *Shāhnāma* is based on oral sources,[11] there can be no doubt, as De Blois rightly points out, that the poem is based on written sources, though we cannot necessarily presume that it is all based on one single source.[12] This last point is more obvious in the case of the chapter featuring Alexander in the *Shāhnāma*, which is an amalgam of independent sources, but nevertheless uniform and coherent. In order to analyse the sources and origins of Alexander's chapter in the *Shāhnāma* of Firdawsī, we first need to examine a brief summary of its contents.

Summary of the *Alexander Romance* in the *Shāhnāma*

Dārā(b)'s Reign

(1) In a war between Philip and Dārā(b), Philip is defeated and agrees to pay tribute in the form of golden eggs.[13] He also gives his daughter, Nāhīd, in marriage to the Persian king.
(2) From this union, Alexander is born, but Dārā(b) is unaware of this because he had sent Nāhīd back to Philip on account of her bad breath.
(3) Meanwhile, Dārā(b) has another son with another woman, and calls him Dārā.

Dārā's Reign

(1) Dārā delivers a speech on ascending the throne of Persia.
(2) Alexander ascends the throne after Philip's death and makes Aristotle his advisor.[14]
(3) Dārā's ambassadors demand the tribute of golden eggs.[15] Alexander refuses and replies: 'The hen that laid those golden eggs has died.' This leads to war between Dārā and Alexander.
(4) Alexander goes to Dārā's court disguised as his own ambassador. At a banquet, he hides some golden cups inside his clothes. When Dārā discovers this, he queries Alexander's strange behaviour. Alexander answers that it is a Greek custom.[16] Thus the Persian king gives the golden cups to Alexander, full of jewellery. The ambassadors who were sent to demand the tribute are present; they recognise Alexander and he has to flee.[17]
(5) Dārā and Alexander exchange letters.[18]
(6) The first battle takes place on the bank of the Euphrates and lasts eight days. Dārā is defeated and has to flee the battlefield.
(7) Dārā tries to gather more troops and a second battle takes place over three days. However, he is defeated again and flees to Jahrum and then to Iṣṭakhr (Persepolis).
(8) In a third battle, Alexander defeats Dārā and conquers Iṣṭakhr. Dārā flees to Kirmān (south-eastern Iran).
(9) Dārā writes a letter to Alexander offering him the treasures of Persia. At the same time, he also writes a letter to Fūr

(Porus), the Indian king, in order to ask him for help against Alexander.[19]

(10) In a fourth battle, the Persians surround Alexander. Dārā is killed by two of his own men. According to Firdawsī, they are Māhyār and Jānūsyār,[20] one a *mubed* and the other a *vazīr* ('minister').[21]

(11) Alexander finds the king as he lies dying and weeps for his misfortune.[22] He hears Dārā's last words and concords with his plea for Alexander to marry his daughter, Rawshanak (Roxana), punish the king's murderers and allow Persian customs and Zoroastrian feasts.[23]

(12) Alexander punishes the murderers. He is accepted as the legitimate king of Persia. He writes a letter to the Persian nobles.[24]

Alexander's Reign

(1) Alexander delivers a speech on ascending the throne.[25] He also writes a letter to Rawshanak (Roxana) and her mother.[26]

(2) Alexander asks his mother, who is in Amorium, to come to Iran and prepare the wedding.[27] There is a detailed description of Rawshanak's dowry.

(3) Kayd, the Indian king, gives four fantastic gifts to Alexander. During ten nights Kayd, the king of Qānūj, has different dreams. Mihrān, his vizier (*vazīr*) interprets them to mean that Alexander will attack Kayd's kingdom unless he gives Alexander four marvellous things the like of which no noble has ever seen in all the world (Kayd's daughter, a philosopher, a physician and a magic cup). The two kings exchange letters and finally Alexander sends nine wise men to examine the gifts. Having had the authenticity of the gifts appraised and verified by the wise men, they bring them to Alexander, who personally tests them too. He marries Kayd's daughter according to Christian custom.[28]

(4) Alexander writes a letter to the Indian king Fūr.[29] A battle takes place between the two kings in which Alexander uses iron horses, with iron saddles and iron riders, filled with black oil. They are mounted on wheels and look like cavalry. Alexander orders that the iron horses be set on fire on the battlefield.[30] Alexander challenges Fūr to single combat, and he manages to kill the Indian king.[31]

(5) Alexander marches towards Mecca to liberate the descendants of Ismael, son of Abraham.[32]

(6) From Jidda he sails to Egypt, where he stays for one year. Here he learns of the Queen Qaidāfa (Candace) of al-Andalus (Spain) and decides to visit her kingdom.[33]

(7) Alexander visits Queen Candace and her sons (this is given in a very detailed account, very close to the Greek *Alexander Romance*).[34]

(8) Alexander meets the Brahmans in order to learn ancient practices from these ascetics.[35]

(9) Alexander marches to the East and undergoes strange and marvellous experiences (fabulous tales are related belonging to the *mirabilia* genre).[36]

(10) Alexander reaches the 'Western sea' and Abyssinia (Ḥabash). A battle with Abyssinians takes place.

(11) Alexander visits the land of *narm-pāyān*, who are creatures with 'soft feet' (with no bones).[37]

(12) Alexander slays a dragon by feeding it five oxen, which he had killed and filled with oil and poison.[38]

(13) Alexander sets out to visit Harūm, the Land of Women.[39] Marching towards this land, he has to face many adventures.

(14) Alexander enters the Land of Darkness.[40] His adventures in the Land of Darkness comprise four stories:

a. His search for the Water of Life.

b. His dialogue with two enormous green birds that speak the Greek language.

c. His encounter with the angel Isrāfīl (the Angel who trumpets the Day of Resurrection).

d. His visit to the Valley of Diamonds.

(15) Alexander builds a wall against Gog and Magog.[41]

(16) Alexander sees a corpse in the Palace of Topaz[42] and also a talking tree,[43] which foretells his death.

(17) Alexander marches towards Chīn (China). He writes a letter to the Chinese Emperor and receives a response, then goes to the Chinese court disguised as his own ambassador.[44]

(18) A battle takes place against the people of Sind.[45]

(19) Alexander reaches Yemen.

(20) Returning to Babylon, he comes across a creature called Gūsh-bastar (literally 'ear-bed'), who has ears so large that he sleeps on them.

He describes a city in which the houses are adorned with portraits of Afrāsīyāb and Kay Khusraw – two ancient kings from the Persian tradition.

(21) Alexander writes a letter to Aristotle informing him that he wants to kill the Persian nobles. Aristotle advises him not to, and that he should instead divide the Persian kingdom among the Persian nobles so that they will not rebel against Rūm.

(22) A woman bears a child that is half-human half-monster, with a lion's head, hooves and a bull's tail. It dies at birth. Alexander's astrologers interpret it as a sign of Alexander's death.[46]

(23) Alexander writes a letter of consolation to his mother.[47]

(24) Alexander dies in Babylon. The Persians and the Greeks argue about where they should bury him. At last, a man advises them to pose their question to a mountain, which responds to each question by way of an echo. The mountain answers that they should bury him in Alexandria, in Egypt.[48]

(25) Philosophers lament Alexander's death with wise sayings.[49]

(26) Firdawsī concludes that Alexander killed 36 kings, established ten cities and reigned for 14 years.[50]

From this summary of the contents of Firdawsī's *Alexander Romance* we may conclude that the story of Alexander in the *Shāhnāma* has some important characteristics that can help us understand the development of the *Alexander Romance* in the Persian tradition, and its transition from the pre-Islamic period to the Islamic era. Firdawsī's account represents an amalgam of various sources (as mentioned above), which contains different parts; the five key points can be enumerated as follows:

(1) The chapter on Alexander in the *Shāhnāma* represents the first complete adaptation of the *Romance*, and contains detailed parts of the Greek original not found in any previous source. The best example is the scene in which Alexander goes to Darius's court disguised as his own envoy, and tries to take some golden wine cups. A comparison between the Greek and Persian versions demonstrates an astonishing similarity. Another example is the episode of Queen Candace and her sons. The *Shāhnāma* is the most complete version and the closest to the Greek original extant in the Arabo-Persian tradition.

(2) The *Shāhnāma* contains parts from the *Khudāynāmag* discussed previously (such as Alexander's Persian ancestry and the tribute of golden eggs), as well as elements that must be based on a Persian source, such as Gūsh-bastar (the creature with enormous ears) and the city with Kay Khusraw's portraits.

(3) The *Shāhnāma* also contains parts from the Syriac sources discussed in the first chapter of this book: the Syriac *Alexander Romance* (such as the dragon slaying and the journey to Chīn), episodes from the Syriac *Legend* and *Poem* (such as Gog and Magog, and the Water of Life) and the philosophers' laments over Alexander's tomb.

(4) Beside the Syriac material, Firdawsī's version contains stories (such as that of Kayd, the Indian king) that must have been independent tales in circulation, especially in the eastern parts of the Iranian world; this will be discussed in detail later in this chapter.

(5) In addition, Firdawsī's text contains episodes that must have been developed only during the Islamic period (such as Alexander's journeys to Mecca and to al-Andalus in Muslim Spain).

Furthermore, it is clear that Alexander's story in Firdawsī's *Shāhnāma* contains various layers that must have been incorporated gradually into the *Khudāynāmag* version after the Arab conquest of the Persian world. Therefore, in order to better trace the development of the *Alexander Romance* from pre-Islamic Persian literature to the *Shāhnāma*, we need to first examine the most important characteristics of Firdawsī's version.[51]

Distinguishing Characteristics and Motifs of Firdawsī's *Alexander Romance*

The figure of Alexander in Firdawsī's *Shāhnāma* has some of the following distinguishing characteristics, which are not found in any other Arabic or Persian source of the Islamic period:

(1) He is a Christian and a legitimate Persian king, whose descent is traced back to the great hero Isfandīyār. Firdawsī's Alexander is well integrated in Persian legends; his ancestor Isfandīyār has much in common with certain figures from Greek mythology, in particular Achilles.[52] It is also interesting that Isfandīyār, like Alexander, is the descendant of a 'Caesar of Rūm' through his mother.[53]

(2) The name Dhū'l-Qarnayn ('the Two-Horned One') is an essential component of Alexander's legend in the Islamic world. However, since Firdawsī's Alexander is a Christian, the epithet Dhū'l-Qarnayn is not attributed to him in the *Shāhnāma*. The prophetic side of Alexander is not dealt with at all by Firdawsī. Nevertheless, we can assume that the source Firdawsī used belonged to a period when Islamic legends concerning Dhū'l-Qarnayn had not yet mixed with the *Alexander Romance* tradition. Through a closer study of the *Alexander Romance* in the *Shāhnāma* we will hopefully be able to identify this period, which may be at the end of the Sasanian period or very early in the Arab conquest of Persia (in the seventh and eighth centuries).

(3) It is clear that Firdawsī's source definitely passed through an Arabic intermediary because of the usage of Arabic terms, such as *tanīn* for dragon instead of the Persian *izhdahā*,[54] and *muḥibb-i ṣalīb* ('lovers of the Cross', that is, Christians).[55] Even though his source was written in Arabic, it must have belonged to a period in which Islamic legends about Alexander had not yet been formed; firstly, because his account is Christianised and not Islamised and, secondly, because Alexander is not called Dhū'l-Qarnayn in any part of the *Shāhnāma*, as mentioned above.

Based on the appearance of the above words, motifs and references in the story, as well as the information that Firdawsī himself gives us, we can now divide Alexander's story in the *Shāhnāma* into three principal layers that show the historic transmission of the legend. All three contain Christian references.

(1) The parts that contain the same common accounts that are also reported in Arabic by historians (including Ṭabarī and Dīnawarī), as discussed in the previous chapter. These parts were originally in the *Khudāynāmag* tradition and formed the basis of the legend.[56]

(2) The material from Syriac sources, which also contains elements from the Persian tradition such as the creature Gūsh-bastar and the city with Kay Khusraw's portraits.

(3) Certain inherently Islamic words and other elements (such as Alexander's journey to Mecca and to al-Andalus in Muslim Spain), which have no specifically Islamic reference. For example, even in

> the story of Candace, who is Queen of al-Andalus, there are only Christian references.

How can we explain such a combination of materials? What do they reflect of Firdawsī's sources in Alexander's chapter in the *Shāhnāma*? When and how was all this material brought together? The remainder of this chapter will try to answer these questions.

Firdawsī's Christian References

Beside Persian proper names (such as Nāhīd, Alexander's mother), there are some references in the *Shāhnāma* to Christian customs (such as for wedding ceremonies), which can be seen throughout the tale from beginning to end. The first Christian reference appears in the marriage of the Persian king Dārāb to Nāhīd, the daughter of Philip of Macedon. She is accompanied by churchmen: 'The beautiful Rūmī [princess] remained in her litter, guided by a bishop and a monk.'[57] The poet also claims that the bishop handed over the princess to Dārāb: 'The bishop gave the beautiful princess['s hand] to Dārāb / And the treasures [of her dowry] were counted out to the king's treasurer.'[58] Another Christian reference appears in the episode of Kayd, the Indian king: Alexander marries King Kayd's daughter according to Christian custom: 'he asked her [in marriage] with proper ceremony according to the custom of the Messiah.'[59]

In the episode relating his visit to Queen Qaidāfa (Candace), Alexander offers a very Christian oath that he will not send his army to invade her kingdom:

> By the faith of the Messiah and Truthful speech, by the knower who stands witness to my words, by the rites and the faith of the Great Cross, by the life and head of the mighty prince, by the deacon's belt (*zunnār*) and by the Holy Spirit.[60]

He also holds the Cross in reverence: 'Your well-wisher will be my brother; your throne will be as the Cross to me.'[61] It is even said that after his death, 'a Christian priest' washed Alexander's body and prepared him for the funeral: 'A bishop washed the corpse with musk and rosewater and sprinkled pure camphor over his body.'[62]

Such Christian references appear throughout the poem's account of Alexander, and it seems that Firdawsī quoted them directly from his source.[63] If we consider the Persian proper names (such as Dārā and Nāhīd) in conjunction with these Christian references, it is likely that the original Middle Persian version was also Christianised. Regarding Christian writings in Middle Persian, it is important to point out that they consisted largely of translations from Syriac.[64] This means that the Middle Persian *Vorlage* must have been based on a Syriac source (or sources). This supports the claims of Boyce and Tafaḍḍulī that the authors of the *Khudāynāmag* used Syriac materials for Alexander's chapter.[65] The most interesting proof of this assumption is that these Christian references generally appear in the episodes that have a Persian context, like the wedding of Nāhīd and the Persian king, or the episode of Kayd, the Indian king.

The Indian King Kayd

According to Firdawsī himself, the episode of the Indian king Kayd and his marvellous gifts to Alexander has a Pahlavi origin.[66] It consists of two principal parts: King Kayd's dreams and their interpretation, and the gifts whose authenticity Alexander examines. This narrative, which is found neither in the Greek nor in the Syriac *Alexander Romance*, also appears in three Arabic sources: the *Qiṣṣat al-Iskandar* (*The Story of Alexander*)[67] of 'Umāra (d. *c.*902),[68] the *Murūj al-dhahab* of al-Masūdī (896–956)[69] and the *Tārīkh Ghurar al-sayr wa Akhbār Mulūk al-Fars* of Tha'ālibī Nīshābūrī (961–1038).[70] However, only Firdawsī and 'Umāra include King Kayd's dreams.

We will study this story by comparing its various sources, in order to verify whether Firdawsī's claim that the source of this story was written in 'Pahlavi' is true. We will mainly focus on the *Shāhnāma* and 'Umāra's tale because they are the most complete versions.

King Kayd in the Kārnāma ī Artakhshīr (The Deeds of Ardashīr)

As an initial step in this comparison, we must take note of some important points concerning King Kayd's name and his appearance in the Pahlavi book *Kārnāma ī Artakhshīr ī Pāpakān* (*The Deeds of Ardashīr,*

Son of Bābak), which is practically the only extant secular work from the Sasanian period. In this Pahlavi text (Chapter XI, number 4)[71] he appears as *Kaīt Hindū* (which is similar to his name in the *Shāhnāma* of Firdawsī: *Kayd-i hindī*). The Pahlavi transcription *Kaitān Kandākān konūshkān*[72] without doubt refers to Kidara, the founder of the Kidarite dynasty,[73] who emerged in Khurāsān in around AD 380 with the Sasanian title *Kushānshāh* 'King of the Kushans'.[74] He is referred to in Sanskrit as Kidara or Kidāra,[75] and in Persian as Kīdār or Kaydar,[76] which explains the transformation of the name into Qaydar in 'Umāra's work. Kayd also appears in the story of Ardashīr in Firdawsī's *Shāhnāma*, where he is a wise man who foretells Ardashīr's destiny.[77] The appearance of King Kayd in the Pahlavi *Kārnāma* and the *Shāhnāma* proves that this personage existed in pre-Islamic Persian literature.

Kayd and Dandamis

Nöldeke[78] was the first scholar to postulate that the story of Kayd is linked to Alexander's meeting with the *gymnosophist* Dandamis.[79] However, this supposition is not correct because Alexander's meeting with the Brahmans is another tale in the *Shāhnāma* in which Dandamis does not appear.[80] Doufikar-Aerts points out: 'It is still not clear, however, by which channel this motif reached the Arab author; as Dandamis does not appear in the Syriac Pseudo-Callisthenes.'[81] The reason for this is that the story of Kayd was an independent tale in Pahlavi, as Firdawsī affirms,[82] which was added to the *Alexander Romance* tradition after the Arab conquest.

King Kayd's Dreams and their Interpretation

It is worth mentioning that the study of dreams and their interpretation were an integral part of the Persian world view.[83] In the *Shāhnāma*, 18 dreams are reported and the episode involving that of Kayd is the most elaborate one.[84] King Kayd recounts his dreams in the *Shāhnāma* as follows:

(1) I dreamed of a huge room like a palace in which there was a huge elephant. It had a door like a tiny hole. The formidable elephant passed through the hole without damaging its body. Its body managed to get out but its trunk was trapped inside the room.

(2) Another night, I dreamed that I was not on my throne; instead a monkey[85] was sitting on my ivory throne with the shining crown on its head.

(3) The third night, I dreamed of a canvas. Four men were pulling the canvas and the effort of stretching it made their faces blue. But neither did they become tired nor did the canvas break.

(4) The fourth night, I dreamed of a thirsty man by a river. A fish poured water on him but the man turned his face and ran away from the water. He was running and the water was following him. O wise man! What is the interpretation of this dream?

(5) The fifth night, I dreamed of a city by the sea. All its inhabitants were blind but yet they were not angry at being blind. It was so crowded as if there was a battle in the city.

(6) The sixth night, I dreamed of a city in which all the people were ill. They went to greet healthy people, and looked at their urine to diagnose the sicknesses.

(7) In the middle of the seventh night I dreamed of a horse with two heads, two hooves and two paws. It was rapidly eating all the plants because it had two mouths. But in its body there was nowhere for which the food to come out.

(8) The eighth night, I dreamed of three jars, all of them similar. Two were full and the one in the middle remained empty for many years. Two men poured cold water from [the] full jar[s] into the empty one, but they never became empty and the empty jar never became full.

(9) The ninth night, I dreamed of a cow lying on the grass in the sun. There was a thin calf beside it. The thin calf was feeding the fat cow.

(10) The tenth night, I dreamed of a spring on a vast plain. The plain was full of water but everything was dry around the spring.[86]

The interpretation of the second dream is very interesting, for Firdawsī refers to four religions:

> Regarding the canvas and four men, in the future a renowned man will rise from 'the plain of lancer riders'. A good man who will cause the division of God's religion into four branches. One is the *dihqān*,

> the old fire worshipper, another is Moses's religion called *juhūd* (Judaism), which says that no other religion deserves to be worshipped. Another is the Greek (*yūnānī*) religion, which will bring justice to the king's heart. The fourth is the religion of that benevolent man[87] who will raise the wise men up from the dust.

While Firdawsī describes ten dreams, 'Umāra's text reduces them to six, as follows:

(1) Kayd dreamed of his demise and the end of his kingdom.
(2) Another of his dreams involved a calf nursing a cow.
(3) He dreamed of blind people in a city buying and selling, eating and drinking, and fighting.
(4) He dreamed of people obliging a huge man with two heads, who ate everything in his path.
(5) He dreamed of an elephant enclosed in a small space that managed to get out, all but its tail. He was surprised to see that the elephant's head and body were able to come out but its little tail could not.
(6) He dreamed of a thirsty man who was dying from thirst as he drowned in water.[88]

But it is notable that during his interpretation of the above six dreams, 'Umāra mentions the existence of a few more dreams, such as the three jars with the middle one empty or the water flowing dry. This means that in 'Umāra's own source there were other dreams similar to those seen in the *Shāhnāma*.

The man who interprets the dreams in 'Umāra's text is described as a 'spiritual leader', while in the *Shāhnāma* he is called 'Mihrān', a man who has reached the heights of knowledge and lives far from people among wild and domestic animals. Firdawsī's description of Mihrān coincides with the figure of the Indian ascetic monk, a spiritual leader mentioned by 'Umāra.

King Kayd's Four Marvellous Gifts

The second part of the story of King Kayd comprises a description of the four wonders or marvellous gifts given by the king to Alexander, during which Alexander and Kayd exchange letters and Alexander assesses the four gifts. All four sources agree on the nature of the four wonders: Kayd's daughter (although according to Mas'ūdī, she is his servant), his philosopher, his physician and a goblet that is always full. Tha'ālibī is the only source that gives names to the three people among these marvellous gifts: Kayd's daughter is *Kanka*, the philosopher is *Shanka* and the physician is *Manka*.[89]

King Kayd's Daughter. Kayd's first marvellous possession is his daughter. According to Firdawsī and Mas'ūdī, when the wise men sent by Alexander to verify the gifts' authenticity saw Kayd's beautiful daughter, they were so astonished that each of them could only write a description of a single part of her body for Alexander.[90] Khaleghi-Motlagh rightly points out that the similarity of Firdawsī's and Mas'ūdī's accounts indicates that this story is based on a written source.[91]

King Kayd's Philosopher. In order to verify the knowledge of King Kayd's philosopher, Alexander puts him to the test by sending him several objects within which are secreted a special message. Each time, by means of a gesture or an alteration to the object, the philosopher shows that he has outwitted Alexander.

For instance, during the exchange of symbolic objects, Alexander sends a dark piece of iron to the Indian philosopher, who turns it into a mirror. In the *Shāhnāma*, the dialogue between Alexander and the Indian philosopher presents the symbolic meaning of a mirror as a reflection of his heart.[92] In these encounters with the philosopher, Alexander is always reproached for his greed for warfare and bloodshed, which 'darkened his heart'.[93] The Indian philosopher is the first person to offer him a solution to 'brighten' Alexander's heart: like a dark piece of iron that becomes a bright mirror by polishing, his heart can become as crystal clear as water by polishing it with divine knowledge (*dānish-i āsmān*).[94] The mirror motif becomes an important element of later Persian versions of the *Alexander Romance*; in fact, it would appear that from this basic motif later Persian poets derived and developed the mystical aspect of Alexander's legendary personality.

The Magic Goblet. Among the wondrous objects Kayd gifted to Alexander was a magic goblet that never ran dry. Firdawsī gives the following explanation as to why it never runs dry:

> Think of what happens here as analogous to magnetism, which attracts iron. In a similar way, this cup attracts moisture from the turning heavens, but it does so in such a subtle fashion that human eyes cannot see the process.[95]

The magic goblet or cup was to become a key component of Alexander's legend in the later Persian poetic tradition.[96] The most famous magic cup in Persian literature is that of Kay Khusraw, in which he was able to contemplate the whole world. In the first part of his *Iskandarnāma*, the poet Niẓāmī relates that Alexander finds Kay Khusraw's magic cup, whose secrets enabled the Greeks to invent the astrolabe.[97]

The Indian Physician. According to the *Shāhnāma*, King Kayd's physician was able to diagnose any illness by examining the sufferer's urine.[98] This part of the story contains advice on eating and drinking and resembles Alexander's dialogue with the Brahmans.[99] Alexander asks the Indian physician: 'What is the most painful illness?' The physician's reply in the 'Umāra and Tha'ālibī versions is 'indigestion'; in the *Shāhnāma* he replies, 'Whoever overeats and does not watch what he consumes during meals, will grow ill; a healthy person will not eat too much, and a great man is the one who seeks to be healthy.'[100]

The Indian physician is able to prepare a remedy that prevents any kind of illness and disease, including old age.[101] Thanks to this remedy, Alexander remains healthy for years. However, the most important part in this story relates to Alexander's sexual affairs and the illness caused by them. The story according to Firdawsī is as follows:

> Then the king began to devote his nights to carousing rather than to sleep. His mind was filled with the desire for women, and he sought out soft, enticing places to be with them. This way of life weakened the king, but he gave no thought to the harm he was doing to his body.[102]

'Umāra's text does not include this part of the story, but there is a sentence that symbolically expresses the same theme: the physician warns Alexander that 'there is no sickness worse than torture by fire. You indulge yourself in your desires more than you should.'[103]

The *Shāhnāma* links Alexander's illness directly with his devotion to overindulgence in sexual relations. In 'Umāra's text the illness is called *sulāl*, which means 'consumption or tuberculosis'.[104] The word Firdawsī uses is *kāhish*, which literally means 'decrease' and indicates an illness that consumes the body and causes the sufferer to lose weight.[105]

In both Firdawsī's and 'Umāra's texts, the physician prepares a remedy against Alexander's illness. In the *Shāhnāma*, Alexander sleeps alone for one night, unaccompanied by any of his beautiful women.[106] When the physician examines Alexander's urine the next day, he finds no sign of illness. He thus throws away the remedy he had prepared for the sovereign.

In 'Umāra's *Qiṣṣat al-Iskandar*, the physician prepares a medicine against *sulāl*. There are some sentences similar to the above account in this narrative. 'Umāra says:

> Before drinking the medicine, Dhū'l-Qarnayn had to go to relieve himself. While in the toilet, a vision came to him and said: 'I am the *sulāl* that was planning to stay inside you for four years. However, I saw the medicine the doctor had prepared and decided to leave you instead of being tortured by his medicine.'[107]

Alexander's sexual affairs are omitted in 'Umāra's account, and the story finishes in a completely different way. 'Umāra is the only source in which the disease called *sulāl* causes Alexander's death:

> Once the doctor returned to India, the disease quickly returned with a vengeance. Now *sulāl* became personified and told Alexander: 'I shall torture you, making you weep as you cause the weeping of mothers and fathers over the deaths of their children.' Soon Alexander felt the burning fire which the doctor told him was the worst of deaths, and he dies in Babylon.[108]

Zuwiyya interprets this denouement as a moral:

> The lesson Alexander could have taken away from the Angel of the Horn, and from his disputations with the Brahmans did not improve his character. The trio of the Indian king, the philosopher and the physician with their humble wisdom, and some divine aid in the way of *sulāl*, managed to trick Alexander with a riddle he could not solve. Consequently, he died and they kept their kingdom.[109]

It is not clear which version, Firdawsī's or 'Umāra's, constitutes the original form of the tale. As we saw above, the original form of this story must have been added to the *Alexander Romance* tradition through a Pahlavi source, just as Firdawsī claimed. There are a number of reasons for this. Firstly, the fact that Kayd is mentioned in the Pahlavi *Kārnāma ī Artakhshīr ī Pāpakān* indicates that this character was known in Sasanian literature. Secondly, as this story appears in Mas'ūdī's *Murūj* as an independent chapter on Alexander in India, it is probable that Kayd's tale was originally an independent story that was integrated into the *Alexander Romance* tradition during the Islamic period. Khaleghi-Motlagh postulates that this passage was an independent story preserved in Sanskrit, which was added to the *Alexander Romance* that had been translated into Pahlavi.[110] However, as this Kayd episode is not mentioned by Ṭabarī, Dīnawarī or the anonymous *Nihāya*, it did not feature in the *Khudāynāmag* tradition. On the other hand, it is included in Tha'ālibī's *Ghurar*, which is also based on the same prose text of the *Shāhnāma* of Abū Manṣūr as the verse composition of the *Shāhnāma* of Firdawsī.[111] All of this demonstrates that it is probable that this independent story was added to the Alexander episode of the *Shāhnāma* of Abū Manṣūr from a Pahlavi source.

Syriac Materials in the *Shāhnāma*

Most of the parts of the Alexander episode in the *Shāhnāma* are based on the Syriac sources mentioned in the first chapter. There are two main themes in most of these stories:

(1) Alexander's adventures in wondrous lands, which were originally part of his letter to Aristotle about the wonders of India.[112]

(2) Alexander's concern with his own death.[113] Alexander is not just a world conqueror. His expeditions become campaigns in search of something more: knowledge, wisdom and immortality. The tone

> of the last parts of Alexander's legend in the *Shāhnāma* changes, and there are high moral themes, as mentioned, and reprimands addressed to Alexander for his greed (*āz*) and his insatiable desire for conquest.

By examining these materials we can shed light on the development of the *Alexander Romance* in the Persian tradition from the pre-Islamic to the Islamic period.

Alexander's Adventures in Wondrous Lands

Alexander in the Land of Creatures with 'Soft Feet'

Alexander's adventure with the soft-footed creatures appears in the Syriac *Alexander Romance* as part of his letter to Aristotle about the marvels of India.[114] In the Persian tradition these creatures with soft feet or legs are also known as *davāl-pā* ('hidden/leather foot or leg').[115] The *Shāhnāma* seems to be the earliest source in which there are references to such creatures: they feature not only in the Alexander section of Firdawsī's epic poem but also in another story, in the adventures of another Kayānid king, Kay Kāvūs, in Māzandarān, where they are also called *sust-pāyān* ('limp-footed creatures').[116]

Alexander the Dragon-Slayer

The story of Alexander slaying a dragon in the *Shāhnāma* is based on an episode in the Syriac version of the *Alexander Romance*. In the Syriac Pseudo-Callisthenes the story takes place in a region close to Prasiake in India.[117] Fighting a dragon is an archetypal labour of many kings and heroes in the *Shāhnāma*, including Alexander's ancestors Isfandīyār and Bahman Ardashīr.[118] However, as Ogden points out, 'it is possible to find Greek precedents' behind these dragon-slaying tales in the *Shāhnāma*.[119] Ogden studied the origins of this motif in the α-recension and earlier Greek dragon-slaying narratives,[120] and also examined the symbolism of the dragon in the Zoroastrian tradition.[121] The *yasht* collection of Avestan hymns lists various types of dragons and killers of dragons, transmitted mainly from the Indo-Iranian period.[122] According to the later Zoroastrian scriptures of the *Vidēvdāt* (or *Vendidād*), the 'law against the *daevas*' divided 'creation into two mutually antagonistic halves – the creatures of the Ahūrā Mazdā (the Great

Wisdom) on the one hand and the creatures of the Ahrīman (the Evil Power) on the other'.[123] According to this understanding, serpents or dragons (*azhi-* in Avestan, and *azh-* in Pahlavi) were identified as creatures of the 'hostile spirit' Ahrīman. They were defined as evil, noxious and harmful to man and his animals and crops (*khrafstra* in Avestan),[124] and thus deserving of death.[125] Firdawsī indeed uses the Avestic term *khrafstra*[126] in the tale of the 'night of terror',[127] when, after pitching camp in India by a freshwater lake, Alexander's army has to endure scorpions, huge beasts and serpents (Pseudo-Callisthenes, III, 7–16).[128]

However, the dragon-slaying legends in the later epic tradition of Persian poetry seem to have largely lost their religious (that is, Zoroastrian) importance. In the national legends, the meaning of the dragon-slaying motif becomes a royal or heroic act required as proof of the king's/hero's legitimacy.[129] As Khaleghi-Motlagh affirms:

> The requirement that every king or hero should demonstrate the legitimacy of his status by slaying a dragon or doing some other fabulous deed or receiving miraculous aid prompted not only the tendency to historicize mythology but also a contrary tendency to mythologize history ... In the case of Alexander, unlike the Zoroastrian priests who never acknowledged the Macedonian conqueror, the court historians attempted to justify Alexander's rule in Iran with all sorts of arguments for his legitimacy ... from stories which the Iranians themselves had invented for the purpose of legitimizing Alexander: Alexander's Iranian lineage and his slaying of a dragon.[130]

The method used by Alexander to slay the dragon is also found in other Persian legends. In the *Shāhnāma*, Alexander kills the dragon by feeding it five oxen stuffed with poison and naphtha.[131] This method is also used by the hero Rustam in the *Shāhnāma*, curiously in India, where he slays a dragon called Babr-i Bayān.[132] According to Firdawsī, Rustam fills oxhides with quicklime and stones and carries them to the place where the dragon comes out of the sea once a week. The dragon swallows them and its stomach bursts. Rustam then has the dragon flayed and makes a coat from its skin, which is also called *babr-i bayān*.[133] A similar method is also used by Farāmarz, Rustam's son, to slay a dragon called *Mār-i jawshā* ('the hissing snake'), which lives on a mountain in India.

Farāmarz slays the dragon with the help of another hero (Bīzhan). They hide in two boxes and allow themselves to be swallowed by the dragon.[134] In general, as Ogden points out, 'the motif of the killing of the dragon by feeding it burning or combustible material may well be best considered a folktale motif'.[135]

Gūsh-bastar and Apocalyptic Figures

Creatures with enormous ears appear constantly in the Persian tradition, not only in various stories of Firdawsī's *Shāhnāma*, but also in other epics.[136] In the *Shāhnāma*, on his return to Babylon, Alexander finds the aforementioned creature Gūsh-bastar,[137] who has such huge ears that he uses one as a mattress and the other as a blanket. Curiously, in many sources, Gog and Magog are described with enormous ears and also referred to as *pīl-gūsh* ('elephant ears') or *gilīm-gūsh* ('carpet ears').[138] Firdawsī also uses this description for Gog and Magog: 'their breast and ears are like those of an elephant. If they go to sleep, one of the ears serves as a bed, while the other is folded over their bodies.'[139]

It is also worth mentioning that similar creatures appear in the *Ayādgār ī Jāmāspīg* (*Memorial of Jāmāsp*), a Zoroastrian apocalyptic work[140] in Middle Persian,[141] also known as the *Jāmāspnāma*. These figures are called Bargūsh (or Vargūsh), which means people with long ears or with ears on their chest.[142] Firdawsī also uses the same word (Vargūsh) for Gūsh-bastar in a verse where Alexander calls the creature Gūsh-var.[143]

Another interesting issue regarding the Persian aspects of the tale of Gūsh-bastar appears on Alexander's way to Babylon, when a Gūsh-bastar creature speaks of an island on which there are images of Afrāsīyāb and Kay Khusraw painted on bones. It is an island where the only food is fish. In the Greek *Romance* (Pseudo-Callisthenes, III, 7), Alexander's letter to Aristotle about the wonders of India recounts that when they reached the city of Prasiake, they discovered people on 'a conspicuous promontory in the sea' who looked like women and fed on fish. Alexander also discovered that they were barbarian in speech. They pointed out an island where there was the grave of an ancient king.[144] This passage appears in two different parts of the *Shāhnāma*. In the passage 'Alexander travels to the East and sight of its wonders', after his encounter with the Brahmans, he reaches a deep ocean where there 'lived men who veiled themselves like women. Their language was not Arabic, Persian, Turkish, Chinese or Pahlavi. Their diet consisted of fish.'[145] In another passage, in Gūsh-bastar's tale, there is a similar description of a city whose buildings are covered with fish skins and fish bones, and the people eat fish.[146] Curiously, the grave of the 'ancient king' from the Greek *Romance* becomes in the *Shāhnāma* the faces of Kay Khusraw and Afrāsīyāb, two ancient kings from the Persian tradition, whose portraits were painted on bones.

As we can see here, in these fabulous legends and tales the description of Gog and Magog is mixed with the apocalyptic figures of Persian tradition (Vargūsh). The legends also feature other Persian elements, such as the mention of ancient Iranian kings. It is thus possible to deduce that these legends were added to the Persian Pseudo-Callisthenes tradition at an early point, when the tale of Gog and Magog was not yet linked to the Qur'ānic figure of Dhū'l-Qarnayn.

Alexander's Concern with his Own Death

Alexander's Encounter with the Brahmans

The narrative of Alexander's encounter with the Brahmans is found in a papyrus preserved in Berlin (*Pap. Berol.* 13044 = F. Gr. Hist., 1539), as well as in all extant works of historians of Alexander.[147] In the Greek *Alexander Romance* (III, 5–6) it features between the battle with Porus and the talking tree episode,[148] and it is expanded in the work of the fifth-century Palladius, *De gentibus Indiae et de Bragmanibus*.[149]

The structure of this episode in the *Shāhnāma* coincides with that found in the Greek Pseudo-Callisthenes. In the *Shāhnāma*, the Brahmans write Alexander a letter, which is similar in content to that in the Greek Pseudo-Callisthenes. Firdawsī also describes the Brahmans as naked (*birahna*), and their diet as consisting of seeds, fruits and plants.[150] Alexander visits them and asks them a series of riddles. At the end, he offers them the chance to ask him for whatever they want. They ask for immortality. He explains that this is impossible since he himself is a mortal, and he justifies his greed as being his fate.

The *Shāhnāma* contains all the same riddles and questions that Alexander poses to the Brahmans in the Greek Pseudo-Callisthenes. However, the questions and the answers become more sophisticated in the *Shāhnāma*, where they cover more than 30 verses. They contain Persian beliefs and demonstrate a familiarity with Firdawsī's source with such profound Persian concepts as *khirad* ('wisdom') and *āz* ('greed') – terms with a pre-Islamic derivation.[151] The best example of the similarity and yet greater sophistication of the Persian version is Alexander's question about kingship. The question in the Greek Pseudo-Callisthenes is simply: 'What is kingship?' (Pseudo-Callisthenes, III, 6). In the *Shāhnāma*, the poet develops the theme further: 'Who is the king of our souls? Who always accompanies us towards evil?' The Indian ascetic answers:

> Greed is the king, the ground of vengeance and the place of sin . . . Greed and need are two demons [*dīv*], wretched [*patyāra*] and malevolent; one is dry-lipped from longing, the other passes sleepless nights from excess. Time passing hunts down both, and blessed is the man whose mind accepts wisdom [*khirad*].[152]

Henceforth, Alexander's story in the *Shāhnāma* contains constant concern with the vanity of this world, and with death, and takes on a cautionary tone of reproach about Alexander's greed. As Charles-Henri de Fouchécour observes, Firdawsī's story of Alexander is really, to a certain extent, 'an anthology of counsels woven into the weave of a narrative that gives it sense . . . each king is placed in the presence of a vanity in which there is the desire to possess a world that death will strip from him.'[153]

Alexander's Dialogue with Two Giant Green Birds

According to the Greek Pseudo-Callisthenes (II, 40), these two birds have human faces and speak Greek. In the *Shāhnāma*, Firdawsī also mentions that the birds speak in Greek (*rūmī*). The green birds live on top of two ebony columns that reach into the clouds, beside a high mountain. While Alexander is the one who asks the questions in his encounter with the Brahmans, in his dialogue with the birds it is he who is interrogated. In this scene, the birds ask Alexander certain questions to verify his wisdom in order to decide whether he has the aptitude and capability to ascend to the heavens. The focus of their dialogue is on mundane pleasures and worldly lifestyles. This passage is so vivid and explicit that when reading the verses, the scene comes alive in one's imagination. Having verified Alexander's knowledge, the birds let the king ascend to the heavens, mounting 'up to the summit of that mountain, without any companions to see something that would make any happy man weep'.[154] The terrible sight Alexander sees at the top of the mountain is the angel Sirāfīl (Isrāfīl),[155] waiting for God's order to blow his trumpet and start the Day of Resurrection.

Alexander's Encounter with the Angel Isrāfīl

In the Greek Pseudo-Callisthenes (II, 41), after speaking with the birds, Alexander constructs a flying machine in order to explore the skies. Although in the *Shāhnāma* the same method of flying is used by Kay Kāvūs,[156] it is absent from Firdawsī's account of Alexander. Instead, after speaking with the birds, Alexander also ascends to the heavens when he climbs the mountain where the birds live. In the Greek Pseudo-Callisthenes he comes across a 'flying creature in the form of a man', who reproaches him by saying 'you have not yet secured the whole earth, and you are now exploring the heavens?'[157] In the *Shāhnāma*, this 'flying creature' is transformed into Isrāfīl, 'the Angel of the Trumpet of Judgement Day',[158] who reproaches Alexander 'with a voice like thunder': 'Stop struggling, slave of greed!'[159] The angel also warns him to prepare himself for death.

While in the Greek Pseudo-Callisthenes, Alexander does not attempt to justify himself or defend his deeds when faced by the flying creature's reproaches, in the *Shāhnāma* he says to Isrāfīl: 'I will never know another fate than this incessant wandering around the world.'[160]

Alexander in the Topaz Palace

Another time that Alexander receives an oracle about his death is when he is on a mountain whose crest is of lapis lazuli, in a palace built of topaz (*yāqūt-i zard*, 'yellow ruby'). The palace is filled with crystal chandeliers and in the middle there is a fountain of saltwater, next to which there is a throne. On the throne stretches a wretched corpse whose head is like that of a boar. When Alexander sets foot within the palace, hoping to take something from it, he finds himself rooted to the spot; his whole body begins to tremble and he starts to waste away. A cry comes from the saltwater: 'O king, still filled with longing and desire, don't play the fool much longer! You have seen many things that no man ever saw, but now it's time to draw rein. Your life has shortened now, the royal throne is without its king.'[161]

This scene is probably based on a similar passage in the Greek version (Pseudo-Callisthenes, III, 28), in which Alexander comes to the harbour of Lyssos. On top of a high mountain there is a circular temple ringed by a hundred columns of sapphire. In the Greek *Romance*, there is also a precious stone that lights up the whole place. However, instead of a saltwater fountain, it is a bird that warns Alexander in 'a human voice, in Greek' to return to his own palace and not strive to climb the paths of heaven.[162]

Alexander and the Talking Tree

As we have seen from these last three encounters with fabulous beings possessed of oracular wisdom, oracles were important to the historical Alexander.[163] In the Greek *Alexander Romance*, the most extended encounter with an oracle occurs in the course of Alexander's adventures in India, when the wise men of Prasiake (Porus's kingdom) invite him to visit two talking trees.[164] Firdawsī's narration of the story is very close to the Greek version. In the *Shāhnāma*, the talking tree is found at the end of the world (*karān-i jahān*). Instead of two trees, there is one tree that has two separate trunks, one female and the other male. At night the female trunk speaks and, when the daylight comes, the male speaks. When Alexander approaches the talking tree, he sees that the soil is covered with the pelts of wild animals. The guide (and interpreter) explains that the tree has many worshippers, and that when they come to worship, they feed on the flesh of wild animals. The interpreter tells Alexander that the tree says: 'However much Alexander wanders in the world, he has already seen his share of blessings; when he has reigned for fourteen years, he must quit the royal throne.' At midnight the female trunk says: 'Do not puff yourself up with greed; why torment your soul in this way? Greed makes you wander the wide world, harass mankind and kill kings.' Alexander asks: 'Will this fateful day come in Greece, will my mother see me alive again, before someone covers my face in death?' The female trunk tells him: 'Few days remain ... neither your mother nor your family in Rūm will see your face again. Death will come soon and you will die in a strange land.'[165]

After all these passages full of warnings and reproaches, Alexander finally dies in Babylon. Alexander's last days in the *Shāhnāma* take a very similar form to the Greek *Romance.* Firdawsī's version even contains such interesting details as Alexander's order to position his bed where all the army will be able to march past and see him (see also Pseudo-Callisthenes, III, 32).[166]

Conclusion: Firdawsī's Sources and his Portrayal of Alexander

Firdawsī's poem clearly supports the case for the existence of a Middle Persian intermediary. Firdawsī's account of Alexander is not only the first version of the *Romance* in New Persian, but also the work in which most of the Syriac sources, Persian legends and independent stories concerning Alexander the Great are reflected. It follows the *Khudāynāmag* tradition, including Alexander in the Kayānid cycle. In addition, its Christian references juxtaposed with Persian elements indicate that the authors of the *Khudāynāmag* used Syriac sources, as Boyce and Tafaḍḍulī affirm.[167] It also indicates that the motifs of Gog and Magog and the Water of Life were also added to the *Romance* at an early stage (probably at the end of the Sasanian period) from Syriac sources.[168] Hence, the *Shāhnāma* of Firdawsī is the closest version to what the Middle Persian *Vorlage* of the *Alexander Romance* might be. It is probable that Abū Manṣūr[169] combined in his prose *Shāhnāma* all the material that was in circulation, particularly in Greater Khurāsān, the land of the Parthians.

As Meisami points out, Firdawsī was working with an older model of history writing in which an authentic bloodline conferred virtue on kings.[170] However, Firdawsī's account of Alexander has two different characteristics. The first parts of the story concern the legitimacy of Alexander's kingship, putting emphasis on his Persian lineage and his deeds following Dārā's advice. However, after Alexander's ascent to the throne of Persia, Firdawsī is no longer concerned with whether the king is legitimate, but rather with what his life shows about royal legitimacy. This part of the legend presents Alexander as the son of the demon Āz (greed), and it deals mostly with reproaches of Alexander's greed and warnings of his death. This makes Firdawsī's *Shāhnāma* a source of metaphors and exemplary anecdotes that became the stock-in-trade of later authors who composed works in the 'Mirrors for Princes' genre. We will look at this in the following two chapters, which are devoted to the portrayal of Alexander in the *Iskandarnāma* of Niẓāmī.

CHAPTER 4

ALEXANDER IN THE *ISKANDARNĀMA* OF NIẒĀMĪ GANJAVĪ (1141–1209)

چنان دان که شاهی و پیغامبری
دو گوهر بود در یک انگشتری

You should know this: that monarchy and prophecy
Are like two precious stones set in a single ring.

Firdawsī (d. 1020)[1]

Almost two centuries after Firdawsī (940–1019 or 1025), on the other side of the Persian world in the trans-Caucasian city of Ganja on the border of Byzantium (in modern-day Azerbaijan), another Persian poet chose to recast the life of Alexander the Great as his last work.[2] Niẓāmī Ganjavī is known primarily for his five long narrative poems,[3] known collectively as the *Khamsa* (*Quintet*) or *Panj Ganj* (*Five Treasures*), which were composed in the late twelfth century AD. They were widely imitated for centuries by poets writing in Persian as well as in Urdu and Ottoman Turkish.[4] In particular, his *Iskandarnāma* became an inspiration for poets in every corner of the Persian world, including Amīr Khusraw of Delhi in India (1253–1325) with his *Ā'īna-yi Iskandarī* (*Alexander's Mirror*),[5] and Jāmī (1414–92) with his *Khiradnāma-ye Iskandarī* (*The Alexandrian Book of Wisdom*).[6]

This chapter will look at Niẓāmī's version of the *Alexander Romance*, exploring its sources, content and characteristics in order to demonstrate how the *Iskandarnāma* served as a mirror for princes. We will start with a summary and general description of Niẓāmī's *Iskandarnāma*,[7] which contains many pre-Islamic stories concerning Alexander, particularly from the Sasanian period. In this regard, it is an important component of the overall intention of this chapter to show how pre-Islamic Persian stories about Alexander persisted and were elaborated during the Islamic period.

Literary and Historical Contexts of Alexander's Personality in Niẓāmī's *Sharafnāma*

As the first poetic treatment of Alexander's tale in Persian, Niẓāmī's *Iskandarnāma* is a heroic romance based on the Greek Pseudo-Callisthenes tradition. It also contains political and ethical advice for rulers,[8] to whom it was evidently dedicated, explicating the ideal of perfect kingship in the first part of the work (the *Sharafnāma*), and correlating that with the concept of the Perfect Man (*insān-i kāmil*) as the true vicegerent of God (*khalīfat Allāh*) in the second part (the *Iqbālnāma*). Thus, Niẓāmī's version of the tale is in fact a multilayered work of practical ethical wisdom, incorporating major elements of the Perso-Islamic tradition of advice literature[9] – particularly that ascribed to Sasanians, which had the most significant bearing on the subsequent development of Perso-Islamic mirrors for princes.[10]

To substantiate precisely how the *Iskandarnāma* fits within the literary genre of Persian mirrors for princes,[11] the influence of four essential works on Niẓāmī's *Iskandarnāma* – all written during the Saljūq period – should first be underlined here:[12]

(1) The earliest known Persian mirror, the *Qābūsnāma* (1083), was written by the Ziyarid ruler Kay Kāvūs b. Iskandar b. Qābūs for his son.[13]

(2) The *Siyar al-mulūk* (also known as the *Sīyāsatnāma*) was commissioned by the Saljūq Sultan Malikshāh and written by his powerful *vazīr* Niẓām-al-Mulk[14] (d. 1092), and was designed to instruct the sultan in statecraft and governance.[15]

(3) Abū Ḥāmid Ghazālī's (d. 1111) *Naṣīḥat al-mulūk* (1109) was possibly written for the Saljūq Sultan Sanjar (1118–57) or for Muḥammad b. Malikshāh, or for both.[16]

(4) The *Sindbādnāma* or the *Seven Sages* of Ẓahīrī Samarqandī is a book of counsel contained within a frame story, and was written some time after 1157.[17]

These books all combine moral counsel with a variety of other materials – pious sayings, exemplary anecdotes and practical advice – to form a condensed exposition of all that an upright nobleman of the twelfth century AD could wish to present to a Muslim ruler. In all of them, Alexander is a fertile source of *exempla* and is frequently mentioned in various anecdotes.[18] By highlighting their common statements concerning concepts such as kingship, religion, justice and counselling, we can see that these manuals of practical advice form antecedent expressions of some of the ideas contained in the *Iskandarnāma* of Niẓāmī.

Given the lack of a good critical English translation of the *Iskandarnāma*, the most important verses and passages will be translated into English here below,[19] with notes on their significance for the subsequent development of the *Alexander Romance* in Persian Literature. Regarding earlier translations of the *Iskandarnāma* into Western languages, the following merit mention here:

(1) There is a literal, but barely readable, translation of the *Sharafnāma* (the first part of the *Iskandarnāma*) into English prose, with copious extracts from Indian commentators, by H. Wilberforce Clarke.[20]
(2) There are complete translations of both parts of the *Iskandarnāma* into Russian verse[21] and prose.[22]
(3) J. Christoph Bürgel also published a poetic translation of the *Iskandarnāma* into German,[23] with some omissions in both the prologues and epilogues of both books.

Although this book on occasion draws on the first and third versions above in the translation of selected passages from the *Iskandarnāma* in this and the following chapter, it undertakes an independent interpretation of this text.

Alexander's Personality in Niẓāmī's Iskandarnāma

The *Sharafnāma* comprises about 6,800 couplets and the *Iqbālnāma* about 3,680 couplets, making the *Iskandarnāma* the longest poem in Niẓāmī's *Khamsa*, constituting about 10,500 couplets penned in the *mutaqārib* metre.[24] The *Iskandarnāma* is considered to be Niẓāmī's final and most mature poetic work. The *Sharafnāma* can be ascribed to the years between 1196 and 1200, and the *Iqbālnāma* to the years between 1200 and the poet's death in 1209.[25] The *Sharafnāma* (*The Book of Honour*)[26] recounts Alexander's adventures during his conquest of Asia, from the Persian Empire to India and China. Niẓāmī states that he chose this title because he considered it 'the most honourable, and the best' of his works:

> And thus, by the mighty points of these witty quills,
> This book has honour [*sharaf*] over all other books.
> That royal Khusrawian wine that in this book's cup was poured,
> Has made it the 'Book of Honour' [*Sharafnāma*] of kings.[27]

In the second part, the *Iqbālnāma* (*The Book of Fortune*) or *Khiradnāma-yi Iskandarī* (*The Book of Alexandrian Wisdom*), Alexander is represented as a sage and prophet who assembles a great library and is surrounded by the greatest philosophers of the ancient world. Through their guidance and instruction, he is transformed from a king into a sage, effectively becoming the 'Perfect Man'. The dual aspects of kingship – temporal and spiritual – can thus be found in the portrayal of Alexander in both books of the *Iskandarnāma*.

In general, Niẓāmī develops three different aspects of Alexander's legendary personality in the *Iskandarnāma*: as a world conqueror or *Kosmokrátor* (κοσμοκράτωρ), as a sage or king constantly surrounded by philosophers and finally as a prophet in the Islamic tradition. Two distinct but interrelated structural patterns provide complementary ways of organising events in the poem (in both its narratives and tales) and of unifying its tripartite form: the first is the linear pattern of Alexander's life through time, the second is his spiritual progress towards the realisation of wisdom and the third is the process of the evolution of his character from a state of temporal kingship to one of spiritual kingship.[28]

Niẓāmī expounds his methodology as well as his reasons for choosing Alexander as his main subject at the beginning of the *Sharafnāma*. After a dream he found himself 'ablaze and inspired':

> It thus became necessary for me to make this my task,
> To compose such a lovely book as this.[29]

He gives three key reasons for choosing Alexander as his principal theme. Firstly, Niẓāmī claims to have had an inspirational encounter with the enigmatic immortal prophet-saint Khiḍr[30] after 40 days' seclusion:

> 'I've heard you plan to write a book of kings,' he said,
> 'With verse that runs as smooth as a stream.
> Do not repeat what the ancient sage {Firdawsī} said,
> For it is wrong to pierce a single pearl twice.
> Except when a passage is reached where thought
> Demands you repeat what's been said before.
> You're of the *avant-garde*, fresh in this business of verse:
> You must not mimic any bygone master's works!
> You are a miner of jewels in the Alexandrian mine;
> Alexander himself shall come to you to shop for jewels.'[31]

The main thing that Khiḍr insists on here is poetic originality. We may speculate that Niẓāmī himself was probably worried that he would be considered an imitator, especially because an earlier poet, Firdawsī, had already set Alexander's story to verse.[32] Indeed, many modern scholars fault him for this.[33] This is Niẓāmī's second reason, as he himself notes on various occasions:

> That great poet of yesteryear, the sage of Ṭūs {Firdawsī},
> Who'd painted the countenance of belles-lettres in bridal hues,
> Who in his book {*Shāhnāma*} had pierced so many pearls of verse,
> Yet left unsaid many things that need be said.
> If he had writ down all he'd heard from the ancients,
> Indeed this romance {of Alexander} would have become long.
> He left unsaid whatever was not pleasing to him;
> And just that which demanded telling wrote down.
> For his friends some of the banquet's leftovers he saved,
> Ill-suited as it is to consume sweet desserts in private.
> Though Niẓāmī here has strung many a pearl on the thread of verse,
> Those tales' pearls that pens of yore have writ he's left unstrung.
> He took those pearls he found in the treasury unpierced,

And so appraising pearls obtained his balance weighing his verses' worth.[34]

Niẓāmī wanted to complete what Firdawsī left unsaid.[35] He claimed to write something new, which would differ from the work of the older poet:

He [Niẓāmī] made the *Sharafnāma* famed far and wide,
And so made a tale grown old, fresh and new![36]

In this regard, Khiḍr's instructions to Niẓāmī on how to recount the legend of Alexander are very significant. Khiḍr enables Niẓāmī to create a new story. However, Khiḍr's appearance is not just significant for the poet personally: he plays a prominent role in the Islamic legend of Alexander insofar as he figures as Alexander's guide in the expedition into the darkness in the episode of the Fountain of Life. Thus, Niẓāmī's *Iskandarnāma* is not simply a repetitive reproduction of Alexander's tale, but a complete poetic recreation and inspired reconsideration of the old material under the eternal prophet's guidance.

Finally, Niẓāmī affirms that he also chose this subject because:

Since none of the good and great deride this tale,
By design, I've set my hand to tell this romance.
There is no tale more pleasing, more right or apposite
That enjoys the approval of those who're upright.
Other legends you may seek and study, but from the start,
You'll find that all the various nations disagree on their wrong and right.
But of such a tale as this no perplexity may be raised,
Writ down as it was by so many quills sharp of wit.[37]

On another occasion, he insists on the importance of Alexander's legend:

Helpless in that place where I was dazed and dazzled,
I cast my lot and found Alexander's name among the great and grand.
Every mirror that I burnished bright in thought of him,
Alexander's imaginal form I found reflected therein.

Do not regard that ruler with a perfunctory, thoughtless gaze,
for he was both a swordsman and one who wore the crown.[38]

In general, in the *Iskandarnāma*, under the protective shade of Khiḍr's inspiration, Niẓāmī tries to tell tales of Alexander that are fresh and original. In this process he combines three aspects of the Macedonian king as an exemplar of the ideal king: conqueror (*vilāyat-sitān*), philosopher (*ḥakīm*) and prophet (*payghambar*):

One company calls him holder of the insignia of the royal crown,
A conqueror of kingdoms, or rather, one who secured frontiers.
Another company, due to the minister he had at court [Aristotle],[39]
Have writ him down as having the philosopher's mandate.
Another group regard his spotless character and cultivation of religion
And so accept him among the prophets.[40]

He then declares:

I shall plant a tree bearing many abundant fruits,
From all these grains of truth these sages have sown.
First I will knock on the door of royalty and kingship;
I will discourse on the conquest of lands far and wide.
Next will I speak of wisdom and philosophy;
I'll make ancient histories seem like a fresh statement.
Then shall I pound my fist on the door of Prophethood –
For God Himself has called him a prophet.
I have made three pearls, in each a mine full of treasures;
Many pains and cares have I taken to create each pearl.
For each door I've knocked upon, and for each pearl of verse,
All the limits of the earth I'll fill with treasure.[41]

From these verses it is clear that Niẓāmī's conception of Alexander's kingship thus incorporates the dual function of prophet and king, echoing both the ancient Iranian ideal of kingship and the Islamic Sufi concept of the king as a Perfect Man.[42] Indeed, it would seem that it was by following the lead of Fārābī's works on political philosophy[43] that Niẓāmī incorporated not only the qualities of a philosopher but also ultimately those of a prophet into Alexander's personality. In this respect, in the *Iskandarnāma* Niẓāmī puts flesh on the figure of Alexander as the ideal ruler who then became, in later centuries, a symbol of the perfect king.[44]

Niẓāmī also penned these interesting verses on the chronology of his account of Alexander in the *Iskandarnāma*:

> I spoke in such a way [in my verse] concerning what I regarded as wondrous
> Such that all hearts would take it on faith and be convinced.
> Yet I did not feel compelled to set in verse
> Accounts that seemed far-fetched or irrational.
> I garnered a grain of truth from each idle pearl.[45]
> I ornamented my poem like an idol temple.
> I thus laid down that temple's foundations from the start
> So its walls, raised up, would remain upright and straight.
> Criticise me not about the events' antecedence or subsequence
> For no historian you'll find who's flawless in chronology.[46]

Sources of Niẓāmī's Iskandarnāma

Niẓāmī also draws attention to the fact that composing the *Iskandarnāma* was an onerous task because of the great diversity and wide variety of sources on Alexander available to him:

> As I planned to tell this tale [of Alexander], my speech came out
> Simple and straightforward, yet the way tortuous and meandering.
> The works of that king who'd trekked to the corners of the globe
> I could never find written down in a single book or tract.
> The discourses I found were full of precious treasures,
> A myriad pearls strewn about in every text.[47]

He emphasises how carefully he selected the tales and *topoi* from his sources:

> From each and every book I adopted different material
> And decked them out in the ornament of verse.[48]

Regarding those same sources, he adds:

> Not only the recent, modern histories did I peruse:
> I studied Jewish, Christian, and Pahlavi sources too.
> I selected naught but the *crème de la crème* from those sources;
> I took only the kernel from the husk of each and every text.[49]

These verses are as important as they are ambiguous. On one hand, they do not refer to any specific source by name. On the other, the poet affirms that besides contemporary histories, he consulted a great range of texts. The main question here is *which sources* is he referring to in this statement? In order to answer this question, we have to consider the region where Niẓāmī lived. It is important to take into account the fact that he lived almost his entire life in his home town of Ganja, located in the Caucasus on the border of Byzantium. This crossroads town was home to diverse peoples, and was a cultural beehive where many languages were spoken and various religions were practised. This is why, in the episodes set in the Caucasus, the *Iskandarnāma* features a great deal of local colour.

Given his geographical location, it is likely that the poet would have been familiar with Byzantine sources, as well as those of Armenian and Georgian provenance or language. We may well also speculate that it is probable that Niẓāmī's 'Jewish and Christian' sources were the Armenian and Georgian legends about Alexander that were in circulation in the Caucasus. Stories and legends about Alexander the Great were probably very popular in Niẓāmī's home town.[50] The Caspian Gates, as well as Darband (in Persian) and *Bāb al-abwāb* (in Arabic),[51] are often identified with the Gates of Alexander.[52] Its 30 north-facing towers, which used to stretch for 40 kilometres between the Caspian Sea and the Caucasus Mountains, effectively blocked the passage across the Caucasus. Alexander actually marched through Darband[53] in pursuit of Bessus, a manoeuvre described by Arrian (*Anabasis* 3.20), although he probably did not stop to fortify it.[54] In this respect, it may be pointed out that *Dar-band*, which means 'pass' in Persian, is often identified with the wall of Gog and Magog. We will revisit this point later on in this chapter.

It was also believed that the legendary 'City of Women' (Harūm in the *Shāhnāma* and Barda' in the *Iskandarnāma*) was located in the Caucasus, which is actually found in modern Azerbaijan.[55] Niẓāmī even replaced Queen Candace of al-Andalus with Queen Nūshāba of Barda',[56] perhaps because the latter name was more familiar to his audience, and perhaps because, according to François de Blois, she 'belongs to that area, as does the Armenian princess who is the heroine of *Khusraw u Shīrīn*'.[57] In conclusion, it is highly probable that many episodes in the *Iskandarnāma* were well known and popular among the Caucasian people, and that Niẓāmī made ample use of such local materials in his poem.

Besides the Jewish and Christian (or, as Niẓāmī says, '*Naṣrānī*/ Nestorian') sources, Niẓāmī refers to 'Pahlavi' works. This is ambiguous. It is not clear whether he is referring to Persian sources relating to the pre-Islamic era or indeed to Pahlavi texts themselves. Through our analysis of the *Iskandarnāma* below we will venture to identify Niẓāmī's possible pre-Islamic Persian sources. From the determined and confident tone used by Niẓāmī in the following verses, there can be no doubt, at least in the poet's own mind, of the historical reliability of these sources:

I selected naught but the *crème de la crème* from those sources;
I took only the pith from the husk of each and every text.
My discourse from the tongues of many treasures of speech was knit;
I created a unified whole from all these motley tongues.
Whosoever's acquainted with these different tongues
Will hold his own from finding fault with my tale.
I crumpled and pleated my speech like curly locks
From those historical scenarios I found factual and true.[58]

However, he admits that there is one fault in his work, though one that encapsulates the very essence of the poetic art:

But if it's 'truth' and 'facts' you'd seek,
It's wrong to look for the plain truth in embellished verse.[59]

In another passage, he clarifies this assertion by adding:

My labour's to make gracious, beauteous speech –
This poetry of mine's an art of lies and deviance –.[60]

However, he states:

> But yet, indeed, whatever seemed incredible in the tale
> Or unreliable, I dismissed at once from my verse.
> I gazed within myself to assess what should be said,
> Apprising what the readers would think delectable.
> If one concentrates on wonders overmuch
> The reins of speech run to extravagance.
> Tales that don't dazzle, related without marvel,
> Make the antique fable seem nothing novel.
> So speak your speech with care and moderation
> So it carries the weight of faith and corroboration.[61]

Therefore, in an attempt to balance historical fact and poetic fiction, he declares:

> But should I reduce the poetic ornaments and frills,
> The whole romance would come to but one meagre verse.
> Thus all the deeds of that errant king who traversed the earth
> I have wrapped up *in toto* within a single vellum roll.[62]

Near the beginning of his poem, Niẓāmī in this respect furnishes us with a precis of the history of Alexander on a single sheet (*Fihrist-i tārīkh-i Iskandar dar yik varaq*), where he gives us a list of the key exploits, feats and accomplishments attributed to the Macedonian king by legend or history. Before examining each chapter of the *Iskandarnāma* in detail, it will be helpful to look at the following translation of the key verses of this important passage.

Precis of the History of Alexander

> Alexander, who journeyed to the farthest reaches of the earth, in the business
> Of travel was adept; the wares of all his voyages were well prepared.
> He journeyed and beheld all four corners of the world
> For no kingdom without four directions can be bought.
> In whatever kingdom's capital he set his foot,

He upheld the rites of the great kings.
He never paid homage to any other rite or ritual
Except the custom and religion of Zoroaster, votary of fire.
He was the first person to establish the use of jewellery;
The first to mint golden coins in the land of Rūm [Anatolia].
At his command the agile goldsmith
Embossed sheets of silver with golden leaves.
He commanded that translations of texts of Persian philosophy
Be made so that they were attired in Grecian robes.
He directed drumbeats to mark the watches of dusk and dawn,
And thus gave time its substance by his court's watches.
It was he who invented the mirror by which he led men –
Which brought that brilliant gem forth from darkness.
He freed the world of the revolt of Zanzibar;
He snatched both crown and throne from Darius.
He cleansed the earth of both the fury of India
And Russia's irascibility and made it like a bridal palace.
His judgements were as bright and clear as a Chinese mirror;
He set up his kingdom in the canton of Cyrus's throne.[63]
When at first the book of his life turned its leaf to twenty
The kettledrum of kingliness with mighty strokes was struck.
In the second place, when he came to twenty-seven years of age
He broke camp and set out on the way of prophecy.
The very day he adopted the rite of prophecy,
The calendar of Alexander recorded its first date.
As he became learned in God's religion, like a gracious kingdom
His conquests came to stretch to the ends of the earth.
He adduced abundant proofs to substantiate the true Faith;
He constructed numerous edifices over the earth's face.
He laid down foundations of several capital cities
With the rotation of each cycle of the compass of time.
In every land and clime he founded cities
From the lands of India all the way to Anatolia [*Rūm*].
It was he who gave Samarqand its fabled loveliness –
Not Samarqand alone, but many such cities.
The founding of cities like Herat was his deed.
How fabulous it is to establish cities such as these!
It was in Darband that he built his first great wall;

He set its foundation down with wisdom and reason.
Go beyond Bulgaria, whose founding was his doing:
Its original foundation was the pit of his cave [*bungār*].
He constructed walls to fend off Gog
By coupling mountains together as a barrier.
Above and beyond this, he established many institutions –
The sum and size of which exceed all mention.
When that well-framed man made his will and pleasure
To divide and share out the face and frame of the earth,
Across the world's face he drew a line like a cross –
Long before either cross or Christian ever was!
Like an atlas of maps composed of four directions
He set up geometry's scores, figures and calculations.
Tent-like he divided up the earth's surface into four parts;
His reign struck the drum of the nine heavens in five watches.
One peg of his reign was hammered into the North Pole;
Another peg struck deep to traverse the south.
One rope of the tent he pulled eastward hither;
Another tent-rope was stretched westward thither.
Who else like him has reigned and held court
In the atelier of the earth's length and breadth?
When he betook himself to voyage about the earth
He undertook to compute its length by yardstick tape.
He surveyed the earth by mile, furlong, waystation – gauged
All bounds and left not one spot of the earth uncalibrated.
He had cartographers and topographers measure its bounds;
A myriad of inspectors were charged with checking and fixing standards.
By log-lines the earth's coordinates were marked up,
The distances between each waystation plotted out.
Wheresoever on the earth he planted his royal tent
He'd count and calibrate each stage and station of the way.
Then, when a voyage by sea became his lot in life,
He calculated water's ways and surveyed the waves!
Once upon the water, he'd lash two ships together –
Between the two he strung a rope for measurement:
Ship one, anchored on the seafloor, stood firm in place,
And ship two tugged forward to the log-line's end.

And so it went – the second ship now moored itself,
And ship one weighed anchor, and took up her lead.
He compassed waves with ships' ropes as micrometres
Who's ever seen any ropewalker enact such wild play?
Alexander the Oceanographer well knew these stages and degrees:
He marked out the sea's width and breadth from shore to shore.
He turned the world's grief and woe to joy and cheer
By fixing standards and coordinates through geometry.
With wise deliberation he made the earth's crooked calculations straight,
Assessed aright how far each road, how long each highway stretched.
He showed us where the earth's 'inhabited quarter' was.
Who else amongst us obtained the domain that he attained?
He brought weal and welfare to all and sundry
In every land and clime through which he drove his steed.
Upon both hill and dale, he lent help and succour to all,
He was – alas! – succourless at the advent of death.
What's said above must suffice to recount the history
Of that king endowed with crown and diadem.
More or less than this is mere captious giddiness:
To say aught else just makes the pen gnaw and fret.
I took the path of verse to pen this romance;
Albeit in verse deviance is always found.
... Now Alexander, the sovereign of the seven climes, has gone.
Once Alexander passed away, no man of worth was left.

The key deeds that Niẓāmī attributes to Alexander in the above passage may be enumerated as follows:

(1) Alexander was the first man to establish the use of jewellery.
(2) He was the first king to mint golden coins in the land of Rūm (Anatolia), and the first to emboss sheets of silver with golden leaves.
(3) He ordered the translation of Persian philosophical texts into Greek.
(4) He directed drumbeats to mark the watches of dusk and dawn, and thus was the first to measure time.
(5) He invented the mirror from dark iron.

(6) He battled against Darius, the natives of Zanzibar, the Russians and the Indians.
(7) At the age of 20 he became a king, and at 27 he became a prophet.
(8) The Alexandrian calendar begins with his becoming a prophet.
(9) He established many cities from western Anatolia to southern India, including Samarqand, Herat and Darband. He is presented as the founding father of Bulgaria and Tbilisi, and the builder of the wall against Gog.
(10) Through geometrical methods he divided the earth into four quarters by drawing a cross. He also discovered that only a quarter of the earth was inhabited. While travelling around the world, he measured its length and breadth by various methods of mathematical calculation. He also measured distances at sea.

Most of these accomplishments, feats and inventions that Niẓāmī attributes to Alexander will now be discussed and analysed.

Alexander's Mirror

One motif crucial to comprehending the prophetic aspect of Alexander and his progress towards the realisation of spiritual kingship is the 'invention of the mirror' that is attributed to him. Alexander's mirror has two meanings. In Platonic terms, it symbolises the mirror of the Unseen World in which reality is reflected, being analogous to the Cup of Kay Khusraw or the Goblet of Jamshīd (*jām-i jam*), a *topos* upon which Niẓāmī elaborates in some detail in the *Sharafnāma*. In Sufi mystical terms, the mirror symbolises theophany (*tajallī*) in the mystic's polished heart, where the Divine is reflected.[64] Plato instructs us: 'Looking at God we should be using the best mirror of mortal things for the virtue of the soul, and thus we should best see and know ourselves.'[65]

As we will see, Alexander's first step in his inner journey in the *Sharafnāma* towards the attainment of spiritual kingship is to obtain self-knowledge. Once he becomes aware of the qualities of his soul, he is able to enter the Land of Darkness for 40 days, where he remains like a Sufi in *chilla-nishīnī* (a 40-day seclusion); he does this not to achieve immortality, but to realise self-knowledge in order to be ready for the final step of his inner journey towards becoming a prophet. Stoneman rightly points out: 'Niẓāmī's account of Alexander's life (among other things) is a reflection of a divine unchanging truth, not of the ephemera of the visible world. The world is in fact God's mirror, a projection of the active intellect, sometimes perceived as an angel.'[66]

Therefore, the fact that Alexander possesses this magic mirror signifies his possession of *gnosis* and the power of insight into the Unseen World and the Divine, which is a characteristic of the prophets – as indeed he is. At the same time it signifies his possession of a polished heart, and also that he is able to polish the hearts of others – his erstwhile subjects and followers – by summoning them to monotheism. Understanding the philosophical and mystical significance of the motif of Alexander's mirror is essential if we are to comprehend the spiritual formation of his personality.

Four Stray Motifs: Jewellery, Coinage, Alexander's Calendar and the Visit to Jerusalem

Turning back now to the historical dimension of the tale, before plunging into the actual text of the *Sharafnāma*, it will be useful to briefly examine the historical veracity – or lack thereof – of four motifs mentioned in the above precis that are absent from the *Shāhnāma* of Firdawsī but present in Niẓāmī's version of the *Alexander Romance*. We will therefore now investigate the nature of the possible texts and sources from which Niẓāmī obtained his information.

As far as jewellery is concerned, it is true that the conquests of Alexander the Great (between 333 and 322) transformed the economy of the Greek world. With his conquests, and later during the Hellenistic period of his domination in the Middle East, gold became more plentiful in Greece, and the artistic designs, motifs and techniques of Persian court artists were widely imitated there.[67] Thus, Niẓāmī's claim that Alexander introduced jewellery to Greece may perhaps relate to the fact that many types of jewellery became popular in the Hellenistic period, and Greek goldwork was considered to be the best.[68]

Regarding the issue of minting coins, Philip II was the first Greek ruler to issue gold coins uninterruptedly due to the wealth of gold mines in the Pangaeum district.[69] However, Niẓāmī's statement may reflect the fact that prior to the Macedonian conquest, silver, which abounded in Greece, was the only currency used for commercial transactions. It was only after Alexander's conquests, which raised the Greek economy (in both its Asian and European provinces) to a higher level, that one finds the minting and circulation of gold coins as well as silver, and also a mixture of the two.[70]

On the subject of Alexander's calendar, al-Bīrūnī affirms in his *Chronology* that it was established in the year that Alexander entered Jerusalem, at the age of 27. Thus the Jewish calendar was replaced with Alexander's calendar.[71] In the passage in question, al-Bīrūnī writes:

> This era is based upon Greek years. It is in use among most nations. When Alexander had left Greece at the age of twenty-six, he prepared to fight with Darius, the king of the Persians, and marching upon his capital, he went down to Jerusalem, which was inhabited by the Jews. Then he ordered the Jews to give up the era of Moses and David, and to use his era instead, and to adopt that very year, the twenty-seventh of his life, as the epoch of this era.[72]

As we can see, Niẓāmī's statement about the origin of Alexander's calendar more or less coincides with al-Bīrūnī's. However, the historical accuracy of both accounts is doubtful because we know that Alexander was 27 years of age in AD 329, at which point he was in Central Asia and nothing obviously prophetic seems to have happened. His supposed visit to Jerusalem, if it happened, would have been in AD 332, when he was 24 years old.[73]

This visit to Jerusalem is certainly not among Alexander's deeds as narrated in the Pseudo-Callisthenes. However, this episode was included in the Latin *Historia de Preliis* and in various vernacular Alexander traditions based upon it.[74] The connection between Alexander's entrance to Jerusalem and his prophethood must have had its origin in the Jewish tradition, since one can already find a prophetical aspect of Alexander's personality in the *Book of Daniel* (7.8; 8.3–26). Likewise, the story of Alexander's visit to Jerusalem features in the Talmud.[75] However, the best-known version of Alexander's visit to Jerusalem is in a narrative by Josephus.[76] It thus seems likely that, as Niẓāmī himself stated, the Jewish religious tradition influenced his work.

* * *

Some of the other points relevant to the history, legend and romance of Alexander will now be discussed in order to illustrate precisely how

Niẓāmī presented them in his poem. In order to present a structured analysis of the *Sharafnāma*, its contents are divided here into four different categories:

(1) Information already mentioned by Firdawsī or other sources with some variants (e.g. Alexander's Persian campaigns and Dārā's murder by his own officers)
(2) Information on Alexander's lineage, tutors, conquests and battles.
(3) The Caucasian episodes (e.g. Alexander in Azerbaijan, Abkhaz, Mount Alburz and Darband)
(4) Marginal stories (e.g. the invention of the mirror, and the competition between the Rūmī and Chinese painters)

Although it is not possible to cover each and every tale and detail of Niẓāmī's version of the Alexander legend in this volume, a fairly comprehensive overview of the poem's view of the conqueror is presented below.

Episodes Common to the Sharafnāma, *Firdawsī's* Shāhnāma *and Other Sources*

As Niẓāmī himself admitted in the prologue of the *Sharafnāma*, though he wanted to compose a new version of the Alexander legend, sometimes there was no choice but to repeat what had been said before him.[77] His poem thus echoes and shares certain material with certain passages in the *Shāhnāma* of Firdawsī, which Niẓāmī tried to complete and 'correct'. He added some other variants to the Alexander legend that had been left unsung by Firdawsī.

It should be taken into account that at the time Niẓāmī was writing his version, Alexander's image had become highly Islamised in the Muslim historical imagination. This Islamised depiction of Alexander first appears in the *Sharafnāma.* Niẓāmī's Alexander destroys fire temples and liberates people from Persian oppression. He is no longer portrayed as a descendent of Darius, nor is he linked to great Persian heroes such as Isfandīyār. This change of view is not unique to Niẓāmī but can be seen in works by other authors, such as Bal'amī's *History.*[78] Indeed, Niẓāmī and Bal'amī[79] coincide on most points of the Alexander legend, and both add supplementary material to their sources, some of which is not found elsewhere.

In order not to repeat the discussion of episodes treated in previous chapters, we will here look at summaries of passages common to the *Sharafnāma*, the Pseudo-Callisthenes and Firdawsī. Niẓāmī's account of the Persian campaigns is the only part of his work that coincides with Firdawsī's *Shāhnāma*. More interestingly, these common episodes are also the only parts that are found in the Greek *Romance*. The various common motifs can be enumerated in Table 4.1.

While these motifs will be examined in the present chapter wherever they appear in the narrative, the emphasis will be on the differences and novelties that Niẓāmī introduced in his work. As we shall see, each episode represents an increasingly more advanced stage in Alexander's progress towards perfect kingship. At the heart of Alexander's progress from temporal to sacred kingship lies an inner journey symbolised by his relinquishing of worldly achievements. We will now focus on two aspects of the narrative of the *Sharafnāma*: firstly, highlighting the

Table 4.1 Sixteen Motifs of the *Alexander Romance* found both in Firdawsī's *Shāhnāma* and Niẓāmī's *Sharafnāma*

Motif	Pseudo-Callisthenes	Firdawsī	Niẓāmī
1. Tribute of golden eggs	✓	✓	✓
2. Alexander in disguise at Darius's court	✓	✓	-
3. Exchange of letters	✓	✓	✓
4. Exchange of symbolic gifts	✓	-	✓
5. Darius's retreat	✓	✓	-
6. Darius's letter to Indian king Porus	✓	✓	-
7. Darius's murder by his own generals	-	✓	✓
8. Alexander's reaction to Darius's death	✓	✓	✓
9. Darius's will	✓	✓	✓
10. Alexander's marriage to Rawshanak	✓	✓	✓
11. Alexander in Mecca	-	✓	✓
12. Queen Candace	✓	✓ (Qaidāfa)	✓ (Nūshāba)
13. Alexander in India	✓	✓	✓
14. The Indian king Kayd	-	✓	✓
15. Alexander in China	-	✓	✓
16. Alexander and the Water of Life	✓	✓	✓

development of the tale in the Persian tradition and its sources, and secondly analysing Alexander's progression towards enlightenment.

Alexander's Birth and Early Years in Niẓāmī's *Sharafnāma*

The key elements that Niẓāmī includes in his work on Alexander's life must be compared with other sources in order to determine the poet's sources. The question of the identity of Alexander's father, and whether he was divine or human, was an important component of the Alexander legend in the sources from antiquity.[80]

Alexander's Ancestry and Birth

Niẓāmī opens his narrative with this theme, providing different narratives or variant readings regarding Alexander's ancestry: the Roman variant (Alexander as an exposed child), the Persian variant (Alexander as a descendent of Darius) and the Greek variant (Alexander as Philip's son). Commencing with the Greek variant, Niẓāmī begins his story by introducing Alexander's father as Philip of Macedonia, whom he calls Fīlikūs.[81] He declares that the rulers of Greece, Anatolia (Rūm) and Russia (Rūs) followed Fīlikūs's command. Niẓāmī describes him as 'the world's best king' and a 'descendant of the grandson of Esau, the son of Isaac'.[82]

Such a biblical ancestry for Philip of Macedonia can also be found in the *History* of Bal'amī (the *vazīr* of the Samanids).[83] Al-Bīrūnī also mentions this version of Alexander's ancestry as being agreed on by 'the most celebrated genealogists', adding definitively: 'that Alexander was the son of Philip is a fact too evident to be concealed'.[84] Al-Mas'ūdī mentioned this variant too.[85] This Old Testament genealogy of Philip is probably based on the identification of Edom/Edumea as Rome in the Jewish tradition,[86] which made Philip (of Rūm) a descendant of Esau.[87]

After presenting the Greek variant of Alexander's ancestry from Philip, Niẓāmī continues:

> How many claims and counterclaims on Alexander's birth
> Exist, to each of which I've lent my ear to find the truth.[88]

He then provides two other variants of Alexander's ancestry. Firstly, he cites a Roman variant:

As has been related by the wise sages of that land,
There was once the wife of a pious man in Greece[89]
Who found herself distressed in pangs of childbirth
Outcast from hearth, home, husband – in dire straits.
When the time to give birth approached, the strain
And labour's woe overmastered her with pain,
She crept off into a corner, gave birth and died.
She fret to death in the distress of childbirth and cried:
'Who shall nurse and nurture you, I know not;
What beast or brute will devour you, who knows'. . .[90]

Philip then finds the abandoned child on his way back from a hunting expedition:

One day while hunting game, King Philip surveyed
The plain and saw a dead woman lying there
Before his feet, a living baby boy's head rose up
From his mother's deathbed; in want of her breast
And milk the infant bit his thumb in grief.
Philip ordered his men to take the lady's corpse;
They gave to her last rites as she deserved.
The servants of the king took the child from
The dust of the way and bore him away –
All were left to marvel at the game of that day.
So Philip took, reared and raised the boy,
And in the end anointed him his heir.[91]

Niẓāmī next explains the Persian variant, though he adds that he does not believe it. Considering Niẓāmī's reference to 'the *dihqān* who adore the fire', one may speculate that this version is based on his 'Pahlavi' source, a Zoroastrian version preserved by the noble *dihqān*s (landowners of noble Sasanian families)[92] mentioned in the verses:

The *dihqān* who adore the fire relate the legend
Of Alexander a different way: they say he was kith
And kin of Darius through ties of blood. Yet when
I perused all these tales and yarns, then regarded
What Firdawsī, the holy master, had to say, those two

Romances appeared like chimera, flights of fancy
Or foolish fictions made of dream and moonshine.[93]

Lastly, Niẓāmī returns to the Roman variant, which he believes to be the 'true history' of Alexander's birth:

In every tongue what's right and true of this legend
Of Alexander is this – that he was of Philip's kin.
Since other tales are incredible and lack veracity,
No poet can pledge his word to them.
That hoary-headed elder relates a tale
He'd read in the history of the kings of yore
That in the revels of King Philip there was
A stainless young bride of alluring loveliness,
Promising in appearance, exalted in eminence,
Whose fetching glances, shot from her eyebrow's
Bow, felled men – her tresses all like lassos.
. . . One night the king took her in love's embrace –
A date palm then arose from his royal seed,
A pearl of great price from his spring rains
Made the ocean oyster engender majesty.
When all nine months of her pregnancy were up
The infant sought his way from out the womb.[94]

Alexander's Horoscope

Niẓāmī relates in detail the astronomical information[95] of the horoscope for the moment of Alexander's birth. He tells us that King Philip ordered his astrologers to determine the infant's star sign, which might reveal his child's future. Deciphering the mysteries of the heavenly constellations, the astronomers examined what the stars held in their balance,[96] finding that:

The ascendant star Leo ruled the day
And blinded with envy every enemy's eye.
The sun in Aries gained lustre and glory,
Attesting a man of practice, not theory.
As Mercury hastened towards Gemini,

The moon and Venus consorted in Taurus;
By Jupiter, Sagittarius was embellished,
Saturn caroused in Libra's Balance
While Mars in Capricorn took his place
Just like a lackey employed in chores.
Such a horoscope so radiant with fortune
Outloud I'd say: 'Preserve him from the Evil Eye!'[97]

According to these verses, Leo, the sign of power, was in the ascendant at the moment of Alexander's birth, while the sun was located in Aries, the sign of wisdom and its practice. Plutarch (*Alex.* 3.3) indicates that Alexander was born in the Greek month Hecatombaeon (July/August).[98] We can also find similar details (on measuring the courses of the heavenly bodies when Alexander's mother went into labour) in the Pseudo-Callisthenes (I, 12).[99] However, according to the Pseudo-Callisthenes, Jupiter was in the ascendant when Alexander was born, 'turning into horned Ammon between Aquarius and Pisces'.[100] Niẓāmī also mentions the constellations of other signs of the horoscope indicating Alexander's future fortune and prosperity, concluding that:

The constellations of heaven's seven stars proclaim:
The world had given him the key to fortune and fame.[101]

The horoscope given by Niẓāmī is quite different from the Greek account with which it has been compared. The passage on the conqueror's horoscope in the Syriac Pseudo-Callisthenes (I, 12) is quite different too, attesting that Alexander was born 'over Aquarius and Pisces of Egypt'. Comparing this horoscope in the *Sharafnāma* with certain horoscopes found in the Zoroastrian *Bundahishn* (such as the fifth and sixth chapters in which the birth of Gayomarth is discussed), it seems evident that Niẓāmī's method was based on Sasanian genethlialogy (natal astrology), which was itself 'essentially an imitation of the Hellenistic, onto which were grafted some Indian features'.[102] Alexander's horoscope was typical of that of a great man, with all the planets aligned in the best astrological positions.[103]

One source that may have been accessible to Niẓāmī is the *Kitāb al-mawālīd al-kabīr* (*Book of Great Births*) by Māshā'allāh ibn Atharī (d. *c.*815), a Jew who may well have been Persian; this book is known only from its Latin translation.[104] It is possible that Niẓāmī based his version of Alexander's horoscope on this book. In general, as S. Ḥ. Naṣr points out, Niẓāmī had an impressive knowledge of traditional astronomy and astrology, such that his erudite references to the principles of astronomy throughout his *Quintet* are unique among the poets of the Persian language.[105]

Alexander's Education

The next piece of biographical information that Niẓāmī provides concerns Alexander's education. It is interesting that Niẓāmī's *Sharafnāma* is the only source in the Persian tradition where a so-called Naqūmājus is mentioned as Alexander's tutor. According to Niẓāmī, he was Aristotle's father, while Aristotle was Alexander's classmate.[106] Nicomachus (Νικόμαχος; fl. *c.*375 BC) was indeed the father of Aristotle. However, he was the physician in Philip's court and not Alexander's tutor. According to Plutarch (*Alex*. 5.5), the man who assumed the character and title of tutor of Alexander was a certain Lysimachus. These two names (Nicomachus and Lysimachus) may have been conflated in their Arabic transcriptions in the sources.[107]

According to the *Sharafnāma*, Naqūmājus/Nicomachus asks Alexander to accept his son (Aristotle) as his minister and counsellor when he becomes king. Nicomachus gives Alexander 'geometrical letters' (*hindisī ḥarf*), that is, a talismanic ring (circle) based on the occult sciences[108] in which the name of the conquered and the conqueror magically appear.[109] Thus, even before each battle, Alexander already knows whether he will win or lose. Nevertheless, despite this foreknowledge, Alexander is always conscious of the power of Fate over his successes and failures, as Niẓāmī affirms:

He'd gain news about his triumph and success
Through what he wrote upon that magic diagram,
And thus with wisdom and intelligence he lived.
From every art he gleaned some lore fit for use.
Although his will was omniscient in expertise,
He also kept on hand the counsel of the wise.
He followed the commands of the erudite: in this
Way Fortune favoured him through his own mindfulness.[110]

Of Banquets and Battles (*bazm u razm*): Alexander as a Warrior

A major part of the *Sharafnāma* deals with the battles through which Alexander tries to liberate the people of various lands, or else guide them on the path of the primordial religion of Abraham (*dīn-i ḥanīfī*).[111] Before each battle there are episodes in which letters are exchanged between Alexander and the enemy king. The exchange of letters between the kings before and during the battle is a characteristic of the *Alexander Romance* tradition from its very beginning.[112] However, Niẓāmī only includes two letters: Darius sends a letter to Alexander, to which he responds.[113] In the *Sharafnāma*, Darius's letter contains material from a pre-Islamic Persian tradition, which indicates that it is based on Niẓāmī's 'Pahlavi' source: Darius swears on the 'bright fire', on the texts of the '*Zand* and *Avestā*' and 'Zoroaster';[114] he also compares himself to the great heroes and kings of the Persian tradition (Isfandīyār and Bahman).[115] Alexander's response similarly contains material that indicates that it was derived from the Persian tradition, such as where he warns Darius that if he compares himself to Isfandīyār, Alexander will be like Rustam.[116]

During every battle and normally after them as well, there are episodes of feasts and symposia. The main point of these banquets is to remind the conqueror – and, by extension, the reader – of the moral lessons to be gleaned from the practice of warfare and conduct on the field of battle. In this respect, the *Sharafnāma* can be seen to have been composed quite deliberately as a mirror for princes.

Overall, Alexander waged three great wars. The first was against the *Zangī*s (black people, known as Zanj in Arabic, who were the African population of the western part of the Indian Ocean);[117] the second was against the Persians; and the third was against the Russians (altogether there were seven battles waged against the Russians). After his conquest of Persia, Alexander conducted some other minor battles or wars, especially in the Caucasus (such as in Azerbaijan, Abkhaz and Armenia). The important passages that memorialise these wars will now be discussed.

The Battle against the Africans

According to Niẓāmī, because the fame of Alexander's justice reached everywhere, people wanted him to liberate them from the tyranny of their kings. Niẓāmī emphasises that Alexander owed his fame to the wise counsel of Aristotle, who was his 'court minister' (*dastūr-i dargāh*) and confidante in all matters. Following Aristotle's wise counsel, within only a few years, Alexander's conquests extended over all the boundaries of the world.[118]

In the passage on the relationship between Alexander and Aristotle, Niẓāmī insists on the indispensability of a good counsellor (*vazīr*) for the aspiring prince. He states that the greatest kings owed their fame to their *vazīrs*,[119] citing a series of illustrious advisors who served their princes with sound advice, and referencing authors of courtly mirrors. In this respect, it should be remembered that Aristotle's letters to Alexander the Great on matters of kingly conduct were well known in their Arabic versions and would have been familiar to the poet.[120] Other great *vazīrs* known to Niẓāmī include Buzurgmihr, minister of the Sasanian king Khusraw I Anūshīrvān the Just (r. 531–79), to whom was attributed a work preserved in Arabic known as the *Ādāb Buzurjmihr* (*The Ethics of Buzurgmihr*);[121] and Niẓām al-Mulk, minister to the Saljūq king Malikshāh, Niẓāmī's predecessor by some hundred years and author of the *Siyar al-mulūk* (*Rules for Kings*). Justifications for counselling rulers are abundant in the Persian mirrors for princes: Niẓām al-Mulk devoted one of the chapters of the *Siyar al-mulūk* to the importance of 'consulting with wise and experienced men',[122] while Ghazālī recommended that a good king constantly study the books of counsel (*pandnāma*) given to the kings who preceded him, referring to anecdotes about Khusraw I Anūshīrvān and his minister.[123] This episode of the *Sharafnāma* explores the relationship between counselling and kingship, and specifically the role of the *vazīr* as the source of that wisdom, which leads to both justice and harmony.

According to the *Sharafnāma*, Alexander's first battle takes place when the Egyptians accuse the people of Zang of tyranny, and Aristotle advises the king to help:

Perchance the king may gain strength should he lend
To this affair of the Egyptians a helping hand,
Thus Egypt and all its surrounding lands to him would
Become subject, his name as champion become
Renowned and all his foes in dust cast down,
All his friends triumph, his foes be overthrown.[124]

Among the sources to which Niẓāmī might have had access, Bal'amī is the only author to mention Alexander's battle against the people of Zang (Zangistān).[125] In the Greek *Alexander Romance*, there is an episode devoted to Alexander's voyage to Africa and traversal of Libya (Pseudo-Callisthenes, I, 30) before be hastens towards Egypt (Pseudo-Callisthenes, I, 34), but there is no account of any war against the African people. Niẓāmī offers much more detailed information about the African campaign: he relates that 'Alexander, following the counsel of his guide (*dastūrī rahnamūn*) took the battle standard from Macedonia . . . He ordered his troops to leave the banks of the River Nile and march towards the desert.'[126] Niẓāmī then describes the battle with the African army in a single verse as follows:

> On the right flank the Abyssinians fought; on left
> The men of Barbary and at the battle's heart
> The wild African army [the Zangī] raged, a demon horde.[127]

The episode of the war against Zangistān in the *Sharafnāma* contains more than 430 verses in which Niẓāmī develops the story with details of individual battles and heroic acts. Just as in the *Alexander Romance*, each battle usually starts with an exchange of letters between the two leaders; in Niẓāmī's version, one also finds episodes in which Alexander sends a message to the other king before a battle and receives an answer back.[128] Normally, victory is not easy and Alexander must personally exert himself on the battlefield to ensure success.[129] At the end of one of the battles against the Africans, Niẓāmī provides some interesting information on how Alexander ordered that the Abyssinians be branded because they helped the people of Zang in a battle in which the Zang army suffered defeat, which is why (according to Niẓāmī) the Abyssinians were slaves.[130]

After the battle against the people of Zang, Alexander rested in a camp near the battlefield for about a week.[131] Niẓāmī also relates how Alexander built bridges over the Nile in order to transport the treasure he obtained as tribute from the people of Zang.[132] The *Sharafnāma* is one of the few sources in Persian[133] that mentions the foundation of the city of Alexandria. The poet mentions how Alexander 'came to Egypt and cherished the Egyptians, building a city there according to his own rule and custom (*ā'īn-i kh^{w}ud*)'. He then went down to the sea and rested a while, and 'everywhere he planted his standard, some edifice or structure was built'. Niẓāmī continues: 'Many a city was built there according to the Greek style [*bih rasm-i rūm*]'. which thus made much of the barren land of Egypt prosperous:

The first city he built was by the ocean's side,
Raised up as lovely and delightful as spring,
It was as spacious and luminous as paradise
With bustling markets and fields with farms.
When Alexander finished work on that city
The name they gave to it was Alexandria.[134]

According to the Pseudo-Callisthenes (I, 35), after founding Alexandria, Alexander leads his army on to Syria; in the *Sharafnāma*, however, Alexander returns to Greece. Comparing this episode in Niẓāmī's *Sharafnāma* with the Greek *Alexander Romance* suggests that Niẓāmī replaced Alexander's battle against the Tyrians found in the Pseudo-Callisthenes with the battle against the Zang. This seems a reasonable supposition, since this episode in the Pseudo-Callisthenes is interpolated between the episodes of Alexander in Egypt and his Persian campaigns.[135] This motif was most likely inserted into the Alexander literature before the eighth century AD through Arabic channels, since a letter in the work known as *Rasā'il* (*Epistolary Romance*)[136] deals with 'fighting the Zanj'. Thus it appears possible, if not probable, that Niẓāmī based his account of the battle against the people of Zang on these *Rasā'il* or on a common Hellenistic source.

Persian Campaigns: Alexander's Battle with Darius and Conquest of Persia

According to Niẓāmī, Alexander's second battle was against the Persians. Most of his account of the Persian conquest coincides with that of Firdawsī's *Shāhnāma*, with some minor divergences. Following his successful campaign against the people of Zang, in the *Sharafnāma* Alexander distributes the treasures he obtained from the war:

The countless treasures from the African campaign
In plunder that he gained, he sent away at once
Without taking weight or measure of their worth

To other lands. With those treasures Providence
Favoured him, all other treasuries he enriched.[137]

Niẓāmī records how as a matter of kingly courtesy and royal largesse, Alexander sent booty from his campaign to the Persian king Dārā (Darius), who treated his gifts contemptuously: 'Darius took fright at this largesse, for the barb of envy just pricked him sharper', the poet relates. Although Darius accepted these gifts from Alexander, he failed to acknowledge them with due thanks. Darius's lack of appreciation was expressed in 'an improper answer [*nih bar jā-yi kh*^{w}*ud*]' sent to Alexander, thus opening 'the door of his secret rancour'. Although he kept his feelings hidden, this offhand acknowledgement of his gifts sorely distressed Alexander. Niẓāmī identifies Darius's ingratitude and lack of courtesy as what soured their relationship and filled the young conqueror with spite and malice towards him.[138] Partly because of Darius's ingratitude and lack of appreciation for his gifts, Alexander decided to stop paying tribute to the Persian king:

He now refused all gifts and boons to Darius
And he recanted his tribute of former times.
For being as he was in the glow of youth
And filled with lust for conquest of lands
To buckle off the Persian armour, his men
He turned, and girt his loins to subdue Iran.[139]

The Symbolic Gifts of Darius and Alexander

A crucial episode establishes both protagonists' character. This is a scene in which Niẓāmī narrates several interesting episodes concerning the exchange of symbolic gifts between Alexander and Darius. The gifts mentioned in the Greek *Romance* (Pseudo-Callisthenes, I, 36) are a whip, a ball and a chest of gold, while in the Syriac version[140] the episode is more elaborate, and adds some sesame and mustard seeds to these gifts. The motif of symbolic gifts is altogether absent from the *Shāhnāma* of Firdawsī. In the *Sharafnāma*, the gifts mentioned are a ball, a polo mallet and some sesame seeds. Niẓāmī elaborates the episode as follows:

Despite all his excuses, Alexander knew that the messenger
Brought with him a coarse, rude message from King Dārā.

'Bring on the message,' he cried with contempt.
The messenger unclasped his lips to express his purpose
And brought forth the wares he had in his case:
He laid them out, one by one, before the king.
When he'd laid each and every item before Alexander,
He opened his lips to relay the message of Darius.
First he spoke of polo mallet and ball, saying
'You're just a child – so learn to play with these aright;
But if war be your wish, you'll naively fill your heart with woe';
– A myriad sesame seeds he then cast before the king –
'We'll urge against you an army more plentiful than these.'
Alexander the wise, discerning judge of the world's ways,
Saw augury of great victory in those symbols manifest –
And voiced this maxim: 'Whoever flees away
With this same mallet may be caught and snared. –
The king bestowed this polo mallet upon me perchance
That I may wrest his kingdom away from him!
– As for this ball, since masters of geometry reckon
The earth itself has a ball's form and shape, it seems
Quite clearly the king has offered up this globe to me:
I'll win this sport! I'll carry off the ball from the field of war!'
Once that mindful man duly honoured these two favours
Bestowed on him, he turned to meditate on the sesame.
He strewed its seeds upon the palace courtyard stones
And saw how birds pounced at once upon them
And instantly cleared the yard of every grain.
'What clear guidance is betokened by this portent!' he exclaimed,
'For just as sesame seeds compressed make oil,
When Darius drives an army as vast as a myriad sesame seeds
At me, just like those birds my troops shall devour them.'
He rewarded the messenger with a handful of wild rue seeds,
And said: 'The king's army may be a battalion of sesame seeds,
Yet know my troops are as abundant as the wild rue.'[141]

As can be seen from these verses, the 'whip' in the Greek and Syriac versions has in the *Sharafnāma* been transformed into a polo mallet (*chawgān*). The Greek version has Darius affirm in a letter, 'Alexander still needs to play. Therefore, the whip and the ball are to show that he still ought to be at play' (Pseudo-Callisthenes, I, 36). The transformation of the 'whip' into a *chawgān* in the Persian tradition[142] seems to have a more genuinely historical ring to it, and also makes more sense in terms of being an appropriate gift to express Darius's contempt for Alexander's youth.

The motif of the sesame and mustard seeds was not originally in the Greek *Romance*, although it was added to later Greek narratives.[143] In the Syriac version, there is a similar episode in which Alexander takes a handful of the sesame seeds and puts them into his mouth, saying: 'they are numerous, but they have no taste.'[144] In response, Alexander sends Darius a bushel of mustard seeds as a symbol of his Greek and Macedonian troops. Darius, in turn, put the mustard seeds into his mouth and reportedly says: 'they are small, but pungent'.[145] Although the interpretations vary slightly, the same passage and motif can also be found in the histories of Ṭabarī and[146] Bal'amī[147] and in the anonymous *Nihāya*.[148]

Omens, Oracles and Auguries

In order to have an augury of the future and determine whether he will be victorious in his battle with the Persian king, Alexander resorts to divination through the observation of two fighting mountain partridges. He interprets the outcome of their struggle as a sign of success in his impending conflict with Dārā:

> One partridge he betokened with his own name,
> – That bird's success made an omen of good outcome.
> The name of Darius he gave the other bird.
> Intent as to how befell their lots, he gazed:
> Both bold birds scratched and pecked their opponent;
> The king took judgement from their bitter contest.
> The partridge whose feathers and pinions won
> The match was the bird of Alexander in the end.
> The monarch, seeing the day was won by that
> Brave bird, understood at once his army's fate:
> That strutting partridge happily flew away
> From the bird he'd thrashed in victory;
> Aloft he soared to perch upon a mountain ridge;
> An eagle then pounced on him and split his head.[149]

Taking this as an omen, Alexander understands that he will defeat the Persians. However, he realises that despite this victory, he is still subject to mortality, and his life will not be long-lasting. Nevertheless, this omen is not enough to give Alexander full assurance of his victory, so he visits a sacred mountain that is considered to be an oracle. Niẓāmī describes the oracle as being built 'atop a granite mountain, [and] its temple had a lofty vaulted turret of heavenly grandeur'. Pilgrims came to the oracle and 'with their own voices asked about the outcome of mysterious events of their own lives'. From the echo that came back from the mountain they then performed a divination and so discerned their future fortune.[150]

The answer Alexander receives from the mountain oracle is again definitive: that he will conquer the world and defeat the Persian King Dārā.[151] Oracles and omens are an important component of the *Alexander Romance* throughout its transmission (such as Pseudo-Callisthenes, I, 30, 32). Alexander's visit to Delphi (Pseudo-Callisthenes, II, 1) may also be cited in this context. In the Greek *Romance*, other episodes following the foundation of Alexandria feature Alexander resorting to oracles and omens to divine the outcome of conflicts with his enemies, such as, for example, his contemplation of an eagle upon a mountain (Pseudo-Callisthenes, I, 33), although this account is different from the episode above in the *Sharafnāma.* In the Syriac Pseudo-Callisthenes (I, 45) Alexander goes to the temple of Apollo, where he interprets an augury from an oracle there. It is unclear whether these episodes in the *Sharafnāma* are Niẓāmī's own inventions; they do not seem to appear in any other source for the *Romance* in any language or literature.

Alexander's Battle with Darius

Niẓāmī affirms that the Persian army was composed of 'nine hundred thousand fighting horsemen, skilful of stirrup'.[152] Darius reaches Armenia and catches Alexander off guard, who was unaware of his approach.[153] When Alexander receives the news, he prepares an army of 300,000 men of Rūm, Egypt, *Afrang*[154] and Russia (Rūs).[155] According to Niẓāmī, Darius is destined to be defeated because he is an oppressor:

> The iniquity of Darius was a cosmic curse. The glad news
> Of Alexander's march made the world renewed.
> All Iran lay upon the rack and suffered sorely
> From Darius's evil ways and lack of equity.

Since for their king the Persians held no esteem,
With love they made Alexander welcome.[156]

Most of the classical Islamic sources mention the tyranny of Darius, including Bal'amī[157] and the *Letter of Tansar*,[158] among others. Both kings asked for advice from their counsellors. While Alexander's courtiers urged him to attack Darius, the Persian counsellors kept silent.

Interestingly, in Niẓāmī's account of Darius's final war, there is a man named Farīburz who counsels him against fighting Alexander, alluding to an old prophecy. Farīburz' grandfather had told him that before Kay Khusraw went off to his death by disappearing into the cave (upon Mount Alburz), after which he was seen no more, the king used his magic goblet to look into the future, and uttered this prediction:

> In the heavens I see a star constellated that will soon appear in the heavens of our empire and descend from zenith to nadir. There shall come an arrogant ruffian out of Greece who will set all Iran's fire temples alight. He will conquer the entire land of Iran and then reign on the throne of the Kayānid kings. Although he may seize the entire world, what he gains will not last, and one day he will be cast down.

At the end of the passage, Farīburz then moralises:

It's wrong if Iran from him should stagnate
Like some poor wretch who loses life for treasure's sake.
I counsel you to dupe him and try to take him in
So that one Greek kingdom might sate and surfeit him.
. . . One may rule the earth by law and reason [*nāmūs*][159]
And thence raise high the standard of good custom.[160]

Such omens of impending catastrophe issued by the ancient kings of Persia can also be found in the Greek *Romance*, such as when a statue of King Xerxes suddenly falls through the ceiling of Darius's court (see Pseudo-Callisthenes, II, 15). However, no one's counsel could dissuade the Persian king from calling off his battle against Alexander. While Firdawsī's *Shāhnāma*[161] cites three battles between Alexander and the Persians, according to Niẓāmī there was only one – just as in the Pseudo-Callisthenes's account. He describes how, after the customary exchange of letters, the two armies meet in 'the land of *Jazīra*,[162] which is Mosul {*Mūṣul*},[163] a delightful place of rest and sweet relaxation'. As Richard Stoneman points out: 'indeed, it is not incorrect to say that the battle took place in al-Jazīra, which is Arbela. This indicates that Niẓāmī's source contained more reliable historical information than Firdawsī,'[164] who mentioned the banks of the Euphrates[165] as the first battlefield. Bal'amī also mentions the land of Jazīra (*Mūṣul*) as the first battlefield.[166] It is thus possible that Bal'amī and Niẓāmī had a common source.

Niẓāmī describes the contest between the two armies as a battle that makes mountains tremble, before concluding dryly:

Now would you seek for sign of both those kings
Upon that ground are strewn about the bones![167]

Contrary to most of the sources,[168] in which Darius is usually portrayed as cravenly fleeing from the battlefield, in the *Sharafnāma* he appears as a brave warrior:

Commanding his legions from the centre, Darius
Raged on like a dreadful black lion on the loose.
He wielded his sword about his head and cut
And cast his foes headlong before his feet.
He passed nobody by and left nobody alive –
In that mad frenzy so much Greek blood he shed
A thousand scarlet Greek corpses lay there dead.[169]

At one point, Alexander becomes injured and is about to lose the war. Niẓāmī describes how 'he took fright at his fearless foe, and reckoning his enemy's courageousness, decided to turn his reins and flee his foes, to save himself from their spears.' At this juncture, the poet tells us that battle-hardened Persian troops cut off the Greek army's advance, so that it seems that all is lost:

The Greeks were trounced and crushed by Persian troops.
Persians made Greeks captive by Death's good auspices.[170]

However, Alexander knows that he will defeat the Persians thanks to the numerological diagram given to him by Nicomachus:

Once more he pinned his hopes on Providence
And pressed on there and held his ground and place.
He knew his luck was great; against the enemy
He would prevail – thus had said the augury.
He knew by fate the upper hand was his
And so he reinforced his arms and forces
To overwhelm Darius in the balance.[171]

Darius's Betrayal by His Generals

At this desperate moment, two of Darius's generals (*sarhang*) propose to Alexander that they will kill their king in return for financial recompense that would reward their 'golden work with gold'.[172] Although Alexander does not believe that 'the unjust officers would commit such a crime against their own lord', he agrees to make a compact with them: 'anyone will gladly obtain the jewel by which he may defeat his enemy.' Such iniquity appears to be justified. Niẓāmī has Alexander cite a well-known Persian proverb to assuage his moral misgivings: 'In that path where justice seemed obtained only by means of injustice, an ancient adage sprang to his mind':

No marvel it is that the hare of every clime
Is only caught by dogs of that same domain![173]

Darius is slain by his two generals. Alexander reaches him just at the moment of his death and listens to his last words. The passage in which Darius is slain by his own generals appears in the *Romance* (Pseudo-Callisthenes, II, 20), as well as in the *Shāhnāma* and most Arabic histories.[174] The difference between the accounts is that neither in the Greek version nor in the *Shāhnāma* is there any mention of a deal being negotiated for Darius's murder between Alexander and the rebel generals. In fact, in the Pseudo-Callisthenes, when 'the traitors heard that Alexander was coming, they fled, leaving Darius dying'.[175] In the *Sharafnāma*, having arranged the deal with the generals, Alexander regrets it and punishes the traitors:

Alexander gave them all the gold he'd promised them
From his treasury just as he had first of all agreed.
But when he put before them the coin in cash
He gainsaid his pledge; he broke his oath
And commanded they be treated with contempt,
And had both of them strung up on the gallows.[176]

At Darius's Deathbed: Alexander the Great and Darius's Last Will

Niẓāmī also relates an elaborate and poignant dramatic dialogue between the two kings, in which Alexander appears to hear his last words before the Persian monarch dies from the mortal wounds inflicted by his two generals. This narrative is apparently based on a passage that originally appeared in the Greek *Romance* (Pseudo-Callisthenes, II, 20–1) and the *Shāhnāma* of Firdawsī. However, Niẓāmī's *Sharafnāma* describes Darius's will in less detail than the *Shāhnāma*. In the former, Darius begs Alexander to grant him three wishes:

Since you asked about my will, to make my last wish
At this time when over me tears should be shed:
There are three things I secretly desire to have from you
By your good fortune – now king of my realm –
The first regards the slaying of innocent men: I ask
That you be just and fair in all your judgements.
Second, I ask you: let not the Persian throne
And Iran's crown that now you wear, fall into disrepute;
Make your heart devoid of spite and malice;
Do not eliminate my offspring from the earth.
And third and last, I entreat you take care of all
My servants, my wives treat well, don't violate them,
And take my daughter Rawshanak, nurtured by me
With human tenderness in hand to share your bed
And be your wife. Kingdoms are made for the flexible.[177]

Several of the ancient sources concur on Darius's will and last words, and coincide with the account given by Niẓāmī in the *Sharafnāma*.[178]

The Destruction of Zoroastrianism by Alexander

However, according to Niẓāmī, despite Alexander's promise not to hurt the Persians, his first deed as King of Persia is to destroy the fire temples and wipe out the Zoroastrian religion.[179] Niẓāmī relates the episode according to 'the narrator of former tales who spoke of earlier epochs'. He states:

> When a fire was set in the Zoroastrian faith [*dīn-i dihgān*], so that its flame was snuffed out and the fire's votaries themselves set ablaze, Alexander commanded that the Persians cease to obey the precepts of their fire-worshipping faith [*ātash-parastī*]. They should instead regenerate their ancient faith [*dīn-i dīrīna-yi kh^{w}ud naw kunnad*], and adopt the faith of their king [Alexander]. He ordered the Magians to throw all their goods and wherewithal into the fire, and instructed the Iranians to hinder the activities of the [votaries of] the fire temple.[180]

This passage is largely based on a Zoroastrian tradition frequently mentioned in Middle Persian texts,[181] in which Alexander is presented as responsible for two important calamities: the destruction of *Ērānšahr* (the Land of the Aryan Iranians) and the burning and/or stealing of the *Avesta* and its commentary.[182] These Middle Persian texts say that he slew many Zoroastrian priests (*herbad*s and *mobad*s) and quenched the sacred fires of many Zoroastrian temples.[183] However, since Niẓāmī writes from a Muslim point of view, the destruction of Zoroastrianism and its scriptures and institutions is presented as an admirable act in the *Sharafnāma*. Niẓāmī also reports two interesting customs in the Zoroastrian tradition. Being long and convoluted, the verse passages concerning these customs have been translated into prose below:

> During that age [of the Kayānid kings], according to custom taught [by their religious tradition], in all the fire temples of the day treasures were secured and stored to which no one had access. Men of wealth who had no heirs would donate their money [upon their death], dedicating their goods to the keepers of these temples. This tradition created discontent and desolation in every direction, and filled the fire temple houses with useless treasures. When Alexander laid waste to those temples, the treasures, thus

> released, flowed out like a sea. He tore down every temple he passed, dug up its treasures and carried them away.
>
> Another misfortune [*āfāt*] was that the [priests among the] fire worshippers would take a different bride to wed each year. At the royal festivals of Nawrūz and Saddah, during which the religious practices of the fire temple were revived and reanimated, every virgin bride who had never seen a husband would hasten out of their houses into the street [to visit the priests at the fire temple]. From the hearths of the Zoroastrians and through the conjuring cant of the *Zend-Avesta*, smoke thus rose up into the highest firmament. Everything those virgins did was alluring and captivating, charming at times by voice, enchanting sometimes with the flesh ... For a whole day, from every mountainside and palace seraglio they flocked and filled the streets to play around and do as they pleased. Every girl caroused and made merry in her own way, from which arose much wickedness and trouble.[184]

Thus, according to Niẓāmī's source, Alexander destroyed the fire temples because he wanted to obtain the treasure hidden in the shrines. From a Muslim point of view, perhaps Niẓāmī perceived the second custom regarding the freedom of women among the Zoroastrians to stand in contrast to the religion of Alexander's ancestor (Abraham).[185] This view is attested by the following verses of this passage, in which Alexander ordered 'that darling chaste girls should display their face only to their mother or husband'.[186] As far as historical factuality is concerned, no attribution of any such act to Alexander appears in any extant Middle Persian,[187] Persian or Arabic source.[188]

According to the *Sharafnāma*, following his successful campaign against and defeat of Darius, Alexander leaves the area of Mosul in Iraq and heads towards Babylon, where he battles with and subdues the sorcerers who are followers of Hārūt, the great Magician of Babylon. He then quenches the sacred fire and destroys 'the sorcery-book of *Zand*'.[189] Alexander also 'offered religious guidance to the Babylonians by proffering them the faith of his ancestor [Abraham], wiping clean the soot and smoke of fire [worship] from their hearts'.[190] Then he marches towards Adharābādigān (Azerbaijan, Niẓāmī's homeland), where he also destroys and extinguishes 'that fire of ancient times'.

In an interesting passage here, Niẓāmī narrates a story in which a Zoroastrian sorceress named Azarhumāyūn, of the lineage of Sām, turns into a dragon to protect her fire temple. Alexander's minister, Balīnās (Apollonius of Tyana),[191] a 'master of sorcery', knows the remedy against this enchantment; he thus confounds all her tricks and overcomes her deception and trickery.[192] When her dragon form is dissolved and Balīnās sees the beautiful sorceress, he falls in love with her. He stops Alexander's soldiers from killing her and protects her. Then Balīnās presents the sorceress to Alexander, who gives her to him as his wife. Niẓāmī says that from her 'Balīnās learned all kinds of sorceries, and because of her today he bears the name of "Balīnās, the Magician".'[193]

Alexander Marries Rawshanak, Visits Mecca and Establishes Tbilisi

Alexander then marches towards Isfahan, where he formally marries Rawshanak, Darius's daughter.[194] Finally, he is crowned in Iṣṭakhr (Persepolis).[195] However, in contrast to the *Shāhnāma* of Firdawsī, Niẓāmī has Alexander send Rawshanak, accompanied by Aristotle, back to Rūm, where she gives birth to a son named Iskandarūs.[196] Then he marches west, to Arabia.[197] He visits Yemen and Mecca, where he performs a religious ceremony in the Ka'ba, the account of which is similar to the *Shāhnāma*, although Niẓāmī's passage in the *Sharafnāma* is far more elaborate:

His face shining with joy, he marched then
Towards the Ka'ba with all due rites performed.
He set his foot upon the navel of the earth
– How many a knot indeed that navel unravels! –
Like the circling compass of Heaven's Wheel
He stepped to its centre on devotion's feet,
Circumambulating that shrine that all adore
He grasped the door ring of the holy house:
First he kissed with reverence the Ka'ba's gate,
Recollecting God-the-Protector with all his heart.
He laid his head on that holy portal to pray
And to the poor gave copious alms from his treasury.
His coins flowed out like treasures manifold!
How plentiful were the camels that he sacrificed!
When in the House of the Righteous he'd made his place

And showed his devotion to God with both heart and hand
The Ka'ba was filled with treasure and jewels galore;
Its roof and door adorned with musk and ambergris.[198]

This motif is probably a literary imitation and parallel of Alexander's entrance to Jerusalem recounted by Muslim authors. If Alexander goes to Jerusalem, according to the Jewish tradition, there is no reason that he should not go to Mecca, according to the Islamic tradition. However, Niẓāmī does not use the word *ḥajj* (pilgrimage); neither does he attribute any pilgrimage to Alexander, nor any performance of the rituals at Mecca that traditionally form part of the Muslim *ḥajj*.[199] This is important, since the Arabic sources do use the word *ḥajj*.[200] For instance, Dīnawarī in his *Akhbār al-ṭiwāl* says that Alexander performs the *ḥajj* to the House of God.[201] It is more likely that what Niẓāmī had in mind was a visit to the ancient shrine erected at Mecca by Abraham.[202] Indeed, in the *Sharafnāma*, Alexander is portrayed as Abraham's descendant. Niẓāmī refers to Alexander's religion as being *ḥanīfī* (which, according to the Qur'ān, is a kind of monotheism characteristic of Abraham).[203]

After his visit to Mecca, Alexander marches towards Iraq and then Azerbaijan, where he is informed that the people of nearby Armenia still follow Zoroastrianism. He then leads his army from Babylon to Armenia,[204] where he destroys the fire temples.[205] Thence he makes 'an assault against Abkhaz', where the ruler, a Kurdish man named Dawālī, offers him his land and his loyalty.

Alexander then founds the city of Tiflīs (Tbilisi, in modern-day Georgia) there, an event that Niẓāmī quotes from 'the old *dihqān*'.[206] Traditionally, the founding of Tbilisi is attributed to King Vaxtang Gorgasali (r. 447–522).[207] Brosset dates the city's origin to AD 455 or 458, when the capital of Georgia was transferred there from nearby Mtskheta (Ptolemy, *Geography*, 5.10: Μεστλῆτα = Μεσχῆτα).[208] According to a medieval (ninth- to fourteenth-century) collection of Georgian historical texts known as *Kartlis Tskhovreba*, a Sasanian force was sent against Varaz-Bak'ar (*c.*379–93) by the King of Georgia (Xuasrovanis, descended from the Sassanians),[209] who built Tiflis 'between the Gates of the Caucasus [between Darial and Darband] to serve as a bulwark against Mtskheta'.[210] Hence, it is likely that the designation of Alexander as Tbilisi's founding father was simply a way to emphasise the city's antiquity. According to the Georgian historical tradition, Alexander installs the first sovereign of Georgia at Tiflis after subjugating the country,[211] but there is no mention of him founding the city.

The Further Adventures of Alexander: Journeys to China, Russia, India and the Land of Darkness

Alexander at the Court of Queen Nūshāba (Candace)

The following passages in the *Sharafnāma* narrate the episode of Queen Nūshāba at some length. Queen Nūshāba replaces the Pseudo-Callisthenes's Queen Candace,[212] and Firdawsī's Queen Qaidāfa.[213] Niẓāmī locates Nūshāba's kingdom in Barda' (Partaw in Caucasian Albania), a city that was in Niẓāmī's neighbourhood. Khāqānī of Shirvān (*c.*1127; d. 1186–1199),[214] a contemporary poet who lived near Niẓāmī's home town, devoted many verses of his *Dīvān* to the story of Queen Candace.[215] Khāqānī's verses indicate that the story of Queen Candace was popular in Azerbaijan, where both poets lived. The fact that Khāqānī named the queen Qaidāfa (Candace) demonstrates that Niẓāmī's naming her Nūshāba was deliberate, perhaps reflecting a choice to present a more familiar name to his audience.[216]

The tale consists of two parts. Firstly, Alexander goes in disguise to Nūshāba's court, but she recognises him because she had his portrait painted. Secondly, there is a banquet in honour of the queen. Niẓāmī dedicates more than 50 verses to the description of Nūshāba's country, palace and court:

> A thousand virgin girls were at her service and, besides damsels skilful in riding, there were thirty thousand swordsmen in her army. However, no men had access to her court, except those who were close to her. Her counsellors were all women who had no husband ... Her throne was made of crystal [*bulūr*] embedded with so many precious stones that they shone at night like the moon. Besides worshipping God, they had no other occupation except drinking, eating and sleeping. She spent the night worshipping, and the day drinking accompanied by music and the songs of minstrels.[217]

Upon hearing the tale of this fabulous queen and her court, Alexander becomes eager to visit Nūshāba's country. Along with a small entourage, Alexander camps near the borders of her kingdom. When Nūshāba learns of this, every day she sends him a different kind of food made from the local produce of her land. Her charming and hospitable behaviour naturally only increase Alexander's desire to visit her, although – typical military strategist that he is – he also wants to obtain news of the secrets of her kingdom's administration in order, in Niẓāmī's words, to 'discover whether the tale was true or false'.[218]

To this end, he travels in disguise to her court, impersonating his own ambassador. When Nūshāba is informed that the 'King of Rūm' (*shah-e rūm*) is in her country, she sits on her throne with a 'ball of amber' (*ma'anbar turanjī*) in her hand.[219] When she receives Alexander, he neither removes his sword nor kneels before her, as is the customary protocol among messengers. Nūshāba, who has a painting of Alexander, immediately sees through his disguise. However, she does not show that she has recognised him until Alexander has delivered his 'king's' message to her in a bold and arrogant manner. She then reveals to him that she knows who he is. When Alexander brazenly continues to deny his identity, she becomes insistent and speaks sharply to the conqueror, commanding her courtiers to bring forth the piece of silk on which Alexander's image has been painted. Alexander turns pale and becomes frightened when he sees his own image, being forced now to disclose his true identity. At this moment, Queen Nūshāba relents and softens towards him, speaking gently to him.

The first part of the Nūshāba episode has crucial importance for Alexander's progress towards perfect kingship. The parallel episode in the *Shāhnāma* (which concerns Qaidāfa, Queen of al-Andalus) is very close to the Greek version (Pseudo-Callisthenes, III, 18–23). However, Niẓāmī's treatment of the story differs both in the attention and importance accorded to the queen (Nūshāba) and in the alteration of some details. The ethical significance of this episode is indicated in Nūshāba's speech, where she accuses Alexander of immaturity and arrogance.[220] Niẓāmī has her show 'him first his own image so that he might recognise and appreciate hers'.[221]

Without self-knowledge, one cannot perceive the Divine. Here, the queen character represents the divine immanence: the Lady Beloved as theophanic receptacle.[222] Thus, Nūshāba becomes a mirror in which

Alexander may contemplate and apprehend the qualities of his own soul, which are first symbolised by his painted image. As he finally accepts Nūshāba's superiority, Niẓāmī presents her queenly wisdom as incarnating divine guidance for Alexander in his quest for moral perfection and self-knowledge.

Alexander in Darband

At this juncture, Niẓāmī tells us that Alexander has assembled such a vast amount of treasure that it becomes difficult for him to continue his expeditions. Thus, after burying his treasure in the ground following Apollonius's advice, Alexander marches towards the Alburz Mountains, passing through Shirvān to Darband:[223]

> When Alexander drove his troops towards the Alburz Mountains, in every place and province he set up an administrator. Through mountain passes difficult of access he pushed his army's supplies – he charged like a lion through Shirvān. The purpose of his forced march was to press on and reach the road to Darband.[224]

In Darband there is a fortress said to be full of treasure, against which Alexander's army battles for 40 days to open, but to no avail, for 'they could not knock down even one clod from its ramparts'.[225] Wearying of the fruitless siege, Alexander summons a new meeting (*majlis*) of his generals and head officers. One of his men informs him that in a certain cave there is a pious devotee who might know how to conquer the fortress. The ascetic supplicates in such a way that the mountain is shattered and the fortress collapses.[226]

While Alexander is in Darband, the Khazar folk (Khazrānyān), who 'dwelled in the vicinity of that mountainous fortress, accused the people of Qipchak [Qafchāq] of tyranny at the king's court', and entreated Alexander to build a gate against them.[227] Thus the king summons the Khazars together to close the mountain passes against the people of Qipchak:

> They erected a barrier on that narrow pass, making use of granite, steel and tin. Master builders in stone, adept in the precepts of their trade, versed in the fortification of fortresses, were

summoned. He called up a multitude of men and set them to the task of closing the mountain pass [from the Qipchak people].[228]

Darband (literally 'pass') – also known as the 'Caspian Gate' and as *Bāb al-abwāb* (the 'Supreme Gate' or 'Gate of Gates')[229] in Arabic – is erroneously identified by some historians as the Gate of Alexander.[230] The Darband fortress was certainly the most prominent Sasanian defensive construction in the Caucasus.[231] The anonymous author of the twelfth-century *Mujmal al-tavārīkh* was aware of this fact and stressed: 'He who built the *Bāb al-Abwāb* [Gate of Gates] was Khusraw I, Anūshīrvān ... to protect [his kingdom] from the Turks. Of course, those who do not know the history well attributed that gate to Alexander.'[232] The Syriac traditions also locate Alexander's Gate in the Caucasus Mountains.[233]

The *Sharafnāma* mentions two different gates or barriers, and according to Niẓāmī, Alexander's gate in Darband is not related to the wall he built against Gog and Magog. The passage on the construction of the Wall of Gog (Magog is not mentioned by the poet) comes in an episode in the *Iqbālnāma* (the second part of the *Iskandarnāma*), which will be discussed in the next chapter.[234] Thus, although Niẓāmī was indeed aware of the fact that Darband (the Caspian Gate) was not the same as the Wall of Gog and Magog, there was evidently some confusion in his sources.[235]

Historically speaking, while Alexander did indeed pass through the Caspian Gates, these gates – as described by Arrian (*Anabasis* 3.19.2) – are to be identified with a defile in the Alburz Mountains in the vicinity of Rhagai (Ray).[236] There is also, incidentally, an 'Iron Gate' on the route from Termez to Shahrisabz in Uzbekistan, through which he probably passed.[237]

Niẓāmī's mistake might have stemmed from the fact that the same name (Darband) was applied to two locations in the Caucasus: the 'Pass of Derbend' between the Caucasus Mountains and the western shore of the Caspian Sea, and the 'Dariel Pass' (from the Parthian *Dar i Alān*, Gate of the Alāns), which runs north–south through the Caucasus Mountains from Tbilisi to Ordzhonikidze. In classical Greek geography, the location of the Caspian Gates was fixed at the Dariel Pass.[238] This is the tradition followed by the *Alexander Romance* of the Pseudo-Callisthenes, so the movements of Alexander following the death of

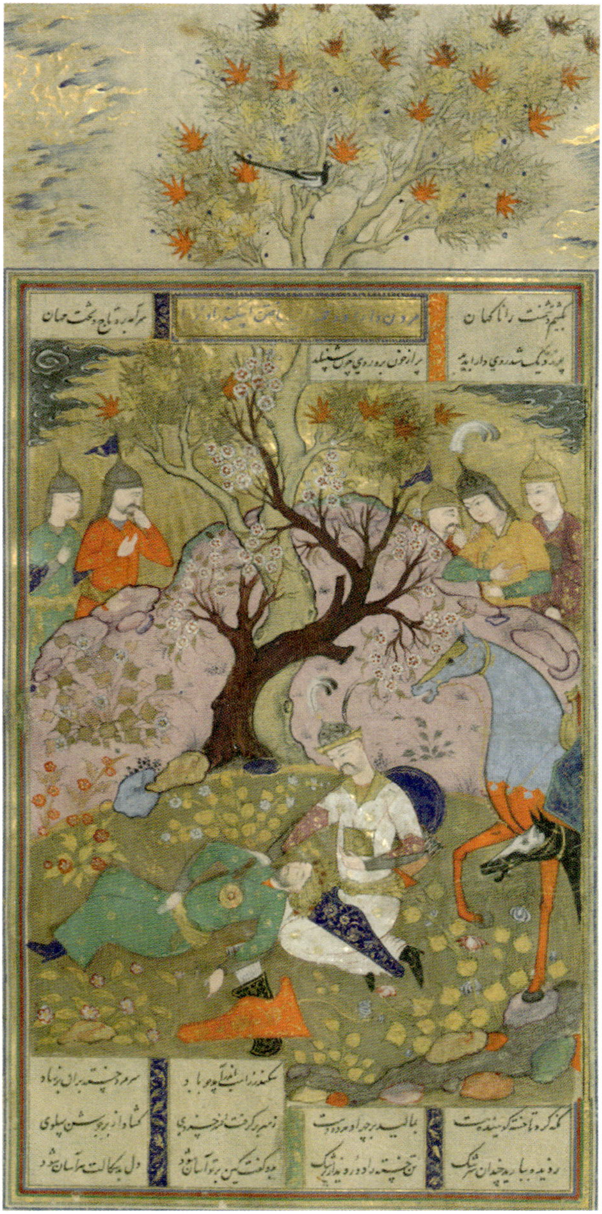

Plate 1 Alexander the Great Mourns the Dying Darius.

Plate 2 Alexander and his Men Watch Naked Girls Swim in the Black Sea.

Plate 3 Battle of Alexander the Great with the Ethiopians.

Plate 4 Alexander the Great Admires his Portrait Commissioned by Queen Nūshāba.

Plate 5 Alexander the Great at the Fountain of Life with the Prophets Khiḍr and Ilyās (Elias).

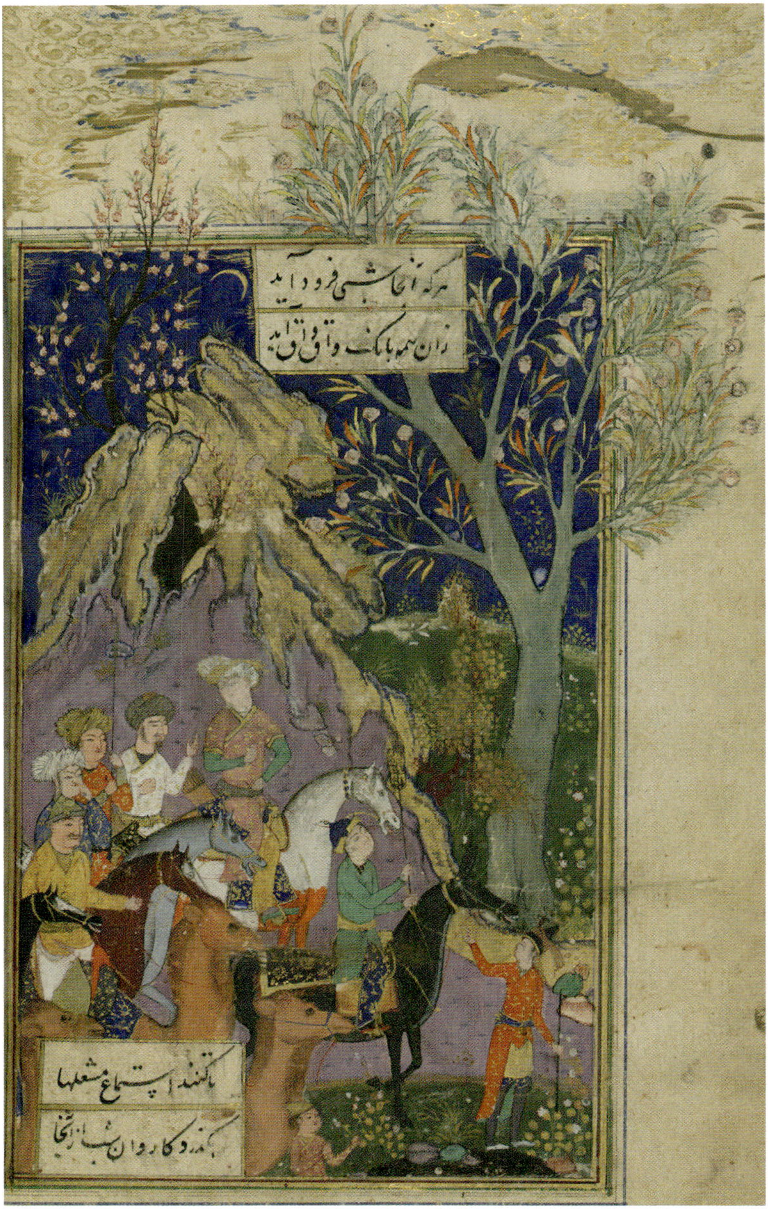

Plate 6 The Talking Tree.

Plate 7 Birth of Alexander the Great.

Plate 8 Invention of the Mirror in the Presence of Alexander the Great.

Plate 9 The Invention of the Mirror.

Plate 10 Kay Khusraw Crosses Lake Zarah in Pursuit of Afrāsiyāb.

Plate 11 Alexander and the Seven Philosophers.

Darius are attached to mountains of the Caucasus region rather than to those of the Hindu Kush.[239]

This in fact corresponds exactly to the situation outlined in the *Sharafnāma*, which no doubt reflects Niẓāmī's source. He rightly locates this episode in the Alburz Mountains, between the episode of Queen Nūshāba of Barda' (Partaw in Caucasian Albania), and Sarīr (in Dāghistān, ancient Albania). Thus, the word *Darband* in this episode most probably refers to the Dariel Pass (also known as the Gate of Alān). However, it is interesting that Niẓāmī clearly distinguishes it from the Wall of Gog and Magog.

The Competition between the Byzantine and Chinese Painters

Following in the virtual footsteps of Kay Khusraw, but in a contrary direction,[240] Alexander is then depicted by Niẓāmī as marching towards Ray and Khurāsān, where he destroys many fire temples and founds the city of Herat.[241] He passes through Balkh, Ghazna and Ghūr on the way to India. Niẓāmī describes Alexander's march to Tibet and then to China.[242] His account differs from that of the *Shāhnāma* insofar as Niẓāmī says the Chinese Emperor goes to Alexander in disguise (as an ambassador), while the other sources say Alexander goes to the Emperor in disguise. This episode permits Niẓāmī to tell some lovely stories about Chinese painting and the prophet Mānī.[243] It is worth mentioning that the Persian word *Chīn* is applied to Chinese or eastern Turkistan, while *Māchīn* refers to Great China. Therefore, in Persian literature, if and when Alexander is depicted as a traveller to Chīn (Turkestan), this theme is probably simply an echo of his expedition to Central Asia. This explains why the building of such cities as Samarqand, Balkh and Merv is also included in this episode.

This passage permits Niẓāmī to insert into the narrative two beautiful tales that appear to be unconnected to the *Alexander Romance* in its original form.[244] He had a philosophical purpose in doing so. The two tales narrate a competition between Chinese and Byzantine painters on the one hand, and the tale of Mānī, the painter prophet, on the other. Both tales concern the role of imagination in Sufi *gnosis*, and the mystical theme that spiritual 'contemplation' and 'reflection' of certain images leads to knowledge of the heart.[245] Niẓāmī's source for the first tale is Ghazālī's (1058–1111) allegory in *Iḥyā 'ulūm al-Dīn* (*Revitalisation of the Religious Sciences*).[246] Here follows the tale according to Niẓāmī.

During Alexander's banquet with the Emperor of China (*Khāqān-i Chīn*), the rulers praise the most famous experts of their respective lands. Alexander proclaims that Byzantine (*rūm*) painters are the best in the world, while the Emperor insists that Chinese painters are better. An altercation arises. Finally, they decide to build a dome, where the two halves of the interior are separated by a curtain down the middle, and on either side Chinese and Byzantine painters respectively paint their half of the dome. When the curtain is removed and their images are revealed, they turn out to be identical in every respect. They are mirror images of each other (*ki īn mīpaḍīruft u ān mīnimūd*). Alexander is unable to judge which group of painters – Chinese or Byzantine – is the more expert. The mage Balīnās, Alexander's wise minister, then interposes a veil once again between the two paintings in such a way that while the delineations of the Byzantine painting do not lose their lustre and colour, obscurity (*zang*) falls upon the polished surface of the Chinese painting. The secret of the two groups of artists is then revealed: while the Byzantine painters were actually engaged in painting, the Chinese were polishing their half of the dome into a mirror.[247]

According to Ghazālī, the story is an allegory of the difference between the theoretical knowledge of philosophers (Byzantine painters) and the intuitive wisdom of Sufi mystics (Chinese painters). While philosophers try to explain the divine mysteries technically, intuitive mystics perceive the same cosmic truth and vision immediately through the 'reflection' of divine inspiration, 'because they can contemplate the Divine mysteries in the polished mirror of their purified hearts'.[248]

The polished heart as a mirror of the Unseen world is one of the characteristics of the *awlīya* (friends of God, Sufi saints). This motif becomes a very important aspect of the *Alexander Romance* and the conqueror's spiritual personality in the second part of the *Iskandarnāma*, since it is a crucial stage in his process of attaining divine kingship.[249] This motif is particularly significant in Niẓāmī's poetry as well; indeed, in another poem he boasts of being so adept in the 'licit magic' of poetry that he himself has become a veritable 'Mirror of the Invisible Realm'.[250]

Alexander's Russian Campaigns

We can now turn to examine Niẓāmī's account of Alexander's campaign against the Russians. The poet relates that 'after Alexander's visit to China, he was keen to come back to his homeland ... even though his dominions spanned innumerable lands'.[251] At this juncture, the ruler of Abkhaz comes to Alexander and complains to him about the tyranny of the Russians:

> Those quarrelsome Russian tribes, the Alān and Gark
> Ambushed and attacked us hard like a barrage of hail!
> They've overthrown all Bardaʿ's kingdom and carried
> Off by pillage many cities full of wealth with them!
> They've borne away in rapine Nūshāba, our queen.
> Upon the stones of war her flagon lies broken![252]

In order to release Queen Nūshāba and help the people of Abkhaz defend themselves against Russian attack, Alexander marches from the Jayḥūn River – the Turkish name for the Amū Daryā (its Arabic name) and the Oxus (its Greek name) – towards Khwārazm until he reaches the Steppe of Qipchak (*dasht-i Qafchāq*). Here he engages the Russians in seven battles. For each battle, Niẓāmī narrates the heroic acts of soldiers from both armies. However, perhaps the most interesting point[253] here is Niẓāmī's description of the people of Rūs:

(1) They are said to comprise seven tribes, five of which he names: the Burṭās, Alāns, Khazars, Isū and Args.
(2) They are renowned for their endurance and tolerance of difficult conditions.
(3) Alexander describes them as renowned rogues and expert bandits: 'Only when engaging in thieving, treachery and highway robbery do they display manliness or are [they] battle-hardy.'[254]
(4) They fight naked and without any weapons.

Niẓāmī also mentions a hatred that prevails between the Russians and the Turks, an enmity that Alexander uses to his own advantage:

> Although the Turks are not allied with Greeks by kinship ties, yet their rage and rancour towards the Russians is far greater than that towards the Greeks. On this strong battle footing, by the sharp darts of the Turks one may cast blisters on the feet of the Russians as they fly! Many a toxin there is that destroys the body, the cure of which is another kind of poison.[255]

Niẓāmī describes the seven battles in detail; he even names the heroes of each army (such as Zarīvand of Māzandarān, an Alān named Faranja and a Russian named Ṭarṭūs, who claims that in the Russian language he is called 'Rustam of Russia').[256] Niẓāmī affirms that the people of Burṭās wear helmets or hats of fox fur, adding that the fox fur of that land was very well known. He also tells us that they wear a fox-fur garment called a *purṭās*.[257]

The Giant Russian Ghoul

Among the accounts of these battles, the appearance of a giant ghoul in the Russian army during the sixth battle is worth mentioning. Niẓāmī describes him as follows:

> Like the Leviathan arising from the depths of the sea, one warrior came forth clad in an old hide. In the maelstrom of action he was huge as a mountain on feet and in bulk his might far greater than five hundred horsemen. As he flexed his gnarled, gritty fists to maul his foes, he made hard diamond seem soft as dough. He attacked like a bloodthirsty devil flying out of the mouth of hell. Although his legs were shackled by a chain, his stature and strength were immense. His sole weapon was an iron mace curved at the top, with which he could sweep up and cast down a mountain.[258]

Astonished at the sight of this wild giant, Alexander asks after his origins. One of his men, who knows the area quite well, describes the ghoul as follows:

> Near the Land of Darkness lies a mountain, the way to which is narrow as the breadth of a hair. On that mountain live men of this immense bodily frame, their flesh of earthly origin but their strength like iron. No one really knows their true origin, their homeland or where was their first haunt and habitat. All have ruddy faces and blue eyes, and when enraged they fear not even lions. One of them can fight a whole battalion, so strong and sure-footed are they in battle. Whether these ghouls be male or female matters not: the day one goes to war with them one summons up the end of the world. Fighting fit, in every contest they come out

> on top, their religion is the art of combat. No one has ever seen one of these ghouls dead: only alive and even these one rarely sees. Each ghoul owns a herd of sheep, by which they make their living. Their strength in trade lies in marten pelts and wool; they value no other goods than these. None of them stores up any wealth, for the only thing they recognise and cherish as riches is the black sable, which can be found nowhere else but in that land. From each ghoul's brow springs a horn like that of the rhinoceros. And if the horn were not part of their bodily form, what difference would there be between their form and the ugly Russians' shape? When one of them is overcome by the desire to sleep, like the vagrant eagle he retreats to a tree where, driving his horn into its trunk, the ghoul falls asleep like a demon in devilish arrest.[259]

The man also explains that if the Russians manage to capture one of these wild people while asleep, they convey him or her with caution to Russia to use in battle. It may be useful in this context to compare Niẓāmī's account of Alexander's campaign against the Russians with that of the *Shāhnāma*, where after the passage on Hārūm, the Land of Women (called Beroe in the Pseudo-Callisthenes), Alexander reaches a land of warriors with fair hair and ruddy faces.[260] In contrast to Niẓāmī's account of the Russian battle, the Russians all surrender to Alexander, so there is no war at all. This description coincides with information given by Viking traders, which is available in the works of Arab geographers and travellers who wrote about northern lands and peoples.[261] In particular, comparison shows that Niẓāmī's 'Russian episode' in the *Sharafnāma* resembles the *Risāla* of Ibn Faḍlān,[262] probably because there were no other (or very few) sources on the Russians and their customs in the Islamic tradition. Regarding the giant ghoul in the sixth battle against the Russians, we find a parallel description in the *Risāla* of Ibn Faḍlān, who also mentions the fur trade and the use of sable pelts by this people.[263]

Alexander in Love: The Tale of the Chinese Slave Girl

In the seventh battle, Alexander falls in love with a warlike woman who is a Chinese slave. Niẓāmī dedicates a whole episode to their love affair.[264] In a long, beautiful passage – quite unusual and remarkable in Persian epic poetry for its celebration of the domination and superior erotic power of female martial prowess over the male's, as well as for its detailed descriptions of Alexander's lovemaking with her – Niẓāmī describes her as an epiphany of the Eternal Feminine, to whom even a world conqueror succumbs.[265] Niẓāmī thus claims that neither heroic actions nor clever statecraft are sufficient to make the perfect king. Rather, the true ruler needs the informing power of love to display valour and dispense justice. It is only through love that he reaches self-knowledge, which is, after all, the explicit goal of the quest undertaken by the protagonist in his journey towards spiritual kingship.

* * *

Alexander finally defeats the Russians and releases Queen Nūshāba. He is very impressed by the fur trade that flourishes in that land.[266] Historically speaking, we know that Alexander never fought against the people of Rūs (including the Khazars, the Alāns and so on), so it is unclear how this episode came to be interpolated in Niẓāmī's *Alexander Romance*. In some sources prior to Niẓāmī, Alexander's expeditions in the Caucasus are often mentioned in relation to the wall he built against the so-called 'Unclean Nations',[267] who are normally identified with the pagan tribes of the Khazars, Huns and Turks.[268] This motif emerged in the Jewish Hellenistic circles in Alexandria at the beginning of the Christian era.[269]

Flavius Josephus (d. *c.*100) linked the biblical Gog and Magog with the Hellenistic Alexander tradition in his *Jewish War* (*Bellum Judaicum*, VII: 7, 4).[270] St Jerome (d. 420) mentions Hun invasions across the Caucasus, as well as the barrier with which Alexander fends them off (Epistula 77, 6–8).[271] However, a fusion of the motif of Alexander's barrier with the uncouth pagan 'Unclean Nations' of the Caucasus Mountains appears in the Syriac Alexander legend (possibly composed in 629–30, after the victory of Emperor Heraclius over the Sasanian king Khusraw II Parvīz).[272]

Christian of Stavelot's commentary on Matthew (*Expositio in Matthaeum Evangelistam*) identifies the Khazars as those whom Alexander confined, and one of the seven tribes[273] mentioned by Niẓāmī. In general, in the Persian and Arabic traditions there is much local lore and ethnohistorical information that amalgamates the Khazars, Alāns and other northern people with the Rūs folk.[274] In conclusion, notwithstanding its nonexistence in Alexander's actual biography and the historical inaccuracy of Niẓāmī's account of this episode, it is clear that it is a motif found in several early Christian sources relating to the Alexander legend.

In his *Tārīkh-i Ṭabaristān* (*Chronicle of Ṭabaristān*), Ibn Isfandīyār makes mention of the Rūs attack on the Caspian Sea as taking place in AD 909.[275] Khāqānī Shirvānī (*c*.1106–90), who lived in the vicinity of Niẓāmī and also spent all his life in the Caucasus, mentions the Rūs's attacks (including the Rūs, Khazars, Alāns and Sarīr) quite frequently in his *Dīvān*.[276] Especially relevant in this respect is the Persian geographic work entitled the *Ḥudūd al-ʿālam*, which affirms the Rūs's attacks on a large village on the outskirts of Bardaʿ (which is, interestingly enough, the city of Queen Nūshaba in the *Sharafnāma*).[277] This mass of information has persuaded scholars of Niẓāmī that the Rūs wars related by the poet in the *Sharafnāma* reflect Russian attacks on Azerbaijan in the tenth century AD.[278]

In the Land of Darkness: Alexander's Quest for the Water of Life

We now come to the Water of Life, the last motif that the *Sharafnāma* shares with the *Shāhnāma* and the Pseudo-Callisthenes's *Alexander Romance* (II, 39–40). The quest for the Water of Life prepares Alexander for the transition from temporal to spiritual kingship, and as a didactic device, the tale functions to remind the reader of human mortality and the transience of worldly glory.[279]

Niẓāmī relates the story of a banquet in which every man is tasked with telling strange tales of his own land. An old man informs Alexander that in the Land of Darkness there is a fountain containing the Water of Life, which he describes in these verses:

> In what is called the 'Land of Darkness' is found,
> Behind the scenes, the purest, limpid *aqua vitae*.
> ... The way is short from here to there: it's just
> One tenth of the distance that you've come so far.[280]

The Greek *Romance* also locates the Water of Life 'in the direction of the constellation of the Plough' (Pseudo-Callisthenes, II, 32), at 'the end of the world' in a region where the sun never shines (Pseudo-Callisthenes, II, 39).[281] Mario Casari believes that this episode can be reconstructed as part of a collection of ancient themes concerning the exploration of the northern lands and seas of Eurasia.[282] However, it is most likely that

Niẓāmī had a mystical purpose in presenting this episode rather than any desire to discuss geographical phenomena,[283] insofar as the tale occurs at a crucial moment in Alexander's progress towards spiritual kingship, as mentioned above. As a mystical motif, the journey to the Land of Darkness to find the Water of Life symbolises the inner journey of man through the darkness of his ego to the ultimate realisation of divine knowledge and the acquisition of eternal wisdom (*philosophia perennis*).

As the tale in the *Sharafnāma* goes, on his way to the North Pole in search of the Water of Life, Alexander reaches a cave where he leaves most of his army and heavy equipment. Niẓāmī calls it a '*Bun-ghār*' (basement-cave), which according to many sources is the etymological origin of the name of Bulgaria:[284]

> Because the conqueror [Alexander] gave it the name
> Of 'Bunghār', the land of 'Bulgaria' gained fame.
> The men of rank and state who now reign there
> Are all the royal sons and heirs of Alexander.[285]

Niẓāmī offers three versions of the legend of the Water of Life in the *Sharafnāma*. He indicates that the first version is derived from the *Tārīkh-i Dihqān* (*Sasanian Tradition*), which probably means his 'Pahlavi' source, at least in its general framework. This version also coincides with Firdawsī's version of the Water of Life episode.

The second version Niẓāmī traces back to '*Rūmīyān-i kuhan*', perhaps meaning an ancient Byzantine/Greek source, in which Ilyās (the biblical Elijah)[286] accompanies Khiḍr. Although Niẓāmī claims that this is a 'Rūmī' tradition, no extant Greek or Byzantine author ever mentions Khiḍr.[287] What does Niẓāmī mean by referring to the 'ancient *Rūmī*s'? Niẓāmī writes that Ilyās and Khiḍr find the fountain accidentally because the salted fish they had for dinner fell into the water and came back to life. This version makes no mention of Alexander at all or, at least, Niẓāmī says nothing of him here. It is thus possible that Niẓāmī is referring to a biblical tradition. Ilyās corresponds to the biblical Elijah, and Khiḍr may be connected to Ahasuerus, the wandering Jew[288] (Ασουηρος in Greek, and *Assuerus* in Latin).[289] Does Niẓāmī's reference to the 'Rūmī' origins of this version perhaps indicate that he had access to the Greek or Latin version of the Jewish Bible?

Finally, the third version comes from the Arabic tradition (*Tārīkh-i tāzī*), the Qur'ānic tale of the fish that accidentally fall into the fountain containing the Water of Life and come back to life.

However, Niẓāmī maintains that the first two versions are incorrect: 'Both the Zoroastrian (*majūsī*) and the Byzantine historians missed the path [of the true narrative].'[290] In the first version (the pre-Islamic Persian one), Niẓāmī writes that Alexander enters the Land of Darkness on the first night of the month of *Urdībihisht* (21 April).[291] Khiḍr, his guide, gives Alexander a magic stone,[292] which he says will start to shine when he comes close to the fountain. Khiḍr finds the fountain and bathes in it. The fountain then promptly disappears from sight. The Arabic tradition, according to Niẓāmī, relates the tale differently. After drinking from the Water of Life, Ilyās and Khiḍr desert Alexander and his army. Khiḍr goes to sea and Ilyās to the desert, while Alexander wanders lost and in vain for 40 days in the Land of Darkness. This version also contains the tale of the Valley of Diamonds found in the Pseudo-Callisthenes (II, 40).[293] Alexander marches on for 40 days until at last he manages to leave the darkness. In none of these versions is Alexander able to find or partake of the Water of Life.

The episode of the Water of Life is one of the most studied motifs in the literature of Alexander Studies, and has also been frequently depicted in Persian miniature painting.[294] It is furthermore a popular motif in various mythologies, from the Indian[295] to the Babylonian (in which it appears as a 'Plant of Life').[296] This passage in the *Sharafnāma* has been interpreted from different viewpoints – the mystical[297] and the cosmographical,[298] among others.

However, since he is a Muslim, the true version of the legend for Niẓāmī is (as he affirms) that of the Arabic tradition (*Tārīkh-i tāzī*), which is based on the Qur'ānic account of Moses and the Servant of God (*Sūrah* 18:60–82), who is identified by Qur'ānic commentators with the prophet Khiḍr in most of the canonical collections of commentaries. Friedländer was the first scholar to use the fish episode to demonstrate the connection between the Alexander stories and the Qur'ān (18:60–5).[299] The earliest references to the fish episode are in the Greek β-recension and the Babylonian Talmud. The most important stage in the evolution of the *Alexander Romance* is the development of the commentaries on the Qur'ān (18:60–101). As Wheeler rightly demonstrates:

> There is no evidence to make Q 18:60–82 dependent on a particular Jewish or Christian source ... earlier scholarship does not make an adequate distinction between the information contained in the Quran and what is said by the Muslim exegetes about these verses ... it is clear that, in time, the exegetes identified all of Q 18:60–101 with the Alexander stories. The exegetes' source for the Alexander stories would have been Jacob of Serugh's sermon that contained the fish episode and Alexander's building the gate against Gog and Magog.[300]

With a more discerning look at the exegesis of such details as the fish and the journey to the ends of the earth, Wheeler shows how Muslim exegesis purposefully incorporated these extra-Qur'ānic materials. The Muslim exegetes seem to have used these details to conflate Moses in the Qur'ān (18:60–82) with the character of Dhū'l-Qarnayn in the Qur'ān (18:83–101), and to associate them with stories of Alexander the Great and Gilgamesh.[301] *Sūrah* 18 (*Kahf*, 'The Cave') in the Qur'ān relates legends that must have had their origin in Oriental Christian circles and biblical tradition (the Seven Sleepers, the Bicorn Dhū'l-Qarnayn, and Moses in the Fountain of Life).[302]

In the *Romance* tradition, however, Alexander replaces Moses. In order to understand why Alexander replaced Moses, it is important to explain the association of Moses with elements from Alexandrian literature. One possible connection between Moses and Alexander is that both are said to have been 'horned'. The earliest known reference to Moses being horned is found in the Latin recension of the Bible.[303] Alexander is also identified as the 'Two-Horned One' (*dhū'l-qarnayn*) in the Qur'ān. Another similarity between Alexander and Moses is that just as Alexander searches for and fails to obtain immortality, Moses is denied entry into Eden.[304] In general, we can conclude that Niẓāmī's version of Alexander's search for the Water of Life was highly influenced by his studies of commentaries on the Qur'ān.

Finally, as Niẓāmī states, it seems that Alexander's search for the Water of Life was not vain after all, for it drove him to advance to the last and most difficult stage of his progress – that of becoming a prophet – thus effecting his transition from temporal to spiritual kingship. It is at this juncture that Niẓāmī brings the *Sharafnāma* to a close and starts the second part of his poetic epic on Alexander, the *Iqbālnāma*. This deals with two general traditions: that of the Qur'ān and that of the portrayal of Alexander in Islamic wisdom literature.

Conclusion

One of the key surprising[305] discoveries made in this chapter is that the *Sharafnāma* includes a great variety of *pre-Islamic* Persian stories about Alexander from the Sasanian period. We thus find that for many, if not most, of the episodes of the *Sharafnāma*, Niẓāmī has drawn from the so-called '*Nāma-yi Khusrawī* (*Book of Kings*), the *Daftar-i Khusruwān* (*Register of Kings*), the *guzāranda-yi darj-i Dihqān-navard* (narrator of the scroll of the *Dihqān*), the *Tārīkh-i Dihqān* (*History of the Dihqān*), the *guzāranda-yi dāstān-i Darī* (narrator of the Persian tale), and the *mūbad-i mūbadān* (Great Zoroastrian priest), among others. Niẓāmī's source or sources are certainly different from those found in the *Shāhnāma* of Firdawsī, to whom he normally refers as '*Dānā-yi Ṭūs*' (the Sage of Ṭūs). These sources may possibly be his 'Pahlavi' source and the Zoroastrian texts from which he extracted his information concerning the destruction of the fire temples and Zoroastrian books (the *Zand* and *Avesta*).

Āzarbāyjān/Azerbaijan (Āturpātakān, as the province appears to have been officially called throughout the Sasanian period) was an important religious centre during the Sasanian period, being the homeland and hearth of one of the empire's three most sacred fires.[306] Because of this great fire temple, Azerbaijan must have had a powerful influence on the elaboration of Zoroastrian tales and the creation of Sasanian culture and religious lore. This may perhaps account for the great variety and novelty of Niẓāmī's information and tales, which were probably based on Zoroastrian tradition and non-religious Sasanian/Azerbaijani literature that had not yet vanished in Niẓāmī's day.

Since Niẓāmī normally provides three different versions of each tale (such as Alexander's ancestry and the Water of Life) throughout the *Sharafnāma*, his sources are likely to have been:

(1) The Sasanian tradition, both religious (Zoroastrian) and non-religious (epic, folklore).
(2) The biblical tradition, referred to as '*tārīkh-i Rūm*' (Byzantine/Greek history) or as his Jewish and Christian/Nestorian (*naṣrānī*) sources.

(3) The Islamic tradition (Arabic and Persian sources).

In sum, our study of the *Sharafnāma* proposes a powerful cumulative argument that a great deal of material from Pahlavi sources that is now lost to us was available to Niẓāmī. It also demonstrates that Niẓāmī's account is much closer to the Greek *Alexander Romance* than to his predecessor Firdawsī, and also that it contains more reliable historical information. The question that arises here is: how and from where did Niẓāmī manage to gather such a great variety of information? The local culture of the Caucasus was shaped by the cultures of the nations that had political influence in the region: the Greeks, Romans, Byzantines and Persians.[307] Therefore, there was a considerable amount of bilingualism and multilingualism among ethnic minorities of adjacent communities.[308] It is highly likely that Niẓāmī, as a native of Ganja, was multilingual. Furthermore, certain information gleaned from his works proves his familiarity with Greek and Byzantine culture and literature.[309]

In transferring part of Alexander's exploits to the Caucasus, Niẓāmī combined local lore with a large and extensive *Alexander Romance* tradition in order to create a hero who encapsulated his own ideas of kingship. The *Sharafnāma* illustrates not only the great diversity of Niẓāmī's sources and his knowledge of the *Alexander Romance* tradition, but also his underlying preoccupation with the veracity of his sources. As he rightly points out:

In this consummate verse of mine, I've always tried
To follow minds with acumen – men wise and shrewd;
So not a single work of history I left unread,
Each word of theirs I perused. Those legends of Alexander –
Those clustered treasures in quartos dispersed
Are here collected in just one book of verse.
This wondrous treasure casket amazes all:
There's alchemy disguised behind these words.[310]

Another important point revealed by this chapter is the diversity of Niẓāmī's sources. Many pieces of information found in the *Sharafnāma* do not seem to appear in any other extant sources (at least in neither Persian nor Arabic). One can mention in this respect (among many other examples), the depiction of Aristotle's father as Alexander's tutor, and Alexander's founding of Tbilisi and Bulgaria. Whether this diversity of source material was derived from local folklore and tales of Niẓāmī's homeland is unclear, and will probably remain so unless new manuscripts or unknown works are discovered that shed light on motifs that do not appear anywhere else.

As we have seen throughout this chapter, Niẓāmī's *Sharafnāma* functions practically as a mirror for princes, providing useful moral advice for princes and kings, and inculcating such vital qualities as justice, generosity and fairness. The poem also contains strong Sufi elements, emphasising *inter alia* the role of music as a means of achieving self-knowledge, and the importance of love and the practice of various disciplines to perfect and refine the soul. Although the *Iskandarnāma* can and should be treated within the framework of the mirror for princes genre, Niẓāmī's ideal of kingship transcends simple statecraft and political strategy – the art of governance by temporal ways and means – to affirm the possibility of becoming a king in the spiritual realm.[311]

Finally, of all the diverse traditions relating to the *Alexander Romance* in the Persianate world (including the Caucasus), it is perfectly clear that in his *Iskandarnāma* Niẓāmī created a harmonious and attractive tale combining Christian and Jewish traditions while drawing on his local knowledge of life on the border of the Byzantine world. All these characteristics served to make Niẓāmī's *Book of Alexander* the most imitated *Alexander Romance* in Persian poetry and an inspiration for all later Muslim poets who aspired to recast the life of Alexander in verse. Niẓāmī himself asserts that his *Iskandarnāma* is a source of immortality. Although Alexander did not manage to drink the Water of Life, Niẓāmī has 'made him immortal by his own Water of Life [his verse]'.[312]

CHAPTER 5

ALEXANDER IN THE *IQBĀLNĀMA* OF NIẒĀMĪ GANJAVĪ

زنگ ظلمت بود از آب زندگانی قسمت
تا سکندر روی در آیینهٔ اقبال داشت

From the water of immortal life his fate
And lot were but the rust of pitch-black night
Once Alexander turned his face to gaze
on Fortune's looking glass.

Ṣā'ib Tabrīzī (d. 1676)[1]

Introduction

The *Iqbālnāma* (*Book of Fortune*),[2] otherwise known as the *Khiradnāma-yi Iskandarī* (*Book of Alexandrian Wisdom*), contains the new and ongoing adventures of Alexander. However, in this poem Niẓāmī presents him as a seeker of Truth, not as a conqueror as in the *Sharafnāma*. With about 3,680 couplets, the *Iqbālnāma* is a little over half the length of the *Sharafnāma*, which is 6,800 couplets long.[3]

The *Iqbālnāma* is a heroic romance, which, as discussed in the previous chapter, should be read (at least on a purely literary level) as part of the mirror for princes genre, to which all of Niẓāmī's *mathnawī*s belonged.[4] At the same time, the poem's mystical dimensions quite transcend the limitations of that genre, providing yet another perspective on its protagonist's actions by conveying his inner spiritual experiences. The *Iqbālnāma* also focuses on the problem of spiritual kingship and the manner in which this is established in the course of Alexander's quest to become the Perfect Man.[5] For this reason, the tale is organised around this theme and divided into two principal parts. The first part is dominated by lengthy philosophical discourses delivered by Niẓāmī or the philosophers in his retinue, as well as extensive dialogues in which the characters declare their thoughts. Interspersed with such passages of discourse are marginal tales,[6] through which Alexander is inculcated with the required wisdom that will eventually enable him to become a prophet.

The second part of the poem consists of Alexander's further adventures and his voyages around the world, made in order to call people to the true monotheistic faith. His quest here is to find Utopia, the perfect kingdom.[7] His adventures contain tales from what is commonly known as the 'marvels of the world' (*mirabilia*) or *'Ajāyib* genre,[8] much of which is derived from the Hellenic–Syriac tradition as will be discussed below.

In what follows, we will survey the key stories and motifs related to Alexander in the *Iqbālnāma*, analyse Niẓāmī's probable sources for each of them and attempt to highlight the poet's original contribution to the elaboration of the *Alexander Romance*. In order to put this analysis of the poem in context, a brief (but by no means comprehensive) 'table of contents' of the various stories therein is presented here:

(1) The poem begins with a discussion of why Alexander is identified with the prophet Dhū'l-Qarnayn (Bicorn or the Two-Horned One).
(2) An encounter takes place between Alexander and Socrates.
(3) There is a dialogue between Alexander and the Indian sages.
(4) There is a symposium on the Creation of the World with seven philosophers: Aristotle, Wālīs (Vettius Valens),[9] Balīnās (Apollonius of Tyana), Socrates, Furfūrīyus (Porphyry),[10] Hermes and Plato.
(5) Alexander becomes a prophet, and each of his three philosophers (Aristotle, Plato and Socrates) dedicates a Book of Wisdom (*Khiradnāma*) to him.[11]
(6) Alexander begins his journey around the world in order to summon people to monotheism. He comes across many wonders and marvels during his journey.

(7) Alexander travels south, where he encounters skull worshippers (*sar-parastān*).
(8) Alexander returns to India and China, where he sails the seas and encounters marvellous marine wonders, and also enters and escapes from deadly deserts.
(9) Alexander travels north and builds a wall against Gog (Magog is not mentioned).
(10) Alexander visits a utopian city in which everything is perfect and whose inhabitants live in harmony with their neighbours.
(11) Alexander receives God's message to return from the north to Greece.
(12) Alexander becomes ill and writes his will.
(13) Alexander writes a letter of consolation to his mother.
(14) Alexander dies in Shahrazūr, near Babylonia.
(15) Alexander's son, Iskandarūs, weeps for his father's death and abandons his kingship.
(16) The deaths of Alexander's seven philosophers (Aristotle, Hermes, Plato, Valens, Apollonius of Tyana, Porphyry and Socrates) are recounted.
(17) Niẓāmī closes the poem with a discourse on his own age, finally dedicating it to his patron, Malik 'Izz al-Dīn Mas'ūd Ibn Arsalān, the Governor of Muṣūl.[12]

As we can see from this summary, the three key themes of the *Iqbālnāma* are separate yet related branches (which also figure as separate literary genres) of the *Alexander Romance*. The first of these is 'Alexander in wisdom literature', the second is 'Alexander in the Dhū'l-Qarnayn tradition' and the third is 'Alexander's adventures with the marvels of the world', each of which will be examined in turn in this chapter. We will look at how Niẓāmī incorporated material from various historical and literary sources drawn from all three of these genres into his poem. Hence, a precis of the *Iqbālnāma* might take the following form:

(1) Niẓāmī first details how Alexander is prepared to become a prophet through his own efforts to achieve wisdom, and also by his assembling, associating with and consulting some of the greatest philosophers of the ancient world.

(2) After Alexander has mastered all the sciences of the world, including the occult sciences (*'ulūm-i nahān*), he receives God's message telling him of his vocation, which is to travel throughout the world and liberate people from ignorance.

(3) During this journey, Alexander encounters and experiences many wonders, which ultimately lead him to the final step of discovering the ideal city (Utopia).[13]

(4) His spiritual quest now completed, and there being no reason for him to continue to wander around the world, Alexander is ordered by the Divine to return to Greece. However, he does not manage to return to his homeland; he dies near Babylon, in a city called Shahrazūr.

* * *

In what follows, the many motifs related to Alexander will be explored in order to highlight their influence on Niẓāmī's understanding of Alexander in the *Iqbālnāma*, and the probable sources accessible to Niẓāmī during the composition of his poem will be examined. We will also explore the development of Alexander's personality and discuss the meaning, historical background and sources of the various stories and anecdotes about divine kingship. Lastly, we will see how the *Iqbālnāma* has contributed to our knowledge of the *Alexander Romance* in world literature in general, and in Islamic literature in particular.

Alexander in Wisdom Literature

Traces of texts related to Alexander written in the Hellenistic and Byzantine periods in the genre known as 'wisdom literature' can be found in Syriac and Arabic literature.[14] Wisdom literature is encapsulated in the terms *andarz* (precept, instruction, admonition, advice, or counsel) and *pand* (counsel, advice), and denotes a popular branch of Pahlavi literature that was continued in classical Persian literature.[15] The ethical content of a great number of Persian works in this genre shows the wide dispersal of ideas common to Iranian and Greek thought.[16] These fundamental ideas, especially those based on Aristotle's *Politics*, reflect the principle that a just ruler requires an advisor to produce a virtuous society, and that the aim of all politics and all laws is 'to accomplish what is good'.[17] The genre of the mirror for princes, to which Niẓāmī's *Iskandarnāma* belongs, is an important subcategory of this literature that comprises works explicitly designed for the instruction of rulers.[18]

There are three main sources among the wisdom literature that had an important influence on the creation of Alexander's image as a wise ruler:

(1) Yuḥanna Ibn al-Bitrīq's *Sirr al-asrār*,[19] known in Europe under its Latin title, *Secretum Secretoru.*
(2) Ḥunayn Ibn Isḥāq's *Kitāb Nawādir al-falāsifa*,[20] which was translated into Spanish and introduced into Western literature as *Libro de los Buenos Proverbios*.[21]
(3) Ibn Fātiq's *Mukhtār al-Ḥikām wa Maḥāsin al-Kalim*,[22] which was also translated into Spanish as *Bocados de Oro*, known in Latin as *Liber philosophorum moralium antiquorum* and in English as *The Dicts and Sayings of the Philosophers*, originally published in 1477.[23]

Doufikar-Aerts has summarised and described the main texts of the wisdom literature in Arabic in which Alexander figures.[24] As she points out, some of the motifs in this genre later appeared in the *Alexander Romance* tradition.[25] According to Doufikar-Aerts, the great variety of Arabic texts on Alexander in the wisdom literature 'must rest on a tradition that already existed in the Byzantine collections of *apophthegmata*, drawing a clear line between Byzantine gnomic literature and Arabic Wisdom Literature'.[26] The stories found in the *Iqbālnāma* implicitly or explicitly drawn from this genre include those of Alexander's library, Alexander and the philosophers, and the seven philosophers, which will now be discussed.

The Library of Alexander

Niẓāmī begins the *Iqbālnāma* by quoting 'the head of the Greek philosophers' (*sar-i fīlsūfān-i Yūnān*),[27] who relates that when Alexander comes back to Greece, he dedicates his life to knowledge and wisdom (*dānish*), with the guidance of a tutor.[28] In order to unveil the secrets of universe, Alexander commands that the philosophers of 'the Greek, Pahlavī and Darī languages' gather and translate every book regarding wisdom (*dānish*), including 'that Persian Book of Kings' (*az ān Pārsī daftar-i Khusravān*) and 'even any Greek or Latin book' (*chi az jins-i Yūnān ... chi Rūm*).

Niẓāmī states that the fruits of Alexander's translations were three books: the *Gītī-shinās* (*Cosmography*), the *Daftar-i ramz-i ruḥānīyān* (*Book of the Secrets of Divine Beings*) and the *Sifr-i Iskandarī* (*Alexandrian Tome*).[29] In addition, he states that of all three translations only traces have survived in the work of 'Antiochus' (*Anṭīyākhus*).[30] Niẓāmī asserts that if Greece is well known for philosophy, this is thanks to Alexander's love of wisdom (*ān Shāh-i dānish-pasand*), for even 'after passing its glorious period' Greece has maintained its fame.[31]

The three works identified by Niẓāmī are probably general titles on geography/cosmography, occult science and philosophy. Regarding 'Antiochus', it is possible that the poet was referring to Antiochus of Ascalon, who had schools in Alexandria and Syria.[32] However, since there were a total of 13 Seleucid kings who bore this name, it is probable that Niẓāmī's source related to the role of Seleucids in transmitting Alexander's legacy.

Alexander and the Philosophers

Niẓāmī had extensive knowledge of Greek philosophy in Arabic translation. At the time that he started to compose the *Iskandarnāma* the Aristotelian school predominated, but this was to be superseded by Neoplatonic Sufi movements represented by Muḥyī al-Dīn ibn al-'Arabī (Shaykh al-Akbar, d. 638/1240) in the West and Shihāb al-Dīn Yaḥyā Suhrawardī ('Shaykh al-Ishrāq', d. 1191) in the Persianate world.[33] Alexander's preparation to reach the degree of philosophy detailed by Niẓāmī in the *Iqbālnāma* effectively represents the conqueror's initiation into the judicious use of prophetic power and wisdom.

In the *Iqbālnāma* Niẓāmī has the opportunity to explore different philosophical discourses through the encounters he presents between Alexander and other philosophers and sages. Niẓāmī makes use of these encounters to discuss moral issues, and Alexander, who utters wise maxims to make his points, himself becomes a fertile source of *exempla*. The poet thus provides a positive evaluation of Alexander's kingship by admiring the depth of his wisdom and the scope of his achievements.

There is an encounter between Alexander and Socrates that recalls the meeting of Diogenes and Alexander.[34] The tale was well known in the Middle Ages and was retold in various versions.[35] In some versions, which Niẓāmī probably drew upon, Socrates is indeed substituted for Diogenes. For instance, the *Disciplina Clericalis* and the *Gesta Romanorum* present an encounter between an unnamed king and Socrates, and between Alexander and Socrates respectively.[36] Niẓāmī includes a dialogue between Alexander and Socrates that contains some remarkable similarities with the classical Greek and Latin sources.[37]

Niẓāmī affirms that during the age of Alexander, the Greeks tended towards cultivating asceticism (*zuhd*).[38] They were dedicated to the philosophy of ascetical abstinence (*rīyāḍat-garī*) and ate very little. In the path of abstinence they reached such a stage of enlightenment that they vanished (because they did not have relations with women).[39] This affirmation is quite interesting, if not rather strange, because it is probable that Niẓāmī is referring to the Pythagorean ascetic tradition.[40] He may have come to know this tradition due to his interest in neo-Pythagorean philosophy[41] or through Apollonius of Tyana,[42] who appears in many episodes of the *Iskandarnāma* (both parts). Then again, there are also Greek sources that identify Alexander with views characteristic of the Cynic school,[43] though the Cynics did not abstain from sex.[44]

Niẓāmī continues the tale as follows. One morning, Alexander commands that a banquet be prepared for an assembly of sages.[45] He issues a command that Socrates be brought to the symposium (he has been invited several times, but has always refused). At last, Alexander has no alternative but to visit him in person. He finds Socrates asleep, enjoying the sunshine. At this juncture, Niẓāmī offers a dialogue between the king and the philosopher, the theme of which is to illustrate the vanity of the conqueror, who is accustomed to boasting of his generosity. The message in this episode is that the less you possess in this journey (of life), the less you will suffer.[46] Socrates reproaches Alexander for his greed, telling him: 'Although you possess this world, you would not be happy even if the entire tablecloth of the world belonged to you.'[47] He also affirms that he himself has great perseverance and high aspiration (*himmat*), while Alexander is a lowly slave of his own ambition and caprices. Socrates advises Alexander to polish his heart in order to realise 'divine secrets'.[48] This is evidently an allusion to the Sufi practice of polishing the heart through divine invocation (*dhikr*), as was elaborated by Niẓāmī in the first part of the *Sharafnāma* (as discussed in the previous chapter; see the sections 'Alexander's Mirror' and 'The Competition between the Byzantine and Chinese Painters').

The ensuing tales in the *Sharafnāma* also provide instances of how Alexander achieves this ability to realise 'divine secrets' by putting Socrates's advice to 'polish his heart' into practice. He stops drinking wine because now 'he sees that there is no permanence to the joys [of this world]'.[49] He gives so generously of his wealth to the people that poverty is eradicated throughout Greece (*Rūm*).[50] He reaches such a degree of wisdom that by the power of reason (*khirad*) he attains an intuitive understanding of the unseen realm.[51] Niẓāmī's presentation of Alexander's personality as an inspired Sufi mystic rather than a philosopher becomes more visible in the subsequent tales of the *Iqbālnāma*.

The Seven Philosophers

According to Niẓāmī, there were seven philosophers in Alexander's retinue, and he was 'the centre point of their compass'.[52] The origin and provenance of the motif of seven philosophers/sages surrounding a king is both ancient and obscure. The earliest extant mention of it seems to be traced back to the Achaemenid period, when Artaxerxes reportedly had seven counsellors.[53] There is also mention of the Seven Sages of Hellas in the Greek tradition.[54] The *Sindbādnāma* (*The Book of Syntipas, the Philosopher*) additionally played an important role in the development of the motif of seven philosophers counselling a king, and may be the source of the motif of the so-called 'Seven Sages of Rome'.[55]

In the *Iqbālnāma*, the seven philosophers in Alexander's court are named as Aristotle, Wālīs (Vettius Valens), Balīnās (Apollonius of Tyana), Socrates, Furfūrīyus (Porphyry), Hermes and Plato.[56] However, it might be said that the origin of this motif is less important than its significance for the study and understanding of Alexander's personality in the *Iqbālnāma*. It is this last issue that we are principally concerned with here, since our focus here is on understanding why Niẓāmī's conception of Alexander in his poem places him in the realm of Sufi wisdom (*ma'rifa*) and general wisdom (*khirad*) and effectively beyond the sphere of philosophy (*falsafa* in the Peripatetic sense of the word).

In this episode, a crucial characteristic that Niẓāmī establishes for Alexander is that his belief and faith are mystical, transcending rationalistic philosophical discourse. In this context, Alexander asks the seven philosophers to discuss the causes of the First Creation (*āfarīnish-i nakhust*). Each philosopher advances a different philosophical view, but

Alexander trumps them all by humbly admitting his inability to understand either the ways of Providence or the causes of creation, proclaiming:

> It's lacking in propriety to state more than this:
> 'Without a Designer, no design in creation exists.'[57]

According to Niẓāmī, Alexander had a pure enlightened heart (*rawshan-dil*),[58] and furthermore was able to see the Unseen World. Alexander's knowledge is the key to unlocking supernatural mysteries, being of a magical nature, for he is acquainted with the 'occult sciences' (*'ilm-hā-yi nahān*).[59] This characteristic is well established during his encounter with the Indian sage (*ḥakīm-e Hind*),[60] during which Alexander's superiority becomes demonstrably apparent. The episode deals with certain theological questions that the Indian sage asks Alexander on the nature of creation and the Creator, on the world after death, the soul, dreams, the evil eye, fortune telling and the reasons for different skin colours (black and white), among other subjects. Alexander answers his questions in such a way that the Indian sage 'became humbled' (*zabūn shud*) before Alexander's wisdom. In this episode, Niẓāmī aims to show that practical worldly wisdom without divine knowledge has no merit. Alexander's wisdom represents a synthesis of knowledge and faith, and this is why he is superior to the Indian sage, who represents mere sophistry and casuistry.

Alexander's encounters with the chief of the Indians (Dandamis) and the Indian Brahmans form an important episode in the *Alexander Romance* (Pseudo-Callisthenes, 3.5 ff.); they also feature in the extant accounts given by all historians on Alexander.[61] However, Niẓāmī's version of this episode is totally different from all other known historical accounts of Alexander, and from any known legends relating to the *Alexander Romance*. While in Greek sources it is always Alexander who poses a series of questions or riddles to the Indians, in Niẓāmī's *Iqbālnāma*, it is the Indian sage who asks the questions and Alexander who delivers the wise responses.

In brief, it is clear that in the first part of the *Iqbālnāma* Niẓāmī establishes Alexander's character: he is presented as an enlightened mystic and sage who has mastered the occult sciences – an adept whose wisdom transcends the sort of rationalistic discourses that are normally associated with Greek philosophy. The Alexander of the *Iqbālnāma* no longer questions the causes of creation; instead he seeks the Creator:

No longer did he talk of creation's causes
Because for him to seek the Creator sufficed.[62]

As a result, he is deemed worthy of receiving God's message (*waḥy*), and he becomes a prophet.

Alexander in the Dhū'l-Qarnayn Tradition

In the Islamic tradition, Alexander is identified with the prophet Dhū'l-Qarnayn mentioned in the Qur'ān (*Sūrah* 18:82). This identification created an important branch of Alexander literature in Arabic, and consequently in Persian, which Doufikar-Aerts appropriately calls 'the Dhū'l-Qarnayn tradition'.[63] This genre, in contrast to other branches of Alexander literature, which are mainly based on Byzantine and Greek works (such as Alexander wisdom literature and the *Alexander Romance* tradition), represents a separate and independent development within the framework of Arabic literature itself.[64] The main motif of the Dhū'l-Qarnayn tradition, which can also be partially traced back to the *Alexander Romance* tradition, is the wall built by the conqueror against Gog and Magog (mentioned in the Qur'ān, *Sūrah* 18:92–8).

More important than the identification of Dhū'l-Qarnayn himself, or the reliability of traditions ascribed to him, is the fact that in the Islamic world, Alexander was identified as the prophet Dhū'l-Qarnayn in both historical and Romance traditions from the ninth century AD onwards. According to Doufikar-Aerts, the Dhū'l-Qarnayn tradition reflects a development that can be traced back to previous Middle Eastern Alexander traditions (such as the Syriac Christian legend), alongside sub-recension γ of the Pseudo-Callisthenes and the oldest Arabic commentaries on the Qur'ān (for example, 18:82–98).[65]

The first episode of the *Iqbālnāma* deals with the question of why Alexander was identified as Dhū'l-Qarnayn (Bicorn). Niẓāmī gives seven possible reasons, which take into account various connotations of the term *qarn*:

(1) Alexander is Dhū'l-Qarnayn because he reached both extremes (*qarn*) of the world: the East and the West.[66]

(2) Alexander is Dhū'l-Qarnayn because he could fight with both hands (*qarn* as arm/hand).

(3) Alexander is Dhū'l-Qarnayn because he fastened his hair (*qarn* as hair) into braids on both sides of his head.[67]

(4) Alexander is Dhū'l-Qarnayn because he dreamt that he held the two poles of the sun (*qarn* as pole).

(5) Alexander is Dhū'l-Qarnayn because his life spanned two different centuries (*qarn* as century).

(6) According to Abū Ma'shar (Albumasar) in his book *al-Ulūf* (*Book of Thousands*)[68] when Alexander died, due to the great love the Greeks felt for him, they drew or painted a portrait of him with two angels bearing horns on either side of his head. When the Arabs saw this painting they incorrectly thought that these angels were Alexander himself, and thus came to call him 'the Two-Horned One' (*ṣāḥib daw qarn*).[69]

(7) Alexander was called 'the Two-Horned One' because his ears were overlarge;[70] this was told to Niẓāmī by 'a wise man' (*khudāvand-i hūsh*).

In the verses in the first episode of the *Iqbālnāma* that discuss the epithet Dhū'l-Qarnayn given to Alexander, Niẓāmī offers a thorough summary of the long tradition of dispute over its meaning.[71] Different writers have given similar summaries and explanations. For instance, Bīrūnī (d. after 1050) dedicates a whole chapter of his *Kitāb al-Āthār al-bāqī'a 'an al-qurūn al-khālī'a* (*Book of Vestiges from Past Centuries*) to discussing 'the different opinions of various nations regarding the king called Dhū'l-Qarnayn'.[72] Although Bīrūnī does not endorse the theory that Alexander should be identified with the prophet Dhū'l-Qarnayn, it is worth noting that most of the themes relating to Alexander as a historical personage in Niẓāmī's *Iskandarnāma* can also be found in this chapter of Bīrūnī's work. The account given in Bal'amī's *History* furthermore coincides with that of Niẓāmī regarding the different connotations of the epithet Dhū'l-Qarnayn; it also enumerates a number of historical persons who might be identified with him.[73]

It is interesting that the seventh interpretation above, that of Alexander's ears being 'overlarge', soon developed into a legend in which

Alexander was said to have had ears as long as a donkey's. The Persian poet Sanā'ī (d. *c.*1130) commented on this motif in his epic poem *The Enclosed Garden of Truth* (*Ḥadīqat al-ḥaqīqa*).[74] Thus, two of the greatest Persian poets, Niẓāmī and Sanā'ī, affirmed that Alexander used to hide his overlong ears under his crown. According to the legend, the only person who knew Alexander's secret was his barber. One day, the barber went to a well and confided the secret of the conqueror's donkey-like ears to it. When reeds grew out of that well, a shepherd cut one of them to make it into a flute. The reeds, which had picked up the barber's words, exposed the secret: 'King Alexander has donkey's ears.' This legend is obviously based on the variant of the myth of King Midas, who was said to possess a donkey's ears.[75] During the transmigration of this legend into Persian poetry, Midas's long ears replaced Alexander's 'horns'. Taking into account Niẓāmī's words '*juz īn guft bā man*' ('I was told in another manner'), we can deduce that his source was an oral one.[76]

The Prophet Alexander

Niẓāmī informs us that once Alexander has mastered all the sciences, he realises that what he was seeking is not there. The above-cited verse merits repetition here:

> No longer did he talk of creation's causes
> Because for him to seek the Creator sufficed.[77]

Niẓāmī emphasises the transcendental scope of Alexander's knowledge, which enables him to penetrate into the realm of the Unseen and apprehend what is beyond the ken of ordinary mortals:

> In seeing the sights that are visible to the eye
> His aim was but to find what was 'impossible'.[78]

Finally, his attempt to reveal 'secrets' bears fruit. Alexander receives a summons from God informing him of his vocation, which henceforth is to travel around the world, calling people to the true religion and releasing them from tyranny and ignorance.[79]

When Alexander asks the angel (*surūsh*) who has brought him this news for some miracle that might serve as proof of his prophethood for those who may be sceptical of his mission, the angel answers that his miracle will be his wisdom, and that he will be able to speak and understand every language of the world:[80]

> You will be aided, given guidance so by inspiration
> You'll have foreknowledge of all dialects of men.
> In every land for every tongue you'll be a dragoman,
> No lingo, no parole there'll be that you don't know.
> Likewise, whenever you talk to men in Greek
> They will decipher all you say without an interpreter.[81]

Niẓāmī then tells us how the three greatest philosophers of classical antiquity, namely Aristotle, Plato and Socrates, each writes a Book of Wisdom (*khiradnāma*) for Alexander. The contents of their tomes deal with the main themes of Islamic statecraft, natural philosophy and moral philosophy, and also feature typical advice on subjects drawn from the mirror for princes genre (such as justice, fear of God, sending wise ambassadors, how to keep the army satisfied, eating little and modesty).[82]

In order to fulfil his mission as a prophet and invite people to the true path, Alexander leaves the throne to his son, Iskandarūs.[83] He abandons Macedonia and passes through Alexandria.[84] He reaches Jerusalem, and the people there ask Alexander to release them from the tyranny of their king, who is 'an enemy to the friends of God'. Alexander accedes to their wishes, kills the tyrant and hangs him on the gate of Jerusalem.[85] After liberating the people of Jerusalem, he continues his journey towards the West (*maghrib*), and reaches Europe (*afranja*) and Spain (*al-Andalus*).[86]

At this point, the *Iqbālnāma* details a number of Alexander's adventures that belong properly to the *'ajāyib* (*mirabilia*) genre. Niẓāmī narrates many of the marvellous adventures and wonders of the world that Alexander encounters during his travels as a prophet. The poet's recourse to the *mirabilia* genre here functions as a didactic device. The protagonist of the poem can only acquire knowledge, both of himself and of the supernatural divine realm, through strange encounters and marvellous experiences that transcend rational understanding. Such incredible experiences not only serve to further his quest for divine kingship, but ultimately enable him, in his role as prophet and spiritual guide of the people, to interpret the laws of the cosmos and uncover higher laws sustaining both the natural and supernatural realms.

As stated in the *Cosmography* of Aḥmad Ṭūsī (possibly written between 1160 and 1177),[87] man should exert himself to study and contemplate God's wondrous and wisely conceived creation, in order to reflect upon it in wonder and astonishment and to understand as much as is possible. In this way, man will gain the delights of both this world and the hereafter.[88]

Mirabilia: Alexander and the Marvels of the World

The last part of the *Iqbālnāma* contains tales from the *'Ajāyib* (*mirabilia*) genre, which was influenced in great part by Greek sources of the great Hellenic scientists and philosophers,[89] and also by the Qur'ān, which points out the marvels of creation as proof of God's power. Representative works of this genre in Persian and Arabic are mainly known under titles such as *'Ajāyib al-makhlūqāt wa-gharāyib al-mawjūdāt* (*Prodigies of Things Created and Miraculous Aspects of Things Existing*) or *Cosmography*,[90] or *'Ajāyib al-Buldān* (*Wonders of the Lands*).[91] At the time that Niẓāmī was composing the *Iqbālnāma*, this genre had reached its peak in the Persian tradition at the hand of Aḥmad Ṭūsī in the twelfth century AD. The sources of Ṭūsī's *Cosmography*[92] may also have been used by Niẓāmī, since it contains various wondrous tales about Alexander that also appear in the *Iqbālnāma*.

The marvels are found in two parts of the Greek *Alexander Romance*. Firstly, in the *Epistola Alexandri Magni ad Aristotelem de mirabilibus Indiae* (*Alexander's Letter to Aristotle about the Wonders of India*), which describes many monstrous beasts and strange races of men.[93] The Greek original of this text is lost, although it is preserved in abridged or truncated forms in all the Greek versions of the *Romance*.[94] Secondly, in the letter to Olympias (II, 23–40), which contains other marvellous adventures that took place mainly in Jerusalem and Egypt (sub-recension γ), while repeating adventures that take place in Book II, 8.[95]

The Lighthouse of Alexandria

The first marvel that Alexander encounters in the *Iqbālnāma* is the Lighthouse of Alexandria, from which the Alexandrian people can see an approaching enemy fleet a month before it arrives. This lighthouse thus effectively enables them to protect the city against any seaborne enemy.[96] Niẓāmī attributes its construction to Alexander, who places his 'mirror' on the Pharos.[97] Curiously, Abū Ṭāhir Ṭarsūsī relates a similar story in the *Dārābnāma* about a tower with a mirror that offers a view all the way to Constantinople. According to Ṭarsūsī, Ptolemy first tried to build this tower, but failed. Then Plato resumed its construction, which is described quite extensively by Ṭarsūsī.[98] Aside from being one of several quasi-supernatural 'marvels' attributed to Alexander, the building of the lighthouse also demonstrates his military abilities, showing the conqueror as 'a clever inventor of defensive stratagems which give him both knowledge and control of the world at large'.[99]

The construction of the lighthouse of Alexandria also appears in the *'Ajāyib al-makhlūqāt* of Aḥmad Ṭūsī, but he distinguishes between 'Alexander, son of Philip' – to whom he attributes its construction – and 'Alexander Dhū'l-Qarnayn.'[100]

Marine Monsters and Deadly Deserts

Most of the other marvels related by Niẓāmī about Alexander deal with the wonders he experiences while crossing oceans and deserts. We are told that he navigates seas for three months and visits many inhabited islands. He comes across a desert that is composed entirely of sulphur, and crosses this desert for a month until he reaches an enormous sea, which 'the Greeks call *Uqyānūs* [ocean]'.[101] There is no sunset on this ocean. Being eager to unveil the secret of this ocean and to explore what lies beyond it, Alexander approaches it, only to find that its water is so dense that it does not evaporate and form cloud. It is also impossible to navigate the waters of this ocean. Experts warn Alexander that in this 'silver' water is a fearsome sea monster – a whale as terrible as a dragon, whose name is 'the Killer' (*Qaṣṣāṣa*).

He is also warned, however, that worse than this monstrous whale are the dangers of the shore of an island on the far side of the ocean. This is a shining shore on which lie colourful stones. However, if any man gazes on these stones, he immediately starts to laugh and cannot stop, until he laughs himself to death. For this reason it is called the 'deadly shore' (*pahna-yi jānguzāy*).[102] To protect himself from the dangers presented by this deadly shore, Alexander uses a ruse. He orders blindfolded men mounted on drunken camels to go to the island and bring back some of its stones and its yellow soil. The stones are covered in canvas so they cannot hurt anyone's eyesight. Then he orders that a castle be built with them, covered with mud made from the yellow soil. As the years pass, the canvas wears away and the stones come to light. Everyone who enters the castle dies, for the stones capture life like a magnet attracts metal.[103]

A very similar story is told in the Pseudo-Aristotelian *De lapidibus*, a sober geological treatise. This describes a stone called Elbehecte, which is yellow in colour, and makes anyone who looks at it completely witless and unable to stop gazing at it.[104] In the Persian literary tradition, this story is known as *Shāristān-i rū'īn* (the City of Brass) and in Arabic as *Madīnat al-ṣifr.*[105] At the end of this tale, Niẓāmī adds: 'he heard that a ruler wanted to verify the existence of this city'. According to the author of the anonymous *Mujmal al-tavārīkh*, that 'king' was the caliph 'Abd al-Malik Ibn Marwān (d. 705), who, after finding a book in which this tale appeared, sent his troops to find the city.[106]

When Alexander completes the construction of his deadly castle, he marches through deserts for a period of six months until he reaches the spring of the River Nile. He follows the flow of the river until he reaches a green musky mountain. The Nile cascades down from this mountain like a waterfall, but the mountain itself is unscalable and covered in thorns. Even if any climbers do manage to scale the mountain's peak, they invariably go to the other side of the mountain, where they disappear and never return. In order to solve the mystery of the mountain, Alexander sends out various men as scouts to its top, but none of them return. Eventually, he sends a father and son who are writers. The son follows his father, lagging a few steps behind him. When the man reaches the peak, he writes down everything he sees on the far side of the mountain and sends his son back with his report. However, the father himself does not return. The son gives Alexander the report, which reveals that what lies on the other side of the mountain is Paradise. Alexander refrains from divulging the content of the report, fearing that, if his followers heard about it, they would all go to this Paradise and never return.

In addition to the above legendary episode, Alexander's search for the source of the Nile is based on historical sources.[107] The legend that the source of the Nile was in Paradise has its origin in a *ḥadīth* attributed to the Prophet Muḥammad (and explained in the anonymous *Mujmal al-tavārīkh*), which relates the tale of a man in search of the source of the Nile.[108] The story of Alexander's visit to Paradise was first told in the Talmud, then in Arabic sources (Wahb Ibn Munabih), and was finally presented in a twelfth-century Western version in Latin as *Alexander the Great's Journey to Paradise*.[109]

Niẓāmī continues the poem with another Paradise-like place. Alexander leaves the source of the River Nile, and traverses a desert until he reaches the Iram Garden.[110] In this marvellous garden, he finds the tomb of Shaddād (the son of 'Ād), on which there is an inscription carved in rubies warning the reader to beware of human mortality and death. This story seems to echo the episode of Alexander's encounter with the dead King Cyrus in the City of the Sun (related in Pseudo-Callisthenes, III, 28) and his concern about death. The content of the inscription in the *Iqbālnāma* also bears a great resemblance with that found on Cyrus's tomb.[111] This episode highlights the vanity of worldly goods and power. As Stoneman points out, 'Alexander is the epitome of the man who has everything, yet it profiteth him nothing for he is doomed to die.'[112]

Niẓāmī next says that Alexander begins his journey through another desert, in which he encounters desert men who live in caves, and whose skin is blacker than tar. Their food is crocodile meat and they can survive without water. Alexander teaches them his customs and wisdom, and they guide him out of the poisonous desert towards a more prosperous land. Emerging from the desert, Alexander and his followers come to another sea. They build a ship for themselves and set sail. After a month's voyage, they reach a land where they rest for a month.

The Village of the Skull Worshippers (sar-parastān)

Next, Alexander marches south from the East, until he reaches a prosperous village that is 'green as Paradise'. However, its inhabitants worship skulls and all look insane. They have no king, and everyone has a vat full of sesame oil. When they come across lost travellers, they kill them and put them in their vats. After 30 to 40 days, they cut off the dead person's head and ask the skull to foretell the future, which it does, through a prophetic voice that issues from it.[113] When Alexander sees the evil of this practice, he realises that it is the work of demons (*dīv*). He orders that the vats be smashed and he removes the sesame oil from their houses. Then he teaches them the correct way to worship God.

A similar tale is described in the *Fihrist* (ch. IX) of Ibn Nadīm, who reports it as '*Hikāyat al-ra's*' ('the Skull's Tale'). Ibn Nadīm attributes this custom to the *Ṣābi'ūn* (Sabians), a name applied in Arabic texts to the pagans of ancient Greece and other polytheists.[114] Ibn Nadīm explains:

> The skull was that of a man whose appearance was that of Mercury, corresponding to what they believe regarding the appearance of stars. When they found a man whose appearance corresponded to that of Mercury, they captured him ... and placed him in oil for a long time until his joints softened ... They did this each year when Mercury was in ascension. Those people believed that the soul moved between Mercury and the skull, and thus could foretell the future and would respond to whatever one asked of it.[115]

Ibn Nadīm quotes a book called the *Kitāb al-ḥātifī*,[116] in which these people and their customs regarding the use of skulls are mentioned. This tale is also mentioned in the Hermetic *Ghāyat al-ḥakīm* (*Goal of the Sage*) attributed to Majrīṭī,[117] known in medieval Europe under its Latin title, *Picatrix*.[118] 'Talking heads' were also used in Greek and Roman necromancy.[119] However, Niẓāmī's reference to the *sar-parastān* and the notion of prophetic skulls might hark back to a Jewish tale, because the Teraphim consulted by the ancient Hebrews seem also to be dead heads.[120]

Valley of the Diamonds

The *Iqbālnāma* presents Alexander as the first person to discover a diamond. In his *Mineralogy*,[121] Bīrūnī called the diamond 'the eagle-stone', highlighting that it was discovered by Dhū'l-Qarnayn (whom he does not identify as Alexander) in the Valley of Diamonds. As is well known, all such tales of the discovery of diamonds have their origins in *Alexander's Letter to Aristotle about India*.[122] Niẓāmī relates that Alexander and his army reach a mountain, which circumstances oblige them to cross. When the hooves of their animals are damaged by the hard stones, Alexander commands that they be wrapped in leather and felt. When his guides bring some of the mountain's stones to Alexander, he tries to strike them with his sword and its blade shatters into small pieces. None can break the stone except with lead, which in fact does not break it but only scratches it. Alexander names this stone *almās* (diamond).[123]

When Alexander's men are urged to push on and scale the mountain, they are informed that this stone is the most precious of all minerals. Descending the mountain, they reach a valley full of diamonds and snakes. As Alexander meditates on a workable solution that might enable them to cross the valley, he notices black eagles with game in their beaks soaring in the air. He commands that some sheep be slain and their carcasses cut into small pieces. His men cast the mutton into the valley that is coated with diamonds, so that the diamonds stick to the meat like salt. At this point, the eagles descend into the valley and carry the meat up to the summit of the mountain. The eagles devour the meat, leaving behind the diamonds, which Alexander's men collect. In this manner, they manage to gather the diamonds without risking being bitten by the snakes.

Niẓāmī's account has certain resonances with the Greek *Alexander Romance* (II, 22), where we read that when Alexander and his army enter the Land of Darkness they pass through a valley where they pick up stones. Emerging from the darkness, they realise that they have picked up jewels. However, the story of the Valley of Diamonds in the *Iqbālnāma* is more likely to be based on a version of the tale known from the work of the Bishop Epiphanius of Salamis's *De gemmis* (*On Gems*), written in the fourth century AD.[124] The story is also retold by Qazwīnī in his *'Ajāyib al-makhlūqāt* (*The Wonders of Creation*),[125] and it eventually found its way into the *Thousand and One Nights*, where it is mentioned in the second voyage of Sindbād the Sailor.[126]

After riding for a month, Alexander and his army reach a prosperous land in which they encounter a handsome young man working on a farm with a spade. Attracted by the nobility of his character and his simplicity, Alexander offers to redeem him from manual labour by elevating him to become the ruler of an entire kingdom.[127] The young farmer rejects the conqueror's proposal:

> He said, 'O you to whom all fame and fortune are subject
> And by whom all unmanageable men are managed!
> Let each one take up that task and work which best
> Suits his nature, which requires of him no forethought.
> If this gross flesh, adept at hard labour, were treated gently
> It would be like using gummy frankincense for honey.'[128]

The young farmer is obviously not an average manual labourer, for it transpires that he had foreknowledge of Alexander's arrival, after having dreamt of him. Alexander rests here for a night before continuing on his journey. He and his army then reach a green land, which is devoid of crops due to storms and floods that have afflicted the farmers. Alexander commands that a dam be constructed to irrigate the land, which he calls

Iskandarābād, and declares its inhabitants free from payment of tribute and taxes.[129]

Alexander's Return to India

Upon his return to India, Niẓāmī states that Alexander passes through a city that the Turks call *Kang-Bihisht*.[130] In this city is a temple called Qandahār, and in the temple is a huge golden idol as tall as the ceiling, its eyes two precious stones shining like lamps. Alexander orders that the idol be destroyed, but the inhabitants of the city beg him not to destroy it because of the ancient story behind the sculpture, which one of them relates as follows:

> Before the temple's construction in its present form, there had been a damaged dome there. One day, two birds came to that dome with two precious stones in their beak[s]. They dropped the stones and left. In order to avoid the townsfolk battling over those stones, the people built the golden idol and used the stones for its eyes.

Taking heed of the idol's marvellous origins, Alexander decides not to destroy it and instead commands that an inscription be set at the top of it: 'This is game hunted but let loose by Alexander.'[131] The same story is told in the *Tārīkh-i Bukhārā* (*The Chronicle of Bukhārā*), which locates it in Bukhārā but makes no mention of Alexander.[132]

The Wonders of the Black Sea[133]

Niẓāmī then relates how Alexander is eager to set sail to behold the wonders of the seas, and embark on maritime adventures. He continues his journey until he reaches China. The Chinese Emperor (*khāqān-i Chīn*) receives him at his court, and the poet tells us that he accepts Alexander's religion.

Alexander asks the Chinese Emperor to accompany him on his sea voyage, and he agrees. Alexander chooses 10,000 men from his army, providing them with sufficient rations for the voyage, and they sail for 40 days until they reach the Black Sea (*āb-i kabūd*). They are informed that there is a land where mermaids (*'arūsān-i ābī*) gather on the shore every night,[134] and sing and play music all night. However, at 'the scent of the dawn', they plunge back into the sea. Everyone who hears the mermaids' songs is struck unconscious. In order to verify the truth of this tale, Alexander goes to the shore alone at night and sees the mermaids coming out of the sea. Their long, dishevelled hair, which they let down freely, covers their bodies entirely.[135] When he hears their song, Alexander starts to cry and laugh simultaneously. Having confirmed the veracity of the story and experienced for himself the strange thrills evoked by the mermaids' nocturnal concert, he returns to his army.

In the Greek *Alexander Romance*, the *Letter to Aristotle* (22) features a similar encounter. This letter relates how women with long hair that covers their whole body emerge from a river and drag men from Alexander's army into the water. Niẓāmī's account of the legend seems to be based on recensions of this text (sub-recension ε 33, 3 and sub-recension γ II, 41 only) in which sirens emerge from a lake and dance around it during the night.[136]

Talismanic Statues

The *Alexander Romance* tradition presents several examples of statues located in remote areas of the world, or erected by Alexander at a turning point in his career.[137] This motif seems to symbolise and indicate the conqueror's physical approach to the borders of the inhabited world. Such statues normally bear inscriptions or talismans that serve to draw attention to the existence of imminent danger if a traveller tries to continue towards the land or the sea beyond them. Indeed, one of the characteristics of Alexander as the prophet Dhū'l-Qarnayn is his reaching and surveying the farthest bounds of the earth.

The *Iqbālnāma* includes two episodes in which Alexander builds such statues. In the first, following his encounter with the mermaids, Alexander orders the captain of his vessels to set sail because he has foreknowledge that God wishes him to undertake a maritime mission. At the same time, knowing the dangers of the voyage, he orders the Chinese Emperor to stay on the shore and wait for him. Among the philosophers in his retinue, Alexander chooses only the wise magician Balīnās/Apollonius of Tyana to accompany him on his voyage. They sail towards the deepest part of the ocean, where there is nothing but a vast expanse of salty water. The strong current almost carries them away, so they have no choice but to return. The sailors, being scared, consult their maps, which show that they have reached the very ends of the earth. Suddenly, an island appears as shining like a light. Afraid of the strong currents, they rest on the island, where Alexander orders Balīnās to sculpt a talismanic statue of copper with an extended arm pointing to the dangerous area of the ocean. The statue warned all ships that it was not safe to sail beyond that island.[138] As they return from the ends of the earth, Alexander realises that it was divine Providence that bore him to that dangerous spot in order to place a talismanic statue there and thus save future sailors' lives.

Alexander continues his journey for a period of ten days through a desert until he reaches a city as white as camphor, which has mines of gold and silver. However, the city has only a few inhabitants, and when Alexander asks why, he is informed that every dawn, such a horrible, frightening noise is emitted from the sea that everyone who hears it flees the city. To counteract this noise, Alexander orders the construction of a loud drum, which is to be struck vigorously every dawn until the sun rises, so the inhabitants will hear this and not the terrible noise from the sea.

There are two possible scientific reasons for the clamour from the depths of the ocean, Alexander claims. The first is that at dawn, the sunlight so heats the water that it turns the waves into domes. Thus, as the waves rise and fall, the crests of these dome-like waves smash against each other like mountains, making a horrible sound. His second explanation is that the water may contain mercury (*sīmāb*). Consequently, he speculates, when the water is heated by sunlight at dawn, the mercury floats to the surface. When the water cools, the mercury sinks and makes the terrible sound.[139] In this fashion, Alexander establishes the royal tradition of kings sounding the watches of day with drums in their courts.[140]

In his *Cosmography* Aḥmad Ṭūsī quotes a book called *Tārīkh-i Rūm* (*History of Byzantium*) as the source of this tale. However, according to this version, the horrible sound is produced by strong winds blowing through some tall trees that stand on the shore. He adds that in these trees lives a kind of bird that has a human body and is decked out in exquisite colours.[141]

Alexander's Construction of the Wall of Gog

The episode of the construction of the wall against Gog in the *Iqbālnāma* is very brief. The probable reason for this is that Niẓāmī, as he himself affirms at the beginning of the *Sharafnāma*, does not want to repeat what Firdawsī has already put into verse. In the *Iqbālnāma* the episode takes place after Alexander leaves China and starts heading towards Kharkhīz.[142] Niẓāmī describes how Alexander's army 'marched for a month through a desert whose soil was silver (*sīm*) and whose water contained mercury (*sīmāb*)',[143] such that many men in his army died of thirst.[144]

Finally, they reach a land whose inhabitants, being 'Muslims without a prophet',[145] gladly accepted Alexander as their prophet.[146] Understanding him to be a king adept and skilful in providing solutions for various challenging circumstances, they reveal their problems to him in the hope of finding relief and remedy. They tell him that behind a mountain pass in a stony place nearby is a plain as wide as the sea, which is inhabited by a tribe known as the *Yā'jūj* (Gog).

Although the Gog are descendants of Adam, they have the appearance of demons. The poet describes them as having lions with hearts of iron and claws as sharp as diamonds; they look as wretched as evil wolves. Their hair stretches from head to toe and is draped over their entire bodies, making it impossible even to see their faces. They are semi-vegetarians who usually eat only plants (*rastanī*); in particular, they eat a plant as hot as pepper (*pilpil*) that is found in that land. However, lest his verse lack marvels, Niẓāmī describes how they also eat a dragon that falls out of the sky in springtime, which gives them their lusty vigour and strength. The Gog folk apparently never fall ill until they are close to death. They also possess miraculous powers of reproduction, with each of them spawning no less than 1,000 children! Niẓāmī reports that they also eat the corpses of their dead kinsmen. To protect other human beings against this demonic race of men, Alexander builds a wall of steel around them that will hold them in until the Day of Judgement.

The origin and many of the details of the tale of the Gog folk can be traced back to two Syriac works: the first is known as the 'Christian Legend concerning Alexander the Great', and the second simply as the 'Syriac Poem'.[147] As the tale of the enclosure of Gog and Magog by Dhū'l-Qarnayn appears in the Qur'ān (*Sūrah* 18 (*Kahf*): 92–100), the story is one of the key characteristics of *Alexander Romance* literature in the Arabic tradition.

Alexander in Utopia

After building the wall against Gog, Alexander reaches a city that 'many people seek, but few find'.[148] The city has no gate, and is full of decorated shops without doors or locks. Its inhabitants welcome Alexander and take him to a castle to entertain him and serve him food.

Alexander asks them how they are not afraid to leave their shops and houses open, and why they leave their possessions unprotected and unguarded. They respond:

The truth of the matter is this: we're just one group
Inhabiting these hills and plains and dales. Although
A puny, weak and frail folk, yet still we don't
Swerve one hair's breadth from what is meet and right.
We'll never bend ourselves to follow crooked ways,
Nor have we knowledge of aught but what is fair and good.
We don't pursue the tortuous, errant ways of the world;
Our foliage grows up by such right graces in this world.
We'll never tell a single lie – black or white – and thus
We never have nightmares that haunt our dreams.
We never ask about something unless it serves our good;
We have no care for anything except that it please God.[149]

Alexander has never encountered such a righteous and honest group of people, and is so impressed that he decides not to continue his journey, declaring that all he had ever wanted to learn through travel, he has now learnt from these people, and that the reason for all his voyages throughout the world, and his traversing across deserts and seas, has been simply to meet these people and learn their customs. The poet puts the following words into the mouth of the world conqueror:

I wish no more to travel throughout the world,
Nor place snares in the way to catch my prey.
What lore and *savoir-faire* I've learned from these men
Suffices me for labour and collaboration.
How fine it is that before the Lord of Judgement Day
The world remains in place through these good men!
The mission I set out upon – to cross desert and plain
Had but this one end: that I should meet such men.[150]

The unworldly justice, righteousness and harmonious cooperation of this people depicted by Niẓāmī is truly remarkable. Several similar tales of a 'City of the Blessed' can be found in medieval Islamic and ancient Greek sources.[151] Much the same story of a just and harmonious city, for instance, is told by Rashīd al-Dīn Maybudī (d. 1126) in his Sufi commentary on the Qur'ān, *Kashf al-asrār wa 'uddat al-abrār* (*The Unveiling of Mysteries and Provision of the Righteous*), in the section pertaining to the prophet Dhū'l-Qarnayn.[152] The tale also recalls Alexander's encounter and colloquy with the Brahmans or naked philosophers of India,[153] versions of which are recounted in Greek historical works (such as Strabo 15.1.61 and Plutarch, *Alex.* 64–5).[154] Considering the fact that Niẓāmī locates this utopian city in 'the north', its residents also resemble the legendary Hyperboreans, the people who lived beyond the North Wind, according to Herodotus (*Histories*, IV, 32–6).[155]

The Last Days of Alexander

The final episode of the *Iqbālnāma* deals with the last days of Alexander's life and the circumstances surrounding his death. Niẓāmī's account does not include many of the typical motifs concerning Alexander's death that are found in the *Shāhnāma* (such as the birth of a part-dead, part-living creature that is half-human and half-animal, and the philosophers' lamentations over Alexander's tomb). However, it does include Alexander's final testament and his letter of consolation written to his mother. Instead of the philosophers' lamentations, Niẓāmī adds a stroke of genius with an entirely new episode that describes the final moments of the lives of the seven philosophers in his retinue.

Niẓāmī recounts Alexander's last days as follows. Hearing an angel ordering him to stop his journeys and return to Greece (*Yūnān*),[156] Alexander turns back from 'the farthest edges of the globe'. He finally reaches Kirmānshahān, and then enters Babylonia. When he reaches Shahrazūr, he falls ill.[157] Thinking himself poisoned, he falls into a delusion and experiences hallucinations that make his body burn. He sends a messenger to Greece to summon Aristotle to his court. Aristotle reaches Shahrazūr in the company of several wise men of Greece and Rūm. He feels Alexander's wrist for a pulse and orders doctors to make an appropriate medicine. However, Alexander's body burns, says the poet, because his corporeal being is like a piece of gold placed in an alembic to be purified and cleansed from the dross of this lower world.

The doctors in his entourage can find no remedy to cure Alexander, while the astrologers find that his star has waned. Since Alexander possesses the miraculous mirror mentioned in the last chapter, however, and is thus quite aware of his own fate and state,[158] he gathers all his friends about him and informs them of his coming death. He has wandered throughout every corner of the world yet still his curiosity is not quenched, Niẓāmī moralises:

This world, I've seen it all – far and wide, and high and low
And yet my eyes still hanker after more sights of this earth.
Not thirty-six years, not thirty thousand years suffice
My greed for lands and spaces, my thirst for sights.[159]

Alexander knows that there is no cure for death. Neither Apollonius with his sorcery[160] nor any of his other philosophers can save him.[161] At this juncture, Alexander orders a copyist to transcribe a letter to his mother in order to console her. He reminds her: 'If there is anyone who remains alive forever in this world, then you can continue in your mourning for me.'[162] He also suggests that she prepare a feast and invite 'only people who had never lost any loved one to dine. If anyone does attend her feast, only then should she be permitted to mourn his death'.[163]

The earliest appearance of the letter of consolation in Greek versions of the *Alexander Romance* is in the eighth-century manuscript *L*.[164] Stoneman suggests that it is possible that this motif entered the Greek tradition from Arabic sources, and not the other way around.[165] He also draws attention to the possibility that the detail about inviting to dinner those who have never known sorrow might originate in a Buddhist story. In this story, the Buddha tells a woman that he will restore her son to life if she will bring him a mustard seed from the house of one who has never known sorrow.[166]

It is probable that Niẓāmī has Alexander make use of a number of commonplace wise adages about death found in Stoic philosophy,[167] which were inculcated by philosopher-kings such as Marcus Aurelius.[168] In two couplets, Niẓāmī finally delivers his moral to summarise the conqueror's death:

When Alexander removed his chattels from this house,
Above and beyond this earthly tent his throne was raised.
None matched his righteousness and virtue in this world:
The world nettled him, yet still its harshness he endured.[169]

When Alexander is dead, his men put him in a golden coffin, deliberately leaving one arm hanging over its side. This is because in his last testament, Niẓāmī relates, Alexander decreed that one of his hands should be displayed empty and open outside his tomb in order to show that although he was the king of seven climes and possessed so many treasures, he left the world empty-handed.[170]

Niẓāmī then informs us that Alexander's body was carried from Shahrazūr to Alexandria in Egypt.[171] The poet also affirms that Alexander was not succeeded by one king, but by numerous princelings ruling divided kingdoms (*mulūk al-ṭawā'if*), because Iskandarūs refused his father's throne.[172]

Finally, Niẓāmī concludes the *Iqbālnāma* with a number of anecdotes on the deaths of the seven philosophers in Alexander's entourage. He also informs the reader that he himself is 63 years (and six months) of age when he finishes the poem. Apparently, Niẓāmī did not live long after the *Book of Fortune* reached completion.[173]

Conclusion

As we have seen in this chapter, a vast field of myth, legend and history relating to the themes of Alexandrian wisdom literature, wonders of the world and prophetology is covered in Niẓāmī's account of the world conqueror in his *Iskandarnāma.*

Firstly, in order to expand his investigation into the mythology of the Dhū'l-Qarnayn traditions relating to Alexander, Niẓāmī draws attention to other genres such as wisdom literature and *mirabilia*, and makes them part of his own original mythopoetic vision of Alexander as a prophet. What links these various genres for the poet is their mutual use of similar ethical messages and morals embedded in political theories designed to produce an image of the 'Perfect Man', the 'Perfect Monarch', the 'Wise Prince', and so on.

Secondly, the various tales of the *Iqbālnāma*'s narrative act as vehicles to broach and expatiate on the topos of the Perso-Islamic concept of the king as the 'Shadow of God on Earth'. In this respect, the *Iqbālnāma* can be considered as a complex allegory containing various meanings and messages. In one sense, it can be read politically as a manual of moral advice; that is, simply as a mirror for princes. In another, it can be interpreted mystically as a poetic exegesis of the Sufi Path towards the ultimate goal of the acquisition of gnosis (*ma'rifat*) and divine knowledge (*khirad*). The mystical–political advice contained in the *Iqbālnāma* thus establishes the communication of ideals on medieval statecraft through the esoteric and mystical writings of the Sufis. This is indeed the main contribution of Niẓāmī's *Iqbālnāma* to the development of the *Alexander Romance* in the Persian tradition. The *Khiradnāma-yi Iskandarī* (*The Book of Alexandrian Wisdom*) of the great Sufi poet Jāmī (1414–92) is the best representative of Niẓāmī's legacy in this regard.

In both parts of his *Iskandarnāma* (the *Sharafnāma* and the *Iqbālnāma*) Niẓāmī combines these two senses, merging spiritual and political counsel to create, in the figure of his ideal hero Alexander, a true vicegerent of God on earth, similar to a prophet who combines all the attributes of the Perfect Man. The tales and anecdotes in the *Iqbālnāma* indicate that achieving this degree of perfection requires that the ruler subdue his ego (*nafs*) by acquiring wisdom (*khirad*) and purifying his soul, just as Socrates advises Alexander to do. According to the political and spiritual wisdom that the figure of Alexander represents in Niẓāmī's poem, the true vicegerent of God is the ruler who combines political *savoir faire* and justice with the mystical qualities of a prophet (with knowledge of the Unseen World). Alexander thus serves as both a symbol of ideal kingship and an exemplar of the mystical philosopher and prophet who, being divinely guided, is a true vicegerent of God on earth.[174]

As we have seen, Alexander's goal throughout his adventures in the *Sharafnāma* is largely intellectual and psychological: the acquisition of self-knowledge. In the *Iqbālnāma*, however, his quest has entirely spiritual ends: the attainment of wisdom or divine knowledge. Alexander's development as a prophetic hero, and his quest for divine kingship, could not have been completed and actualised in the *Iqbālnāma* without his acquisition of knowledge of God. Indeed, Alexander's various encounters with monsters, strange creatures, talismanic statues, inexplicable phenomena and other wonders serve to amplify his moral and spiritual understanding and actualise his perfection as a prophet.

* * *

We can now revisit and review some of the key points made in this chapter regarding Niẓāmī's sources for his *Iqbālnāma*. One of the major focal points has been to explore and, wherever possible, disclose the literary and historical origins of the tales and motifs used by Niẓāmī in his description of Alexander and the *Alexander Romance* in the *Iqbālnāma*. From our examination of the *Iskandarnāma* as a whole in this and the preceding chapter, it appears likely that while Niẓāmī was occupied in the composition of part one, the *Sharafnāma*, he used predominantly Sasanian sources, which is clear from the presence of Persian figures and names (such as Kay Khusraw and the Zoroastrian sorceress). However, in the *Iqbālnāma* – as we have seen throughout this chapter – he drew more upon Arabic lore and Islamic sources (as can be seen in Arabic names such as the whale *Qaṣṣāṣa* and the king Shaddād), which is not at all surprising since here he was largely concerned with the spiritual and Qur'anic dimensions of Alexander's personality.

In particular, Niẓāmī's depiction of Alexander seems to owe a great deal, and in fact to share considerable similarity to the portrayal of the conqueror in Bal'amī's *History* and Bīrūnī's *Āthār al-bāqīya*. Both these authors coincide with Niẓāmī on when and where Alexander died, and on the different meanings of Dhū'l-Qarnayn, and both feature similar versions of the exchange of symbolic gifts between Darius and Alexander. It seems clear that this was due to the fact that Niẓāmī was as much concerned with the historical accuracy of his narrative as with its poetic beauty and literary appeal. Niẓāmī, like Bal'amī and Bīrūnī, did not simply transmit what his sources contained, but instead carefully appraised and verified them.

However, the Jewish influence in the *Iqbālnāma* (such as the visit to Jerusalem and the liberation of the Jewish people there) and some motifs (such as the mermaids dancing on the shore) indicate that Niẓāmī had access to a version of the *Romance* close to sub-recension γ or ε. Indeed, he may have had access to such sources through the Jewish works themselves, as he affirmed at the beginning of the *Sharafnāma*.

In addition, among Niẓāmī's possible other sources one can trace Hermetic works in which Aristotle and Alexander play a crucial role.[175] In particular, we can point to the Hermetic *Dhakhīrat al-Iskandar* (*The Treasury of Alexander*);[176] Abū Ma'shar Balkhī's (d. 886) *al-Ulūf* (*The Thousands*), which Niẓāmī mentions once in the *Iqbālnāma*;[177] and other 'Talismanic Pseudo-Aristotelian Hermetica',[178] such as the *Ghāyat al-ḥakīm* (the Latin *Picatrix*), in which Alexander appears frequently.[179] Niẓāmī also mentions a source called *Tārīkh-i Rūm* (*The History of Byzantium*) in various parts of the *Iskandarnāma* (both in the *Sharafnāma* and the *Iqbālnāma*), which is also cited in Aḥmad Ṭūsī's *Ajāyib al-makhlūqāt*, but which so far remains unidentified among Greek, Latin and Arabic sources.

At the beginning of this chapter, attention was drawn to the similarity of the titles of Niẓāmī's *Iqbālnāma* (*The Book of Fortune*) and Plutarch's *Fortune of Alexander* (*Moralia: De Alexandri Magni Fortuna aut Virtute*). The dominance of the motif of 'Fortune' in Alexander's career has always been highlighted in classical Greek sources (such as Quintus Curtius), and in fact underlies the long medieval and renaissance development of the idea.[180] It is unlikely that Niẓāmī had read any of Plutarch's works,[181] but it is nonetheless worth noting that his attitude towards Alexander is similar to Plutarch's: both authors celebrate his great achievements. In his *Iqbālnāma*, like Plutarch in his *Fortuna*, Niẓāmī demonstrates that Alexander was not Fortune's child but the product of his own qualities and efforts. Niẓāmī also suggests that Alexander was superior to other sages who were mere 'philosophers' because his deeds spoke louder than their words. Niẓāmī's notion in the *Iqbālnāma* that the purpose of Alexander's prophethood was the emancipation of the masses from ignorance resembles Plutarch's idea of the 'mission of civilization' in his *Fortuna*.[182] Both authors urge upon us the view that Alexander represented the virtuous man par excellence.

CONCLUSION

به هرکه هر چه سزاوار بود بخشیدند
سکندر آینه و خضر آب حیوان یافت

To each and every one their just due:
Thus Alexander's lot was a looking glass
And Khiḍr was granted the *Aqua Vitae*.

Ṣā'ib Tabrīzī (d. 1676)[1]

The Greek *Alexander Romance* originated in Alexandria (Egypt) in the third century AD and became the most influential source for the deeds and adventures of Alexander the Great, especially in the East. It took up Alexander's dreams and longings and treated them as if they were real.[2] The composition of the Greek Pseudo-Callisthenes itself and its different recensions makes it a difficult source to trace; the work continued to be rewritten and modified throughout antiquity according to the needs and constraints of different authors, historical periods and social conditions. The vast literature on Alexander that was produced in eastern Greece penetrated other literary traditions, among which the Persian corpus is but one of many intersecting branches. This is the issue with which this book has principally been concerned. It has also addressed the question about the extent to which the *Alexander Romance* influenced Persian literature in general. Thus this book has tried to refocus and rethink the debate on the following points:

(1) The development of the *Alexander Romance* in the Persian tradition: was there any Middle Persian translation of the Pseudo-Callisthenes? If so, what characteristics would it have had?
(2) What sort of Syriac and Arabic translations of the Pseudo-Callisthenes existed? What do Persian sources tell us about Syriac and Arabic sources?
(3) The vast influence of the *Alexander Romance* on Persian literature: the *Romance* had a great impact on historiography, epic, storytelling (popular romances), the *mirabilia* genre and wisdom literature – and in particular on the mirror for princes genre.

Although a number of important points have been covered in the conclusions of each chapter, a few of them are quite new and original, and deserve highlighting here in the following summaries.

The Genesis of the Persian *Alexander Romance*

Since the nineteenth century AD, when Theodore Nöldeke launched his theory about the development of the Pseudo-Callisthenes in Syriac, Arabic, Persian and Ethiopic versions, there have been many disputes around how, when and through which channels the Greek Pseudo-Callisthenes entered the Persian tradition.[3] Nöldeke's theory was based on a philological examination of the Syriac text. He affirmed that a Middle Persian version must have preceded the Syriac version of the Pseudo-Callisthenes. His hypothesis is still generally accepted today despite some disagreements on minor points.[4] However, despite different viewpoints regarding the transmission of the Pseudo-Callisthenes in the East, it might now be possible to add a new argument to Nöldeke's hypothesis in light of the new materials that have been discovered over the past century and recent decades. This book has attempted to do precisely this: to review the origins of the Pseudo-Callisthenes tradition and explore its development in light of these new materials.

The main problem in tracing the origins of Persian versions of the *Alexander Romance* emerges when we consider that there is a vast gap between the pre-Islamic period and the appearance of the first example of this work in Persian in the tenth century AD: Firdawsī's *Shāhnāma*. This is because Arabic replaced Middle Persian for almost two centuries after the Arab conquest of Persia, during which time next to no written works survived in Middle Persian. Thus, in order to determine whether there was a Middle Persian version of the Pseudo-Callisthenes, besides later Persian sources, we must rely primarily on Arabic sources. However, it is necessary to take into account the fact that the Persian and Arabic sources studied here were written almost four centuries after the fall of the Sasanians.[5] It is possible therefore that they contain elements and passages that were not in pre-Islamic sources. In view of this, we may ask to what extent Arabic and Persian works really reflect the actual content of pre-Islamic sources? In order to address this question, we should assume that the only motifs that might have been in the Middle Persian *Vorlage* are those that are mentioned in almost all of these sources, and that contain Persian words and elements from Persian epic and mythology.

A second problem arises when we consider the hostility shown towards Alexander by extant Middle Persian writings, which generally consider him to be one of the greatest enemies of Iran: a man who destroyed the country and eradicated its religion, destroying its sacred writings and fire temples. Since there is almost no extant source on Alexander from the pre-Islamic Persian tradition, might it be possible that there was a Middle Persian version of the *Alexander Romance*? Is there any trace of a positive attitude towards Alexander in pre-Islamic Persian sources? And if a Middle Persian version of the Pseudo-Callisthenes did exist, what characteristics did it have?

As a first step towards resolving these questions, this book has explored the Persian versions of the *Alexander Romance*, not from a philological point of view but by examining different motifs and the actual contents of the legends relating to the conqueror in order to find answers. We have departed from a point of view that focuses solely on the Sasanians as an empire that dominated a vast territory of different people with different languages and religions, and who were thus not restricted to the Zoroastrian attitude towards Alexander. Instead, we have assumed that there is a great possibility that a Middle Persian version of the *Alexander Romance* did exist in the pre-Islamic period.

We can now revisit some of the key points made throughout the whole book regarding the existence and the development of the *Alexander Romance* from the pre-Islamic Persian tradition up to the twelfth century AD. Our investigation has focused on the evidence found in Arabic and Persian sources, particularly their historical formation and composition.

Firstly, we can conclude that legends concerning Alexander the Great must have existed in the Iranian world from the Parthian period. It has already been said that the fame and popularity of the Alexander legends in the East was due to the contact and relations between the Iranians and Greeks living in Greek cities in Asia Minor during the Parthian period,[6] the effect of which can be detected in Ṭarsūsī's *Dārābnāma*. Furthermore, apart from cultural materials such as coinage, some texts show that there was a positive attitude towards Alexander among the Parthians, who often tried to link themselves to Alexander's legacy in Iran. For instance, as Daryaee points out, in the Middle Persian manuscript MU29, the Arsacids connected themselves to Alexander and the Irano-Hellenic cultural setting;[7] this unique text shows that besides the hostile Zoroastrian attitude, there were Middle Persian sources with a positive view of the conqueror.

Thus the timeworn opposition between the Pahlavi tradition and the Arabic and Persian traditions should not lead us in the wrong direction. Despite the hostile attitude in the Pahlavi sources, Persian legends concerning Alexander's ancestry and his deeds as a legitimate Persian king might have had their origin among the Parthians. In this context, we also have the testimony of Tacitus (*Annals*, 6.31), who claims that the Arsacid king Ardawān II legitimised his claim over Roman territories by associating himself with Alexander and the Seleucids on one hand, and with the Achaemenids on the other.[8] Therefore, the so-called Persian ancestry of Alexander found in the *Alexander Romance*, which linked him with the Kayānid kings (especially Bahman Ardashīr, Dārāb and Dārā) on one hand, and Philip on the other, might have had its origin in the Arsacid period. These legends must have been circulating orally due to the Parthians' mainly oral cultural tradition.[9]

Secondly, there appears to have been a distinct historical epoch in which the Sasanian Persian legends concerning Alexander the Great came into contact with the Pseudo-Callisthenes tradition. The period of Khusraw Anūshirvān's reign (Chosroes I, r. 531–79) must be considered as the most probable time when these oral legends were amalgamated with the *Alexander Romance*. During his reign, Khusraw Anūshirvān accepted refugees from the Eastern Roman Empire and Alexandria when Justinian closed the Neoplatonist schools of Athens in 529.[10] Thus, it is likely that the Greek tale became known to Persians as a result of the Hellenophiliac interests of this Sasanian king.[11]

Furthermore, the *Shāhnāma* of Firdawsī and Arabic historical accounts such as that of Ṭabarī and Dīnawarī, and the *Nihāya*, incorporated the Persian ancestry variant, which shows that the *Alexander Romance* was modified and adapted for the purpose of creating a coherent history of Iran. As Ḥāfiẓ claims in a famous verse,[12] Alexander's legend among the Iranians subsequently became emblematic of the downfall of the kingdom of Darius III. Thus, the *Alexander Romance* in general and his conquest of Persia in particular became regarded as an integral part of Persian history that was impossible to ignore.

At this juncture, the question arises as to whether there was ever any independent 'written' version of the *Alexander Romance* in Middle Persian. Alexander is always portrayed as part of the history of the Kayānid dynasty in Arabic historical accounts and in the Persian *Shāhnāma* of Firdawsī, the earliest sources in which motifs from the Pseudo-Callisthenes appear. These same sources deal with the *Alexander Romance* as a part of Persian history. It is not until the twelfth century AD that we find independent works on Alexander under the individual title of *Iskandarnāma* (*The Book of Alexander*). This does not mean that such a written text did not exist prior to this. The citation of motifs from the Pseudo-Callisthenes tradition in the poems of Persian poets of the tenth and eleventh centuries shows the popularity of the *Alexander Romance* in Iran, especially in Khurāsān and Sīstān.[13] For instance, Farrukhī Sīstānī (d. 1037) affirmed in the eleventh century AD that Alexander's story was so famous that everyone knew it by heart.[14] Therefore, it is likely that the *Alexander Romance* was known and circulated in oral form, as the popular romance of the *Dārābnāma* itself demonstrates. The romance achieved such popularity and fame that it reached the Arabs, as reflected in the *Sīrat al-Iskandar*, in the same way that the story of Rustam and Isfandīyār was recited in Mecca.[15]

Keeping this in mind, it is possible that the Middle Persian written version of the *Alexander Romance* was included in the Sasanian *Khudāynāmag*, with historians treating it as a part of Persian history. This might be the reason that there is no mention of such an independent individual work in reference works such as Ibn Nadīm's *al-Fihrist*. From this we may also deduce that the first translation of the *Alexander Romance* into Arabic was through this Middle Persian version in the *Khudāynāmag*, since the earliest Arabic versions (of Dīnawarī and Ṭabarī, and the *Nihāya*) contain the Persian ancestry of Alexander, linking him with the Kayānids.

Here another question arises regarding the Syriac translation of the Pseudo-Callisthenes: was it based on a Middle Persian translation of the Greek Pseudo-Callisthenes, as Nöldeke argues,[16] or was it based on a Greek text, as Richard Frye and Claudia Ciancaglini propose?[17] We know, for instance, that Firdawsī's *Shāhnāma* contains Christian references, especially in passages with a strong Persian element (such as that of Alexander's birth). This would indicate that if the Middle Persian version also contained Christian references, it must have been based on the Syriac translation of the Pseudo-Callisthenes;[18] this in turn would explain Boyce and Tafaḍḍulī's affirmation that the authors of the *Khudāynāmag* used Syriac sources for the passage on Alexander.[19] Does it follow that no Middle Persian version of the Pseudo-Callisthenes existed, which is why they had to use 'Syriac sources'?

There is some evidence to suggest that the Syriac *Alexander Romance* was translated under the patronage of the Sasanian king Khusraw I. Budge, for instance, suggests that Syriac was not the translator's native language.[20] In this case, the translator or translators might have been Nestorian Christians who were Persian-speaking subjects of the Sasanian Empire, and who produced Persian and Syriac translations of Greek texts for the Persian court.[21] If we consider this possibility, the presence of Persian elements and the author's familiarity with the history and geography of Iran in the Syriac *Alexander Romance* can be easily explained. This theory is strengthened by a series of literary features, particularly the replacement of the Achaemenid kings' names with the Sasanian title Khusraw (an allusion to Khusraw I or II), which is evidently intentional.[22]

Thus it is likely that both Middle Persian and Syriac versions of the *Alexander Romance* were translated by (one or more) Nestorians in the Sasanian court under the patronage of Khusraw (either I or II) in the second half of the sixth century AD. Since the first appearance of motifs from the *Alexander Romance* can be found in the works of Firdawsī and other historians – works that are supposed to be based indirectly on the Sasanian *Khudāynāmag* – it seems that the Middle Persian translation of the Pseudo-Callisthenes was adopted and integrated into the *Khudāynāmag*. It is likely that an independent Middle Persian version of the *Alexander Romance* 'in written form' did not exist, since it always appeared as a part of Persian history – that is, until the twelfth century AD, when independent works on Alexander appeared. This is only a hypothesis, however, since neither a Middle Persian version of the

Alexander Romance nor the original or any Arabic translation of the *Khudāynāmag* have ever been found, and are presumed lost.

The *Shāhnāma* of Firdawsī

Khaleghi-Motlagh affirms in various studies that the story of Alexander, as we see it in the *Shāhnāma* of Firdawsī, was not included in the *Khudāynāmag*; instead, it was based on an independent translation in Arabic, which was itself based on the Middle Persian version of the Pseudo-Callisthenes, according to Nöldeke's hypothesis.[23] Our analysis of the Alexander passage in the *Shāhnāma* has shown its complexity, which is due to the different sources that inspired the story, which were evidently gradually added to it. The basis of the story of Alexander's birth and the parts that deal directly with 'Persian history' (that is, the reigns of Dārāb and Dārā) must have been derived from the *Khudāynāmag*. In addition, the *Shāhnāma* contains most of the Syriac materials, which were independent sources in their original forms – such as the tales of Gog and Magog, the Water of Life and the philosophers' lamentations. Firdawsī's epic poem contains the story of the Indian king Kayd, which must have been an independent source in Middle Persian too, as the poet himself also claims. It is not clear when all these materials were put together, but Firdawsī's *Alexander Romance* is a coherent and well-integrated tale within the framework of the *Shāhnāma*. However, Tha'ālibī's *Ghurar akhbār*, which was based on the *Shāhnāma* of Abū Manṣūr, contains almost all the same materials found in Firdawsī's work. This indicates that in the *Shāhnāma* of Abū Manṣūr at least – that is, by the tenth century AD – all these materials had probably been collated in the form later seen in the *Shāhnāma* of Firdawsī.

In addition, most of the Syriac materials in Firdawsī's *Shāhnāma*, such as the story of Gog and Magog and the apocalyptic figures, contain elements from the Persian tradition. This demonstrates that they may have been integrated into the tale from the Syriac tradition at an early stage, possibly at the end of the Sasanian period in the early seventh century AD. Thus, Firdawsī's version of Alexander's story represents a valuable clue in identifying terra incognita in the ancient landscape of the *Alexander Romance*.

The *Iskandarnāma* of Niẓāmī Ganjavī

Our examination of the contents of the *Iskandarnāma* has also revealed that Niẓāmī compiled and collated therein a great variety of pre-Islamic Persian stories about Alexander from the Sasanian period. Niẓāmī demonstrates his knowledge of Sasanian tales in his other works, in particular his *Khusraw u Shīrīn* and *Haft Paykar*, which deal with the adventures of two Sasanian kings (Khusraw II and Bahrām V Gōr). Thus it is not at all surprising that his *Iskandarnāma* also reflects Sasanian tales concerning Alexander the Great.

We must also take into account the historical relevance of Niẓāmī's poem to his homeland, Azerbaijan, which was an important religious centre during the Sasanian period, as the hearth and heartland of one of the Persian Empire's three most sacred fires.[24] As a result, Azerbaijan must have had a powerful effect on the elaboration of Zoroastrian tales and the creation of Sasanian culture and religious lore. This may account for both the great variety and the novelty of Niẓāmī's information and tales. These tales were probably based on non-religious Sasanian/Azerbaijani literature, which had not yet vanished in Niẓāmī's lifetime. We thus find Niẓāmī quoting a so-called *Nāma-yi Khusrawī* (*Book of Kings*), a *Tārīkh-i Dihqān* (*History of Dihqān*), a 'guzāranda-yi dāstān-i Darī' (narrator of a Persian tale) and a '*mūbad-i mūbadān*' (chief Zoroastrian priest) in different passages of both parts of the *Iskandarnāma*. All these quotations can probably be taken as referring to his pre-Islamic Persian sources.

But Niẓāmī's *Iskandarnāma* contains even more surprises. While the Eastern versions of the *Alexander Romance* are supposed to be based on the δ-recension of the Pseudo-Callisthenes, the *Iskandarnāma* includes motifs from sub-recension ε, probably due to his use of Jewish sources. We may also assume that while Firdawsī's *Shāhnāma* reflects Eastern (Khurāsānī/Parthian) legends concerning Alexander, which represented him as a Christian, Niẓāmī's Alexander embodies Western (particularly Caucasian) tales of the conqueror, and also reflects the Jewish tradition, as he himself affirms at the beginning of the *Sharafnāma*.

However, such motifs can also be seen as indicative of the literary cross-fertilisation of various thematic elements, such as the story's protagonist travelling further eastwards or westwards and experiencing various fantastic adventures under similar circumstances. Dick Davis has rather convincingly considered the hypothesis that Greek and Persian literary cultures intermingled and borrowed from each other.[25] It is likely that these elements originate from a similar stock of mythological motifs, which over time came to be applied to different heroes.[26] Alexander's celebrity among the Persians and in the Islamic tradition in general is a measure of the esteem Hellenistic culture has always enjoyed in the Persianate world.

The analysis of themes from the *Alexander Romance* in Niẓāmī's *Iskandarnāma* thus highlights the striking extent to which religious traditions and cultures have interpenetrated. Alexander's personality seems to have developed into an amalgam of diverse literary, historical, mythological and religious personages. As John Renard points out, Alexander functions as a transitional figure between royal and religious character types.[27] Alexander's identification with the Dhū'l-Qarnayn of the Qur'ān (18:82 ff.) is a crucial link that distinguishes the royal 'Persian Alexander' from the religious 'Muslim Alexander'. In the Persian tradition, he had two different histories, which might even have existed in parallel. He was considered to be the 'Accursed One' who destroyed the country and religion of *Īrān-zamīn*, and he was also the Persian king and hero – a slayer of dragons who had strange adventures resembling those of Isfandīyār and Kay Khusraw. In the Islamic period, Alexander then became a model of the ideal 'good king', the most elaborate picture of which appears in Niẓāmī's *Iskandarnāma*, where the Macedonian king is turned into a perfect philosopher and ideal monarch – a figure of sacral authority and a 'law-giving' prophet!

In conclusion, there are very few legends in history that aspire to reach different audiences and yet harbour such vast thematic resonances and generic references as the *Alexander Romance*. As we have seen throughout this book, the tale of the Macedonian world conqueror Alexander the Great gave rise to various interpretations in the long history of its reception in Persian history and literature. The *Alexander Romance* thus demonstrates, as Ulrich Marzolph affirms, that 'world literature is not only, and maybe not even primarily, defined by the appeal of a given literary work, but moreover by this work's capacity to link its basic narrative to different cultural contexts and thus become part of a web of tradition that is constantly woven by the creative combination of history and imagination'.[28]

APPENDIX

SUMMARY OF THE SYRIAC *ALEXANDER ROMANCE*

Book I

1. Nectanebo, the last king of Egypt, protected his kingdom through sorcery.
2. A spy told Nectanebo that the enemy would attack Egypt, but he laughed because he thought that he would be able to protect his kingdom by sorcery as he always had.
3. Through his sorcery, Nectanebo saw that Egypt had been betrayed by its gods. He left his kingdom and fled. He came to Pella of the Macedonians. There he dressed like an Egyptian prophet and astrologer. The people asked him questions and he became renowned. Hephaestus sent an oracle to the Egyptians announcing that a young man would come and subjugate all the enemies of Egypt in their service. The Egyptians carved this oracle under the brass tablet on the stone pedestal upon which the statue of King Nectanebo stood.
4. Queen Olympias asked Nectanebo what her future held. Nectanebo fell in love with her. He told her that Ammon, the god of Libya (who had ram's horns on his head), would sleep with her.
5. Nectanebo used his magic to send Olympias a dream in which she slept with the god Ammon.
6. Olympias asked Nectanebo to make it possible for her to sleep with the god in reality. He said that the god would appear various times,

firstly in the form of a serpent, secondly with ram's horns, thirdly in the form of the hero Hercules, fourthly in the form of Dionysus, and finally in Nectanebo's form.

7. Nectanebo slept with Olympias in all these forms.
8. Nectanebo sent Philip a dream in which he learned that Olympias was pregnant by the god Ammon.
9. Philip returned from war. He told Olympias what he had dreamed.
10. Philip accused Olympias of being unfaithful. Using his sorcery, Nectanebo changed his own form and assumed that of a huge serpent. The serpent kissed Olympias and Philip saw it.
11. A hen laid an egg from which sprang a small serpent. The serpent crawled around the egg, and then went back into it and died immediately. The chief of the Chaldeans interpreted this prodigy to Philip as follows: 'the child that is to be born will be a son. He will traverse the whole world and subjugate all men with his power. But when he returns to his own place, he will die.'
12. Nectanebo calculated the stars of heaven at the time of Olympias's delivery (over Aquarius and Pisces of Egypt). The child's birth was accompanied by the sudden noise of thunder and lightning.
13. Philip named the child Alexander, in remembrance of a son he had had with a former wife. His hair resembled the mane of a lion, and his eyes were different colours, one light and the other dark. His tutor was Lekranikos the Pellaean. There were other tutors too: Āpos the Lemnian taught him letters, Philip was his tutor in geometry, Ārespīmōn in the art of speaking, Aristotle the Milesian in philosophy, and his instructor in war was Ardippos the Dmaṭsḳian. The princes of the Cappadocians brought an offering to Philip: the horse Bucephalus ('Bull-head'), which devoured men.
14. When Alexander was 12, he went to war with Philip and he practised horsemanship. Alexander killed Nectanebo by pushing him into a pit. He then realised that he was Nectanebo's son.
15. Philip sent his servants to Polias the diviner at Delphi to ask who would be king after him. The answer was that the future king would make the mighty steed Bucephalus run through Pella.
16. Alexander managed to ride the 'man-eating' horse. Philip realised that the Delphi oracle referred to Alexander.
17. When he became king, Alexander was asked by Aristotle what he would give him. Alexander replied that he would make Aristotle a

ruler. The other tutors asked Alexander the same question. Letters were exchanged between Aristotle and Philip regarding Alexander's education, because his parents had sent him some funds but Alexander gave them to his friends as gifts.

18. When Alexander was 15, he returned home from school. He went to Pisa to enter the horse and chariot races. There was a quarrel between Alexander and Nicolaus, the King of Ārēṭā, who considered Alexander to be 'small in stature'.
19. Alexander won the race.
20. He went back to Pella and discovered that his mother was divorced. Philip was going to marry Cleopatra. Alexander was angry with Philip.
21. Philip wanted to stab Alexander with a knife but he stumbled and fell.
22. Alexander reconciled his father and mother.
23. A certain city called Methone had rebelled against Philip. He sent Alexander to kill all the inhabitants through warfare. Instead, Alexander persuaded them with words to return to Philip's service. They obeyed. When Alexander returned, he saw Darius's ambassadors demanding the customary tribute from Philip. Alexander answered: 'When Philip had no children, his hens used to lay golden eggs, but since I was born, they have been barren and no longer lay eggs.' The ambassadors hired a skilful painter to paint Alexander. They took the picture and returned to their own land. Philip sent Alexander to subdue the Armenians.
24. A man called Theosidos tried to kill Philip because he (Theosidos) was in love with Olympias. Alexander came back after victory against the Armenians and saw Theosidos and Olympias together. He took the man to Philip, who was still alive. Philip killed Theosidos and then died himself.
25. Alexander announced that he would march against the Persians.
26. Alexander's army numbered 270,000 men in all.
27. They embarked on triremes and other large ships, and advanced over the sea from Dithoas and Thrace.
28. Alexander and his army came to Rome. The Romans welcomed him with many gifts, including 600 talents of gold and the golden crown of Zeus. They asked Alexander to take vengeance upon Carthage on their behalf. Alexander accepted the challenge.

29. Alexander set out from Italy and came by sea to Africa. He fought against the Carthaginians.
30. Alexander went to Libya and offered sacrifices there to the god Ammon. In a dream Ammon affirmed that Alexander was his son. The god showed Alexander a place where he should build a city.
31. In the dream, Alexander killed a stag. Around the spot where the stag died, there were 15 (or 12) towns. Alexander remembered his dream.
32. He entered the temple of Zeus and Hera. He read a legend there and realised that the first god was Serapis. He also saw a golden cup that was made for Serapis. He decided to build a city where the first god dwelled, just as Ammon had shown him in his dream. He called this city Alexandria.
33. Aristotle warned Alexander not to build such a great city because even if Alexander stored up all the food in his lands, it would not suffice for the nourishment of all the people in it.
34. Alexander went to Memphis and saw the statue of Nectanebo and the oracle in which it was said that Nectanebo's son would rule the world.
35. He went with his troops to Syria. There was a battle against the Tyrians. Alexander defeated them and built the city of Tripolis.
36. Darius's ambassadors showed him Alexander's painting. Roxana fell in love with Alexander. She carried the picture to her bedchamber. Then Darius sent Alexander some symbolic gifts (a whip, a ball, a box full of gold and a letter).
37. Alexander's troops were terrified. He commanded that the ambassadors be crucified but then he released them to show the superiority of Greeks over the barbarians. The motif of the sesame seeds.
38. Alexander wrote a letter to Darius in which he interpreted the gifts as his own victory over Darius. He also sent a bushel of mustard seeds as a response to the gift of sesame seeds.
39. Darius sent a letter to his satraps ordering them to fight Alexander. The satraps replied that the king should come with a strong force to help them. Darius replied.
40. Darius heard that Alexander had reached the river Estalraglos and wrote a letter to him.

41. Alexander responded. He received a message that his mother was sick, and decided to visit her. On the way, he went to Arabia and fought against one of Darius's generals. The motif of sesame and mustard seeds repeated.
42. Alexander went to Phrygia and offered sacrifices to Hector and Achilles. He gave a speech about Homer.
43. He returned to Macedonia and visited his mother. Then he went to Abdera and set fire to the city.
44. Alexander reached a city of cannibals. He ordered the horses to be killed in order to protect his troops.
45. Then he went to Locri, where he obtained food and horses. He marched towards Aḳranṭīs and went to the temple of Apollo. There he heard an oracle.
46. He began to march towards Thebes. He fought against Theban warriors and killed them all. A singer tried to enchant Alexander and his troops. Alexander expelled from the country all Thebans who remained alive.
47. These Thebans went to Delphi to ask the oracle about their city. The oracle told them that when three athletes held a contest with one another, their city would be rebuilt. Alexander went to Corinth to the Olympic Games. A Theban won the games and Alexander promised to rebuild Thebes.

Book II

1. Alexander set out from Corinth and came to Plataeae, an Athenian city. The Athenians were displeased that Alexander changed the ruler of that city because he had removed a priestess. Alexander wrote a letter to the Athenians.
2. Letters were exchanged between Alexander and the Athenians.
3. The assembly of the Athenians took place.
4. Demosthenes made a speech.
5. The Athenians sent Alexander a golden crown of victory but not the ten orators. Alexander wrote them a letter demanding the ten orators.
6. Alexander came to the border of Persia and camped by the River Tigris. He went on an embassy to Darius. The Persian king thought

that Alexander was the god Mithras who had come to assist the Persians. Alexander presented himself as an ambassador.

7. At the banquet, Alexander hid the golden wine cups in his bosom. When the Persians saw this, they asked him why he had done it. Alexander said that whenever he held a feast, he would give all the golden cups to his guests. Darius gave him the cups. Meanwhile, Alexander was recognised by Darius's ambassadors, who had been to Macedonia. Alexander escaped. A picture of Xerxes in Darius's court fell to the ground.
8. Alexander filled his troops with courage to fight against Darius.
9. A battle was fought between the Persians and Macedonians on the banks of the River Strangas. Darius fled and many Persian soldiers drowned in the river or were slaughtered by the Macedonians. Darius wrote a letter to Alexander offering him Persian treasures. Alexander ordered the palace of Xerxes to be burned, but then relented.
10. Alexander saw the graves of the Persians, including the golden coffin of King Cyrus. He liberated Greek prisoners.
11. Darius wrote a letter to Porus, the King of the Indians to ask him for help against Alexander.
12. Two of Darius's generals, Bāgīz and Ānābdaeh, assassinated him because they thought that they might be rewarded by Alexander with gifts. A dialogue took place between the dying king and Alexander. Darius spoke his last words to Alexander.
13. Alexander buried Darius with honour. Thus, the Persians were filled with love for him. Alexander wrote a proclamation to the Persians. He also ordered Darius's assassins to be impaled on stakes.
14. Alexander wrote letters to Darius's mother and wife. They sent answers to him. He also wrote a letter to Rawshanak, Darius's daughter, and then he took her as his wife.

Book III

1. A war took place against Porus, King of the Indians.
2. Porus wrote a letter to Alexander, who replied.
3. Alexander and his troops were terrified of Porus's army, which had elephants. They fought for 20 days.

4. Alexander fought Porus alone and killed him.
5. The Brahmans, 'the naked sages', wrote a letter to Alexander.
6. Alexander asked them some questions and they answered. Then they asked Alexander about immortality.
7. Alexander wrote a letter to Aristotle on the wonders of India and China.
8. Alexander wished to go to the country of Samrāyē (Semiramis) and see Queen Kundāḳa (Candace). Thus he wrote her a letter. Candace sent him gifts with a letter.
9. A Greek painter painted Alexander's portrait for Queen Candace without his knowledge. One of Candace's sons, named Ḳandāros (Candaules), went to the country of the Amazons with his wife. His wife was captured; he escaped and went to Alexander's camp. Alexander presented himself as Antigonus.
10. Alexander helped Candaules to rescue his wife and went with him to Queen Candace, disguised as his own ambassador.
11. The description of Candace's land. The queen received Alexander and prepared a splendid feast for him.
12. Alexander saw Queen Candace as his own mother, Olympias. The description of Candace's palace. Candace told Alexander that she knew he was Alexander himself and not his ambassador.
13. Candace's other son, whose father-in-law was Porus, wanted to take revenge on Alexander by killing his ambassador. Alexander, still in disguise, promised that he would deliver Alexander into his hands if he did not kill him. The son accepted.
14. Alexander saw an angel (Sesonchosis, the ruler of the world).
15. Alexander went to the country of the Amazons, where the people had one breast like a man's and one like a woman's.
16. Letters were exchanged between Alexander and the Amazons.
17. When Alexander was near the country of the Amazons, Zeus sent a great rain upon them. Then a fierce and powerful heat came upon them. Then came lightning and thunder and mighty sounds from heaven. The Amazons said that this was all happening because of Alexander's presence in the land. They gave 60 mighty elephants to Alexander to abandon that land. He received a letter from Aristotle telling Alexander to sacrifice to the gods who honoured him. He decided to return to Babylon. Near that city, he wrote a letter to his mother to tell her about his journey to the country of the Amazons.

18. The letter to his mother contained the marvels that Alexander had come across throughout his journey.
19. There was a sign of Alexander's death: a certain woman gave birth to a child who from his waist upwards had the form of a man, and from his waist downwards the form of a number of animals – a lion, a leopard, a wolf and a wild dog, all with separate heads.
20. Olympias's letter contained an accusation against Antipater, who then tried to poison Alexander. Alexander drank the poison and felt great pain. He ordered a will to be written.
21. The Macedonians carried Alexander on his bed. They passed before him in their armour. They wept when they saw that Alexander was sick. Alexander gave a speech.
22. Alexander was carried to his palace. Alexander commanded that the will be brought and read before him.
23. When Alexander had given the commands (in his will), he died. Ptolemy made him a tomb in Alexandria, as he had been ordered to do.
24. In summary, Alexander waged numerous battles and great wars. He lived 32 years and seven months. He subdued 22 barbarian kings and 13 Greek kings. He built 13 cities, including Samarqand, Balkh and Merv. Alexander died in Babylon after being poisoned. He reigned as king for 12 years and seven months.

NOTES

Introduction

1. Farrukhī Sīstānī, *Dīvān*, ed. Muḥammad Dabīr Siyāqī, 2nd edn (Tehran, 1970). Interestingly, the quote from Sīstānī bears a great resemblance to Chaucer's (d. 1400) lines in 'The monk's tale'. See *The Canterbury Tales* (London, 1951; repr. 2003), pp. 208–9:

   The story of Alexander is so famous
   That it is known to everyone at least
   In part, unless he be an ignoramus.
   He conquered the wide world from west to east
   By force of arms, and as his fame increased
   Men gladly sued to have him for their friend.
   He brought to naught the pride of man and beast
   Wherever he came, as far as the world's end.

2. Franz Rosenthal, *The Classical Heritage in Islam*, trans. Emile and Jenny Marmorstein (London/New York, 1975; repr. 1994), p. 255.
3. For more information regarding this Persian poet see Dh. Ṣafā, *Tārīkh-i Adabīyāt dar Irān*, 12th edn (Tehran, 1371/1992), vol. I, pp. 531–46; F. de Blois, *Persian Literature: A Bio-Bibliographical Survey, V/1: Poetry to ca. AD 1100* (London, 1992), pp. 108–12.
4. See M. Kayvānī, 'Iskandar dar adab-i fārsī', *Dānishnāma-yi zabān va adab-i fārsī*, ed. Ismā'īl Sa'ādat (Tehran, 1384/2005), vol. I, p. 404.
5. For a translation from Greek to Middle Persian and then to Arabic see Dimitri Gutas, *Greek Wisdom Literature in Arabic Translation: A Study of the Graeco-Arabic Gnomologia* (New Haven, 1975); Gutas, 'Paul the Persian on the classification of the parts of Aristotle's philosophy: a milestone between Alexandria and Baġdād', *Der Islam* lx (1983), pp. 231–67; Gutas, *Greek Thought, Arabic Culture: The Graeco-Arabic Translation Movement in Baghdad and Early 'Abbāsid Society (2nd–4th/8th–10th centuries)* (London/New York, 1998),

especially pp. 25–7; Gutas, 'The "Alexandria to Baghdad" complex of narratives: a contribution to the study of philosophical and medical historiography among the Arabs', *Documenti e Studi sulla Tradizione Filosofica Medievale* x (1999), pp. 155–93. For translations from Middle Persian into Arabic see Antonio Panaino, 'L'influsso greco nella letteratura e nella cultura medio-persiana', *Autori classici in lingue del Medio e Vicino Oriente* (Rome, 2001), pp. 29–45; F. de Blois, 'Tardjama: translations from Middle Persian (Pahlavī)', *EI* [2] x, 231b–2b; Shaul Shaked, 'From Iran to Islam: notes on some themes in transmission', *Jerusalem Studies in Arabic and Islam* iv (1984), pp. 31–67.

6. See Charles-Henri de Fouchécour, 'Alexandre le macédonien iranisé: l'exemple du récit par Nézami (XIIe siècle) de la visite d'Alexandre à la grotte de Key Khosrow', in Laurence Harf-Lancner, Claire Kappler and François Suard (eds), *Alexandre le Grand dans les littératures occidentales et proche-orientales (Actes du Colloque de Paris, 27–29 novembre 1999)* (Paris, 1999), pp. 227–41.
7. Īraj Afshār (ed.), *Iskandarnāma* (Tehran, 1343/1964; repr. Tehran, 1387/2008).
8. On its dating, see Muḥammad Taqī Bahār, *Sabk-shināsī ya tarīkh-i taṭavvur-i naṣr-i fārsī* (Tehran, 1942), vol. II, pp. 128–51.
9. Nöldeke's theory, based on a philological examination of the Syriac translation of the Pseudo-Callisthenes, launched the hypothesis that the Syriac *Romance* must have been translated from a lost Middle Persian version, which in turn depended on a Greek recension of the text. See Nöldeke, *Beiträge zur Geschichte des Alexanderromans* (Wien, 1890), pp. 11–17.
10. See Minoo S. Southgate (trans.), *Iskandarnamah: A Persian Medieval Alexander-Romance* (New York, 1978), which is a translation of the Persian text edited by Afshār (published in 1964 under the title *Iskandarnāma*). See Introduction note 7.
11. See also M.S. Southgate, 'Portrait of Alexander the Great in Persian *Alexander Romances* of the Islamic era', *Journal of the American Oriental Society* xcvii (1977), pp. 278–84.
12. Abū Ṭāhir Ṭarsūsī, *Dārābnāma*, ed. Dh. Ṣafā, 2nd edn (Tehran, 2536 Shāhanshāhī/1977), vol. I, pp. 13–19.
13. Dh. Ṣafā, *Ḥamāsa-sarāyī dar Irān* (Tehran, 1363/1984), pp. 89–90.
14. See Khaleghi-Motlagh, 'Jā-yi Rustam, Arash, Isfandīyār, Gushtāsp, Jāmāsp va Iskandar dar *Khudāynāma*', *Nāma-yi Irān-i Bāstān* ix/1–2 (2009–10), pp. 19–24; Khaleghi-Motlagh, 'Az *Khudāynāma* tā *Shāhnāma*', *Nāme-yi Irān-i Bāstān* vii/1–2 (2007–8), pp. 29–30.
15. William L. Hanaway, 'Persian popular romances before the Safavid period' (PhD thesis, Columbia University, 1970; published 1972).
16. W. L. Hanaway, 'Anahita and Alexander', *Journal of the American Oriental Society* cii (1982), pp. 285–95.
17. Ṭarsūsī, *Alexandre le Grand en Iran: Le Dārāb Nāmeh d'Abū Ṭāhir Ṭarsūsī*, trans. and annotated Marina Gaillard (Paris, 2005), p. 14.
18. Ḥasan Ṣafavī, etc., *Iskandar va adabīyāt-e Irān va shakhsīyat-e madhhabī-ye Iskandar* (Tehran, 1364/1985).

19. Majd al-Dīn Kayvānī, 'Iskandar dar adabīyāt-e Irān' and '*Iskandar-nāmahā*', *Dānishnāma-ye zabān va adabīyāt-e fārsī*, ed. Ismā'īl Sa'ādat (Tehran, 1384/2005), vol. I, pp. 402–10.
20. Bertels, *Roman ob Aleksandre* (Moscow/Leningrad, 1948).
21. F. Doufikar-Aerts, *Alexander Magnus Arabicus: A Survey of the Alexander Tradition through Seven Centuries: From Pseudo-Callisthenes to Ṣūrī* (Louvain, 2010).
22. Doufikar-Aerts, *Alexander Magnus Arabicus*, p. 80.
23. Khaleghi-Motlagh, 'Jāy-i Rustam, Arash, Isfandīyār, Gushtāsp, Jāmāsp va Iskandar dar *Khudāynāma*', pp. 19–24.
24. Khaleghi-Motlagh, 'Az *Khudāynāma* tā *Shāhnāma*', pp. 29–30.

Chapter 1 Greek and Syriac Versions of the *Alexander Romance* and their Development in the East

1. Farrukhī, *Dīvān*, ed. M. Dabīr-Sīyāqī (Tehran, 1335/1957; 2nd edn 1349/1970), p. 66. I thank Dr Lewisohn for the English translation of this verse.
2. For the Greek and Latin historical sources on Alexander see E. Baynham, 'The ancient evidence for Alexander the Great', in J. Roisman (ed.), *Brill's Companion to Alexander the Great* (Leiden, 2003), pp. 3–29. See also A. B. Bosworth (1994), 'Alexander the Great, part 1: the events of the reign', in D. M. Lewis et al. (eds), *The Cambridge Ancient History* (Cambridge, 1994), pp. 791–845.
3. R. Merkelbach, *Die Quellen des griechischen Alexanderromans* (Munich, 1954; 2nd edn 1977), pp. 88–92; R. Stoneman (trans.), *The Greek Alexander Romance* (London/New York, 1991), p. 8.
4. For a study of the production of this *Romance* see Merkelbach, *Die Quellen des griechischen Alexanderromans*; G. Cary, *The Medieval Alexander* (Cambridge, 1956; repr. 1967), p. 9; R. Stoneman, 'Primary sources from the classical and early medieval periods', in Z. David Zuwiyya (ed.), *A Companion to Alexander Literature in the Middle Ages* (Leiden/Boston, 2011), pp. 1–9; Stoneman, *Alexander the Great: A Life in Legend* (New Haven, 2008), pp. 2–3; Stoneman, *Il Romanzo di Alessandro*, trans. T. Gargiulo (Milan, 2007); Stoneman, *The Greek Alexander Romance*, pp. 1–23.
5. See R. Stoneman, 'The author of the *Alexander Romance*', in M. Paschalis, S. Panayotakis and G. Schmeling (eds), *Readers and Writers in the Ancient Novel* (Groningen, 2009), pp. 142–54.
6. Stoneman, 'Primary sources', pp. 3–9; Stoneman, *The Greek Alexander Romance*, pp. 8, 28–32.
7. In the Bibliothèque Nationale in Paris (Parisinus graecus 1711).
8. W. Kroll, *Historia Alexandri Magni* (Berlin, 1926).
9. It was edited and translated into English by A. Wolohojian, *The Romance of Alexander the Great by Pseudo-Callisthenes* (New York, 1969).
10. See Appendix I in Stoneman, *A Life in Legend*, p. 232.

11. Julius Valerius, *Res gestae Alexandri Macedonis translatae ex Aesopo Graeco*, ed. M. Rossellini, 2nd edn (Munich, 2004). See also Stoneman, *A Life in Legend*, pp. 230, 236; Stoneman, 'The Latin Alexander', in H. Hofmann (ed.), *Latin Fiction* (London, 1999), pp. 167–8.
12. It was edited (with full details of all the manuscripts) by L. Bergson, *Der griechische Alexanderroman rezension Beta* (Stockholm, 1965). See also Stoneman, 'Primary sources', p. 7; Stoneman, *A Life in Legend* (Appendix I), pp. 230–1.
13. Epsilon's edition: J. Trumpf, *Vita Alexandri regis Macedonum* (Stuttgart, 1974).
14. Lambda's edition: H. Van Thiel, *Die Rezension Lambda des Pseudo-Kallisthenes* (Bonn, 1959).
15. For editions see Stoneman, *A Life in Legend*, p. 232; for description and editions see Stoneman, 'Primary sources', p. 9.
16. For an edition and German translation see H. Van Thiel, *Leben und Täten Alexanders von Makedonien: Der griechische Alexanderroman nach der Handschrift L* (Darmstadt, 1983); for an English translation see Stoneman, *The Greek Alexander Romance*.
17. See Stoneman, 'Primary sources', pp. 17–19; Stoneman, *A Life in Legend*, p. 237; Stoneman, 'The medieval Alexander', in H. Hofmann (ed.), *Latin Fiction: The Latin Novel in Context* (London, 1999), pp. 238–40.
18. See Chapter 5 on the *Iqbālnāma* (*Book of Fortune*).
19. Amīr Khusraw Dihlavī, *Khamsa*, ed. A. Aḥmad Ashrafī (Tehran, 1362/1983), pp. 533–9.
20. The variations are added as supplements to Stoneman's English edition of the *Romance*; see Stoneman, *The Greek Alexander Romance*, pp. 161–88.
21. The *Apocalypse* of Pseudo-Methodius was translated into Greek from Syriac. The motif of Alexander enclosing Gog and Magog entered into Western versions of the *Alexander Romance* through this text. See F. J. Martínez, *Eastern Christian Apocalyptic in the Early Muslim Period: Pseudo-Methodius and Pseudo-Athanasius* (Ann Arbor, 1996), pp. 18–19; G. J. Reinink, 'Alexander the Great in seventh-century Syriac "apocalyptic" texts', *Byzantinorossica* ii (2003), pp. 150–78; Stoneman, 'Alexander the Great and the end of time: the Syriac contribution to the development of the *Alexander Romance*', paper given at Mardin Artuklu University, April 2012.
22. This originally independent treatise is a fifth-century Christian rewriting of a Cynic diatribe written before the second century AD. See Stoneman, *A Life in Legend*, pp. 97–102, for editions and a translation see p. 232.
23. K. van Bladel, 'The Syriac sources of the early Arabic narratives of Alexander', in H. Prabha Ray and D. T. Potts (eds), *Memory as History: The Legacy of Alexander in South Asia* (New Delhi, 2007), pp. 54–75.
24. See J. P. Monferrer-Sala, 'Alexander the Great in the Syriac literary tradition', in Z. David Zuwiyya (ed.), *A Companion to Alexander Literature in the Middle Ages* (Leiden/Boston, 2011), p. 42.

25. S. Gero, 'The legend of Alexander the Great in the Christian Orient', *Bulletin of the John Rylands University Library of Manchester* lxxv (1993), pp. 1, 5.
26. E. A. Wallis Budge, *The History of Alexander the Great, Being the Syriac Version* (New York/London, 1889; repr. New Jersey, 2003).
27. A summary of the Syriac Pseudo-Callisthenes with a reordering of its structure can be found in J. P. Monferrer-Sala, 'Alexander the Great in the Syriac literary tradition', pp. 60–3.
28. This part of the Syriac Pseudo-Callisthenes bears a great resemblance to the parallel stories of Alexander in the *Shāhnāma* of Firdawsī.
29. Other episodes only found in Syriac versions, as Stoneman points out, are 'Aristotle's advice to Alexander about the building of Alexandria; Nectanebo's and Olympias's discussion of Philip's disaffection from his wife (I.14); the metaphor of the golden eggs (I.23); and the symbolic gifts of the mustard seeds (I.36 and 39). The commissioning of a painting of Alexander by the ambassadors from Darius is properly motivated only in this version, where it is shown to Darius's daughter. But there is a large lacuna at II.6–14, presumably the result of a defective Greek original' (Stoneman, *A Life in Legend*, Appendix I, p. 233).
30. For an English translation see W. Budge, *The History of Alexander*, pp. 144–58. In this book I will refer to this work as the *Christian Legend.*
31. K. Czeglédy, 'The Syriac legend concerning Alexander the Great', *Acta Orientalia* vii (1957), pp. 245, 249.
32. Reinink underlines the political setting of the *Legend*, which clearly displays pro-Byzantine propaganda. See G. J. Reinink, 'Die Entstehung der syrischen Alexanderlegende als politisch-religiöse Propagandaschrift für Herakleios' Kirchenpolitik', in C. Laga, J. A. Munitiz and L. van Rompay (eds), *After Chalcedon: Studies in Theology and Church History, Offered to Professor Albert van Roey for His Seventieth Birthday* (Louvain, 1985), pp. 263–81.
33. See E. Donzel and A. Schmidt, *Gog and Magog in Early Syriac and Islamic Sources: Sallam's Quest for Alexander's Wall* (Leiden, 2010), p. 17.
34. Budge, *The History of Alexander*, pp. lxxix–lxxxiii, 163–200. In this book I will refer to this work as the *Alexander Poem.*
35. The authorship of Jacob of Serūgh (d. 521), to whom the text is ascribed by the majority of the Syriac manuscripts, is definitely out of the question. See Reinink, *Das Alexanderlied: Die drei Rezensionen* (Louvain, 1983), vol. II, pp. 1–15.
36. Reinink, 'Alexander the Great in seventh-century Syriac "apocalyptic" texts', pp. 165–8; Reinink, *Das Alexanderlied*, vol. II, p. 12.
37. See van Bladel, 'The early Syriac sources', p. 58; Donzel and Schmidt, *Gog and Magog*, p. 22.
38. S. P. Brock, 'The laments of the philosophers over Alexander in Syriac', *Journal of Semitic Studies* xv (1970), pp. 205–18; see also J. P. Monferrer-Sala, 'Alexandri magni de anima dictum fictitum apud philosophos enuntiavit', *Hikma* 5 (2006), pp. 155–69. For editions and translations see Monferrer-Sala, 'Alexander the Great in the Syriac literary tradition', p. 50.

39. Yaʿqūbī, *Tārīkh al-Yaʿqūbī* (Beirut, 1960), vol. I, pp. 143–4.
40. See Brock, 'The laments', pp. 211–14.
41. Masʿūdī, *Murūj al-dhahab*, ed. Ch. Pellat (Beirut, 1966–79), vol. II, pp. 11–13.
42. Firdawsī, *Shāhnāma*, ed. Khaleghi-Motlagh and M. Omīdsālār, 3rd ed. (Tehran, 1389/2010), vol. VI, pp. 125–8.
43. Th. Nöldeke, 'Die von Guidi herausgegebene syrische Chronik übersetzt und commentiert', *Sitzungsberichte der kaiserlichen Akademie der Wissenschaften, Phil.-Hist. Classe* 128 (1893), pp. 1–48.
44. It is also occasionally referred to as the *Anonymous Nestorian Chronicle*, see S. P. Brock, 'Syriac historical writing: a survey of the main sources', *Journal of the Iraqi Academy* (Syriac Corporation) xxv/302 (1979–80), p. 5; Pierre Nautin, 'L'auteur de la '*Chronique Anonyme de Guidi*': Élie de Merw', *Revue de l'Histoire des Religions* cxcix/3 (1982), pp. 303–14.
45. The influence of Yazdīn in the Sasanian court is discussed in James Howard-Johnson, *Witnesses to a World Crisis: Historians and Histories of the Middle East in the Seventh Century* (Oxford, 2010), pp. 130–3. We will discuss the importance of the influence of the Nestorians in the Sasanian court in the development of the *Alexander Romance* through this study.
46. The building of Merv is attributed to Alexander in the *Syriac Romance* and also in the *Legend*; see Budge, *The History of Alexander*, pp. 116, 142, 160.
47. This Latin translation of the Syriac *Khuzistān Chronicle* is available online at http://booksnow1.scholarsportal.info/ebooks/oca7/52/chronicaminorapa00guid/chronicaminorapa00guid.pdf.
48. Ignacio Guidi, 'Chronicon anonymum', *Chronica Minora* (Paris, 1903), vol. I, 15–39 (Syriac text); vol. II, 15–32 (Latin trans.), pp. 28–9.
49. Guidi, *Chronica Minora*, p. 22.
50. Ṭabarī, *The History of al-Ṭabarī: An Annotated Translation*, Vol. IV: *The Ancient Kingdoms*, trans. Moshe Perlmann, notes by Shaul Shaked (New York, 1987), p. 94.
51. For instance, see Ṣafā, *Ḥamāsa-sarāyī dar Irān*, pp. 198–200; R. N. Frye, 'Two Iranian notes', *Papers in Honour of Professor Mary Boyce* (Leiden, 1985), vol. I, pp. 185–8.
52. On the passages of Pahlavi sources where Alexander appears see the Appendix in Touraj Daryaee, '*Imitatio Alexandri* and its impact on Late Arsacid, Early Sasanian and Middle Persian literature', *Electrum* xii (2007), pp. 93–5. See also M. R. Shayegan, *Arsacids and Sasanians: Political Ideology in Post-Hellenic and Late Antique Persia* (Cambridge, 2011), pp. 295–7; Yuriko Yamanaka, 'From evil destroyer to Islamic hero: the transformation of Alexander the Great's image in Iran', *Annals of Japan Association for Middle East Studies* viii (1993), pp. 55–87.
53. This fact is also pointed out by C. Ciancaglini in her article 'The Syriac version of the Alexander Romance', *Le Muséon, Revue d'Études Orientales* cxiv/1–2 (2001), pp. 136–7.

54. See K. van Bladel, *The Arabic Hermes: From Pagan Sage to Prophet of Science* (Oxford, 2009), pp. 30–9; Gutas, *Greek Thought, Arabic Culture*, pp. 25–7.
55. Th. Nöldeke, *Beiträge zur Geschichte des Alexanderromans*, pp. 11–18.
56. Frye, 'Two Iranian notes', pp. 185–8.
57. Ciancaglini, 'The Syriac version of the Alexander Romance', p. 140. See also the original Italian chapter: 'Gli antecedenti del Romanzo di Alessandro', in R. B. Finazzi and A. Valvo (eds), *La diffusione dell'eredità classica nell'età tardoantica e medieval: Atti del Seminario internazionale tenuto a Roma–Napoli* (Alexandria, 1998), pp. 55–93.
58. Van Bladel, 'The Syriac sources', pp. 61–4.
59. Ibid., p. 62.
60. Monferrer-Sala, 'Alexander the Great in the Syriac literary tradition', p. 47.
61. Doufikar-Aerts, *Alexander Magnus Arabicus*, p. 13.
62. On the Arabic Pseudo-Callisthenes tradition see Chapter 1 of Doufikar-Aerts, *Alexander Magnus Arabicus*, pp. 13–91, where she examines different historical and geographical Arabic sources, besides the Arabic popular romances that deal with the *Alexander Romance*. She determines the main motifs, sources and the transmission of the Pseudo-Callisthenes tradition in Arabic literature.
63. Doufikar-Aerts, *Alexander Magnus Arabicus*, p. 14.
64. For a detailed study of the Syriac manuscripts see J. P. Monferrer-Sala, 'Alexander the Great in the Syriac literary tradition', pp. 45–8.

Chapter 2 Alexander the Great and the Legacy of Sasanian Historiography

1. Ḥāfiz, *Dīvān*, ed. S. Ṣ. Sajjādī and 'A. Bahrāmīyān (Tehran, 1379/2000), p. 384. See also Ḥāfiz, *Dīvān*, ed. Parvīz Nātil Khānlarī (Tehran, 1359/1980), *ghazal* 264:7.
2. Dīnawarī, *Akhbār al-ṭivāl*, ed. 'A. 'Āmir (Cairo, 1960).
3. Ṭabarī, *Tārīkh al-rusul va al-mulūk*, ed. Dodge (Leiden, 1879–81). English passages are quoted from Ṭabarī, *The History of al-Ṭabarī (Tārīkh al-rusul wa'l-mulūk)*, Vol. IV: *The Ancient Kingdoms*, ed. E. Yarshater, trans. and annotated Moshe Perlmann and Shaul Shaked (New York, 1987).
4. M. T. Dānishpazhūh (ed.), *Nihāya al-'erab fī tārīkh al-furs wa al-'arab* (Tehran, 1374).
5. See Grignaschi, 'La *Nihāyatu-l-'arab fī akhbāri-l-Furs wa-l-'arab*', *Bulletin d'études orientales* xxii (1969), pp. 15–67; Grignaschi, 'La *Nihāyatu-l-'arab fī akhbāri-l-Furs wa-l-'arab* et les *Siyaru mulūki-l-'ağam* du Ps. Ibn-al-Muqaffa'', *Bulletin d'études orientales* xxvi (1973), pp. 83–184. However, Yarshater states that it was probably written in the eleventh century. See Yarshater, 'Iranian national history', in E. Yarshater (ed.), *Cambridge History of Iran* (Cambridge, 1983), vol. III/1, p. 363.

6. Tha'ālibī Nīshābūrī, *Tārīkh ghurar al-sayr*, ed. H. Zotenberg (Paris, 1900; repr. Tehran, 1342/1963).
7. Abū Rayḥān Bīrūnī, *Āthār al-bāqīya 'an al-qurūn al-khālīya*, ed. E. Sachau (Leipzig, 1923).
8. Ḥamza Iṣfahānī, *Tārīkh sinī mulūk al-arḍ wa-l-anbīyā* (Beirut, 1961).
9. This work has been lost, but a summary of it is preserved by Abū 'l-Ḥasan al-Shayzārī (*c.*1022). See Ibn al-Faqīh al-Hamadānī, *Mukhtaṣar Kitāb al-Buldān*, *Bibliotheca Geographorum Arabicorum*, Vol. V: *Compendium Libri Kitab al-boldan*, ed. M. J. de Goeje (Leiden, 1885; repr. 1967).
10. For instance, while Ṭabarī dedicated a whole chapter to the identification and meaning of Dhū'l-Qarnayn in his *Tafsīr* (*Commentary on the Qur'ān*), in his *Tārīkh* (*Annals*) he did not even mention this name. This indicates that in his *Tārīkh* he was working with sources older than the compilation of the Qur'ān.
11. Yarshater, 'Iranian national history', pp. 359–477. See also his entry 'Iran: iii. Traditional history', *EIr* xiii/3, pp. 299–307.
12. J. Khaleghi-Motlagh, 'Az *Shāhnāma* tā *Khudāynāma*', *Nāme-yi Irān-i Bāstān, The International Journal of Ancient Iranian Studies* vii/1–2 (2007–8), pp. 3–119. See also Khaleghi-Motlagh, 'Jāy-i Rustam, Ārash, Isfandīyār, Gushtāsp, Jāmāsp va Iskandar dar *Khudāynāma*', *Nāme-yi Irān-i Bāstān* ix/1–2 (2009–10), pp. 3–24.
13. See Yarshater, 'Iranian national history', p. 359.
14. See M. Boyce, 'Middle Persian literature', *Iranistik II: Handbuch der Orientalistik* 1. IV. 2.1 (Leiden, 1968), pp. 57–9; A. Tafaḍḍulī, *Tārīkh-i adabīyāt-i Irān pīsh az Islam*, ed. Zh. Āmūzgār (Tehran, 1376/1997), pp. 269–74.
15. Touraj Daryaee, *Sasanian Persia, the Rise and Fall of an Empire* (London/New York, 2009), p. xvii.
16. Sh. Shahbazi, 'On the *Xwadāy-Nāmag*', *Iranica Varia: Papers in Honor of Professor Ehsan Yarshater* (Leiden, 1990), pp. 218–23.
17. Agathias (*c.*530–82) was a Greek poet and historian of the Roman emperor Justinian I. For a detailed and comprehensive treatment of Agathias's life see Averil Cameron, *Agathias* (Oxford, 1970), pp. 1–11.
18. See Averil Cameron, 'Agathias on the Sasanians', *Dumbarton Oaks Papers* xxiii–xxiv (1969–70), p. 128.
19. See Khaleghi-Motlagh, 'Az *Shāhnāma* tā *Khudāynāma*', pp. 3–71; Vladimir Minorsky, 'The older preface to the *Shāhnāma*', *Studi Orientalistici in onore di G. Levi della Vida* (Rome, 1956), vol. II, pp. 159–79.
20. Eight Arabic recensions of the text are referred to by Ḥamza al-Iṣfahānī alone, including the two earliest translations of the *Khudāynāmag*, the first by Ibn al-Muqaffa', the second by Muḥammad b. Jahm al-Barmakī, probably a client of the Barmakids. On the Arabic translation of *Khudāynāmag* see W. Barthold, 'Zur Geschichte des persischen Epos', *Zeitschrift der Deutschen Morgenländischen Gesellschaft* xcviii (1944), pp. 144ff.; Christensen, *L'Iran sous les Sassanides* (Copenhagen, 1944; repr. Osnabrück, 1971), pp. 59ff. Bīrūnī and Bal'amī

name other translations: see Christensen, *L'Iran sous les Sassanides*, p. 61. See also Khaleghi-Motlagh, 'Az *Shāhnāma* tā *Khudāynāma*', pp. 34–7.

21. See Ḥamza Iṣfahānī, *Tārīkh sinī mulūk al-arḍ wa-l-anbīyā*, pp. 15, 19, 43.
22. See Yarshater, 'Iranian national history', pp. 359–66.
23. Barthold, 'Zur Geschichte des persischen Epos', pp. 121–57; Christensen, *L'Iran sous les Sassanides*, pp. 59ff.; Nöldeke, *Das iranische Nationalepos* (Berlin/Leipzig, 1920); Shahbazi, 'On the *Xwadāy-Nāmag*', pp. 218–23; Yarshater, 'Iranian national history'; Boyce, 'Middle Persian literature', pp. 31–66; Tafaḍḍulī, *Tārīkh-i adabīyāt-i Irān pīsh az Islām*, pp. 269–74; M. Macuch, 'Pahlavi literature', in Ronald E. Emmerick and M. Macuch (eds), *The Literature of Pre-Islamic Iran: Companion Volume I to A History of Persian Literature* (London/New York, 2009), pp. 172–7.
24. See Boyce, 'Middle Persian literature', pp. 31–66; E. Yarshater, 'Iranian national history', pp. 359–66; Macuch, 'Pahlavi literature', pp. 172–6.
25. See Shahbazi, 'Historiography: ii. Pre-Islamic period', *EIr* xii/3, pp. 325–30. See also Yarshater, 'Iran: iii. Traditional history' in *EIr* xiii/3, pp. 299–307.
26. Yarshater, 'Chirā dar *Shāhnāma* az pādishāhān-i mād va hakhāmanishī dhikrī nīst?', *Shāhnāma-Shināsī* (Tehran, 1357/1978), vol. I, pp. 268–301.
27. Yarshater, 'Were the Sasanians heirs to the Achaemenids?' in *Academia Nazionale dei Lincei: Problemi attuali de scienza e cultura: Atti congegno internazionale sul themo La Persia nel medioevo* (Rome, 1971), pp. 517–31.
28. Shahbazi, 'Early Sasanians' claim to Achaemenid heritage', *Nāma-yi Irān-i Bāstān, The International Journal of Ancient Iranian Studies* i/1 (2001), p. 69.
29. Touraj Daryaee, 'National history or Keyanid history? The nature of Sasanid Zoroastrian historiography', *Iranian Studies* xxviii/3–4 (1995), pp. 129–41; Daryaee, 'The construction of the past in Late Antique Persia', *Historia: Zeitschrift für Alte Geschichte* lv/4 (2006), pp. 493–503, especially pp. 500–1.
30. Daryaee, 'Memory and history: the construction of the past in Late Antique Persia', *Nāme-ye Irān-e Bāstān, The International Journal of Ancient Iranian Studies* i/2 (2001–2), pp. 12–13.
31. Daryaee, 'National history or Keyanid history?', pp. 129–41.
32. Boyce, 'Some remarks on the transmission of the Kayanian heroic cycle', in R. N. Frye et al. (eds), *Serta Cantabrigiensia* (Wiesbaden, 1954), pp. 45–52; Boyce, 'The Parthian *Gōsān* and Iranian minstrel tradition', *Journal of the Royal Asiatic Society* lxxxix/1–2 (1957), pp. 10–45.
33. Tafaḍḍulī, *Tārīkh-i adabīyāt-i Irān pīsh az Islām*, p. 271.
34. Christensen discerns two traditions: a religious one and a national one. See A. Christensen, *Les Kayanides* (Copenhagen, 1931), pp. 35ff.; Christensen, *Les Gestes des Rois dans les traditions de l'Iran antique* (Paris, 1936), pp. 33ff. See also Yarshater, 'Iranian national history', pp. 395ff.
35. Macuch, 'Pahlavi Literature', p. 176.
36. P. Pourshariati, 'The Parthians and the production of the canonical *Shāhnāmas*: of Pahlavī, Pahlavānī and the Pahlav', in Henning Börm and Josef Wiesehöfer

(eds), *Commutatio et Contentio: Studies in the Late Roman, Sasanian, and Early Islamic Near East in Memory of Zeev Rubin* (Düsseldorf, 2010), pp. 347–92.

37. On these two *Shāhnāmas* and their compilation see Chapter 3.
38. Pourshariati, 'The Parthians and the production of the canonical *Shāhnāmas*', p. 347.
39. The Parthian coins were stamped in the Greek language, and the epithet *philhellene* remained in use until the end of the Parthian period. See D. Sellwood, 'Parthian coins', in E. Yarshater (ed.), *Cambridge History of Iran* (Cambridge, 1983), vol. III/1, pp. 279–98; Sellwood, *Introduction to the Coinage of Parthia*, 2nd edn (London, 1980).
40. Huyse, 'Parthian inscriptions', in R. E. Emmerick and M. Macuch (eds), *The Literature of Pre-Islamic Iran* (London/New York, 2009), p. 86.
41. Quoted from Shayegan, *Arsacids and Sasanians*, pp. 294–5.
42. For more information on this manuscript see Jamasp-Asa and Nawabi, *Ms. MU29. Stories of Kersāsp, Tahmurasp & Jamshed, Gelshah & Other Texts*, Pahlavi Codices and Iranian Researches 26 (Shiraz, 1976) cited in Touraj Daryaee, 'Alexander and the Arsacids in the manuscript *MU29*', *Dabir, Digital Archive of Brief Notes & Iran Review* i/1 (2015), p. 8, n. 7.
43. Daryaee, 'Alexander and the Arsacids in the manuscript *MU29*', pp. 8–10.
44. On the Pahlavi texts where Alexander appears see Shayegan, *Arsacids and Sasanians*, pp. 295–8; Daryaee, '*Imitatio Alexandri* and its impact on Late Arsacid, Early Sasanian and Middle Persian literature', *Electrum* xii (2007), pp. 93–5.
45. See Boyce, 'Parthian writings and literature', *Cambridge History of Iran*, ed. E. Yarshater (London/New York, 1983), vol. III/2, pp. 1154–5.
46. See Boyce, 'The Parthian *Gōsān* and Iranian minstrel tradition'.
47. Regarding these discrepancies see Khaleghi-Motlagh, 'Jāy-i Rustam ... va Iskandar dar *Khudāynāma*', pp. 19–24.
48. See Macuch, 'Pahlavi literature', pp. 175–7.
49. See Gutas, *Greek Thought, Arabic Culture*, pp. 25–7, 54–5; C. E. Bosworth, 'The Persian impact on Arabic literature', in A. F. L. Beeston et al. (eds), *Arabic Literature to the End of the Umayyad Period* (Cambridge, 1983), pp. 483–96.
50. See Gutas, *Greek Thought, Arabic Culture*, pp. 54–7.
51. According to Boyce, this word might refer to the Middle Persian word *ahr*, which means 'strong'. Mario Grignaschi has discussed this issue. See M. Grignaschi, 'La *Nihāyatu-l-'arab fī akhbāri-l-Furs wa-l-'arab* et les *Siyaru mulūki-l-'ağam* du Ps. Ibn-al-Muqaffa'', p. 100.
52. Dīnawarī, *Akhbār al-ṭiwāl*, pp. 28ff.
53. For a discussion concerning all of these accounts see El-Sayed M. Gad, 'Al-Ṭabari's tales of Alexander: history and romance', in R. Stoneman, K. Erickson and I. Netton (eds), *The Alexander Romance in Persia and the East* (Groningen, 2012), pp. 219–31; Southgate, *Iskandarnamah: A Persian Medieval Alexander-Romance*, Appendix III, pp. 193–4.

54. Ṭabarī, *Tārīkh*, vol. II, p. 692. According to Firdawsī, Alexander's mother was named Nāhīd. See Firdawsī, *Shāhnāma*, vol. V, p. 521.
55. Ṭabarī, *Tārīkh*, vol. II, pp. 692ff.
56. See Khaleghi-Motlagh, *Yāddāsht-hā-yi Shāhnāma* (Tehran, 1389/2010), vol. II, p. 353.
57. *Nihāya*, p. 99. The herb is also called 'iskandar' in the *Shāhnāma* of Firdawsī and the *Ghurar* of Tha'ālibī.
58. Firdawsī, *Shāhnāma*, vol. V, p. 523.
59. Stoneman, *A Life in Legend*, p. 25.
60. Grignaschi, 'La *Nihāyatu-l-'arab fī akhbāri-l-Furs wa-l-'arab* et les *Siyaru mulūki-l-'ağam* du Ps. Ibn-al-Muqaffa'', pp. 100–1.
61. Arthur George Warner and Edmond Warner (trans.), *Shahnama of Firdausi* (London, 1912), vol. VI, p. 19.
62. Dihkhudā, *Lughatnāma {Encyclopaedic Dictionary}*, ed. M. Mu'īn and J. Shahīdī (Tehran, 1993–4), vol. VIII, p. 12157.
63. Bīrūnī, *The Chronology of Ancient Nations*, trans. C. Edward Sachau (London, 1879), pp. 44, 48.
64. According to Khaleghi-Motlagh, King Bahman Ardaxshīr represents both Artaxerxes I and Cyrus the Great. See Khaleghi-Motlagh, 'Bahman', *EIr* iii/5, pp. 489–90.
65. When Gushtāsp, Isfandīyār's father, went to Rūm, he married Caesar's daughter, Katāyūn, and from this union Isfandīyār was born. See Firdawsī, *Shāhnāma*, vol. V, pp. 12–24.
66. God's adversary in the Zoroastrian religion; see J. Duchesne-Guillemin, 'Ahriman', *EIr* i/6–7, pp. 670–3.
67. Sh. Shahbazi, 'Haft sīn', *EIr* xi/5, p. 525.
68. On these Greek festivals see M. Detienne, *The Gardens of Adonis: Spices in Greek Mythology*, trans. Janet Lloyd (London, 1977), pp. 80, 93.
69. D. Davis, *Panthea's Children: Hellenistic Novels and Medieval Persian Romances* (New York, 2002), p. 76, n. 59.
70. See Muhammad A. Dandamaev and Vladimir G. Lukonin, *The Culture and Social Institutions of Ancient Iran*, trans. Philip L. Kohl (Cambridge, 1989), p. 296.
71. Davis, *Panthea's Children*, p. 77.
72. In the *Shāhnāma*, there is no reference to the goddess. However, her role in relation to Alexander is obvious in a popular romance known as the *Dārābnāma* of Ṭarṭūsī. Regarding the goddess Ānāhītā and Alexander the Great in the *Dārābnāma* see W. Hanaway, 'Anahita and Alexander', *Journal of the American Oriental Society* cii/2 (1982), pp. 285–95.
73. Ṭabarī, *Tārīkh*, vol. II, p. 666.
74. See Touraj Daryaee, '*Imitatio Alexandri* and its impact on Late Arsacid, Early Sasanian and Middle Persian literature', *Electrum* (Krakow, 2007), vol. XII, pp. 89–97, especially pp. 92–3. The effect of *Imitatio Alexandri* on the Middle Persian literature is also studied in Shayegan, *Arsacids and Sasanians*, pp. 295–8.

75. Ṭabarī, *Tārīkh*, vol. II, pp. 692ff.
76. Firdawsī, *Shāhnāma*, vol. V, p. 532.
77. See Budge, *The History of Alexander*, p. 31.
78. Firdawsī, *Shāhnāma*, vol. V, p. 521.
79. Ibid., p. 533.
80. Ṭabarī, *Tārīkh*, vol. II, p. 694ff.; Tha'ālibī, *Ghurar*, pp. 403ff., *Nihāya*, pp. 116ff. Bal'amī, in his *History* (vol. I, pp. 485ff.), and Niẓāmī Ganjavī, in his *Sharafnāma*, also dedicate a whole passage to the exchange of symbolic gifts. Instead of 'mustard seeds', Niẓāmī and Bal'amī have *sepandān* (wild rue).
81. Budge, *The History of Alexander*, vol. I, chapters XXXVI–XLI.
82. *Nihāya*, pp. 116ff.
83. Ṭabarī, *The History of al-Ṭabarī*, vol. IV, pp. 89–90.
84. See Budge, *The History of Alexander*, vol. I, chapters XXXVI–XLI, pp. 46–54.
85. Ṭabarī, *The History of al-Ṭabarī*, vol. IV, p. 89.
86. Ibid., pp. 90–3.
87. This will be discussed further in the next chapter, where the *Shāhnāma* provides more proofs of the authenticity and antiquity of its source.
88. See Francis Joseph Steingass, *A Comprehensive Persian–English Dictionary* (London, 1963), p. 403.
89. W. J. van Bekkum (ed. and trans.), *A Hebrew Alexander Romance according to MS London, Jews' College no. 145*, Orientalia Lovaniensia analecta 47 (Leuven, 1992), pp. 16–33; W. J. van Bekkum, *A Hebrew Alexander Romance according to MS Héb. 671.5 Paris, Bibliothèque nationale*, Hebrew Language and Literature Series 1 (Groningen, 1994).
90. W. J. van Bekkum, 'Medieval Hebrew versions of the Alexander Romance', in A. Welkenhuysen, H. Braet, W. Verbeke (eds), *Medieval Antiquity* (Leuven, 1995), p. 296.
91. W. J. van Bekkum, *A Hebrew Alexander Romance according to MS Héb. 671.5 Paris, Bibliothèque nationale*, p. 32 (fol. 249a, line 6).
92. Ibn al-Faqīh, *Bibliotheca Geographorum Arabicorum*, vol. V, p. 219.
93. Indeed, it is not incorrect to say that the battle took place in al-Jazīra, which is Arbela. This indicates that Ṭabarī's source contained more reliable historical information than any other Arabic account. In concordance with Ṭabarī, Bal'amī (and Niẓāmī) also mentioned the land of Jazīra (*Mūṣul*), 'which is near the banks of the Tigris', as is the first battlefield. See Bal'amī, *Tārīkh-i Bal'amī, Tarjoma-yi Tārīkh-i Ṭabarī*, ed. M. T. Bahār and M. P. Gunābādī, 2nd edn (Tehran, 1353/1974), vol. II, p. 696.
94. Firdawsī, *Shāhnāma*, vol. V, p. 541.
95. In total, four battles take place: the first by the Euphrates over eight days; the second in a vast camp over three days; the third near Iṣṭakhr (Persepolis), where Dārā is defeated and flees to Kirmān; and the fourth where Dārā is murdered by his own guards. See Firdawsī, *Shāhnāma*, vol. V, pp. 540–54.
96. Firdawsī, *Shāhnāma*, vol. VI, p. 392.

97. Budge, *The History of Alexander*, pp. 79–80.
98. Firdawsī, *Shāhnāma*, vol. V, p. 554.
99. Ṭabarī, *The History of al-Ṭabarī*, IV, p. 91.
100. *Nihāya*, p. 121; Firdawsī, *Shāhnāma*, vol. V, p. 554.
101. Dīnawarī, *Akhbār al-ṭiwāl*, p. 32; Ṭabarī, *Tārīkh*, vol. II, p. 696; Tha'ālibī, *Ghurar*, p. 408.
102. The names in the Greek Pseudo-Callisthenes are Besso and Ariobarzanes, satraps of Darius (II, 20). In the Syriac Pseudo-Callisthenes, their names are Bagiz and Anabdeh (II, XII). No other source names the murderers.
103. He adds that it is ironic that a murderer should bear such a name. See Khaleghi-Motlagh, *Yāddāsht-hā-yi Shāhnāma* (Tehran, 1389/2010), vol. II, p. 364.
104. Bīrūnī, *Chronology*, p. 44.
105. Ṭabarī, *The History*, vol. IV, pp. 91–2.
106. *Nihāya*, p. 123.
107. According to Arrian, Darius was already dead when Alexander found him. Alexander did not find Darius alive, as the *Romance* describes.
108. Bīrūnī, *Chronology*, p. 44.
109. Stoneman, *The Greek Alexander Romance*, p. 109.
110. Firdawsī, *Shāhnāma*, vol. V, pp. 555–6. Bīrūnī affirmed that Alexander called Dārā 'brother'. See Chapter 4 of *Chronology*, p. 44.
111. However, this scene can be an alleged feature of Greek tragedy; for similar examples see David Konstan, *Pity Transformed* (London, 2001), especially Chapter 3: 'Pity and power', p. 91, n. 36.
112. Alexander did indeed marry a woman called Roxana, but nearly three years after the death of Darius (in the spring 327 BC), and she was not the daughter of Darius, but of a Bactrian chieftain named Oxyartes.
113. Ṭabarī, *The History*, vol. IV, p. 91.
114. Firdawsī, *Shāhnāma*, vol. V, p. 559. Tha'ālibī also makes a brief mention of preserving the Zoroastrian texts and faith. See Tha'ālibī, *Ghurar*, p. 411. On the interpretation of this passage in the *Shāhnāma* see Shayegan, *Arsacids and Sasanians*, pp. 299–303.
115. This is developed by Niẓāmī in the *Sharafnāma*, the first part of his *Iskandarnāma*. See Chapter 4.
116. Ṭabarī, *The History*, vol. IV, p. 93.
117. See Shayegan, *Arsacids and Sasanians*, pp. 295–8; and the appendix in Daryaee, '*Imitatio Alexandri*', pp. 93–5.
118. Quoted in S. M. Afnan, *Philosophical Terminology in Arabic and Persian* (Leiden, 1964), pp. 77–8.
119. Quoted in D. Pingree, *The Thousands of Abū Ma'shar* (London, 1968), pp. 9–10.
120. Ḥamza Iṣfahānī, *Tārīkh sinī mulūk al-arḍ wa-l-anbīyā*, p. 24.
121. Daryaee, '*Imitatio Alexandri*', p. 90.
122. Ṭabarī, *The History*, vol. IV, p. 92.

123. On the Middle Persian version of this tale see T. Daryaee, 'Šegafty va Barjestegī-ye Sīstān, Matn-e be zabān-e pahlavī', *Iranshenāsī* viii/3 (1996), pp. 534–42. The *Shāhnāma* of Firdawsī provides the epic narrative of this division of the world. See Firdawsī, *Shāhnāma*, vol. I, pp. 270–80.
124. See Firdawsī, *Shāhnāma*, vol. V, pp. 562–5.
125. Tafaḍḍulī, *Tārīkh adabīyāt-i Irān pīsh az Islām*, pp. 238–9.
126. For instance, Ṭabarī provides Khusraw I Anūshirvān's speech (*Tārīkh*, vol. I, pp. 896–7); Dīnawarī reports the speech of Hurmuz, Khusraw I's son (*Akhbār al-ṭiwāl*, p. 77) and the *Nihāya* contains Ardaxshīr's speech (*Nihāya*, pp. 193–6).
127. Dīnawarī, *Akhbār al-ṭiwāl*, pp. 34–9.
128. Ṭabarī, *Tārīkh*, vol. II, pp. 696ff.
129. *Nihāya*, pp. 117ff.
130. Budge, *The History of Alexander*, p. 142.
131. Dīnawarī, *Akhbār al-ṭiwāl*, pp. 39–40.
132. See Shayegan, *Arsacids and Sasanians*, pp. 295–7; Daryaee, '*Imitatio Alexandri*', pp. 90, 93–5.
133. See Shahbazi, 'Arsacids: vi. Arsacid chronology in traditional history', *EIr* ii/5 (New York, 1987), p. 542. See also M. Morony, 'Mulūk al-ṭawā'if: i. In pre-Islamic Persia', EI^2 vii, pp. 551–2.
134. Firdawsī, *Shāhnāma*, vol. VI, pp. 116–18.
135. Budge, *The History of Alexander*, pp. 142–3.
136. Guidi, 'Chronicon anonymum', *Chronica Minora* (Paris, 1903), vol. I, pp. 15–39 (Syriac text); vol. II, pp. 15–32 (Latin trans.), pp. 28–9.
137. Yarshater, 'Iranian national history', p. 377.
138. This summary of Alexander's deeds is also found in the *Shāhnāma* of Firdawsī, the best representation of the *Khudāynāmag* tradition. See Chapter 3.
139. Khaleghi-Motlagh, 'Az *Shāhnāma* tā *Khudaynāmag*', pp. 29–30; Khaleghi-Motlagh, 'Jāy-i Rustam ... va Iskandar dar *Khudāynāmag*', pp. 19–20.
140. Tafaḍḍulī, *Tārīkh-i adabīyāt-i Irān pīsh az Islām*, pp. 270–1; Boyce, 'Middle Persian literature', p. 59.
141. Yarshater points out that the fame of the Alexander legend was due to the relations between the Iranians and Greeks living in Greek cities in Asia Minor during the Parthian period. See Yarshater, 'Chirā az pādishāhān-i mād va hakhāmanishī dar *Shāhnāma* dhikrī nīst', p. 194. See also Shayegan, *Arsacids and Sasanians*, p. 306.
142. Agathias, *The Histories*, trans. J. D. Frendo (Berlin, 1975), II, p. 31. See also Daryaee, *Sasanian Persia*, p. 30.
143. Ḥafiẓ's verses, cited in the epigraph of this chapter, explain this subject very well: Alexander's story was a means for remembering what happened to Darius III. It was regarded as a part of Persian history.
144. Stoneman, *A Life in Legend*, p. 31; Daryaee, '*Imitatio Alexandri*', p. 89.
145. Budge, *The History of Alexander*, p. lx.
146. See C. Ciancaglini, 'The Syriac version of the Alexander Romance', *Le Muséon, Revue d'Études Orientales* cxiv/1–2 (2001), p. 139.

147. Stoneman, *A Life in Legend*, p. 32; Daryaee, '*Imitatio Alexandri*', p. 90.
148. It is possible that the Syriac version was prepared for the Nestorians and a non-Zoroastrian audience, and that the Middle Persian translation was a courtly version that was used in Persian historiography in order to create a continuous history of the Persian Empire.
149. See Doufikar-Aerts, *Alexander Magnus Arabicus*, pp. 77–9.
150. *Nihāya*, p. 110; See also Doufikar-Aerts, *Alexander Magnus Arabicus*, p. 30.
151. This anonymous work, written in the eleventh century, but subsequently altered with later additions, provides some popular tales about the ancient epic from the Sīstān cycle. See M. T. Bahār (ed.), *Tārīkh-i Sīstān* (Tehran, 1314/1935; 2nd edn 1352/1973), pp. j–ṭ (introduction).
152. The word in Latin is actually *arx*.
153. *Tārīkh-i Sīstān*, p. 11.

Chapter 3 Alexander the Great in the *Shāhnāma* of Firdawsī

1. Ṣā'ib Tabrīzī, *Dīvān*, ed. Muḥammad Qahrimān (Tehran, 1370/1991), vol. VI, pp. 3011–12. This verse was translated by Dr Leonard Lewisohn.
2. On the historical value of the *Shāhnāma* see J. S. Meisami, 'The past in service of the present: two views of history in medieval Persia', *Poetics Today* xiv/2 (1993), pp. 252–72.
3. J. S. Meisami, 'History as literature', in Ch. Melville (ed.), *A History of Persian Literature*, Vol. X: *Persian Historiography* (London/New York, 2012), pp. 8–10.
4. See Yarshater, 'Iranian national history', in E. Yarshater (ed.), *Cambridge History of Iran* (Cambridge, 1983), vol. III/1, p. 361.
5. Other works on Alexander's legend that antedate the *Shāhnāma* normally contain a summary and a brief mention of motifs from the Pseudo-Callisthenes tradition, as discussed in Chapter 2.
6. Firdawsī, *Shāhnāma*, vol. V, pp. 518–65 and vol. VI, pp. 3–129.
7. D. Davis, 'The aesthetics of the historical sections of the *Shahnama*', in Ch. Melville (ed.), *Shahnama Studies* (Cambridge, 2006), vol. I, p. 115.
8. See M. Qazwīnī, 'Muqaddama-yi qadīm-i *Shāhnāma*', *Bīst Maqāla* ii (1313/1934), pp. 20ff.; V. Minorsky, 'The older preface to the *Shāhnāma*', *Studi Orientalistici in Onore di Giorgio Levi Della Vida* (Roma, 1956), vol. II, pp. 159–79; Th. Nöldeke, 'Ein Beitrag zur Schahname-Forschung', *Hizāra-yi Firdawsī*, 2nd edn (Tehran, 1362/1983), pp. 58–63; A. Khaṭībī, 'Yikī nāma būd az gah-i bāstān: justārī dar shinākht-i manba'-i *Shāhnāma*-yi Firdawsī', *Nāma-yi Farhangistān* iii/5 (1381/2002), pp. 54–73.
9. See Khaleghi-Motlagh, 'Dar pīrāmūn-i manābi'-i Firdawsī', *Irānshināsī* iii (1377/1998), pp. 512–13.
10. See J. Khaleghi-Motlagh, 'Az *Shāhnāma* tā *Khudāynāma*', *Nāme-yi Irān-i Bāstān, The International Journal of Ancient Iranian Studies* vii/1–2 (2007–8), pp. 3–119.

11. Olga M. Davidson, *Poet and Hero in the Persian Book of Kings* (London, 1994); Davis, 'The problem of Ferdowsi's sources', *Journal of the American Oriental Society* cxvi (1996), pp. 48–57.
12. F. de Blois, *Persian Literature, A Bio-Bibliographical Survey: Poetry of the Pre-Mongol Period* (London/New York, 2004), vol. V, p. 110. De Blois also affirms: 'the *Shahname* as it was written by Firdausi, was not oral poetry, but book-literature. However, almost as soon as it was written down, it most certainly did turn into oral poetry on the tongues of the rhapsodists, who developed and elaborated the epic orally and have continued to do so to the present. The tremendous degree of disagreement already between the oldest manuscripts of the poem cannot be explained purely in terms of the carelessness and unscrupulousness of generations of scribes. It is quite clear that from a very early date the scribal and oral textual traditions have constantly influenced one another. But this is an oral tradition which does not (as is assumed to have been the case with the Homeric poems) culminate and end with a book. In Iran the book is the point of departure.' See De Blois, *Persian Literature: A Bio-Bibliographical Survey*. Vol. V, Part 1: *Poetry to ca. AD 1100* (London, 1992), p. 58.
13. Curiously, this motif is not in the Greek *Alexander Romance*. However, the tribute of golden eggs is mentioned in one scene (Pseudo-Callisthenes, I, 23). See Stoneman, *The Greek Alexander Romance*, p. 54: 'One hundred golden eggs ... each weighing 20 pounds of solid gold'. According to Herodotus (V. 17–20), Xerxes's ambassadors demand that Amintas, the Macedonian king, pay tribute to the Persians. Plutarch (*Alex.* 5, 1) affirms that the Persian king demands tribute, considering himself the king of all lands by divine right.
14. Aristotle is mentioned three times in the *Shāhnāma*: the first time at Alexander's ascent to the throne, as his counsellor; the second time almost at the end of the story, when Alexander sends him a letter telling him that he wants to kill the Persian nobles; and the third and last time, where Aristotle is one of the philosophers who speaks at Alexander's tomb.
15. There is a similar scene in the Greek *Alexander Romance* (Pseudo-Callisthenes, I, 23). However, Philip is still alive in this scene in the Greek Pseudo-Callisthenes. For an English translation see Stoneman, *The Greek Alexander Romance*, pp. 54–5.
16. Stoneman's commentary on the *Alexander Romance* (II, 15, 5–6) gives several parallels: see Richard Stoneman, *Il Romanzo di Alessandro*, trans. Tristano Gargiulo (Milan, 2012), vol. II, p. 399.
17. Exactly the same scene features in the Greek *Alexander Romance* (Pseudo-Callisthenes, II, 14).
18. The letters are an important component of the *Alexander Romance*, and have been since its origins. There are some papyri containing the correspondence between Alexander and Darius, which demonstrates the antiquity of these letters as a component of the *Alexander Romance*. See Papyrus Italian Society 1285, Florence, edited by Dino Pieraccioni in 1951, and the Papyrus

Hamburg 129, studied in Merkelbach, *Die Quellen des griechischen Alexanderromans* (Munich, 1954), pp. 193ff.

19. There is also a similar letter to Porus in the Pseudo-Callisthenes (II, 19).
20. According to Khaleghi-Motlagh, 'Janūsyār must be the term gyān-abespār in Pahlavi, which means guard. The fact that Darius is killed by his own guard is an irony.' See Khaleghi-Motlagh, *Yāddāsht-hā-yi Shāhnāma {Notes on the Shāhnāma}*, vol. II, p. 364.
21. In the Greek *Alexander Romance*, the two assassins are Darius's satraps, Bessus and Ariobarzanes (Pseudo-Callisthenes, II, 20).
22. On the moralistic content of Alexander and Darius's dialogue in this passage of the *Shāhnāma* see Charles-Henri de Fouchécour, *Moralia: Les notions morales dans la littérature persane du 3/9 au 7/13 siècle* (Paris, 1986), pp. 57–79.
23. There is a similar passage in the Greek *Alexander Romance* (Pseudo-Callisthenes, II, 20), without the Persian elements. Shayegan studied this scene of the *Shāhnāma* in parallel with the Pahlavi texts. See Shayegan, *Arsacids and Sasanians*, pp. 299–300.
24. On the content of this letter and its comparison with Pahlavi texts see Shayegan, *Arsacids and Sasanians*, pp. 300–3. There is a similar letter from Alexander to the Persians in the Greek *Alexander Romance* (Pseudo-Callisthenes, II, 21).
25. There is a similar passage in the Greek *Alexander Romance* (Pseudo-Callisthenes, II, 21).
26. In the Greek *Alexander Romance*, Alexander writes letters to Darius's mother, wife and daughter (Pseudo-Callisthenes, II, 22).
27. In the Greek *Alexander Romance*, Alexander writes a letter to his mother and asks her to send back the jewellery, garments and robes of Darius's mother and wife to Roxane as bridal gifts on his behalf (Pseudo-Callisthenes, II, 22). See also Stoneman, *The Greek Alexander Romance*, p. 114.
28. According to Firdawsī, this tale came from a Pahlavi source (*Shāhnāma*, vol. VI, p. 11). In this chapter we will see that this story was likely to be an independent tale integrated into the Persian Alexander romances through a pre-Islamic Persian source.
29. There is a similar passage in the Greek version (Pseudo-Callisthenes, III, 2).
30. A similar passage in the Greek version (Pseudo-Callisthenes, III, 3) reads: 'Alexander had all the bronze statues he possessed and all the armour he had taken as booty from the soldiers heated up thoroughly until they were red-hot, and then set up in front of the army like a wall.' Stoneman, *The Greek Alexander Romance*, p. 129.
31. There is a similar passage in the Greek version (Pseudo-Callisthenes, III, 4).
32. This passage may be an imitation of Alexander's journey to Jerusalem as told by sub-recension γ.
33. In the Greek version she is the Queen of Meroe (Pseudo-Callisthenes, III, 18).
34. Pseudo-Callisthenes, III, 18–23.
35. There is a similar passage in the Greek version (Pseudo-Callisthenes, III, 5–6).

36. In the Greek version, this is a letter to Aristotle about the wonders of India (Pseudo-Callisthenes, III, 7–16) added as Supplement I in Stoneman's English translation (*The Greek Alexander Romance*, pp. 181–5). On the *mirabilia* genre see Chapter 5.
37. This passage is based on the Syriac *Alexander Romance* (Budge, *The History of Alexander the Great*, vol. III, p. 99). The Syriac version describes these creatures as 'the people whose feet are twisted'.
38. This passage is also based on the Syriac version (Budge, *The History of Alexander*, pp. 107–8). In the Syriac version there are two oxen instead of five.
39. There is a similar passage in Alexander's journey to the land of the Amazons in the Greek Pseudo-Callisthenes (III, 25–6).
40. This passage is in the β-recension, sub-recension γ, and manuscript *L*, but absent from the α-recension (see Chapter 1). This passage is also found in the Syriac *Poem* edited by Budge (*The History of Alexander*, pp. 163–76).
41. This passage is based on the Syriac sources. See Budge, *The History of Alexander*, pp. 176–200.
42. This passage may be based on a scene in the Greek version (Pseudo-Callisthenes, III, 28) in which Alexander goes to the palace of Cyrus, and on the top of a high mountain he sees a circular temple ringed by a hundred columns of sapphire. See Stoneman, *The Greek Alexander Romance*, pp. 147–8.
43. In the Greek version there is a similar passage (Pseudo-Callisthenes, III, 17).
44. This is based on the Syriac version (Budge, *The History of Alexander*, vol. III, pp. 109ff., VI).
45. The older Indian Sindhu, the name for the region around the lower course of the Indus River. On Alexander's campaigns in this region see Pierre H. L. Eggermont, *Alexander's Campaigns in Sind and Baluchistan and the Siege of the Brahmin Town of Harmatelia* (Leuven, 1975).
46. There is a similar passage in the Greek version (Pseudo-Callisthenes, III, 30) in a letter to Olympias. See Stoneman, *The Greek Alexander Romance*, pp. 148–9.
47. In the Greek version, Alexander writes a similar letter to his mother (Pseudo-Callisthenes, III, 33). This part of the *Shāhnāma* contains some elements from Alexander's will (Pseudo-Callisthenes, III, 32), such as the destiny of Roxane's child and how the funeral is to be organised.
48. In the Greek version it is Ptolemy who suggests consulting an oracle of the Babylonian Zeus. The oracle says that Alexander should be buried in Memphis, Egypt (Pseudo-Callisthenes, III, 34).
49. This part was originally an independent source in Syriac; see Chapter 1 of this book and also S. P. Brock, 'The laments of philosophers over Alexander in Syriac', *Journal of Semitic Studies* xv (1970), p. 207. There is a similar passage in Niẓāmī's *Iqbālnāma*; see Chapter 5.
50. The Greek *Alexander Romance* also finishes with a similar passage (Pseudo-Callisthenes, III, 35) in which, 'Alexander lived thirty-two years. He was king for ten years. He made war for twelve years. He overcame twenty-two

barbarian nations and fourteen Greek peoples. He founded twelve cities.' See Stoneman, *The Greek Alexander Romance*, p. 158.

51. Some of the common related legends that are also told by Niẓāmī in his *Iskandarnāma* will be discussed in depth and detail in Chapters 4 and 5 in order to avoid repeating them, such as the stories of the Water of Life and the Valley of Diamonds, for example.
52. Some scholars have devoted studies to the similarity between the two figures. See Ismaelpūr, *Barrisī taṭbīqī shakhsīyat-i Āshīl va Isfandīyār* (Teheran, 1388/2009); Omīdsālār, 'Isfandīyār va Ashīl', *Irānshināsī* iv (1377/1998), pp. 734–44; Amīrqāsimī, 'Ashīl va Isfandiyār du hamzād-i usṭūriī', *Adabiyāt va zabān-hā* lxxxvi/7 (1368/1989), pp. 433–48.
53. Firdawsī, *Shāhnāma*, vol. V, pp. 12–24: Isfandīyār's father Gushtāsp is angry at his father, so he goes to Rūm, where he marries the Caesar's daughter, Katāyūn, who falls in love with him through a dream.
54. Firdawsī, *Shāhnāma*, vol. VI, p. 98.
55. Firdawsī, *Shāhnāma*, vol. V, p. 533.
56. These parts were discussed in the previous chapter.
57. Firdawsī, *Shāhnāma*, vol. V, p. 522:

    دلای رومی به مهد اندرون   سکوبا و راهب ورا رهنمون

58. Ibid.,

    سقف خوب رخ را به دارا سپرد   گهرها به گنجور او برشمرد

59. Firdawsī, *Shāhnāma*, vol. VI, p. 28:

    نشستند و او را به آیین بخواست   به رسم مسیحا و پیوند راست

60. Ibid., p. 69:

    به دین مسیحا و گفتار راست   به داننده کو بر زبانم گواست
    به آیین صلیب بزرگ   به جان و سر شهریار سترگ
    به زنار و شماس و روح القدس

61. Ibid.,

    برادر بود نیک خواهت مرا   به جای صلیب ست گاهت مرا

62. Ibid., p. 123:

    سکوبا بشستش به روشن گلاب   پراگند بر تنش کافور ناب

63. As Qamar Āryān points out, 'as a native of Ṭūs, Firdawsī must have been in touch with the Christian community, which in his time had a quarter of its own, called *kūy-i tarsāyān* ("the Christian town") in the city. Nevertheless, the Christian references in the *Shāhnāma* generally echoed statements and sentiments that the poet found in his sources.' See Qamar Āryān, 'Christianity: vi. In Persian literature', *EIr* v/5, pp. 339–42.
64. See N. Sims-Williams, 'Christian literature in Middle Iranian languages', in Ronald E. Emmerick and Maria Macuch (eds), *The Literature of Pre-Islamic Iran* (London/New York, 2009), pp. 266–70.

65. Tafaḍḍulī, *Tārīkh-i adabīyāt-i Irān pīsh az Islām*, pp. 270–1; Boyce, 'Middle Persian literature', *Iranistik* ii, p. 59.
66. Firdawsī, *Shāhnāma*, vol. VI, p. 11. The story begins with this verse:

    چنین گفت گوینده ی پهلوی (Thus the Pahlavi narrator told ...).

67. On the characteristics of this Arabic romance see Zuwiyya, *Islamic Legends Concerning Alexander the Great* (New York, 2001), pp. 24–7; Doufikar-Aerts, *Alexander Magnus Arabicus*, pp. 35–45.
68. Zuwiyya, *Islamic Legends Concerning Alexander the Great*, p. 25. I would like to thank Dr Zuwiyya for letting me have a copy of 'Umāra's manuscript, Codex London B.M. Add. 5928, ff. 2–81. Although I use the Arabic manuscript to compare 'Umāra's text with the *Shāhnāma*, the English translation of 'Umāra's tale is based on Zuwiyya's translation, which is included as Appendix I in his *Islamic Legends Concerning Alexander the Great*, pp. 163–6.
69. Mas'ūdī, *Murūj al-dhahab wa ma'ādin al-jawhar {Meadows of Gold and Mines of Gems}*, ed. Ch. Pellat (Beirut, 1966), vol. I, pp. 14–23.
70. Tha'ālibī, *Ghurar Akhbār Mulūk al-Fars {Histoire des Rois des Perses}*, ed. and French trans. H. Zotenberg (Paris, 1900), pp. 424–31.
71. According to the edition of Dastur Darab Pashutan (Bombay, 1896–; repr. Tehran 1369/1990). *Kārnāma-yi Ardashīr-i Bābakān*, ed. Muḥammad Javād Mashkūr (Tehran, 1369/1990). The references in this chapter belong to this edition.
72. *Kārnāma*, p. 98.
73. The Kidarities, a dynasty that ruled a residual north Indian kingdom, perhaps in Swat, until AD 477. See E. V. Zeimal, 'The Kidarite Kingdom and Central Asia', in B. A. Litvinsky (ed.), *History of Civilizations in Central Asia* (Paris, 1996), vol. III, pp. 119–33.
74. His name appears as Kidaro on Greco-Bactrian script on Kushano-Sasanian type gold coins. See A. D. H. Bivar, 'Hephthalites', *EIr* xii/2, pp. 198–201.
75. See Frantz Grenet, 'Regional interaction in Central Asia and north-west India in the Kidarite and Hephthalite periods', in N. Sims-Williams (ed.), *Indo-Iranian Languages and Peoples*, Proceedings of the British Academy 116 (London, 2002), pp. 203–5.
76. *Kārnāma*, p. 102.
77. Firdawsī, *Shāhnāma*, vol. VI, pp. 204–5.
78. Nöldeke, *Beiträge zur Geschichte des Alexanderromans*, p. 47.
79. On this character see Beverly Berg, 'Dandamis: an early Christian portrait of Indian asceticism', *Classica et Mediaevalia* xxxi (1970), pp. 269–305.
80. This tale will be studied later in this chapter.
81. Doufikar-Aerts, *Alexander Magnus Arabicus*, p. 22, n. 34.
82. Firdawsī, *Shāhnāma*, vol. VI, p. 11. However, the phrase at the beginning of this story in the *Shāhnāma* ('Thus the Pahlavi narrator said') recalls the manner in which some Buddhist *sutras* ('It is heard thus by me') and Sogdian texts ('It is heard thus') begin. See Y. Yoshida, 'Buddhist literature in Sogdian', in Ronald E. Emmerick and M. Macuch (eds), *The Literature of Pre-Islamic Iran*:

Companion Volume I to *A History of Persian Literature* (London/New York, 2009), p. 312.

83. H. Ziai, 'Dreams and dream interpretation: ii. In the Persian tradition', *EIr* vii/5, pp. 549–51. See also A. Sh. Shahbazi, *Ferdowsi: A Critical Biography* (Costa Mesa, 1991), p. 81n.20.
84. Khaleghi-Motlagh doubted the authenticity of the dreams episode, but as it was included in almost all of the *Shāhnāma* manuscripts, he finally included it in his edition. See Khaleghi-Motlagh, 'Az *Shāhnāma* tā *Khudāynāma*', p. 60. However, a comparison of the dreams mentioned in the *Shāhnāma* with 'Umāra's version demonstrates that the dreams episode was an original part of this story.
85. Khaleghi-Motlagh reads this word as *Kapī* (in Pahlavi *kabig*), which means 'monkey', while in the Moscow edition it is read as *kasī* ('someone'). See Khaleghi-Motlagh, *Yaddāshthā-yi Shāhnāma {Notes on the Shāhnāma}* (Tehran, 1389/2010), vol. III, p. 5.
86. The dreams are numbered in order to be able to compare them more easily with 'Umāra's version. This part of the story is translated in full in the French translation of the *Shāhnāma* by Jules Mohl (Paris, 1877), vol. V/1, pp. 88–97.
87. It is not clear what the fourth religion referred to is. There is no direct mention of it, but it is probably Christianity. Mohl translated 'that benevolent man' into 'Arab', supposing that the fourth religion was Islam, but there is no reference to Islam nor is an Islamic phrase used here.
88. Zuwiyya, *Islamic Legends Concerning Alexander the Great*, Appendix I, pp. 163–4.
89. In this regard see 'A. Parīsh-rūy, *Barābar-nahād-i Shāhnāma-yi Firdawsī wa Ghurar al-sayr Tha'ālibī* (Tehran, 1390/2011), pp. 643–5.
90. Firdawsī, *Shāhnāma*, vol. VI, p. 26.
91. See Khaleghi-Motlagh, *Yaddāsht-hā-yi Shāhnāma {Notes on the Shāhnāma}*, vol. III, p. 8.
92. Firdawsī, *Shāhnāma*, vol. VI, pp. 30–1.
93. In the *Shāhnāma* there is constant reproach of Alexander's greed; for instance, see Firdawsī, *Shāhnāma*, vol. VI, pp. 30, 78, 95, 101. In the Greek *Alexander Romance* there are various passages in which Alexander is reproached for his avaricious behaviour too; for example, see Pseudo-Callisthenes, III, 6.
94. Firdawsī, *Shāhnāma*, vol. VI, p. 30.
95. Ibid., p. 35. See the English translation of Dick Davis (*The Book of Kings*, p. 482).
96. See M. Murtaḍavī, *Maktab-i Ḥāfiz, Muqaddama bar Ḥāfiz-shināsī* (Tabriz, 1383/2004), pp. 207–25.
97. Niẓāmī, *Sharafnāma*, ed. V. Dastgirdī, re-ed. S. Ḥamīdīyān, 3rd edn (Tehran, 1378), pp. 335–6.
98. Firdawsī, *Shāhnāma*, vol. VI, p. 31.

99. Alexander's encounter with the Brahmans will be discussed later in the present chapter.
100. Ibid., p. 32. There is similar advice in Tha'ālibī's *Ghurar*: Alexander asks the physician: 'What is the best method to preserve someone's health?' The physician replies: 'Eating, drinking and engaging in sexual relations with moderation.'
101. Firdawsī, *Shāhnāma*, vol. VI, pp. 32–3.
102. Ibid., p. 33.
103. It is worth noting a similar argument that Palladius (d. 341) puts into the speech of Dandamis, as follows: 'You indulge your greed. Your greed makes you ill.' See Stoneman, 'Who are the Brahmans? Indian lore and Cynic doctrine in Palladius' *De Brahmanibus* and its models', *Classical Quarterly* xliv/2 (1994), p. 507. For the edition of Palladius's *On the Life of the Brahmans* see J. Duncan M. Derrett, 'The history of Palladius on the races of India and the Brahmans', *Classica et mediaevalia: revue danoise de philologie et d'histoire* xxi (1960), pp. 64–135, especially pp. 100–35. See also Stoneman, *A Life in Legend*, pp. 97–8.
104. Zuwiyya, 'The riddles of kings and philosophers in 'Umāra ibn Zayd's *Qiṣṣat al-Iskandar*', in R. G. Khoury, J. P. Monferrer-Sala and M. J. Viguera Molins (eds), *Legendaria Medievalia* (Cordoba, 2011), p. 293.
105. Khaleghi-Motlagh, *Yāddāshthā-yi Shāhnāma*, vol. III, p. 10.
106. Firdawsī, *Shāhnāma*, vol. VI, p. 33.
107. Zuwiyya, *Islamic Legends Concerning Alexander the Great*, p. 166.
108. Ibid.
109. Zuwiyya, 'The riddles of kings and philosophers in 'Umāra ibn Zayd's *Qiṣṣat al-Iskandar*', p. 294.
110. Khaleghi-Motlagh, 'Az Shāhnāma tā Khodāynāma, Jastārī darbāri-yi Ma'khaz-i Mustaghīm va ghayr-i mustaghīm-i *Shāhnāma*', *Nāma-yi Irān-i Bāstān* vii/1–2 (2007–8), p. 60.
111. See Omidsalar, 'Could al-Tha'alibi have used the *Shāhnāma* as a source?', *Der Islam* lxxv/2 (1998), pp. 338–46.
112. See Stoneman, *A Life in Legend*, pp. 73–7.
113. This theme is also studied by Olga M. Davidson, 'The burden of mortality: Alexander and the dead in Persian epic and beyond', in David Konstan and Kurt A. Raaflaub (eds), *Epic and History* (Oxford, 2010), pp. 212–22.
114. Budge, *The History of Alexander the Great*, p. 99.
115. An imaginary evil anthropoid creature characterised by flexible legs (*pā*) resembling leather straps, which he uses as tentacles to grip and enslave human beings, who then have to carry him on their shoulders or back and labour for him until they die of fatigue. See H. A'lam, 'Davāl-pā(y)', *EIr* vii/2, pp. 128–9.
116. Firdawsī, *Shāhnāma*, vol. II, p. 46.
117. Budge, *The History of Alexander*, pp. 107–8.
118. Firdawsī, *Shāhnāma*, vol. V, pp. 42–7, 232–6.

119. See Daniel Ogden, 'Sekandar, dragon-slayer', in Richard Stoneman, Kyle Erickson and Ian Netton (eds), *The Alexander Romance in Persia and the East* (Groningen, 2012), pp. 277–94.
120. See ibid., pp. 279–83. Ogden claims that 'the motif of the killing of the dragon by feeding it burning or combustible material may well be best considered a folktale motif'; see ibid., p. 290.
121. Ibid., pp. 288–90.
122. See M. Rastigār Fasāyī, *Azhdahā dar asāṭīr-i Irān* (Tehran, 1379/2000), pp. 259–62. See also Christensen, *Les Kayanides* (Copenhagen, 1931), trans. F. N. Tumboowalla (Mumbai, 1993), p. 23.
123. Zaehner, *The Dawn and Twilight of Zoroastrianism* (London, 1961), p. 162.
124. Boyce, *A History of Zoroastrianism: The Early Period* (Leiden, 1975; repr. 1996), vol. I, pp. 90–1. The custom of killing *khrafstra*s is also mentioned by Plutarch (*De Iside et Osiride* 46; *De Invidia et Odio* 3.537B).
125. This is expressed in the *Vidēvdād* (14.5; 18.73), one of the divisions (*nask*) of the *Avesta*, the holy book of Zoroastrianism. The *Vidēvdād* is a priestly code concerning purity laws and demons; see M. Shākī, 'Dād nask', *EIr* vi/5, p. 549.
126. Firdawsī, *Shāhnāma*, vol. VI, p. 80:

بکشتند چندان خراستر که راه
به یکبارگی تنگ شد بر سپاه

127. Stoneman identified this term as a part of Alexander's letter to Aristotle about India. See Stoneman, *A Life in Legend*, p. 74.
128. See Stoneman, *The Greek Alexander Romance*, pp. 183–4.
129. See Khaleghi-Motlagh, 'Farāmarznāma', *Irānnāma* i/1 (1361/1982), p. 43, n. 23.
130. Khaleghi-Motlagh, 'Aždahā: ii. In Persian literature', *EIr* iii, pp. 199–202.
131. According to the Syriac *Alexander Romance*, Alexander slays the dragon with quicklime, bitumen, lead and sulphur. Daniel Ogden points out the similarity of the Syriac version to the story of Daniel slaying a dragon with balls of bitumen, dough and hair, and the killing of the snake-king Sapor (Shāpūr?) through the use of camel hides stuffed with straw and charcoal. See Ogden, 'Sekandar, dragon-slayer', pp. 281–2.
132. Babr-i Bayān might mean 'Tiger of the Indian city of Bayāna' (suggested by Khaleghi-Motlagh, 'Babr-e Bayān', *EIr* iii/3, pp. 324–5). On the other possible meanings of this word see M. Omidsalar, 'Babr-i Bayān', *Irānnāma* iii (1362/1983), pp. 447–58. For an edition of this story see Khaleghi-Motlagh, 'Babr-i Bayān', *Irannāma* vi/1 (1988), pp. 200–27 and *Irannāma* vi/2 (1988), pp. 382–416.
133. 'It may be significant that in Greek mythology, the lion which Hercules strangled (because its skin was invulnerable), and whose skin he thereafter wore (like Rustam's *babr-i Bayān*) on his shoulders, is called the Nemean lion after the place (Nemea) the lion had infested.' Cited from Khaleghi-Motlagh, 'Babr-e Bayān', p. 325.
134. Khaleghi-Motlagh, 'Farāmarznāma', pp. 22–45.

135. Ogden, 'Sekandar, dragon-slayer', p. 290.

136. Asadī Ṭūsī in the *Garshāspnāma* describes some creatures called *sagsārān* ('dog-headed'), with two enormous ears as big as those of an elephant. He also calls them *pīl-gūshān* ('elephant-eared'). See Asadī Ṭūsī, *Garshāspnāma*, ed. Ḥ. Yaghmāyī, 2nd edn (Tehran, 1354/1975), pp. 174–5. In the anonymous prose *Iskandarnāma*, Alexander fights against creatures called *pīl-gūshān* (*Iskandarnāma-yi manthūr*, ed. I. Afshār (Tehran, 1343/1964), pp. 701–4.) These creatures also appear in the *Kūshnāma*. See Irānshāh Ibn abī al-Khayr, *Kūshnāma*, ed. Jalāl Matīnī (Tehran, 1377/1998).

137. Aḥmad Ṭūsī, *'Ajāyib al-makhlūqāt wa gharāyib al-mawjūdāt*, ed. M. Sutūda (Tehran, 1345/1966), p. 169) and Qazwīnī (*'Ajāyib al-makhlūqāt wa gharāyib al-mawjūdāt*, ed. N. Sabūḥī (Tehran, 1340/1961), p. 458) indeed speak of creatures with enormous ears which they use as a bed.

138. See A. Asghar Seyed-Gohrab, F. Doufikar-Aerts and S. McGlinn, *Gog and Magog: The Clans of Chaos in World Literature* (Rozenberg, 2007), p. 58; E. Van Donzel and A. Schmidt, *Gog and Magog in Early Eastern Christian and Islamic Sources, Sallam's Quest for Alexander's Wall* (Leiden, 2002), p. 231.

139. Firdawsī, *Shāhnāma*, vol. VI, pp. 97–8:

بر و سینه و گوش هاشان چو پیل
بخسبند یکی گوش بستر کنند
دگر بر تن خویش چادر کنند

140. See M. Boyce, 'Apocalyptic: i. In Zoroastrianism', *EIr* ii/2, pp. 154–6.

141. For editions and content of this work see M. Boyce, 'Ayādgār ī Jāmāspīg', *EIr* iii/2, pp. 126–7.

142. See Jalāl Matīnī, 'Kūsh yā gūsh?', *Irānnāma* xxi (1366/1987), p. 7; Khaleghi-Motlagh, *Yāddāsht-hā-yi Shāhnāma*, vol. III, p. 28.

143. Firdawsī, *Shāhnāma*, vol. VI, p. 115:

بدان گوش ور گفت: رو
بیاور کسی تا چه بینم نو

144. Stoneman, *The Greek Alexander Romance*, p. 182.

145. Firdawsī, *Shāhnāma*, vol. VI, p.79:

بسان زنان مرد پوشیده روی ...
زبان شان نه تازی و نه خسروی
نه ترکی، نه چینی و نه پهلوی
ز ماهی بدی شان همه خوردنی ...

146. Ibid., p. 115.

147. See R. Stoneman, 'Naked philosophers: the Brahmans in the Alexander historians and the Alexander romance', *Journal of Hellenic Studies* cxv (1995), pp. 99–114.

148. See Appendix II in Van Thiel, *Leben und Taten Alexanders von Makedonien* (Darmstadt, 1983), pp. 242–5. For an English translation see Stoneman, *The Greek Alexander Romance*, pp. 131–3.

149. See Stoneman, 'Who are the Brahmans?', pp. 500–10. On Palladius (d. 341), the Bishop of Helenopolis and his work *On the Life of the Brahmans* see Stoneman, *A Life in Legend*, pp. 97–8; J. Duncan M. Derrett, 'The history of Palladius on the races of India and the Brahmans', pp. 64–135.
150. Firdawsī, *Shāhnāma*, vol. VI, p. 75.
151. These are terms that can be found in Pahlavi writings, for example in the *Dēnkart*. See R. C. Zaehner, *Zurvan: A Zoroastrian Dilemma* (New York, 1972), pp. 173–4.
152. Firdawsī, *Shāhnāma*, vol. VI, p. 77; see also the English translation of Dick Davis (*The Book of Kings*, p. 504).
153. De Fouchécour, *Moralia*, p. 79.
154. Firdawsī, *Shāhnāma*, vol. VI, p. 95.
155. Firdawsī uses the name of the angel as Sirāfīl due to the rhyme of the poem.
156. Firdawsī, *Shāhnāma*, vol. II, pp. 95–7. See also Dick Davis's comparison of these two scenes in the Greek and Persian versions: *Pantheas' Children, Hellenistic Novels and Medieval Persian Romances* (New York, 2002), pp. 81–2. Kay Kāvūs's flight is probably modelled on Alexander's, but its meaning is quite different; see Firuza Melville, 'Kingly flight: Nimrūd, Kay Kāvūs, Alexander, or why the angel has the fish?', *Persica* xxiii (2009–10), p. 129; Melville, 'A flying king', *The Alexander Romance in Persia and the East*, pp. 40–59.
157. Stoneman, *The Greek Alexander Romance*, p. 123.
158. The name of this angel is probably to be traced to the Hebrew *Serāfīm*, as is indicated by the variants *Sarāfīl* and *Sarāfīn*. See A. J. Wensinck, 'Isrāfīl', *EI* [2] iv, p. 211.
159. Firdawsī, *Shāhnāma*, vol. VI, p. 95.
160. Ibid.
161. Ibid., pp. 100–1. The English translation is by Davis, *The Book of Kings*, pp. 516–17.
162. See Pseudo-Callisthenes, III, 28. For an English translation of this passage see Stoneman, *The Greek Alexander Romance*, p. 147.
163. See Stoneman, *A Life in Legend*, p. 187.
164. See Pseudo-Callisthenes, III, 17. For an English translation of this passage see Stoneman, *The Greek Alexander Romance*, pp. 133–5.
165. Firdawsī, *Shāhnāma*, VI, pp. 102–5. For an English translation see Davis, *The Book of Kings*, pp. 517–18.
166. Firdawsī, *Shāhnāma*, VI, pp. 122–3.
167. Tafaḍḍulī, *Tārīkh-i adabīyāt-i Irān pīsh az Islām*, pp. 270–1; Boyce, 'Middle Persian literature', p. 59.
168. According to N. Sims-Williams, the Middle Iranian Christian literature may be regarded as a branch of Syriac literature. See Sims-Williams, 'Christian literature in Middle Iranian languages', in Ronald E. Emmerick and Maria Macuch (eds), *The Literature of Pre-Islamic Iran*: Companion Volume I to *A History of Persian Literature* (London/New York, 2009), p. 266.

169. In the episode of the search for the Water of Life, Firdawsī mentions his source as *dihqān* ('the noble landowner') and *Pahlavān.* In general, when Firdawsī identifies his source as *dihqān*, he is referring to the prose *Shāhnāma* of Abū Manṣūr.
170. J. S. Meisami, 'The past in service of the present: two views of history in medieval Persia', *Poetics Today* xiv/2 (1993), p. 254.

Chapter 4 Alexander in the *Iskandarnāma* of Niẓāmī Ganjavī (1141–1209)

1. Firdawsī, *Shāhnāma*, vol. VIII, p. 458.
2. De Blois has doubted the traditional chronology of the poems of Niẓāmī's *Khamsa*. Through his comparison of the manuscripts, and his identification of the dedicatees and other textual data, he suggested 590/1194 as the date of completion for the *Iskandarnāma*. See François de Blois, *Persian Literature: A Bio-Bibliographical Survey, Begun by the Late C. A. Storey*, Vol. 2: *Poetry ca.* AD *1100 to 1225* (London, 1994), pp. 438–46; de Blois, Vol. 3 (London, 1997), pp. 585–91. However, in the preface to the *Sharafnāma* (pp. 78–9), Niẓāmī declares that he has already completed four *mathnawī*s. This would indicate that the *Iskandarnāma* was the fifth and last of his epic poems, composed after 593/1197, the date of completion of *Haft Paykar.* At the end of the *Iqbālnāma*, Niẓāmī mentions his age as 60 (p. 290). Taking the year 1141 as his birth, the completion of the *Iqbālnāma* would be *c.* 1200.
3. They are the *Makhzan al-Asrār*, *Khusraw o Shīrīn*, *Laylī o Majnūn*, *Iskandarnāma*, and *Haft Paykar*
4. F. de Blois, 'Nizami', *Persian Literature: A Bio-Bibliographical Survey* (1994), pp. 438–95; see also Ṣafā, *Tārīkh-i adabīyāt dar Irān*, 13th edn (Tehran, 1373/1994), vol. II, pp. 808–9.
5. This work is edited by J. Mirsaidov (Moscow, 1977).
6. For more detail on this work see J. C. Bürgel, 'Jāmī's epic poem on Alexander the Great: an introduction', *Oriente Moderno* xv/76 (1996), pp. 415–38; Ch.-H. de Fouchécour, 'Djāmi, conseiller des princes, ou Le Livre de la Sagesse Alexandrine', *Kārnāma* v (1999), pp. 11–32.
7. This descriptive section is necessary, since there is almost no detailed research on Niẓāmī's *Alexander Romance* and no critical English translation of the *Iskandarnāma.* However, Chelkowski includes a summary of the *Iskandarnāma* in his Niẓāmī's *Iskandarnāmeh*: *Colloquio sul poeta Persiano Niẓāmī e la leggenda Iranica di Alessandro Magno (Roma, 25–26 marzo 1975)* (Roma, 1977), pp. 11–53.
8. On the subject of Niẓāmī's patron of the *Iskandarnāma*, confusion has been created among scholars by the various dates given for the completion of the poem, as well as by the various people to whom the work or parts of it are dedicated in the available manuscripts. Those whose names have come down to us associated with the manuscripts are: Nuṣrat al-Dīn Jahān Pahlawān from

among the rulers of Azerbaijan, 'Izz al-Dīn Mas'ūd from among the rulers of Mawṣil, and Nuṣrat al-Dīn Abū Bakr Pīshkīn (1195–1210) of the Ildeñizids from among the rulers in the Caucasus. On the problems connected with the dedication of the two parts of the *Iskandarnāma*, see Minorsky, 'Caucasica II', *Bulletin of the School of Oriental and African Studies* xiii/4 (1951), pp. 872–3. See also V. Dastgirdī, *Ganjīna-ye Ganjayī*, ed. S. Ḥamīdīyān (Tehran, 1376/1997), p. 71; Rypka, 'Poets and prose writers of the late Saljuq and Mongol periods', in J. A. Boyle (ed.), *Cambridge History of Iran*, V: *The Saljuq and Mongol Periods* (Cambridge, 1968), pp. 582–3.

9. The most well-known work of this tradition is the famous *Kalīla u Dimna*, whose Middle Persian translation of the Sanskrit original (the *Panchatantra*) was commissioned by the Sasanid Khusraw I Anūshirvān the Just. Its translation on the order of Anūshirvān, a type of ideal ruler, established its importance at the outset. Niẓāmī gave it a prominent role in Khusraw's education in his work *Khusraw u Shīrīn.* On the importance of Sasanian sources in the genre of advice literature during the Islamic period see C. E. Bosworth, 'Mirrors for princes', in J. S. Meisami and P. Starkey (eds), *Encyclopaedia of Arabic Literature* (New York, 1998), vol. II, p. 527; J. S. Meisami, 'Genres of court literature', in J. T. P. de Brujin (ed.), *General Introduction to Persian Literature* (New York, 2009), pp. 254–60; on the medieval Perso-Islamic mirrors for princes in general see A. K. S. Lambton, '*Quis Custodiet Custodes?* Some reflections on the Persian theory of government (part 1)', *Studia Islamica* v (1955), pp. 125–48; Lambton, '*Quis Custodiet Custodes?* Some reflections on the Persian theory of government (part 2)', *Studia Islamica* vi (1956), pp. 125–46; Lambton, 'Justice in the medieval Persian theory of kingship', *Studia Islamica* xvii (1962), pp. 91–119; Lambton, 'Islamic mirrors for princes', *Atti del convegno internazionale sul tema, La Persia nel medioevo* (Rome, 1970), pp. 419–42; Lambton, *State and Government in Medieval Islam: An Introduction to the Study of Islamic Political Theory: The Jurists* (New York, 1981); Lambton, 'Changing concepts of justice and injustice from the fifth/eleventh century to the eighth/fourteenth century in Persia: the Saljuq Empire and the Ilkhanate', *Studia Islamica* lxviii (1988), pp. 27–60.

10. It is during the early 'Abbāsid period that the genre of advice literature crystallised around Arabic translations of prose works of Sasanian origin, such as the advice of Ardashīr, Anūshirvān and Buzurgmihr, and the letter of Tansar, for example; see C. E. Bosworth, 'Mirrors for princes', vol. II, p. 527.

11. Meisami believes that Niẓāmī's concern with ideal kingship culminates in his *Iskandarnāma*. See J. S. Meisami, 'Genres of court literature', in J. T. P. de Brujin (ed.), *General Introduction to Persian Literature* (New York, 2009), p. 254. See also C. H. de Fouchécour, *Moralia* (Paris, 1986), especially pp. 79–80. On the ideas of kingship in Niẓāmī's romances see J. S. Meisami, *Medieval Persian Court Poetry* (Princeton, 2014), pp. 192–236.

12. On Saljūq mirrors for princes, see the introduction in Abū Ḥāmid Ghazālī, *Ghazali's Book of Counsel for Kings (Nasihat al-muluk)*, trans. F. R. C. Bagley

(London, 1964), pp. xiii–xvi; Lambton, 'Islamic mirrors for princes', *Quaderno dell'Accademia Nazionale dei Lincei* clx (1971), pp. 424–38; Lambton, *State and Government in Medieval Islam*, pp. 106–29. Although most of Niẓāmī's works are dedicated to local rulers of Transcaucasia and northern Iraq, he had a connection to the Saljūqs insofar as he dedicated the first of his romantic epics, *Khusraw u Shīrīn*, to the Atabeg of Azerbaijan, Muḥammad Jahān-Pahlawān b. Eldigüz.

13. 'Unṣur al-Ma'ālī Kaykāvūs Ibn Iskandar Ibn Qābūs ibn Vūshmgīr, *Qābūsnāma*, ed. Gh. Yūsifī, 2nd edn (Tehran, 1352/1973).
14. The influence of Niẓām al-Mulk on our poet of Ganja is such that he chose his pen name 'Niẓāmī' in honour of the Saljūq *vazīr*. Michael Barry, 'Niẓāmī: mirror of the unseen world', Lecture given at *The Kamran Djam Annual Lectures*, Centre for Iranian Studies, University of London, 2 February 2015.
15. Niẓām al-Mulk, *Siyar al-Mulūk or Sīyasatnāma*, ed. Hubert Darke, 3rd edn (Tehran, 2535 Shāhanshāhī/1976).
16. Abū Ḥamid Ghazālī, *Naṣīḥat al-mulūk*, ed. J. Humā'ī (Tehran, 1351/1972); Ghazālī, *Ghazali's Book of Counsel for Kings*. The influence of this work is much more relevant to the second part of the *Iskandarnāma* (i.e. the *Iqbālnāma*).
17. Ẓahīrī Samarqandī, *Sindbādnāma*, ed. A. Qawīm (Tehran, 1333/1954). The influence of this work will be studied in the next chapter, which focuses on the second part of the *Iskandarnāma*, the *Iqbālnāma*.
18. Kaykāvūs Ibn Iskandar, *Qābausnāma*, pp. 130, 140, 148–9, 238; Niẓām al-Mulk, *Siyar al-Mulūk*, pp. 41–2, 81; al-Ghazālī, *Naṣīḥat al-mulūk*, pp. 85, 87, 93, 128, 153, 159, 166, 188–9, 226, 336–8; Ẓahīrī Samarqandī, *Sindbādnāma*, p. 29.
19. I owe the beautiful poetic translation of Niẓāmī's verses quoted in this chapter to Dr Leonard Lewisohn, to whom I am very grateful. Given the fact that there is no previous intelligible English translation of the *Iskandarnāma* – Wilberforce Clarke's translation being so convoluted as to be almost incomprehensible – these translated selections represent a valuable contribution to Niẓāmī studies.
20. H. Wilberforce Clarke, *The Sikandar Nāma e Bará* (London, 1881).
21. Niẓāmī, *Iskandarnāma*, trans. K. Lipskerov (Baku, 1953).
22. Niẓāmī, *Iskandarnāma*, trans. Y. E. Bertels and A. K. Arends (Baku, 1983).
23. Niẓāmī, *Das Alexanderbuch*, trans. J. Christoph Bürgel (Zurich, 1991).
24. This is the same metre Firdawsī used in the *Shāhnāma*. It is usually used for epics. See Khaleghi-Motlagh, 'Pīrāmūn-i vazn-i Shāhnāma', *Īrānshināsī* v (1369/1990), p. 48; Sa'īd Nafīsī, 'Vazn-i Shāhnāma-yi Firdawsī', *Dānishnāma* ii (1326/1947), pp. 133–48.
25. See Rypka, 'Poets and prose writers of the late Saljuq and Mongol periods', pp. 582–3. Ṣafā dedicated almost two pages on the date of the *Iskandarnāma*'s compilation. However, he does not clarify his opinion. See Ṣafā, *Tārīkh-i adabīyāt dar Irān*, vol. II, pp. 805–6. See also note 1 in this chapter.
26. In India it is known as the *Iskandarnāma-yi barri* (*The Adventures of Alexander by Land*) because most of the adventures take place on land, while the *Iqbālnāma*

is known as the *Iskandarnāma-yi baḥrī* (*The Adventures of Alexander by Sea*) due to the fact that the adventures occur at sea.

27. Niẓāmī, *Sharafnāma*, p. 50. He calls the book *Sharafnāma-yi Khusrowān*.
28. On the distinction between wilful and lawful kingship, see Lambton, 'Islamic mirrors for princes', pp. 426–36.
29. Ibid., p. 49.
30. On the role of al-Khiḍr/al-Khaḍir/al-Khaḍīr in early Near Eastern mythology, see A. J. Wensinck, 'al-Khaḍir', EI^2 iv, pp. 902–5. On the significance of Khiḍr in Niẓāmī's poetry, see P. Franke, 'Drinking from the Water of Life: Nizāmī, Khizr and the symbolism of poetical inspiration in later Persianate literature', in J.-C. Bürgel and Christine van Ruymbeke (eds), *A Key to the Treasure of the Hakīm: Artistic and Humanistic Aspects of Niẓāmī's* Khamsa (Leiden, 2011), pp. 77–125.
31. Niẓāmī, *Sharafnāma*, pp. 51, 52, 53.
32. Three of Niẓāmī's epics (*Khusraw u Shīrīn*, *Haft Paykar* and the *Iskandarnāma*) share themes with the *Shāhnāma* of Firdawsī, and in composing the *Haft Paykar* and *Khusraw u Shīrīn* Niẓāmī shared similar historical concerns with Firdawsī. In *Khusraw u Shīrīn* he thus claimed that he would relate the part of Khusraw's life that was untreated by Firdawsī (*Khusraw u Shīrīn*, 11:46–9, p. 137); in the *Haft Paykar* he likewise declared that he would say what his predecessor had left unsaid (*Haft Paykar*, 4:18–32).
33. Ṣafā, *Ḥamāsa-sarāyī dar Irān*, p. 333; Ṣafā, *Tārīkh-i adabīyāt dar Irān*, vol. II, p. 807.
34. Niẓāmī, *Sharafnāma*, p. 50.
35. He advanced the same reason for his composition of the tale of Sasanian King Bahrām V in the *Haft Paykar* (4:18–32).
36. Niẓāmī, *Sharafnāma*, p. 50.
37. Ibid., p. 49.
38. Ibid., p. 54.
39. The poet refers to the fact that as Aristotle reportedly acted as his counsellor and minister, Alexander is considered a philosopher too.
40. Niẓāmī, *Sharafnāma*, p. 54, VIII, 42–4.
41. Ibid., p. 55, VIII, 45–50.
42. The ideas of the king as the Perfect Man and the ruler as the regent of God, and the concept of man as a microcosm (with the king embodying the highest level of mankind), are reflected in Fārābī's ideal of the philosopher-king. See Lambton, *State and Government*, pp. 69–82, 288–306, 316–25. See also Bürgel, 'Krieg und Frieden im Alexanderepos Nizamis', in M. Bridges and J. Ch. Bürgel (eds), *The Problematics of Power: Eastern and Western Representations of Alexander the Great* (Bern, 1996), pp. 91–107.
43. Abū Naṣr al-Fārābī is known as Alfarabius or Avennasar in medieval Latin texts. His ideas on ideal kingship are reflected in *Aphorisms of the Statesman {Fuṣūl al-madanī}*, ed. D. M. Dunlop (Cambridge, 1961); *On Political Government {al-Siyāsa al-madaniyya}* (Hyderabad, 1346/1927); *On the Perfect*

State {Mabādī' ārā' ahl al-madīnat al-fāḍilah}, trans. Richard Walter (Chicago, 1985).

44. On the political usage of Alexander in the Islamic world, see Paul Weinfield, 'The Islamic Alexander: a religious and political theme in Arabic and Persian literature' (PhD thesis, Columbia University, 2008).
45. The scattered chronicles are each likened to pearls strewn about ('each idle pearl'), which are then gathered and strung together by the poet on the necklace of his poem.
46. Niẓāmī, *Sharafnāma*, p. 68, X, 10–16.
47. Ibid., p. 69, X, 17–18.
48. Ibid., X, 19.
49. Ibid., X, 20–1.
50. This point is mentioned by Bertels in his work *Niẓāmī: The Great Poet of Azerbaijan*. Unfortunately, I have not been able to find the original version of this book. However, I made use of its Persian translation: Bertels, *Niẓāmī: shā'ir-e buzurg-e Adharbāyjān*, trans. Ḥ. Muḥammadzāda Ṣadīq (Tehran, 1357/1978), p. 132.
51. The ancient sources mistakenly identified the pass at Darband with the Dar'yal Pass in the central Caucasus. See Erich Kettenhofen, 'Darband', *EIr* vii/1, pp. 13–19.
52. See A. R. Anderson, 'Alexander at the Caspian Gates', *Transactions of the American Philological Association* v (1928), pp. 130–63; Anderson, *Alexander's Gate, Gog and Magog and the Enclosed Nations* (Cambridge, 1932).
53. Darband, through which Alexander passed, was in the vicinity of Ray. The confusion arises because there are several cities with the same name. See the discussion below in this chapter and the references cited, especially Stoneman, *A Life in Legend*, pp. 77–8.
54. The Darband fortress was certainly the most prominent Sasanian defensive construction in the Caucasus. See M. I. Artamonov, *Istoriya Khazar {History of the Khazars}* (Leningrad, 1962), p. 122.
55. This point will be discussed later on.
56. Niẓāmī did the same with another female character in the *Haft Paykar*: he changed the name of the female harpist who appears in the *Shāhnāma* from Āzāda (Noble) to Fitna (Mischief). Not only did he change her name, but he also reversed the roles of the male and female participants in the drama, making the female its heroine. For more information on this episode in the *Haft Paykar* and its parallel in the *Shāhnāma* of Firdawsī, see Meisami, *Medieval Persian Court Poetry*, pp. 213–19.
57. F. de Blois, 'Eskandar-Nāma of Neẓāmī', *EIr* viii/6, p. 614.
58. Niẓāmī, *Sharafnāma*, p. 69.
59. Ibid.
60. Ibid., p. 74. For an extended discussion of the place of truthfulness versus falsity in Islamic poetry, see Vicente Cantarino, *Arabic Poetics in the Golden Age* (Leiden, 1975), Chapter 3 ('Poetry: lie or truth'), pp. 27–40.

61. Niẓāmī, *Sharafnāma*, pp. 74–5.
62. Ibid., p. 70.
63. Literally, he says: 'Kay Khusraw's throne'.
64. See A. Qamber, 'The mirror symbol in the teachings and writings of some Sufi masters', *Temenos* i (1990), pp. 163–79; Michael Ferber, 'Mirror', *A Dictionary of Literary Symbols* (Cambridge, 1999), pp. 124–5.
65. Plato, *Alcibiades*, 133c, cited by R. Stoneman, 'Alexander's mirror', in *Temenos Academy Review* xix (2016), pp. 46–65. In this paper, Stoneman analyses various types of Alexandrian 'mirrors' and provides an impressive interpretation of each tale ascribed to Alexander concerning mirrors in the *Alexander Romance*, and their Greek and Byzantine parallels.
66. Stoneman, 'Alexander's mirror', p. 57.
67. See the introduction to Herbert Hoffman and Patricia F. Davidson, *Greek Gold: Jewellery from the Age of Alexander* (Von Zabern, 1965). There are also interesting remarks on the jewellery of the Hellenistic period in Reynold A. Higgins, *Greek and Roman Jewellery*, 2nd edn (San Francisco, 1980), p. 153; D. Williams (ed.), *The Art of the Greek Goldsmith* (London, 1998).
68. See Hoffman and Davidson, *Greek Gold*.
69. S. Perlman, 'The coins of Philip II and Alexander the Great and their Pan-Hellenic propaganda', *The Numismatic Chronicle and Journal of the Royal Numismatic Society*, 7th Series v (1965), p. 57.
70. On this issue see Martin Price, *The Coinage in the Name of Alexander the Great and Philip Arrhidaeus* (London, 1991); H. A. Troxell, *Studies in the Macedonian Coinage of Alexander the Great* (New York, 1997).
71. Al-Bīrūnī, *Athār al-Bāqīya*, trans. A. Dānishsirīsht (Tehran, 1363/1984), pp. 45–6. See also the English translation of this text by C. E. Sachau, *The Chronology of Ancient Nations* (London, 1879), pp. 32–3.
72. Al-Bīrūnī, *Chronology*, p. 32.
73. R. Stoneman, personal communication.
74. See David J. A. Ross, *Alexander Historiatus: A Guide to Medieval Illustrated Alexander Literature* (Frankfurt am Main, 1988), p. 50, n. 85; p. 87, n. 120.
75. W. Jac. Van Bekkum, 'Alexander the Great in medieval Hebrew literature', *Journal of the Warburg and Courtauld Institutes* xlix (1986), p. 219.
76. Josephus, *Ant. Xi*, pp. 314ff. See also A. Kleczar, 'The kingship of Alexander the Great in the Jewish versions of the Alexander narrative', in Richard Stoneman, Kyle Erickson and Ian Netton (eds), *The Alexander Romance in Persia and the East* (Groningen, 2012), pp. 342–3.
77. In the *Sharafnāma* (p. 51), as mentioned above, Niẓāmī's muse, the Prophet Khiḍr admonished him:

    Do not repeat what the ancient sage [Firdawsī] said,
    For it is wrong to pierce a single pearl twice.
    Except when a passage is reached where thought
    Demands you repeat what's before been said.

78. Bal'amī, *Tārīkh-i Bal'amī*. The episode on Alexander is in the second volume (pp. 692–720).
79. Bal'amī is best known for his Persian translation of Ṭabarī's history, which was done for Manṣūr b. Nūḥ. Because he adds supplementary material, some of which is not found elsewhere, the work is called *Tārīkh-i Bal'amī*. According to the *Mujmal al-tawārīkh*, Bal'amī began his translation in 352/963 (see *Mujmal al-tawārīkh*, ed. M. T. Bahār (Tehran), p. 180). It is therefore the oldest New Persian prose work, after the preface (all that has been preserved) of the prose *Shāhnāma* of Abū Manṣūr. See Khaleghi-Motlagh, 'Amīrak Bal'amī', *EIr* i/9, pp. 971–2.
80. On Alexander's birth myths in the Greek tradition see the first chapter in Daniel Ogden's *Alexander the Great: Myth, Genesis and Sexuality* (Exeter, 2011), where he analyses their content and chronology. On the Egyptian and Persian origins of Alexander in the *Romance* tradition see Stoneman, *A Life in Legend*, pp. 6–26.
81. The name also appears as Fīlqūs, Fīlfūs or Fīlifūs in the manuscripts of the *Sharafnāma*.
82. Niẓāmī, *Sharafnāma*, p. 80, XV, 2–5.
83. Bal'amī, *Tārīkh-i Bal'amī*, vol. II, pp. 692–3.
84. Bīrūnī, *Athār al-bāqīyya*, pp. 48–9.
85. Mas'ūdī, *Murūj*, vol. I, p. 124.
86. Avishur, Isaac, Moshe David Herr and Carl Stephen Ehrlich, 'Edom', in Michael Berenbaum and Fred Skolnik (eds), *Encyclopaedia Judaica*, 2nd edn (Detroit, 2007), vol. VI, p. 158. The name Edom means 'red' in Hebrew, and was given to Esau, the elder son of Isaac (Genesis 25:30). The Torah, Tanakh and New Testament thus describe the Edomites as descendants of Esau. The identification of Edom with Rome was very widespread, and the overwhelming majority of homilies about Edom speak explicitly of Rome. Thus it was stated that Rome was founded by the children of Esau, and Rome was identified as one of the cities of the chiefs of Esau listed at the end of Genesis 36. At a still later period the term became a synonym for Christian Rome.
87. See K. Aḥmadnezhād, *Taḥlīl-i athār-i Niẓāmī Ganjavī* (Tehran, 1375/1996), p. 64.
88. Niẓāmī, *Sharafnāma*, p. 81, XV, 15.
89. Niẓāmī uses the term 'Hūshyārān-i Rūm' (lit. wise Anatolian/Roman? sages) here, but given the context it seems more likely that his reference is to Greek or Byzantine historians who wrote about Alexander.
90. Niẓāmī, *Sharafnāma*, p. 81, XV, 16–20.
91. Ibid., pp. 81–2, XV, 25–30.
92. See A. Tafaḍḍolī, 'Dehqān', *EIr* vii/2, pp. 223–4 and vii/3, pp. 225–6.
93. Niẓāmī, *Sharafnāma*, p. 82, XV, 31–3.
94. Ibid., XV, 34–47.
95. Regarding the influence of astrology in Niẓāmī's works see Meisami, *Medieval Persian Court Poetry*, p. 233, n. 63. There is useful information on the usage of

science in general in Niẓāmī's work in Christine van Ruymbeke, *Science and Poetry in Medieval Persia: The Botany of Nizami's Khamsa* (Cambridge, 2007), pp. 13–14. However, the best example of Niẓāmī's astrological knowledge is found in his *Haft Paykar (The Seven Princesses)*, on which, see Julie Scott Meisami (trans.), *The Haft Paykar: A Medieval Persian Romance* (Oxford, 1995), pp. xxxi–xxxvii.

96. Here Niẓāmī uses the term '*tarāzū-yi anjam*' (balance of stars), which, curiously, is the translation of the Greek word ἀστρολάβος (star-taker).
97. Niẓāmī, *Sharafnāma*, p. 83, XV, 48–56.
98. Indeed, the name of this month in the Persian calendar is derived from the constellation of Leo, which is *amurdād* in Persian and *Asad* (lion) in Arabic. See M. Akramī, *Gāh-shumārī-yi irānī* (Tehran, 1380/2001), p. 29.
99. Stoneman, *The Greek Alexander Romance*, pp. 43–4.
100. There is a discussion of Alexander's horoscope according to the Pseudo-Callisthenes in R. Stoneman, *Il Romanzo Di Alessandro*, trans. T. Gargiulo (Milan, 2007), vol. I. pp. 478–9.
101. Niẓāmī, *Sharafnāma*, p. 83, XV.
102. See David Pingree, 'Mashā'allāh: some Sassanian and Syriac sources', *Essays on Islamic Philosophy and Science*, ed. George F. Hourani (Albany, 1975), pp. 5–14, especially p. 6; Pingree, 'Historical horoscopes', *Journal of the American Oriental Society* lxxxii/4 (1962), pp. 487–502. On the Zoroastrian parts of *Bundahishn* see W. B. Henning, 'An astronomical chapter of the Bundahishn', *The Journal of the Royal Asiatic Society* lxxiv/3–4 (1942), pp. 229–48; D. N. MacKenzie, 'Zoroastrian astrology in the *Bundahišn*', *Bulletin School of Oriental and African Studies* xxvii (1964), pp. 511–29.
103. In the casting of a horoscope it was necessary to evaluate the significance of each sign within the system of 12 constellations (i.e. the 12 Zodiacal 'houses of the signs'). Niẓāmī's horoscope for Alexander resembles this method. He interprets the significance of each sign in relation to each specific house, as for instance where he claims that the sun being in Aries implied the putting of wisdom into practice.
104. The Latin translation was made by Hugo de Santalla under the title *Libellus de navitatibus 14 distinctus capitulis* (Oxford, Bodl. Savile 15, 72 fols). See L. Thorndike, 'The Latin translations of astrological works by Messahala', *Osiris* xii (1956), pp. 49–72; E. S. Kennedy and D. Pingree, *The Astrological History of Māshā'allāh* (Cambridge, 1971).
105. See S. Ḥ. Naṣr, *The Islamic Intellectual Tradition in Persia*, ed. Mehdi Amin Razavi (London: Curzon 1996), p. 184.
106. Niẓāmī, *Sharafnāma*, p. 86, XVI, 15, 23.
107. Neither of these names – Nicomachus and Lysimachus – appears in the Syriac Pseudo-Callisthenes. It is not clear on which source Niẓāmī based his information. As far as this book is concerned, there is no Arabic source where this information appears either!
108. This probably refers to *Sīmiyā'* (from the Greek σημεῖα), one of the branches of occult science in the Islamic tradition concerned with 'the science of the

secret powers of letters'. See D. B. MacDonald [T. Fahd], 'Sīmiyā", *EI* [2] ix, pp. 612–13.

109. The use of occult sciences associated with Alexander the Great is normally found in works attributed to Aristotle, not Aristotle's father; for example, in the *Secret of Secrets*, Aristotle sent four magical stones to Alexander, one of which would always rout the enemy. There are also stones that prevent any army withstanding Alexander. It is also worth mentioning the *Lapidary* of Aristotle, another work devoted to the marvellous properties of stones and tales of Alexander the Great. Regarding Aristotle and Alexander in these two works and the use of occult science see Lynn Thorndike, 'The Latin pseudo-Aristotle and medieval occult science', *Journal of English and Germanic Philology* xxi/2 (1922), pp. 229–58.
110. Niẓāmī, *Sharafnāma*, p. 88, XVI, 49–52.
111. In Islamic texts and contexts, *ḥanīf* refers to one who follows the original and true monotheistic religion, and the term is used especially of Abraham. See W. Montgomery, 'Ḥanīf', *EI* [2] iii, pp. 165–6.
112. Two extant papyri contain the correspondence of Darius and Alexander: the first (*Pap. Sociedad Italiana 1285*) is in Florence and belongs to the second century AD, edited by Dino Pieraccioni in 1951. The second (*Pap. Hamburg 129*) belongs to the first century BC. In the introduction to his translation of the Pseudo-Callisthenes (*Pseudo-Calístenes: vida y hazañas de Alejandro de Macedonia* (Madrid, 1988), pp. 15–16, 19–20), C. Garcia Gual analysed the origins of the letters and quoted C. Erwin Rohde, *Der griechische Roman und sein Vorläufer*, 4th edn (Darmstadt, 1960) and R. Merkelbach, *Die Quellen des griechischen Alexanderromans* (Munich, 1954), pp. 193ff.), among many others. It is believed that the letters probably belong to an 'epistolary novel' about Alexander. See also R. Stoneman's introduction (*The Greek Alexander Romance*, pp. 10–11).
113. On the correspondence between Darius and Alexander in the *Shāhnāma* and the Pseudo-Callisthenes see Chapter 2.
114. Niẓāmī, *Sharafnāma*, p. 185:

    به رخشنده آذر به استا و زند
    به خورشید روشن به چرخ بلند
    به یزدان که اهریمنش دشمن است
    به زردشت کو خصم اهریمن است

115. Ibid., p. 188:

    به من می رسد بازوی بهمنی
    که اسفندیارم به رویین تنی

116. In Persian epic, although Isfandīyār was immortal (*rūyīn-tan*, which means 'iron-body'), Rustam managed to kill him by consulting the fabulous mythological bird, the Sīmurgh, who knew that Isfandīyār had a weak point: his eyes. Alexander wisely uses this comparison to warn Darius of the consequences of the war.
117. I. Lewis, 'Berberā', *EI* [2] i, pp. 1172–3.

118. Niẓāmī, *Sharafnāma*, p. 93.
119. Ibid. There is a similar passage in the *Iqbālnāma* (p. 40) and in the *Haft Paykar* (6:35–40).
120. See Simon Swain, *Themistius, Julian and Greek Political Theory under Rome: Texts, Translations and Studies of Four Key Works* (Cambridge, 2013), pp. 110–23, and the translation of the text at pp. 180ff. See also Emily Cottrell, 'An early mirror for princes and manual for secretaries: *The Epistolary Novel of Aristotle and Alexander*', *Alexander the Great in the East* (Wroclaw, forthcoming); M. Maróth, *The Correspondence between Aristotle and Alexander the Great: An Anonymous Greek Novel in Letters in Arabic Translation* (Piliscsaba, 2006).
121. It is preserved in Miskawayh's *al-Ḥikmah al-Khālidah*. See Daniel Gimaret, *Le livre de Bilawhar et Būḏāsf selon la version arabe ismaélienne* (Paris, 1971), pp. 38–41.
122. Niẓām al-Mulk, *Siyar al-mulūk*, pp. 138–40; English translation, pp. 95–6.
123. Ghazālī, *Naṣīḥat al-mulūk*, p. 112; English translation, p. 63.
124. Niẓāmī, *Sharafnāma*, p. 96, XVIII, 31–3.
125. Bal'amī, *Tārīkh-i Bal'amī*, vol. II, p. 694.
126. Niẓāmī, *Sharafnāma*, p. 96, XVIII, 34 and 38.
127. Niẓāmī, *Sharafnāma*, p. 119.
128. Niẓāmī, *Sharafnāma*, XIX.
129. It was mentioned above that Aristotle's father gave a magical alphabetical ring to Alexander to foretell the outcome of a battle. This is curious because the idea of Alexander using magic to defeat the enemy seems to have aroused some scepticism among medieval readers; one can mention Geoffrey of Waterford (d. *c.*1300) in particular, who translated the *Secret of Secrets* into French. Thorndike notes: 'He wonders why Alexander had to win his battles by hard fighting when Aristotle is supposed to inform him in his book of a stone which will always rout the enemy' ('The Latin pseudo-Aristotle', p. 257).
130. Niẓāmī, *Sharafnāma*, XX, p. 131. Curiously, in the Greek *Romance* (Pseudo-Callisthenes, I, 35), there is a similar sentence regarding the Tyrians: 'To this day the miseries of Tyre is a proverbial expression' (Stoneman, *The Greek Alexander Romance*, p. 70.
131. Niẓāmī, *Sharafnāma*, XXI, p. 135.
132. Ibid., XXI, p. 136.
133. The *Shāhnāma* of Firdawsī does not mention the foundation of Alexandria.
134. Niẓāmī, *Sharafnāma*, XXI, pp. 136–7.
135. The episode of the battle against the Tyrians in the Pseudo-Callisthenes (I, 35) comes after Alexander hastened towards Egypt (I, 34), and his first battle against Darius. The episode of the battle against the people of Zang also appears between these two episodes in the *Sharafnāma*.
136. The *Rasā'il* is one of the earliest works of Arabic literature and was translated or edited by Sālim Abū l-'Alā', secretary to the tenth Umayyad caliph, Hishām ibn 'Abd al-Mālik (r. 724–43). It consists of approximately 16 letters and treatises. See Simon Swain, *Themistius, Julian and Greek Political Theory under*

Rome, pp. 110–23, and his translation of the text at pp. 180ff.; M. Grignaschi, 'Les *Rasā'l d'Arisṭūṭālīsa ilā-l-Iskandar* de Sālim Abū-l-'Alā' et l'activité culturelle à l'époque omeyyade', *Bulletin d'études orientales* xix (1965–6), p. 31. It looks as if the epistolary novel came to be in Arabic through a version in Syriac. See Brock, 'The laments of the philosophers over Alexander in Syriac', pp. 215–18; Van Bladel, 'Syriac sources of the early Arabic narratives of Alexander'.

137. Niẓāmī, *Sharafnāma*, XXI, p. 137.
138. Ibid., XXI, p. 139.
139. Niẓāmī, *Sharafnāma*, XXII, p. 142.
140. Budge, *The Syriac Pseudo-Callisthenes*, pp. 46–52.
141. Niẓāmī, *Sharafnāma*, XXIV, pp. 160–1.
142. Bal'amī also translates the word as 'chawgān' in order for Alexander to play polo (Bal'amī, *Tārīkh-i Bal'amī*, vol. II, p. 695).
143. See García Gual, *Pseudo-Calístenes*, p. 94, n. 67.
144. Budge, *The Syriac Pseudo-Callisthenes*, p. 47.
145. Ibid., p. 50.
146. For a detailed discussion of this passage in Ṭabarī's *Tārīkh* see Gad, 'Al-Ṭabarī's tales of Alexander', p. 221.
147. Bal'amī, *Tārīkh-i Bal'amī*, vol. II, pp. 695–6.
148. *Nihāyat al-'arab fī tārīkh al-fars wa al-'arab*, ed. M. T. Dāneshpazhūh (Tehran, 1374/1995), pp. 116ff. Here the author also adds a golden coffin and a pearl to the symbolic gifts.
149. Niẓāmī, *Sharafnāma*, XXII, p. 143.
150. Ibid., XXII, p. 144.
151. Ibid., XXII, p. 144.
152. Ibid., XXIV, p. 162.
153. Ibid., XXV, p. 163.
154. Niẓāmī uses the word *afranja* (the Arabised form of *Afrang*, which in Persian means 'Europe'). According to Yāqūt Ḥamavī (*Mu'jam al-Buldān*), one of the *Afrang* cities was Rhodes, which lay in front of Alexandria. See Mu'īn, 'Afrang', *Farhang-i Fārsī*, 10th edn (Tehran, 1375/1996), vol. I, p. 314.
155. Niẓāmī, *Sharafnāma*, XXV, p. 164.
156. Ibid., XXVI, pp. 170–1.
157. Bal'amī, *Tārīkh-i Bal'amī*, vol. II, p. 696.
158. *Nāma-yi Tansar*, ed. M. Mīnavī, 2nd edn (Tehran, 1354/1975), p. 86.
159. This Persian word is derived from the Greek νόμος (law, reason, order, tradition).
160. Niẓāmī, *Sharafnāma*, XXVI, pp. 172–3.
161. Firdawsī, *Shāhnāma*, vol. V, pp. 541ff.
162. According to Canard, Jazīra 'is the name used by Arab geographers to denote the northern part of the territory situated between the Tigris and the Euphrates'. See 'al-Djazīra', *EI* [2] ii, pp. 523–4.

163. Mawṣil (or al-Mawṣil) – modern-day Mosul – is a city in northern Mesopotamia (Iraq), some 400 km north of Baghdad. The original city stands 'on the west bank of the Tigris River and opposite to ancient Nineveh'. See E. Honigmann [C. E. Bosworth], 'al-Mawṣil', *EI* [2] vi, pp. 899–901.
164. R. Stoneman, personal communication.
165. Firdawsī, *Shāhnāma*, vol. V, p. 541.
166. Bal'amī, *Tārīkh-i Bal'amī*, vol. II, p. 696.
167. Niẓāmī, *Sharafnāma*, XXVIII, p. 197.
168. Pseudo-Callisthenes, I, 41–2; Firdawsī, *Shāhnāma*, vol. V, pp. 541, 547.
169. Niẓāmī, *Sharafnāma*, XXIX, p. 202.
170. Ibid., XXIX, p. 204.
171. Ibid., XXIX, p. 204.
172. Ibid., XXIX, p. 206.
173. Ibid.
174. For a detailed analysis of this passage in the Arabic histories and the *Shāhnāma* see Chapters 2 and 3 of this book.
175. Stoneman, *The Greek Alexander Romance*, p. 109, II, 20.
176. Niẓāmī, *Sharafnāma*, XXXI, p. 228.
177. Ibid., XXIX, p. 219.
178. Bal'amī also reports these three wishes (*Tārīkh-i Bal'amī*, vol. II, p. 696). See also Stoneman, *A Life in Legend*, p. 43; J. S. Meisami, *Persian Historiography to the End of the Twelfth Century* (Edinburgh, 1999), p. 79.
179. In this regard see the important discussion of C. Ciancaglini, 'Alessandro e l'incendio di Persepoli nelle tradizioni greca e irancia', in A. Valvo (ed.), *La diffusione dell'eredità classica nell'età tardoantica e medievale: Forme e metodi di trasmissione* (Alexandria, 1997), pp. 59–81; K. van Bladel, *The Arabic Hermes*, pp. 33–6; Shayegan, *Arsacids and Sasanians*, pp. 301–2.
180. Niẓāmī, *Sharafnāma*, XXXII, pp. 238–9.
181. Regarding Pahlavi texts in which Alexander is mentioned, see the appendix to Touraj Daryaee, '*Imitatio Alexandri* and its impact on Late Arsacid, Early Sasanian and Middle Persian literature', *Electrum* xii (2007), pp. 93–5; Shayegan, *Arsacids and Sasanians*, pp. 295–7.
182. See T. Daryaee, '*Imitatio Alexandri*', pp. 90–3, where he analyses the content of passages of Middle Persian texts in which Alexander appears. In addition, see Stoneman, 'Alexander the destroyer', in his *A Life in Legend*, pp. 41–4.
183. M. Boyce, *Zoroastrians: Their Religious Beliefs and Practices* (London, 1979), p. 78.
184. Niẓāmī, *Sharafnāma*, XXXII, pp. 239–40.
185. Ibid., XXXII, p. 241.
186. Ibid., XXXII, p. 240.
187. For English translations of fragments of Middle Persian texts mentioning Alexander, see T. Daryaee, '*Imitatio Alexandri*', pp. 93–5.
188. For example, in Bal'amī's *Tārīkh*, which coincides with Niẓāmī in the majority of its content, there is no mention of this custom.

189. Niẓāmī, *Sharafnāma*, XXXII, p. 241.
190. Ibid.
191. On the identification of Balīnās with Apollonius of Tyana see M. Plessner, 'Balīnūs', *EI* ² i, pp. 994–5. His role at Alexander's side will be studied in this and the next chapter. Piemontese believes that Balīnās is Eupalinus of Megara, an ancient Greek engineer who built the Tunnel of Eupalinus on Samos in the sixth century BC. See Amīr Khusraw of Delhi, *Lo specchio Alessandrino*, trans. Angelo M. Piemontese (Catanzaro, 1999).
192. Niẓāmī, *Sharafnāma*, XXXII, pp. 243–4.
193. On the role of Apollonius of Tyana in the *Iskandarnāma* see Manteghi, 'The king and the wizard', in Richard Stoneman (ed.), *The Alexander Romance: History and Literature, Ancient Narratives Supplements* (Groningen, forthcoming).
194. Niẓāmī, *Sharafnāma*, XXXIII, pp. 245–56.
195. Ibid., XXXIV, p. 258.
196. Niẓāmī, *Sharafnāma*, p. 263.
197. Niẓāmī, *Sharafnāma*, XXXVI, p. 271. The direction of his travel was evidently south, but Niẓāmī says west because, according to the Islamic tradition, Alexander reached both extremes of the world: East and West.
198. Niẓāmī, *Sharafnāma*, pp. 272–3.
199. A. J. Wensinck, 'Hadjdj', *EI* ² iii, pp. 31–3.
200. See Stoneman, *A Life in Legend*, pp. 31, 159.
201. Dīnavarī, *Akhbār al-ṭiwāl*, ed. 'Abd al-Mun'im Amīr and Jamāl al-Dīn al-Shiyal (Cairo, 1960), pp. 33–4.
202. Emel Esin, *Mecca the Blessed, Madinah the Radiant* (New York, 1963), pp. 18–22.
203. See W. Montgomery Watt, 'Ḥanīf', *EI* ² iii, pp. 165–6.
204. Actually, according to the *Greek Romance* (Pseudo-Callisthenes, II, 9), 'Alexander was keen to conquer Greater Armenia' and so subdued it.
205. Niẓāmī, *Sharafnāma*, XXXVI, pp. 273–4.
206. Ibid., XXXVI, p. 275.
207. Stephen H. Rapp Jr, *The Sasanian World through Georgian Eyes: Caucasia and the Iranian Commonwealth in Late Antique Georgian Literature* (Farnham, 2014), p. 269.
208. M. F. Brosset, *Histoire de la Géorgie* (St Petersburg, 1849), vol. I, p. 140.
209. On the Sasanians and Xuasrovanis see Stephen H. Rapp Jr, *The Sasanian World through Georgian Eyes*, p. 269.
210. V. Minorsky [C. E. Bosworth], 'al-Kurdj', *EI* ² v, pp. 487–98.
211. Van Donzel and Schmidt, *Gog and Magog*, p. 215.
212. In the Greek *Romance* (Pseudo-Callisthenes, III, 18–23) she is renowned as the Queen of Meroe.
213. Firdawsī, *Shāhnāma*, vol. VI, pp. 51–74. In the *Shāhnāma* she is known as the Queen of al-Andalus. See also Claude-Claire Kappler, 'Alexandre dans le *Shāh Nāma* de Firdousi: De la conquête du monde à la dé couverte de soi', in

M. Bridges and J. Ch. Bürgel (eds), *The Problematics of Power: Eastern and Western Representations of Alexander the Great* (Bern, 1996), pp. 165–90.

214. On Khāqānī's life and works see Anna Livia Beelaert, 'K̲āqānī Šervānī', *EIr* xv/5, pp. 521–9.

215. Khāqānī Shirvānī, *Dīvān*, ed. Sajjādī, pp. 80, 177, 403.

216. See F. de Blois, 'Eskandar-Nāma of Neẓāmī', *EIr* viii/6, p. 614.

217. Niẓāmī, *Sharafnāma*, XXXVII, pp. 277–8, 279–80.

218. Ibid., XXXVII, p. 281.

219. According to S. Ḥamīdīyān (editor of the *Iskandarnāma*), it was customary for kings (or queens in this instance) to hold amber in their hands for its fragrance. See Niẓāmī, *Sharafnāma*, XXXVIII, p. 282, n. 5.

220. Ibid., XXXVII, p. 285:

نظر پخته تر کن که خام آمدی

221. Ibid., XXXVII, p. 287:

به نقش تو زان نمودم نخست
که تا نقش من بر تو گردد درست

222. This motif of the Sophianic Feminine in Niẓāmī's romances has been extensively treated by Michael Barry. See *Farīd-od-Dīn 'Attār: The Canticle of the Birds Illustrated through Persian and Eastern Art*, trans. A. Darbandi and Dick Davis, with commentary by Michael Barry (Paris, 2014), pp. 139–54, where Barry connects the motif of the theophany of the Lady Beloved throughout Niẓāmī's various *mathnawī*s to that found in 'Aṭṭār's *Manṭiq al-ṭayr.*

223. See Erich Kettenhofen, 'Darband', *EIr* vii/1, pp. 13–19; D. M. Dunlop, 'Bāb al-Abwāb', *EI* ^{2} i, pp. 835–6.

224. Niẓāmī, *Sharafnāma*, XLI, p. 316.

225. Ibid., XLI, p. 317.

226. Ibid., XLI, pp. 321–2.

227. Ibid., XLI, p. 323.

228. Ibid.

229. D. M. Dunlop, 'Bāb al-Abwāb', *EI* ^{2} i, pp. 835–6.

230. See A. R. Anderson, 'Alexander at the Caspian Gates', *Transactions of the American Philological Association* lix (1928), pp. 130–63; Anderson, *Alexander's Gate, Gog and Magog and the Inclosed Nations* (Cambridge, 1932). For a long discussion of the symbolism and history underlying Alexander's attack on the castle of Darband and his related adventures (and for a translation of the *Sharafnāma*'s text concerning these), see Michael Barry, *Figurative Art in Medieval Islam and the Riddle of Bihzād of Herāt* (Paris, 2004), pp. 291–300.

231. See R. N. Frye, 'The Sasanian system of walls for defense', in M. Rosen-Ayalon (ed.), *Studies in Memory of Gaston Wiet* (Jerusalem, 1977), pp. 11–12.

232. *Mujmal*, ed. Bahār, p. 76.

233. See the study of Van Donzel and Schmidt, *Gog and Magog*, p. 216. On Alexander's barrier in the Syriac tradition, see pp. 17–30.

234. Niẓāmī, *Iqbālnāma*, ed. V. Dastgirdī, re-ed. S. Ḥamīdiyān (Tehran, 1376/1997), pp. 220–32.
235. On the confusion arising from the ancient sources' mistaken identification of the pass at Darband with the Dar'yal Pass in the central Caucasus see Erich Kettenhofen, 'Darband', *EIr* vii/1, pp. 13–19.
236. See Stoneman, *A Life in Legend*, p. 77.
237. R. Stoneman, personal communication.
238. Particularly important is Suetonius's remark in his biography of Nero (19.1) where the emperor prepares for war against the Albanians, which gives a clear indication that he identified the Caspian Gates with the Darband Pass. See D. C. Braund, 'The Caucasian frontier: myth, exploration and the dynamics of imperialism', in P. Freeman and D. Kennedy (eds), *The Defence of the Roman and Byzantine East* (Oxford: 1986), pp. 31–49; W. F. Standish, 'The Caspian Gates', *Greece & Rome* xvii (1970), pp. 12–24.
239. See R. Stoneman, 'Romantic ethnography: Central Asia and India in the *Alexander Romance*', *Ancient World* xxv (1994), pp. 93–107.
240. In the *Shāhnāma* of Firdawsī, Kay Khusraw pursues Afrāsīyāb from Ray and Khurāsān, and reaches Caucasia passing over the Caspian Sea. In the *Sharafnāma*, Alexander starts his journey from Caucasia and then reaches Khurāsān and Ray.
241. Niẓāmī, *Sharafnāma*, XLIV, pp. 342–50.
242. Ibid., XLVII, p. 366.
243. The founder of Manicheism in the third century AD. See Werner Sundermann, 'Mani', *EIr*, Online edition. Available at http://www.iranicaonline.org/articles/mani-founder-manicheism.
244. These tales (such as the competition between the Chinese and Roman painters, and the painting of Mānī, for example) have been the subject of much learned research and many publications. The best of these studies, which covers all these motifs and their interpretation along with their Greek and Byzantine parallels is Stoneman, 'Alexander's mirror', pp. 53–8. On the comparison of Ghazālī, Niẓāmī, Rūmī and other versions of the tale, see A. Kitābī, 'Qiṣṣa-yi mirī kardan-i rūmīyān va chīnīyān dar 'ilm-i naqqāshī va ṣūratgarī', *Āyīna-yi Mīrāth* xxxvi/7 (1386/2007), pp. 258–71.
245. For a good study of the mystical themes of both these tales in the *Sharafnāma*, see Michael Barry's 'Nizāmī on painters in the Book of Alexander' in his *Figurative Art in Medieval Islam*, pp. 263–8.
246. Abū Ḥāmid Muḥammad Ghazālī, *Iḥyā 'ulūm al-Dīn, Vol. III: Rub' mahlakāt*, trans. M. Muḥammad Khwarazmī, 3rd edn (Tehran, 1368/1989), p. 46.
247. The tale is also told by Rūmī (*Mathnavī*, ed. and trans. R. A. Nicholson (Tehran, 1356/1977), Book I, couplets 3459–99). However, in his version the roles of the Byzantine and the Chinese are reversed and Alexander is left out of the tale, replaced by an anonymous sultan.
248. Barry, *Figurative Art in Medieval Islam*, p. 262.

249. This point will be studied in the next chapter.
250. See Niẓāmī, 'Laylī va Majnūn,' in *Kulliyāt-i Ḥakīm Niẓāmī Ganjavī*, in Vaḥīd Dastgirdī (Tehran, 1378/1999), p. 314.
251. Niẓāmī, *Sharafnāma*, LV, p. 419.
252. Ibid., LV, p. 420.
253. Niẓāmī's description of Russians and their customs is one of the first of its type found in Persian literature, which gives it great historical significance.
254. Niẓāmī, *Sharafnāma*, LVI, p. 433:

به دزدی و سالوسی و رهزنی   نمایند مردی و مردافگنی

255. Ibid., LVI, p. 434:

اگر چه نشد ترک با روم خویش   هم از رومشان کینه از روس بیش

256. مرا مادر من که طرطوس خواند   به روسی زبان رستم روس خواند
257. Ibid., LVIII, p. 439:

ز روسی برون شد به آوردگاه ، یکی شیر پرطاس روبه کلاه

258. Ibid., LXIII, pp. 455–6.
259. Ibid., LXIII, pp. 457–8.
260. Firdawsī does not use the word 'Russians', but he gives a similar description of the people Alexander visits in Hārūm, who are fair-haired and red-faced (*Shāhnāma*, vol. VI, p. 91): همه روی سرخ و همه موی زرد همه از درجنگ روز نبرد
261. On the geographical/historical works in Arabic that describe the northern lands, especially the land of Rūs, see C. Stone and P. Lunde, *Ibn Faḍlān and the Land of Darkness: Arab Travellers in the Far North* (London, 2012), vol. III.
262. This work is of great historical, geographical and ethnographic interest, and shows that Ibn Faḍlān offered a mass of extremely important information on the peoples – including the Rūs and the Khazars – whom he had been able to see himself or of whom he had heard accounts during his journey. On Ibn Faḍlān and his journey to Volga see M. Canard, 'Ibn Faḍlān', *EI* [2] iii, p. 759.
263. R. N. Frye (trans.), *Ibn Fadlan's Journey to Russia: A Tenth-Century Traveler from Baghdad to the Volga River* (Princeton, 2005), pp. 54–7.
264. Niẓāmī, *Sharafnāma*, LXIV and LXVII.
265. Niẓāmī, *Sharafnāma*, pp. 486–98. For a study of the erotic content of this passage, see Khaleghi-Motlagh, 'Tan kāma-sarāyī dar adab-i fārsī', *Majāla-yi Īrānshināsī* viii/1 (1375/1996), pp. 20–2.
266. Niẓāmī describes the inhabitants' opinion of these fur pelts as follows: 'Do not regard with contempt these shrivelled skins, for they are the top currency of this land. This patched leather is in our opinion far more valuable than the softest human hair, for many of those {slaves} with the most beautiful hair found here can be bought with this arid and hairless leather' (*Sharafnāma*, LXVI, p. 480).
267. On the unclean nations see Andrew Colin Gow, 'The unclean nations, Gog and Magog, and the ten tribes', *The Red Jews: Antisemitism in the Apocalyptic Age, 1200–1600* (Leiden, 1995), pp. 23–6, and Appendix B, especially pp. 319ff.

268. See A. Seyed-Gohrab, F. Doufikar-Aerts and A. McGlinn (eds), *Gog and Magog: The Clans of Chaos in World Literature* (Amsterdam, 2007), pp. 69–79.
269. Van Donzel and Schmidt, *Gog and Magog*, p. 10.
270. Ibid., p. 11.
271. Ibid., p. 13.
272. On this work see J. P. Monferrer-Sala, 'Alexander the Great in the Syriac literary tradition', *A Companion to Alexander Literature in the Middle Ages*, ed. Z. David Zuwiyya (Leiden, 2011), pp. 54–5.
273. P. B. Golden, 'The conversion of the Khazars to Judaism', in P. B. Golden, H. Ben-Shammai and A. Róna-Tas (eds), *The World of the Khazars* (Leiden, 2007), p. 139.
274. See Dan D. Y. Shapira, 'Iranian sources on the Khazars', in P. B. Golden, H. Ben-Shammai and A. Róna-Tas (eds), *The World of the Khazars* (Leiden, 2007), pp. 298–305.
275. Ibn Isfandīyār, *Tārīkh-i Ṭabaristān*, ed. 'A. Iqbāl (Tehran, 1320/1941), vol. I, p. 266.
276. Khāqānī, *Dīvān*, pp. 135, 139, 145, 476. See also V. Minorsky, 'Khāqānī and Andronicus Comenus', *Bulletin of the School of Oriental and African Studies* ix (1943–6), pp. 550–78.
277. See *Ḥudūd al-'ālam min al-mashriq ilā al-maghrib*.
278. For example, see Bertels, *Shā'ir-i buzurg-i Āzarbāyjān*, p. 142; K. Aḥmad-Nizhād, *Taḥlīl-i āthār-i Niẓāmī Ganjavī*, 2nd edn (Tehran, 1375/1996), pp. 123–4.
279. For an English translation of this tale, see Michael Barry's 'Alexander wends his way into the Land of Darkness' in his *Figurative Art in Medieval Islam*, pp. 321–6; and on its mystical meaning, see pp. 321–30.
280. Niẓāmī, *Sharafnāma*, LXVIII, p. 500.
281. See M. Casari, 'The king explorer', in Richard Stoneman, Kyle Erickson and Ian Netton (eds), *The Alexander Romance in Persia and the East* (Groningen, 2012), p. 179.
282. Italian scholars have dedicated various works to discussing this subject; among them, see in particular: M. Casari, 'Nizami's cosmographic vision and Alexander in search of the Fountain of Life', in Johann-Christoph Bürgel and Christine van Ruymbeke (eds), *A Key to the Treasure of Hakim, Artistic and Humanistic Aspects of Nizāmī Ganjavī's Khamsa* (Leiden, 2011), pp. 95–105.
283. As elaborated by Barry, *Figurative Art in Medieval Islam*, pp. 327ff.
284. Among the sources that include the same etymology for the name of Bulgaria, we can mention Ibn Khalaf Tabrīzī's *Burhān-i Qāṭi'*. According to this source, Bulgaria is near the Land of Darkness and was founded in Alexander's time. According to Ghīyāth al-Dīn's *Ghīyāth al-lughāṭ*, the name Bulgār derives from the fact that the country is full of caves (*ghār* means cave in Persian). Both works are cited by Dihkhudā, 'Bulghār', *Lughatnāma*, vol. III, p. 4305.
285. Niẓāmī, *Sharafnāma*, LXVIII, p. 501.

286. H. Schwarzbaum, *Biblical and Extra-Biblical Legends in Islamic Folk Literature* (Walldorf-Hessen, 1982), p. 167.
287. R. Stoneman, personal communication.
288. A. J. Wensinck, 'al-Khaḍir', EI^2 iv, p. 904.
289. A poem by Percy Bysshe Shelley (d. 1822) compares Khiḍr and Ahasuerus, as does Shahrastānī's *Majlis-i maktūb* (eleventh century). See: L. Lewisohn, 'From the Moses of reason to the Khidr of the resurrection', in O. Alí-de-Unzaga (ed.), *Fortresses of the Intellect, Ismaili and Other Islamic Studies in Honour of Farhad Daftary* (London, 2011), pp. 423–7.
290. Niẓāmī, *Sharafnāma*, p. 511:

    که بود آب حیوان دگر جایگاه
    مجوسی و رومی غلط کرد راه

291. Ibid., LXIX, p. 508.
292. According to classical Greek tradition, it is Aristotle who gives magical stones to Alexander. See Thorndike, 'The Latin pseudo-Aristotle and medieval occult science', p. 235.
293. The valley of diamonds appears in Firdawsī's *Shāhnāma* (VI, pp. 95–6). The tale of the Valley of the Diamonds will be related in the context of the *Iqbālnāma* in Chapter 5.
294. The following sources may be cited here: Stoneman, *A Life in Legend*, pp. 150–62; Casari, 'Nizami's cosmographic vision', pp. 95–105; P. Franke, 'Drinking from the Water of Life', pp. 77–125.
295. See A. Szalc, 'In search of Water of Life: the Alexander romance and Indian mythology', in R. Stoneman, K. Erickson and I. Netton (eds), *The Alexander Romance in Persia and the East* (Groningen, 2012), pp. 327–38.
296. See the discussion on the myth of Gilgamesh in Stoneman, *A Life in Legend*, pp. 152–3. Jalāl Sattārī compares the myth of Gilgamesh with the Alexander legend in his book *Usṭūra-yi Gīlgamish va afsāna-yi Iskandar* (Tehran, 1384/2005).
297. Ethé has shown that the episode in the *Iskandarnāma* is full of terms that could be understood as allusions to Sufi concepts; cited by Franke, 'Drinking from the Water of Life', p. 115.
298. See Casari's 'The king explorer' and 'Nizami's cosmographic vision'.
299. See Friedländer, *Die Chadhirlegende und der Alexanderroman* (Leipzig, 1913), p. 330.
300. Brannon M. Wheeler, *Moses in the Quran and Islamic Exegesis* (London/New York, 2002), pp. 17–18. Wheeler makes a very detailed study of the motif of 'the lost fish' (pp. 11–19), and a brief summary of his conclusions is presented here.
301. See Wheeler, *Moses in the Quran and Islamic Exegesis*, p. 8.
302. This is mentioned by Aṣghar Mahdavī in a letter to Iraj Afshār, who included it in the prose edition of the *Iskandarnāma* (Tehran, 1387/2008), p. 632.
303. This reference seems to indicate that it originated from a linguistic fault by Bible translators in the Middle Ages. The Torah (Exodus 34:29–35) reports

that when Moses came down from Mount Sinai with the Ten Commandments, the skin of his face was radiant. When the Bible was translated into Latin, the translators attributed 'horns of light' to Moses because the spelling of the Hebrew verb *karan* (to shine) is identical to that of *keren* (horn). See Wheeler, *Moses in the Quran and Islamic Exegesis*, pp. 31–2.

304. Wheeler, *Moses in the Quran and Islamic Exegesis*, p. 117.
305. It is normally assumed that Niẓāmī's *Iskandarnāma* was highly Islamised; this point partially contradicts and subverts that assumption.
306. K. Schippmann, 'Azerbaijan: iii. Pre-Islamic history', *EIr* iii/2, p. 224.
307. Frederik Coene, *The Caucasus: An Introduction* (London/New York, 2010), p. 199.
308. Coene, *The Caucasus*, p. 69.
309. To cite one such example out of many, in the *Iqbālnāma*, Niẓāmī uses the word 'Uqyānūs' and affirms that it is a Greek word. From this statement, S. Ḥamīdīyān, the text's editor, concludes that it is possible that Niẓāmī knew Greek. See Niẓāmī, *Iqbālnāma*, p. 171, n. 4.
310. Niẓāmī, *Sharafnāma*, XXXII, p. 241.
311. See Lambton, *State and Government*, p. 55; Lambton, 'Islamic mirrors for princes', pp. 426–36.
312. Niẓāmī, *Sharafnāma*, p. 79.

    پس از دور هایی که بگذشت پیش
    کنم زنده ش از آب حیوان خویش
    سکندر که راه معانی گرفت
    پی چشمه زندگانی گرفت
    مگر دید کز راه فرخندگی
    شود زنده زین چشمه زندگی

Chapter 5 Alexander in the *Iqbālnāma* of Niẓāmī Ganjavī

1. Ṣā'ib Tabrīzī, *Dīvān*, vol. II, p. 664.
2. This title recalls Plutarch's *The Fortune of Alexander* (*Moralia: De Alexandri Magni Fortuna aut Virtute*). Is this a coincidence? We will briefly discuss this in the conclusion to the chapter.
3. See Peter Chelkowski, 'Niẓāmī Gandjawī', *EI* [2] viii, p. 79.
4. See J. Scott Meisami's chapter 'Romance as mirror' in *Medieval Persian Court Poetry*, pp. 191–234.
5. The idea of the king as the 'Perfect Man' or 'Universal Man' (*al-insān al-kāmil*) is discussed in many different Islamic works. For a survey of some of these doctrines, see S. Ḥ. Naṣr, *An Introduction to Islamic Cosmological Doctrines* (Cambridge, 1964), pp. 66–70.
6. The contents of these tales can be divided into two categories: stories in which Alexander is the protagonist, and independent stories in which Alexander does not play any role or plays only an insignificant one. Christoph Bürgel examines some of the key stories in the *Iqbālnāma* (e.g. the tale of Archimedes and his

Chinese Slave-girl, Mary the Copt, the Seventy Sages Who Deny the Doctrines of Hermes and Perish, Plato Composes Songs to Put Aristotle to Shame, etc.). For a study of some of these tales, see 'Occult sciences in the *Iskandarnameh* of Nizami', pp. 129–39. See also Bürgel, 'Die Geheimwissenschaften im *Iskandarnāme* Nizami', in Bert G. Fragner et al. (eds), *Proceedings of the Second European Conference of Iranian Studies, held in Bamberg, 30th September to 4th October 1991, by the Societas Iranologica Europaea* (Rome, 1995), pp. 103–12; Carlo Saccone, 'The wasteland and Alexander, the righteous king, in Niẓāmī's *Iqbālnāma*', in J. Christoph Bürgel and Christine van Ruymbeke (eds), *A Key to the Treasure of the Hakīm* (Leiden, 2011), pp. 165–79. Among the many interesting studies on these stories in Persian we may mention the following: 'A. Zarrīnkūb, 'Falsafa-yi yūnān dar bazm-i Iskandar: Naẓarī bi *Iskandarnāma-yi* Niẓāmī', *Irānshināsī* xi (1370/1991), pp. 482–98; K. Aḥmad-Nizhād, *Taḥlil-i āthār-i Niẓāmī Ganjavī* (Tehran, 1375/1996), pp. 142–218.

7. Regarding Niẓāmī's use of Alexander in his search for a perfect society see Zarrīnkūb, 'Niẓāmī, a life-long quest for a Utopia', *Colloquio sul poeta Persiano Niẓāmī e la leggenda Iranica di Alessandro Magno (Roma, 25–26 marzo 1975)* (Roma, 1977), 5–10.
8. On the various works of this genre in Arabic see T. Lewicki, 'al-Ḳazwīnī', *EI* [2] iv, pp. 865–7; C. E. Bosworth, "Ajā'eb al-Maklūqāt: i. Arabic works', *EIr* i/7, pp. 696–8. On the Persian works of this genre see Ī. Afshār, "Ajā'eb al-Maklūqāt: ii. Persian works', *EIr* i/7, pp. 698–9. See also the introduction of A. Ṭūsī, in M. Sutūda (ed.), *'Ajāyib al-makhlūqāt va gharāyib al-mawjūdāt* (Tehran, 1345/1966), pp. xv–xvii; P. M. Berlekamp, *Wonder, Image and Cosmos in Medieval Islam* (New Haven, 2011). On the different traditions of this genre see "*Ajāyib* literature', in J. Scott Meisami and P. Starkey (eds), *Encyclopaedia of Arabic Literature* (London/New York, 1998), vol. I, pp. 65–6.
9. Vettius Valens was a Hellenic astrologer. For his works and their importance, see O. Neugebauer and H. B. Van Hoesen, *Greek Horoscopes* (Philadelphia, 1987), pp. 176–85.
10. On Porphyry (233–*c*.304), the renowned Neoplatonic philosopher, disciple, biographer and editor of Plotinus, see 'Furfūrīyus', in M. Saeed Sheikh (ed.), *A Dictionary of Muslim Philosophy*, 2nd edn (Lahore, 1981), p. 80.
11. In fact, the reason the *Iqbālnāma* is also known as the *Khiradnāma* is the existence of these three 'Books of Wisdom' within the book.
12. On the historical information about this patron see, C. E. Bosworth, 'The political and dynastic history of the Iranian World (AD 1000–1217)', in J. A. Boyle (ed.), *The Cambridge History of Iran*, V: *The Saljuq and Mongol Periods* (Cambridge, 1968), pp. 170–1. See also Ḥ. Vaḥīd Dastgirdī, *Ganjīna-yi Ganjayī*, ed. S. Ḥamīdīyān (Tehran, 1376/1997), p. 71.
13. On the Greek utopian tradition in relation to the *Alexander Romance* see Stoneman, *A Life in Legend*, pp. 97–100.
14. For more information on this genre in Arabic and the influence of Greek literature upon it see Franz Rosenthal, *The Classical Heritage in Islam*, trans.

Emile and Jenny Marmorstein (London/New York, 1975; repr. 1994); Dimitri Gutas, *Greek Wisdom Literature in Arabic Translation* (New Haven, 1975), pp. 436–51; Gutas, 'Classical Arabic wisdom literature: nature and scope', *Journal of the American Oriental Society* ci (1981), pp. 49–86. For examples of these texts, see Doufikar-Aerts, *Alexander Magnus Arabicus*, pp. 93–4; H. J. Gleixner, *Das Alexanderbild der Byzantiner* (Munich, 1961), p. 20.

15. On Pahlavi wisdom literature see M. Macuch, 'Pahlavi literature', in R. E. Emmerick and M. Macuch (eds), *The Literature of Pre-Islamic Iran* (New York, 2009), pp. 160–72. For examples of this genre in Persian literature see C. H. de Fouchécour, *Moralia: Les notions morales dans la littérature persane des 3e/9e au 7e/13e siècles* (Paris, 1986).
16. On Greek influence on the Persian wisdom literature see C. van Ruymbeke, 'Hellenistic influences in classical Persian literature', in J. T. P. de Bruijn (ed.), *General Introduction to Persian Literature* (New York, 2009), p. 358.
17. De Fouchécour, *Moralia*, p. 316.
18. See J. Scott Meisami, 'Genre of court literature', in J. T. P. de Bruijn (ed.), *General Introduction to Persian Literature* (New York, 2009), pp. 255–60. Regarding the Greek wisdom literature in the *Iqbālnāma* of Niẓāmī see J. C. Bürgel, *The Feather of Simurgh: The 'Licit Magic' of the Arts in Medieval Islam* (New York/London, 1988), pp. 36–7; Niẓāmī, *Das Alexanderbuch: Iskandarname*, trans. J. C. Bürgel (Zürich, 1991). The mirror for princes genre is discussed in Chapter 4.
19. Yuḥanna Ibn al-Bitrīq, *Sirr al-asrār, al-uṣūl al-Yūnāniyya li naẓariyyat al-siyāsiyya fī'l-Islām*, ed. A. Badawī (Cairo, 1954).
20. Ḥunayn Ibn Isḥāq's original work (*Kitāb nawādir al-falāsifa*) has not been preserved. However, it is known through a version attributed to Muḥammad ibn 'Alī al-Anṣārī. The *'Ādāb al-falāsifa'* was edited by A. Badawī (Kuwait, 1985).
21. Christy Bandak (ed.), *Libro de los buenos proverbios: estudio y edición crítica de las versiones castellana y árabe* (Zaragoza, 2007).
22. Al-Mubashshir Ibn Fātiq, *Los bocados de oro (Mukhtār al-ḥikām wa maḥāsin al-kalam)*, ed. 'Abd al-Raḥmān Badawī (Madrid, 1958). On the relation of this work with the *Alexander Romance* see Emily Cottrell, 'Al-Mubaššir ibn Fātik and the α Version of the Alexander Romance', in Richard Stoneman, Kyle Erickson and Ian Netton (eds), *The Alexander Romance in Persia and the East* (Groningen, 2012), pp. 233–53.
23. On the role Alexander played in wisdom literature there are important annotations in Richard Stoneman, 'The legacy of Alexander in ancient philosophy', in J. Roisman (ed.), *Brill's Companion to Alexander the Great* (Leiden, 2003), pp. 325–46.
24. Doufikar-Aerts, *Alexander Magnus Arabicus*, pp. 96–128.
25. These motifs are in the *Shāhnāma* of Firdawsī and the *Iskandarnāma* of Niẓāmī (such as Alexander's letter of consolation to his mother, the philosophers'

funeral sentences around Alexander's tomb, his relationship with his philosophers, etc.).

26. Doufikar-Aerts, *Alexander Magnus Arabicus*, p. 130.
27. Niẓāmī, *Iqbālnāma*, p. 36.
28. Ibid., p. 37.
29. Ibid., pp. 37–8.
30. Ibid., p. 38:

    کنون زان صدفهای گوهرفشان
    برون ز انطیاخس نبینی نشان

31. Ibid.
32. See Tiziano Dorandi, 'Chronology', in K. Algra et al. (eds), *The Cambridge History of Hellenistic Philosophy* (Cambridge, 1999), pp. 49ff.
33. H. Corbin, *Histoire de la philosophie islamique I: des origines jusqu'à la mort d'Averroës (1198)* (Paris, 1964), pp. 284–304. For Neoplatonic ideas in the Arabic world, see Peter Adamson, *The Arabic Plotinus: A Philosophical Study of the 'Theology of Aristotle'* (London, 2002).
34. Plutarch, *Alex.*, 14.
35. See M. Buora, 'L'incontro tra Alessandro et Diogene: Tradizioni e significato', *Atti dell'Istituto Veneto de Scienze: Lettere ed Arti* 132 (1973–4), p. 247; S. Doloff, 'Let me talk with this philosopher: the Alexander paradigm in *King Lear*', *The Huntington Library Quarterly* liv (1991), pp. 253–5; D. Pinski, *Aleksander un Dyogenes* (Vilne, 1930); Luis E. Navia, *Classical Cynicism: A Critical Study* (Greenwood, 1996), pp. 98–100.
36. Cited from J. D. Burnley, *Chaucer Studies II: Chaucer's Language and the Philosophers' Tradition* (New York, 1979), p. 71.
37. For instance, Niẓāmī describes Socrates 'asleep, enjoying the sunshine' (*mashqūl-e khāb, barāsūda az tābish-e āftāb*), which recalls the famous sentence of Diogenes (Arr. *Anab.* 7.2; Diog. *Ep.* 33), telling Alexander 'Please get out from between me and the sun!'
38. Niẓāmī, *Iqbālnāma*, p. 97.
39. Ibid., p. 98.
40. On the Pythagorean ascetic tradition and sexual abstinence in the pagan and Hellenistic periods see R. Damian Finn, *Asceticism in the Graeco-Roman World* (Cambridge, 2009), pp. 27–55.
41. See Nasr, *The Islamic Intellectual Tradition in Persia*, p. 184.
42. In Philostratus's *Life of Apollonius of Tyana*, Pythagoras was the model by which the author established the life of his protagonist. See Ewen L. Bowie, 'Apollonius of Tyana: tradition and reality', *Aufsteig und Niedergang der Römischen Welt*, Teil II: Principat, xvi/2 (1978), pp. 3–41. The conclusion of the previous chapter suggests that Niẓāmī might have known Philostratus's work or the source(s) of the *Life of Apollonius of Tyana*.
43. For examples of texts that share the Cynic view of Alexander in Antiquity see R. Stoneman, 'The legacy of Alexander in ancient philosophy', pp. 331–45.

44. I am grateful to Dr Richard Stoneman for drawing my attention to the fact that any matters concerning sexual asceticism must come from non-Cynic sources.
45. Niẓāmī, *Iqbālnāma*, p. 98.
46. Ibid., p. 103:

    بران راهرو نیم جو بار نیست
    که او را یکی جو در انبار نیست

47. Ibid., p. 104:

    تو با اینکه داری جهانی چنین
    نه ای سیردل هم ز خوانی چنین

48. Ibid., p. 105:

    دل پاک را زنگ پرداز کن
    برو راز روحانیان باز کن

49. Ibid., p. 108:

    دهن مهر کرد از می خوشگوار
    که بنیاد شادی ندید استوار

50. Ibid., p. 120.
51. Ibid., p. 135:

    ز تعلیم دانش به جایی رسید
    که دادش خرد بر گشایش کلید

52. Ibid., p. 121:

    چنین هفت پرگار بر گرد شاه
    دران دایره شه شده نقطه گاه

53. Ezra 7:14. The identification of Artaxerxes I or II depends on when we date Ezra; see the discussion in Stoneman, *Xerxes: A Persian Life* (New Haven/London, 2015), pp. 58–61.
54. Plato, *Protagoras*, 343 A; Plutarch, *Mor.*, 146 Bff. See J. M. Dillon, *Morality and Custom in Ancient Greece* (Indiana, 2004), p. 190.
55. See 'The seven sages of Rome' in A. Grafton, G. Most and S. Settis (eds), *The Classical Tradition* (Harvard, 2010), p. 877.
56. For a good overview of the motif of the philosophers surrounding Alexander in the Persian romance tradition, see Mario Casari, 'The wise men at Alexander's court in Persian medieval romances: an Iranian view of ancient cultural heritage', in Carlo Cereti (ed.), *Iranian Identity in the Course of History* (Rome, 2010), pp. 67–80.
57. Niẓāmī, *Iqbālnāma*, p. 131:

    از این بیش گفتن نباشد پسند
    که نقش جهان نیست بی نقشبند

58. Ibid., p. 130.

59. Ibid., p. 135.
60. Ibid., pp. 108–20.
61. For references see R. Stoneman, 'Naked philosophers: the Brahmans in the Alexander historians and the Alexander romance', *Journal of Hellenic Studies* cxv (1995), p. 99, nn. 1, 2.
62. Niẓāmī, *Iqbālnāma*, p. 135:

    نزد دیگر از آفرینش نفس
    جهان آفرین را طلب کرد و بس

    I owe the poetic translation of Niẓāmī's verses in this chapter to Dr Leonard Lewisohn, to whom I am very grateful.
63. See Doufikar-Aerts, *Alexander Magnus Arabicus*, Chapter 3.
64. Ibid., p. 135.
65. Ibid., p. 188.
66. Bal'amī also commented on this interpretation. See Bal'amī, *Tārīkh-i Bal'amī*, vol. II, p. 701.
67. Arrian (7.14.4) suggested that Alexander wore his hair long in imitation of Achilles. According to Olga Palagia, there are two silver decadrachm (medallions of Porus) on which Alexander appears with strands of hair hanging down from either side of his helmet over his chest. See Olga Palagia, 'The impact of Alexander the Great in the art of Central Asia', *The Alexander Romance in Persia and the East*, p. 372.
68. Abū Ma'shar al-Balkhī (*c.*787–886), is best known for his astrological writings. See Keiji Yamamoto, 'Abū Ma'shar al-Balkhī', *The Biographical Encyclopaedia of Astronomers*, ed. Thomas Hockey et al. (New York, 2007), p. 11.
69. Niẓāmī, *Iqbālnāma*, pp. 44–5.
70. Ibid., p. 45.
71. On this tradition and the background of various Dhū'l-Qarnayn legends in Islam, see Doufikar-Aerts, *Alexander Magnus Arabicus*, pp. 135–50; K. Aḥmad-Nizhād, *Taḥlīl-i āthār-i Niẓāmī Ganjavī* (Tehran, 1375/1996), pp. 153–8; Ṣafavī, *Iskandar va adabīyāt-i Irān*, pp. 279–310.
72. Bīrūnī, *Āthār al-bāqī'a*, p. 31; English translation, p. 43.
73. See Bal'amī, *Tārīkh-i Bal'amī*, vol. II, pp. 701ff.
74. Sanā'ī, *Kitāb Ḥadīqat al-ḥaqīqa wa sharī'at al-ṭarīqa*, ed. Muḥammad Rawshan (Tehran, 1377/1998), pp. 351–2.
75. In her article 'King Midas' ears on Alexander's head', Doufikar-Aerts explores these oral traditions reflected in the repertoires of preachers and storytellers (pp. 61–79).
76. For instance, Doufikar-Aerts quotes the Darī variant of this story, as preserved by an aged lady from Kabul, beside some Turkish variants. See 'King Midas' ears on Alexander's head', pp. 70–1.
77. Niẓāmī, *Iqbālnāma*, p. 135:

    نزد دیگر از آفرینش نفس
    جهان آفرین را طلب کرد و بس

78. Ibid., p. 136.
79. Alexander's prophethood is discussed in a similar way by Bal'amī (*Tārīkh*, vol. II, p. 711).
80. There is a similar attribution to Alexander in the anonymous *Mujmal al-tavārīkh* (pp. 506–7).
81. Niẓāmī, *Iqbālnāma*, pp. 139–40.
82. Ibid., pp. 142–64.
83. Ibid., p. 166:

    بفرمود تا عبره روم و روس
    نبشتند بر نام اسکندروس

84. Ibid., p. 168:

    ز مقدونیه روی در راه کرد
    به اسکندریه گذرگاه کرد

85. Ibid., p. 170:

    چو بیدادگر دید،خون ریختش
    ز دروازه مقدس آویختش

86. Ibid., p. 170:

    بر افرنجه آورد از آنجا سپاه
    وز افرنجه بر اندلس کرد راه

87. Muḥammad Ibn Maḥmūd Ibn Aḥmad Ṭūsī, *'Ajāyib al-makhlūqāt wa gharāyib al-mawjūdāt {Prodigies of Things Created and Miraculous Aspects of Things Existent}*, ed. M. Sutūda (Tehran, 1391/2012), introduction, p. xvi.
88. See Aḥmad Ṭūsī, *'Ajāyib al-makhlūqāt*, pp. 2–3.
89. Such as Megasthenes and Philostratus. See R. Stoneman, 'The marvels of India', *A Life in Legend*, pp. 69–72; K. Karttunen, *India and the Hellenistic World* (Helsinki, 1997); J. Romm, *The Edges of the World in Ancient Thought* (Princeton, 1992), pp. 82–120.
90. The most important work with this title in Persian is attributed to Aḥmad Ṭūsī (twelfth century) and that in Arabic to Abū Yaḥyā Zakarīyā b. Muḥammad Qazwīnī (*c.*1203–83).
91. On the *Ajāyib al-Buldān* (*Wonders of the Lands*) attributed to Abū al-Mu'ayyid Balkhī (tenth century), see M. T. Bahār, *Sabk-shināsī*, 7th edn (Tehran, 1373/1994), vol. II, pp. 18–19; Dh. Ṣafā, *Tārīkh adabīyāt dar Irān*, vol. I, p. 618.
92. Aḥmad Ṭūsī, *Ajāyib al-makhlūqāt*, introduction, p. xvi.
93. F. Doufikar-Aerts, 'A letter in bits and pieces: "The Epistola Alexandri ad Aristotolem Arabica". A first edition with translation based on four 16th–18th century manuscripts', in Robert M. Kerr and Thomas Milo (eds), *Writings and Writing from Another World and Another Era* (Cambridge, 2010), pp. 91–115.
94. Richard Stoneman, 'Romantic ethnography: Central Asia and India in the Alexander romance', *Ancient World* xxv (1994), pp. 93–107; see also Stoneman, *A Life in Legend*, pp. 73–7, 238.

95. See Supplement F in Stoneman's edition of *The Greek Alexander Romance.*
96. Niẓāmī, *Iqbālnāma*, p. 168:

    که از روی دریا به یک ماهه راه
    نشان باز داد از سپید و سیاه

97. Most of the Islamic sources attributed the construction of the lighthouse of Alexandria to Alexander. For Arabic sources, see F. Doufikar-Aerts, 'Alexander the Great and the Pharos of Alexandria in Arabic literature', in J. Ch. Bürgel and M. Bridges (eds), *The Problematics of Power* (Bern, 1996), pp. 191–201. For Persian sources see *Mujmal al-tavārīkh*, p. 494; Ṣafavī, *Iskandar va adabīyāt-i Iran*, pp. 214–17. See also Amīr Khusraw Dihlavī, 'A'īna-yi Iskandarī', in A. Aḥmad Ashrafī (ed.), *Khamsa* (Tehran, 1362/1983), pp. 495–6.
98. Ṭarsūsī, *Dārābnāma*, vol. II, pp. 531–4.
99. See Stoneman, 'Alexander's mirror', p. 47.
100. Aḥmad Ṭūsī, *Ajāyib al-makhlūqāt*, pp. 180–3, 146.
101. The text reads *ki Yūnānīsh uqyānūs kh^{w}ānd.* The fact that Niẓāmī uses the word *uqyānūs* (from the Ancient Greek Ὠκεανός, *Okeanós*) in this verse may indicate his knowledge of the Greek language, insofar as no other poets or authors in Persian literature had used this word before him. See the editor's note to Niẓāmī, *Iqbālnāma*, p. 171, n. 4.
102. Ibid., pp. 174–5.
103. Ibid., p. 176. There is a similar story in the *'Ajāyib al-makhlūqāt* of Aḥmad Ṭūsī (p. 357).
104. Stoneman, *A Life in Legend*, p. 124.
105. For instance, see Ibn al-Faqīh al-Hamadānī, *Bibliotheca Geographorum Arabicorum*, vol. V, p. 71; Mas'ūdī, *Murūj*, vol. I, p. 369; Yāqūt Ḥamavī, *Mu'jam*, vol. IV, p. 45; Qazwīnī, *'Ajāyib*, vol. II, p. 375. See also A. Hamori, 'An allegory from the Arabian Nights: the city of brass', *On the Art of Medieval Arabic Literature* (Princton, 1974), pp. 145–63.
106. *Mujmal al-tavārīkh*, pp. 501–11.
107. S. M. Burstein, 'Alexander, Callisthenes and the sources of the Nile', *Greek, Roman and Byzantine Studies* xvii (1976), pp. 135–46.
108. *Mujmal al-tavārīkh*, pp. 474–5.
109. Stoneman, *A Life in Legend*, p. 165.
110. This evidently refers to the 'Iram of lofty pillars' mentioned in the Qur'ān (Fajr, 89:7) built by Shaddād, a legendary king of Arabia.
111. On the comparison between Shaddād's inscription and that of Cyrus the Great see Ṣafavī, *Iskandar va adabīyāt-i Irān*, p. 221.
112. See Stoneman, *A Life in Legend*, pp. 163–4.
113. Niẓāmī, *Iqbālnāma*, pp. 189–91.
114. According to Fahd, it is also applied to 'a community following an old Semitic polytheistic religion, but with a strongly Hellenised elite, one of the last outposts of Late Antique paganism'. See T. Fahd, 'Ṣābi'a', *EI*^{2} viii, p. 676.

115. Ibn Nadīm, *al-Fihrist*, trans. M. R. Tajaddud (Tehran, 1343/1964), p. 570.
116. On the possible identification of this book, see T. M. Green, *The City of the Moon God: Religious Traditions of Harran* (Leiden, 1992), p. 180.
117. Abū l-Qāsim Maslama b. Aḥmad al-Majrīṭī (d. 1007), known in Europe as 'Pseudo Picatrix' (the 'Pseudo Hippocrates'). See J. Vernet, 'al-Madjrīṭī', *EI* [2] v, pp. 1109–10.
118. See D. Pingree (ed.), *Picatrix: The Latin Version of the Ghayat al-hakim* (London, 1986); R. Kieckhefer, *Magic in the Middle Ages* (Cambridge, 1989), p. 133. For the version of prophetic skulls in the *Picatrix* see H. Ritter and M. Plessner, *'Picatrix': Das Ziel des Weisen von Pseudo-Majrīṭī* (Studies of the Warburg Institute xxvii) (London, 1962), pp. 146–7.
119. See D. Ogden, *Greek and Roman Necromancy* (Princeton/Oxford, 2001), pp. 210–16. For Greek texts on the use of skulls in necromancy see D. Ogden, *Magic, Witchcraft, and Ghosts*, pp. 202–5.
120. See Stoneman, *The Ancient Oracles*, pp. 67–9.
121. Bīrūnī, *Kitāb al-jamāhir fī ma'rifat al-jawāhir {The Sum of Knowledge about Precious Stones}*, ed. F. Krenkow (Hyderabad, 1355/1936), p. 99.
122. See Stoneman, *A Life in Legend*, pp. 85–6.
123. Niẓāmī, *Iqbālnāma*, p. 192. With 'almās', Niẓāmī must be referring to the word *adámas*, from the ancient Greek ἀδάμας (unbreakable).
124. See Stoneman, *A Life in Legend*, p. 85.
125. Qazwīnī, *Kitāb 'ajāyib al-Makhlūqāt*, ed. F. Wüstenfeld (Göttingen, 1849), vol. II, p. 375.
126. See Y. Yamanaka, 'Alexander in the Thousand and One Nights and the Ghazālī Connection', in Y. Yamanaka and T. Nishio (eds), *The Arabian Nights and Orientalism: Perspectives from East and West* (New York/London, 2006), pp. 93–115.
127. Niẓāmī, *Iqbālnāma*, p. 195.
128. Ibid., p. 196:

    چنان مان به هر پیشه ور پیشه ای
    که در خلقتش ناید اندیشه ای

129. Ibid., p. 198.
130. This must refer to the word mentioned in the *Avesta* (*Ābān Yasht*, 54, 57; *Zāmyād Yasht*, 4) and to 'Kang Dizh' (which can be translated as the Castle of Kang), which appears in the *Bundahishn* (29.10) and in the *Mīnū-yi Khirad* (62.13–14). The castle was said to have been built by Sīyāvajsh, Kay Khusraw's father. See Firdawsī, *Shāhnāma*, vol. II, pp. 308–9.
131. Niẓāmī, *Iqbālnāma*, p. 202:

    نبشت از بر پیکر آن نگار
    که با داغ اسکندر است این شکار

132. Abū Bakr Muḥammad Ibn Ja'far, *Tārīkh-i Bukhārā*, ed. Muddaris Raḍavī, 2nd edn (Tehran, 1363/1984), pp. 62–3.
133. Niẓāmī uses *'āb-i kabūd'*, which means the Black Sea:

چو نزدیک آب کبود آمدند
به پایین دریا فرود آمدند

However, it is ambiguous because in some verses he refers to a 'Chinese Sea' (*daryā-yi Chīn*):

درافگند کشتی به دریای چین

Thus, it is not clear whether he is referring to different seas or applying multiple names to the same one.

134. Niẓāmī, *Iqbālnāma*, p. 205.
135. Ibid.:

پراگنده گیسو بر اندام خویش
زده مشک بر نقره خام خویش

136. See Stoneman, *A Life in Legend*, pp. 145–6.
137. Budge, *The History of Alexander*, p. 97; Budge, *The Life and Exploits of Alexander the Great: Being a Series of Ethiopic Texts* (London, 1896), p. 147.
138. Ibn al-Faqīh al-Hamadānī and Yāqūt mention that Alexander erected an equestrian statue. Others, such as Gharnāṭī and Ṭabarī, also mention this but do not link the statue with Alexander. See G. Ferrand, 'Le *Tuḥfat al-Albāb* de al-Andalusī al-Ġarnāṭī', *Journal Asiatique* ccvii (1925), p. 64; Qazwīnī *Kitāb 'ajāyib al-Makhlūqāt* (1849), vol. I, p. 180; Ṭabarī, *Annales*, p. 684.
139. Niẓāmī, *Iqbālnāma*, p. 217.
140. Ibid., p. 220:

شه آن رسم را نیز بر جای داشت
که هر صبحدم با دهل پای داشت

141. Aḥmad Ṭūsī, *'Ajā'ib al-makhlūqāt*, p. 327.
142. Kharkhīz is a city in Khutan (Chinese Turkistan) famous for its musk and silk. See 'Alī Akbar Dihkhudā, *Lughat-nāma*, vol. VI, p. 8483, s.v. 'Kharkhīz'.
143. Niẓāmī, *Iqbālnāma*, p. 223.
144. This may refer to the crossing of the Gedrosian desert (Plutarch, *Alex.* 66.4–5). Thanks to Professor Lynette Mitchell for this comment.
145. Niẓāmī, *Iqbālnāma*, p. 224:

گروهی بران کوه دین پروران
مسلمان و فارغ ز پیغمبران

146. Ibid.:

چو دیدند سیمای اسکندری
پذیرا شدندش به پیغمبری

147. For the English translation see Budge, *The Syriac Alexander Romance* (repr. Amsterdam, 1976), pp. 144–58, 163–200.
148. Niẓāmī, *Iqbālnāma*, p. 226:

ازان مرحله سوی شهری شتافت
که بسیار کس جست و آن را نیافت

149. Ibid., pp. 228–31.

150. Ibid., pp. 231–2.
151. See Stoneman, 'Tales of Utopia: Alexander, Cynics and Christian ascetics', Paper given at *ICAN IV: International Conference on the Ancient Novel: Crossroads in the Ancient Novel: Spaces, Frontiers, Intersections* (Lisbon, 21–6 July 2008). See also Budge, *The Life and Exploits of Alexander the Great*, p. 422.
152. Maybudī, *Kashf al-asrār wa 'uddat al-abrār*, ed. 'A. A. Ḥikmat (Tehran, 1357/1978), vol. V, p. 75.
153. See Stoneman, 'Naked philosophers', pp. 99–114; Stoneman, 'Who are the Brahmans?', pp. 500–10.
154. For more discussion see Stoneman, *A Life in Legend*, pp. 92–102.
155. See Timothy P. Bridgeman, *Hyperboreans: Myth and History in Celtic–Hellenic Contacts* (London/New York, 2005).
156. Niẓāmī, *Iqbālnāma*, p. 236.
157. Alexander is also said to have died in a city called 'Shahrzūr' by Bal'amī (*Tārīkh*, vol. II, p. 700) and Bīrūnī (*Āthār al-bāqīyah*, pp. 60–1). The Persian verses in Niẓāmī are as follows:

به کرمان رسید از کنار جهان
ز کرمان درآمد به کرمانشهان
وز آنجا به بابل برون برد راه
ز بابل سوی روم زد بارگاه
چو آمد ز بابل سوی شهرزور
سلامت شد از پیکر شاه دور

158. Niẓāmī, *Iqbālnāma*, p. 242:

چو اسکندر آیینه در پیش داشت
نظر در تنومندی خویش داشت

159. Ibid., p. 245:

جهان جمله دیدم ز بالا و زیر
هنوزم نشد دیده از دید سیر
نه این سی و شش، گر بود سی هزار
همین نکته گویم سرانجام کار

160. Ibid., p. 246:

بلیناس کو تا به افسونگری
کند چاره جان اسکندری؟

161. For an excellent survey (and partial translation) of the extensive literature in Arabic on 'Sayings on Alexander's Death' see Rosenthal, *The Classical Heritage in Islam*, trans. Emile and Jenny Marmorstein (London/New York, 1975; repr. 1994), pp. 120–4.
162. Niẓāmī, *Iqbālnāma*, p. 255:

اگر ماندنی شد جهان بر کسی
بمان در غم و سوگواری بسی

163. Ibid., p. 256:

که: آن کس خورد این خورشهای پاک
که غایب نباشد ورا زیر خاک
اگر زان خورشها خورد میهمان
تو نیز انده من بخور در زمان

164. Stoneman, *A Life in Legend*, p. 191.
165. Ibid.
166. Stoneman also suggests the possibility that Democritus, who had travelled in the East, may have introduced the motif into Greek literature. See Stoneman, *A Life in Legend*, p. 192.
167. See Pierre Hadot, *What is Ancient Philosophy?* (Cambridge, 2002), index, s.v. 'death', where a number of philosophical meditations from the Stoics and other Greek philosophical schools similar to these adages can be found.
168. For adages resembling the maxims on death that Alexander addressed to his mother, see Marcus Aurelius, *Meditations*, trans. Maxwell Staniforth (Middlesex, 1964), Books II: 14; III: 10; IV: 5–6; VI: 47, 56.
169. Niẓāmī, *Iqbālnāma*, p. 258:

سکندر چو بربست ازین خانه رخت
زدندش به بالای این خیمه تخت ...
اگرچه ز ره تافتن تفته بود
رهی رفت کان راه نارفته بود

170. Ibid., p. 259:

ز تابوت فرموده بد شهریار
که یک دست او را کنند آشکار ...
که: فرمانده هفت کشور زمین
همین یک تن آمد ز شاهان، همین
ز هر گنج دنیا که در بار بست
بجز خاک چیزی ندارد به دست

171. Ibid., pp. 259–60:

سوی مصر بردندش از شهرزور
که بود آن دیار از بداندیش دور
به اسکندریش وطن ساختند
ز تختش به تخته در انداختند

172. Ibid., pp. 263–8. This is also known from Ṭabarī (*Tārīkh*, vol. II, p. 494).
173. Niẓāmī, *Iqbālnāma*, p. 280 (see also n. 2):

فزون بود شش مه ز شصت و سه سال
که بر عزم ره بر دهل زد دوال

174. On this tendency see Lambton, 'Sufis and the state in medieval Persia', in C. van Dijk and A. H. de Groot (eds), *State and Islam* (Leiden, 1995), p. 23.
175. In these works Aristotle reveals talismanic secrets and Hermetic magic rituals to his pupil Alexander. See F. E. Peters, *Aristoteles Arabus: The Oriental Translations and Commentaries of the Aristotelian Corpus* (Leiden, 1961), p. 58.

176. See J. Ruska, *Tabula Smaragdina: Ein Beitrag Zur Geschichte Der Hermetischen Literatur* (Heidelberg, 1926), pp. 68–107. In this work Apollonius (Balīnās) also appears as a contemporary of Alexander the Great.
177. See section two of this chapter.
178. See K. van Bladel, 'Hermes and Hermetica', in Kate Fleet, Gudrun Krämer, Denis Matringe, John Nawas, Everett Rowson (eds), *Encyclopaedia of Islam*, 3rd edn Brill Online.
179. See Pingree, *Picatrix*, pp. 45, 97, 98, 140, 146, 150.
180. R. Stoneman, 'The origins of Quintus Curtius' concept of Fortuna', Paper given at the conference *Curtius Rufus the Roman Historian on Alexander Narrative Technique, Rhetoric, Psychology of Characters*, Wien, 4 October 2014.
181. Franz Rosenthal in *The Classical Heritage of Islam*, pp. 124–26, 142–44 in fact quotes passages of the sayings of Plutarch (Protarchus) that were translated into Arabic. On p. 83, he says that 'a very few of Plutarch's works' were translated into Arabic.
182. T. S. Schmidt, 'Barbarians in Plutarch's political thought', in L. de Blois, J. Bons, T. Kessels and D. M. Schenkeveld (eds), *The Statesman in Plutarch's Works, Vol. I: Plutarch's Statesman and His Aftermath: Political, Philosophical, and Literary Aspects* (Leiden, 2004), p. 229.

Conclusion

1. Ṣā'ib Tabrīzī, *Dīvān*, vol. II, p. 902.
2. Stoneman, *A Life in Legend*, p. 2.
3. Nöldeke, *Beiträge zur Geschichte des Alexanderromans*.
4. Frye, 'Two Iranian notes', *Acta Iranica XI: Papers in Honour of Professor Mary Boyce* (Leiden, 1985), pp. 186–8; Ciancaglini, 'The Syriac version of the Alexander romance', *Le Muséon, Revue D'Études Orientales* cxiv/1–2 (2001), pp. 135–40.
5. The reference here is to the historical accounts of Ṭabarī, Dīnawarī, the *Nihāya*, Tha'ālibī Nayshābūrī and Firdawsī.
6. See Yarshater, 'Chirā az pādishāhān-i mād va hakhāmanishī dar *Shāhnāma* dhikrī nīst', p. 194. See also Shayegan, *Arsacids and Sasanians*, p. 306.
7. Touraj Daryaee, 'Alexander and the Arsacids in the manuscript *MU29*', *Dabir, Digital Archive of Brief Notes & Iran Review* i/1 (2015), pp. 8–10.
8. Quoted from Shayegan, *Arsacids and Sasanians*, pp. 294–5.
9. Boyce, 'The Parthian 'Gōsān' and Iranian minstrel tradition', *The Journal of the Royal Asiatic Society of Great Britain and Ireland* i/2 (1957), pp. 10–45.
10. Agathias, *The Histories*, trans. J. D. Frendo (Berlin, 1975), II.31. See also Daryaee, *Sasanian Persia*, p. 30.
11. On the translations of Greek works into Middle Persian that were commissioned by Khusraw I, see Gutas, *Greek Thought, Arabic Culture*, p. 25.

12. Ḥāfiẓ, *Dīvān*, ed. Ḥasan Dhū'l-Faqār and Abū'l-Faḍl 'Alī Muḥammadī (Tehran, 1381/2002), *ghazal* 3:

    The holy grail of Jamshid is just
    the same as Alexander's looking glass;
    So look therein if you would contemplate
    the affairs of the kingdom of Darius.

13. See M. Kayvānī, 'Iskandar dar adab-i Fārsī', p. 404.
14. Farrukhī Sīstānī, *Divān*, ed. Muḥammad Dabīr Siyāqī, 2nd edn (Tehran, 1970). This verse was cited as the epigraph of the introduction above.
15. See Ṣafā, *Tārikh-i Adabiyāt dar Irān*, vol. I, p. 20; Ibn Hishām, *Sīra al-Nabavīya*, ed. M. Saqā (Cairo, 1355/1936); Dh. Ṣafā, *Hamāsa-sarāyī* (Tehran, 1363/1984), p. 74. See also Lings, *Muhammad*, p. 89.
16. Nöldeke, *Beiträge zur Geschichte des Alexanderromans*.
17. Frye, 'Two Iranian notes', pp. 186–8; Ciancaglini, 'The Syriac version of the Alexander romance', pp. 135–40.
18. According to N. Sims-Williams, Middle Iranian Christian literature may be regarded as a branch of Syriac literature. See his 'Christian literature in Middle Iranian languages', in Ronald E. Emmerick and Maria Macuch (eds), *The Literature of Pre-Islamic Iran*: Companion Volume I to *A History of Persian Literature* (London/New York, 2009), p. 266.
19. Tafaḍḍulī, *Tārīkh-i adabīyāt-i Irān pīsh az Islam*, ed. Zh. Āmūzgār (Tehran, 1376/1997), pp. 270–1; Boyce, 'Middle Persian literature', *Iranistik II: Handbuch der Orientalistik* 1. IV. 2.1 (Leiden, 1968), p. 59.
20. Budge, *The History of Alexander*, p. lx.
21. See also Ciancaglini, 'The Syriac version of the Alexander romance', p. 139.
22. Ibid., pp. 139–40.
23. Khaleghi-Motlagh, 'Az *Shāhnāma* tā *Khudāynāma*', *Nāma-yi Irān Bāstān (International Journal of Ancient Iranian Studies)* vii/1–2 (2007–8), pp. 29–30; Khaleghi-Motlagh, 'Jāy-i Rustam, Ārash ... va Iskandar dar *Khudāynāmag*', *Nāma-yi Irān Bāstān* ix/1–2 (2009–10), pp. 19–20.
24. K. Schippmann, 'Azerbaijan: iii. Pre-Islamic history', *EIr* iii/2, p. 224.
25. Davis, *Panthea's Children*, p. 1.
26. For examples see Ulrich Marzolph, 'The creative reception of the *Alexander Romance* in Iran', in Dominique Jullien (ed.), *Foundational Texts of World Literaure* (New York, 2012), pp. 74–9; Marjolijn van Zutphen, *Farāmarz, the Sistāni Hero, Texts and Traditions of the* Farāmarznāme *and the Persian Epic Cycle* (Leiden, 2014), pp. 512ff.
27. Renard, *Islam and the Heroic Image*, p. 86.
28. Marzolph, 'The creative reception of the *Alexander Romance* in Iran', p. 79.

BIBLIOGRAPHY

Abel, A., 'Iskandar-Nāma', *EI* [2] iv, ed. E. Van Donzel, B. Lewis and Ch. Pellat (Leiden, 1997), pp. 127–8.
Abū Bakr Muḥammad Ibn Ja'far, *Tārīkh-i Bukhārā*, ed. Muddaris Raḍavī, 2nd edn (Tehran, 1363/1984).
Adamson, Peter, *The Arabic Plotinus: A Philosophical Study of the 'Theology of Aristotle'* (London, 2002).
Afnan, S. M., *Philosophical Terminology in Arabic and Persian* (Leiden, 1964).
Afshār, Īraj, "Ajā'eb al-Maklūqāt: ii. Persian works', *EIr* i/7, pp. 698–9.
——— (ed.), *Iskandarnāma-yi manthūr* (Tehran, 1343/1964; repr. 1387/2008).
Agathias, *The Histories*, trans. J.D. Frendo (Berlin, 1975).
Aḥmadnizhād, K., *Taḥlīl-i athār-i Niẓāmī Ganjavī* (Tehran, 1375/1996).
Akramī, M., *Gāh-shumārī-yi īrānī* (Tehran, 1380/2001).
A'lam, H., 'Davāl-pā(y)', *EIr* vii/2, pp. 128–9.
Amīr Khusraw Dihlavī, *Khamsa*, ed. A. Aḥmad Ashrafī (Tehran, 1362/1983).
——— *Lo specchio Alessandrino*, trans. Angelo M. Piemontese (Catanzaro, 1999).
Amīrqāsimī, 'Ashīl va Isfandiyār du hamzād-i usṭūri'ī', *Adabiyāt va zabān-hā* lxxxvi/7 (1368/1989), pp. 433–48.
Anderson, A. R., 'Alexander at the Caspian Gates', *Transactions of the American Philological Association* lix (1928), pp. 130–63.
——— *Alexander's Gate, Gog and Magog and the Enclosed Nations* (Cambridge, 1932).
Artamonov, M. I., *Istoriya Khazar* [*History of the Khazars*] (Leningrad, 1962).
Āryān, Qamar, 'Christianity VI: In Persian literature', *EIr* v/5, pp. 339–42.
Asadī Ṭūsī, *Garshāspnāma*, ed. Ḥ. Yaghmāyī, 2nd edn (Tehran, 1354/1975).
Badawī, A (ed.), *Ādāb al-falāsifa* (Kuwait, 1985).
Bahār, Muḥammad Taqī (ed.), *Mujmal al-tawārīkh* (Tehran, 1318/1939).
——— *Sabk-shināsī ya tarīkh-i taṭavvur-i naṣr-i fārsī*, 3 vols (Tehran, 1942).
——— (ed.), *Tārīkh-i Sīstān* (Tehran, 1314/1935; 2nd edn 1352/1973).
Bal'amī, *Tārīkh-i Bal'amī: Tarjuma-yi Tārīkh-i Ṭabarī*, ed. M. T. Bahār and M. P. Gunābādī, 2nd edn, 2 vols (Tehran, 1353/1974).
Bandak, Christy (ed.), *Libro de los buenos proverbios: estudio y edición crítica de las versiones castellana y árabe* (Zaragoza, 2007).

Barns, J. W. B., 'Egypt and the Greek romance', *Mitteilungen aus der Papyrussammlung der Österreichsichen Nationalbibliothek* v (1956), pp. 29–36.

Barry, Michael, *Figurative Art in Medieval Islam and the Riddle of Bihzād of Herāt* (Paris, 2004).

——— *Farīd-od-Dīn 'Attār: The Canticle of the Birds Illustrated through Persian and Eastern Art*, trans. A. Darbandi and Dick Davis, with commentary by Michael Barry (Paris, 2014).

Barthold, W., 'Zur Geschichte des persischen Epos', *Zeitschrift der Deutschen Morgenländischen Gesellschaft* xcviii (1944), pp. 121–57.

Bausani, Alessandro, 'Aspetti filosofico-etici dellopera di Niẓāmī', *Colloquio sul poeta Persiano Niẓāmī e la leggenda Iranica di Alessandro Magno (Roma, 25–26 marzo 1975)* (Roma, 1977), pp. 149–74.

Baynham, E., 'The ancient evidence for Alexander the Great', in J. Roisman (ed.), *Brill's Companion to Alexander the Great* (Leiden/Boston, 2003), pp. 3–29.

Beelaert, Anna Livia, 'Ḵāqānī Šervānī', *EIr* xv/5, pp. 521–9.

Berenbaum, Michael and Fred Skolnik (eds), *Encyclopaedia Judaica*, 2nd edn (Detroit, 2007).

Berg, Beverly, 'Dandamis: an early Christian portrait of Indian asceticism', *Classica et Mediaevalia* xxxi (1970), pp. 269–305.

Bergson, L., *Der griechische Alexanderroman rezension Beta* (Stockholm, 1965).

Berlekamp, P. M., *Wonder, Image and Cosmos in Medieval Islam* (New Haven, 2011).

Bertels, Yevgeni Edvardovich, *Roman ob Aleksandre* (Moscow/Leningrad, 1948).

——— *Niẓāmī: shā'ir-e buzurg-e Adharbāyjān*, trans. Ḥ. Muḥammadzāda Ṣadīq (Tehran, 1357/1978).

Bidez, J. and F. Cumont, *Les Mages Hellénisés, Zoroastre, Ostanès et Hystaspe d'après la tradition grecque* (Paris, 1938).

Bīgdilī, Gh., *Chihra-yi Iskandar dar Shāhnāma-yi Firdawsī va Iskandarnāma-yi Niẓāmī [The Portrait of Iskandar in Firdawsī's Book of Kings by Firdawsī and Niẓāmī's Book of Alexander]* (Tehran, 1369/1991).

Bīrūnī, Abū Rayḥān, *The Chronology of Ancient Nations*, trans. C. Edward Sachau (London, 1879).

——— *Āthār al-bāqīya 'an al-qurūn al-khālīya*, ed. E. Sachau (Leipzig, 1923).

——— *Kitāb al-jamāhir fī ma'rifat al-jawāhir [The Sum of Knowledge about Precious Stones]*, ed. F. Krenkow (Hyderabad, 1355/1936).

——— *Athār al-Bāqīya*, trans. A. Dānishsirīsht (Tehran, 1363/1984).

Bivar, A. D. H., 'Hephthalites', *EIr* xii/2, pp. 198–201.

Bosworth, A. B., 'Alexander the Great part 1: The events of the reign', in D.M. Lewis et al. (eds), *The Cambridge Ancient History* (Cambridge, 1994), pp. 791–845.

Bosworth, C. E., 'The political and dynastic history of the Iranian world (AD 1000–1217)', in J. A. Boyle (ed.), *The Cambridge History of Iran*, V: *The Saljuq and Mongol Periods* (Cambridge, 1968), pp. 1–202.

——— 'The Persian impact on Arabic literature', in A. F. L. Beeston et al. (eds), *Arabic Literature to the End of the Umayyad Period* (Cambridge, 1983), pp. 483–96.

——— "Ajā'eb al-Maklūqāt: i. Arabic works', *EIr* i/7, pp. 696–8.

——— 'Mirrors for princes', in J. S. Meisami and P. Starkey (eds), *Encyclopaedia of Arabic Literature* (New York, 1998), vol. II, p. 527.

Bowie, Ewen L., 'Apollonius of Tyana: tradition and reality', *Aufsteig und Niedergang der Römischen Welt*, Teil II: Principat, xvi/2 (1978), pp. 3–41.

Boyce, M., 'Some remarks on the transmission of the Kayanian heroic cycle', in R. N. Frye et al., (eds), *Serta Cantabrigiensia* (Wiesbaden, 1954), pp. 45–52.
——— 'Zariadres and Zārer', *Bulletin of the School of Oriental and African Studies* xvii (1955), pp. 463–77.
——— 'The Parthian *Gōsān* and Iranian minstrel tradition', *Journal of the Royal Asiatic Society* lxxxix/1–2 (1957), pp. 10–45.
——— 'Middle Persian literature', *Iranistik II: Handbuch der Orientalistik* (Leiden, 1968), pp. 32–66.
——— *A History of Zoroastrianism: The Early Period* (Leiden, 1975; repr. 1996).
——— *Zoroastrians: Their Religious Beliefs and Practices* (London, 1979).
——— 'Parthian writings and literature', in E. Yarshater (ed.), *Cambridge History of Iran*, Vol. III/2: *The Seleucid, Parthian and Sasanian Periods* (London/New York, 1983), pp. 1151–65.
——— 'Persian religion in the Achaemenid Age', in W. D. Davies and L. Finkelstein (eds), *The Cambridge History of Judaism* (Cambridge, 1984), vol. I, pp. 279–307.
——— 'Apocalyptic: i. In Zoroastrianism', *EIr* ii/2, pp. 154–6.
——— 'Ayādgār ī Jāmāspīg', *EIr* iii/2, pp. 126–7.
Braund, D. C., 'The Caucasian frontier: myth, exploration and the dynamics of imperialism', in P. Freeman and D. Kennedy (eds), *The Defence of the Roman and Byzantine East* (Oxford, 1986), pp. 31–49.
Briant, Pierre, *Darius dans l'ombre d'Alexandre* (Paris, 2003).
——— *Darius in the Shadow of Alexander*, trans. Jane Marie Todd (Cambridge, MA, 2015).
Bridgeman, Timothy P., *Hyperboreans: Myth and History in Celtic–Hellenic Contacts* (London/New York, 2005).
Brock, S. P., 'The laments of the philosophers over Alexander in Syriac', *Journal of Semitic Studies* xv (1970), pp. 205–18.
——— 'Syriac historical writing: a survey of the main sources', *Journal of the Iraqi Academy* (Syriac Corporation) xxv/302 (1979–80), pp. 1–30.
Brosset, M. F., *Histoire de la Géorgie, I* (St Petersburg, 1849).
Budge, E. A. Wallis, *The History of Alexander the Great: Being the Syriac Version of the Pseudo-Callisthenes* (New York/London, 1889; repr. New Jersey, 2003).
——— *The Life and Exploits of Alexander the Great: Being a Series of Ethiopic Texts* (London, 1896).
Buora, M., 'L'incontro tra Alessandro et Diogene: tradizioni e significato', *Atti dell'Istituto Veneto de Scienze. Lettere ed Arti* 132 (1973–4), pp. 243–64.
Bürgel, J. Christoph, *The Feather of Simurgh: The 'Licit Magic' of the Arts in Medieval Islam* (New York/London, 1988).
——— 'Conquérant, philosophe et prophète: l'image d'Alexandre le Grand dans l'épopée de Neẓāmi', in Christophe Balaÿ, Claire Kappler and Živa Vesel (eds), *Pand-o sokhan: Mélanges offerts à Charles-Henri de Fouchécour* (Tehran, 1995), pp. 65–78.
——— 'Die Geheimwissenschaften im *Iskandarnāme* Nizami', in Bert G. Fragner et al. (eds), *Proceedings of the Second European Conference of Iranian Studies, held in Bamberg, 30th September to 4th October 1991, by the Societas Iranologica Europaea* (Rome, 1995), pp. 103–12.
——— 'Jāmī's epic poem on Alexander the Great: an introduction', *Oriente Moderno* xv/76 (1996), pp. 415–38.

——— 'Krieg und Frieden im Alexanderepos Nizamis', in M. Bridges and J. Ch. Bürgel (eds), *The Problematics of Power: Eastern and Western Representations of Alexander the Great* (Bern, 1996), pp. 91–107.

——— 'L'attitude d'Alexandre face à la philosophie grecque dans trois poèmes épiques persans: le Roman d'Alexandre de Nizāmī, l'A'ina-i Iskandarī de Amīr Khusraw Dihlawī et le Khiradnāma-i Iskandari de Djāmī', in Laurence Harf-Lancner, Claire Kappler and François Suard (eds), *Alexandre le Grand dans les littératures occidentales et proche-orientales (Actes du Colloque de Paris, 27–29 novembre 1999)* (Paris, 1999), pp. 53–9.

——— 'Occult sciences in the *Iskandarnameh* of Nizami', in K. Talattof and J. W. Clinton (eds), *The Poetry of Nizami Ganjavi: Knowledge, Love and Rhetoric* (New York, 2000), pp. 129–39.

——— 'On some sources of Nizāmī's *Iskandarnāma*', in Franklin Lewis and Sunil Sharma (eds), *The Necklace of the Pleiades (Studies in Persian Literature Presented to Heshmat Moayyad on his 80th Birthday)* (Amsterdam, 2007), pp. 22–30.

Burnley, J. D., *Chaucer Studies II: Chaucer's Language and the Philosophers' Tradition* (New York, 1979).

Burstein, S. M., 'Alexander, Callisthenes and the sources of the Nile', *Greek, Roman and Byzantine Studies* xvii (1976), pp. 135–46.

Cameron, Averil, 'Agathias on the Sasanians', *Dumbarton Oaks Papers* xxiii–xxiv (1969–70), pp. 67–183.

——— *Agathias* (Oxford, 1970).

Canard, M., 'al-Djazīra', *EI* [2] ii, pp. 523–4.

Cantarino, Vicente, *Arabic Poetics in the Golden Age* (Leiden, 1975).

Cary, G., *The Medieval Alexander* (Cambridge, 1956; repr. 1967).

Casari, Mario, 'The wise men at Alexander's court in Persian medieval romances: an Iranian view of ancient cultural heritage', *Iranian Identity in the Course of History*, ed. Carlo Cereti (Rome, 2010), pp. 67–80.

——— 'Nizami's cosmographic vision and Alexander in search of the Fountain of Life', in Johann-Christoph Bürgel and Christine van Ruymbeke (eds), *A Key to the Treasure of Hakim: Artistic and Humanistic Aspects of Nizāmī Ganjavī's Khamsa* (Leiden, 2011), pp. 95–105.

——— 'The king explorer', in Richard Stoneman, Kyle Erickson and Ian Netton (eds), *The Alexander Romance in Persia and the East* (Groningen, 2012).

Cejpek, J., 'Iranian folk-literature', in J. Rypka (ed.), *History of Iranian Literature* (Dordrecht, 1968), pp. 607–709.

Chaucer, *The Canterbury Tales* (London, 1951; repr. 2003).

Chelkowski, Peter, 'Niẓāmī Gan*dj*awī', *EI* [2] viii, p. 79.

——— *Les Gestes des Rois dans les traditions de l'Iran antique* (Paris, 1936).

——— *L'Iran sous les Sassanides* (Copenhagen, 1944; repr. Osnabrück, 1971).

——— Niẓāmī's *Iskandarnāmeh*: *Colloquio sul poeta Persiano Niẓāmīe e la leggenda iranica di Alessandro Magno (Roma, 25–26 marzo 1975)* (Roma, 1977), pp. 11–53.

Christensen, Arthur, *Les Kayanides* (Copenhagen, 1931), trans. F. N. Tumboowalla (Mumbai, 1993).

Ciancaglini, Claudia, 'Alessandro e l'incendio di Persepoli nelle tradizioni greca e irancia', in A. Valvo (ed.), *La diffusione dell'eredità classica nell'età tardoantica e medievale: Forme e metodi di trasmissione* (Alexandria, 1997), pp. 59–81.

——— 'Gli antecedenti del Romanzo di Alessandro', in R. B. Finazzi and A. Valvo (eds), *La diffusione dell'eredità classica nell'età tardoantica e medievale: Atti del Seminario internazionale tenuto a Roma–Napoli* (Alexandria, 1998), pp. 55–93.

——— 'The Syriac version of the *Alexander Romance*', *Le Muséon, Revue d'Études Orientales* cxiv/1–2 (2001), pp. 121–40.

Coene, Frederik, *The Caucasus: An Introduction* (London/New York, 2010).

Corbin, H., *Histoire de la philosophie islamique I: des origines jusqu'à la mort d'Averroès (1198)* (Paris, 1964).

Cottrell, Emily, 'Al-Mubaššir ibn Fātik and the α version of the *Alexander Romance*', in Richard Stoneman, Kyle Erickson and Ian Netton (eds), *The Alexander Romance in Persia and the East* (Groningen, 2012), pp. 233–53.

——— 'An early mirror for princes and manual for secretaries: *The Epistolary Novel of Aristotle and Alexander*', *Alexander the Great in the East* (Wroclaw, forthcoming).

Czeglédy, K., 'The Syriac legend concerning Alexander the Great', *Acta Orientalia* vii (1957), pp. 231–49.

Dandamaev, Muhammad A. and Vladimir G. Lukonin, *The Culture and Social Institutions of Ancient Iran*, trans. Philip L. Kohl (Cambridge, 1989).

Dānishpazhūh, M. T. (ed.), *Nihāya al-'erab fī tārīkh al-furs wa al-'arab* (Tehran, 1374).

Dārāb Pashūtan, Dastūr (ed.), *Kārnāma-yi Ardaxshīr Pāpakān* (Bombay, 1896; repr. Tehran, 1369/1990).

Daryaee, Touraj, 'National history or Keyanid history? The nature of Sasanid Zoroastrian historiography', *Iranian Studies* xxviii/3–4 (1995), pp. 129–41.

——— 'Šegafty va Barjestegī-ye Sīstān, Matn-e be zabān-e pahlavī', *Iranshenāsī* viii/3 (1996), pp. 534–42.

——— 'Memory and history: the construction of the past in Late Antique Persia', *Nāma-yi Irān-i Bāstān: The International Journal of Ancient Iranian Studies* i/2 (2001–2), pp. 12–13.

——— 'The construction of the past in Late Antique Persia', *Historia: Zeitschrift für Alte Geschichte* lv/4 (2006), pp. 493–503.

——— '*Imitatio Alexandri* and its impact on late Arsacid, early Sasanian and Middle Persian literature', *Electrum* xii (2007), pp. 93–5.

——— *Sasanian Persia: The Rise and Fall of an Empire* (London/New York, 2009).

Davidson, Olga M., *Poet and Hero in the Persian Book of Kings* (London, 1994).

Davis, Dick, 'The problem of Ferdowsi's sources', *Journal of the American Oriental Society* cxvi (1996), pp. 48–57.

——— *Panthea's Children: Hellenistic Novels and Medieval Persian Romances* (New York, 2002).

——— 'The aesthetics of the historical sections of the *Shahnama*', in Ch. Melville (ed.), *Shahnama Studies* (Cambridge, 2006), vol. I, pp. 115–24.

De Blois, François, *Persian Literature: A Bio-Bibliographical Survey, Vol. 1: Poetry to ca. ad 1100* (London, 1992).

——— *Persian Literature: A Bio-bibliographical Survey, Begun by the Late C.A. Storey*, Vol. 2: *Poetry ca. ad 1100 to 1225* (London, 1994–7).

——— *Persian Literature: A Bio-Bibliographical Survey: Poetry of the Pre-Mongol Period* (London, 2004).

——— 'Eskandar-Nāma of Neẓāmī', *EIr* viii/6, p. 614.

——— 'Tardjama: translations from Middle Persian (Pahlavī)', *EI* [2] x, pp. 231b–2b.

De Fouchécour, Charles-Henri, *Moralia: les notions morales dans la littérature persane du 3/9 au 7/13 siècle* (Paris, 1986).

——— 'Djāmi, conseiller des princes, ou Le Livre de la Sagesse Alexandrine', *Kārnāma* v (1999), pp. 11–32.

Detienne, M., *The Gardens of Adonis: Spices in Greek Mythology*, trans. Janet Lloyd (London, 1977).

Dihkhudā, 'Alī Akbar, *Lughatnāma* [*Encyclopedic Dictionary*], ed. M. Mu'īn and J. Shahīdī, new edn (Tehran, 1372–3/1993–4).

Dillon, J. M., *Morality and Custom in Ancient Greece* (Indiana, 2004).

Dīnawarī, *Akhbār al-ṭivāl*, ed. 'A. 'Āmir (Cairo, 1960).

Doloff, S., 'Let me talk with this philosopher: the Alexander paradigm in *King Lear*', *The Huntington Library Quarterly* liv (1991), pp. 253–5.

Donzel, E. and A. Schmidt, *Gog and Magog in Early Syriac and Islamic Sources: Sallam's Quest for Alexander's Wall* (Leiden, 2010).

Dorandi, Tiziano, 'Chronology', in K. Algra et al. (eds), *The Cambridge History of Hellenistic Philosophy* (Cambridge, 1999), pp. 31–54.

Doufikar-Aerts, Faustina, 'Alexander the Great and the pharos of Alexandria in Arabic literature', in J. Ch. Bürgel and M. Bridges (eds), *The Problematics of Power* (Bern, 1996), pp. 191–201.

——— '*Sīrat al-Iskandar*: an Arabic popular romance of Alexander', *Oriente Moderno*, Nuova serie, Anno 22 (83), Studies on Arabic Epics 2 (2003), pp. 505–20.

——— 'The last days of Alexander in an Arabic popular romance of al-Iskandar', in S. Panayotakis, M. Zimmerman and W. Keulen (eds), *The Ancient Novel and Beyond* (Leiden, 2003), pp. 23–35.

——— *Alexander Magnus Arabicus: A Survey of the Alexander Tradition through Seven Centuries: From Pseudo-Callisthenes to Ṣūrī* (Louvain, 2010).

——— 'A letter in bits and pieces: "The Epistola Alexandri and Aristotolem Arabica": a first edition with translation based on four 16th–18th century manuscripts', in Robert M. Kerr and Thomas Milo (eds), *Writings and Writing from Another World and Another Era* (Cambridge, 2010), pp. 91–115.

——— 'King Midas' ears on Alexander's head', in Richard Stoneman, Kyle Erickson and Ian Netton (eds), *The Alexander Romance in Persia and the East* (Groningen, 2012), pp. 61–79.

Drews, Robert, 'Sargon, Cyrus and Mesopotamian folk history', *Journal of Near Eastern Studies* xxxiii–xxxiv (1974), pp. 387–93.

Duchesne-Guillemin, J., 'Apocalypse juive et apocalypse iranienne', in U. Bianchi and M. J. Vermaseren (eds), *La soteriologia dei culti orientali nell'Impero Romano: Atti del Coloquio Internazionale* (Rome/Leiden, 1982), pp. 753–61.

——— 'Ahriman', *EIr* i/6–7, pp. 670–3.

Duleba, W., *The Cyrus Legend in the Šāhnāme* (Krakow, 1995).

Dunlop, D. M., 'Bāb al-Abwāb', *EI* [2] i, pp. 835–6.

Dzielska, M., *Apollonius of Tyana in Legend and History*, trans. Piotr Pieńkowski (Rome, 1986).

Eggermont, Pierre H.L., *Alexander's Campaigns in Sind and Baluchistan and the Siege of the Brahmin Town of Harmatelia*, Orientalia Lovaniensia Analecta 3 (Leuven, 1975).

Esin, Emel, *Mecca the Blessed, Madinah the Radiant* (New York, 1963).

Fahd, T., 'Ṣābi'a', *EI* [2] viii, p. 676.

Fārābī, Abū Naṣr, *On Political Government* [*al-Siyāsa al-madaniyya*] (Hyderabad, 1346/1927).
——— *Aphorisms of the Statesman* [*Fuṣūl al-madanī*], ed. D. M. Dunlop (Cambridge, 1961).
——— *On the Perfect State* [*Mabādī' ārā' ahl al-madīnat al-fāḍilah*], trans. Richard Walter (Chicago, 1985).
Farrukhī Sīstānī, *Divān*, ed. Muḥammad Dabīr Siyāqī, 2nd edn (Tehran, 1970).
Ferber, Michael, *A Dictionary of Literary Symbols* (Cambridge, 1999).
Ferrand, G., 'Le *Tuḥfat al-Albāb* de al-Andalusī al-Ġarnāṭī', *Journal Asiatique* ccvii (1925), pp. 1–148.
Feuillebois-Pierunek, Éve (ed.), *Épopées du monde: pour un panorama (presque) général* (Paris, 2011).
Finn, R. Damian, *Asceticism in the Graeco-Roman World* (Cambridge, 2009).
Firdawsī, *Shāhnāma*, ed., Khaleghi-Motlagh and M. Omīdsālār, 3rd edn (Tehran, 1389/2010).
Franke, P., 'Drinking from the Water of Life: Nizāmī, Khizr and the symbolism of poetical inspiration in Later Persianate literature', in J.-C. Bürgel and Christine van Ruymbeke (eds), *A Key to the Treasure of the Hakīm: Artistic and Humanistic Aspects of Niẓāmī's Khamsa* (Leiden, 2011), pp. 77–125.
Friedländer, *Die Chadhirlegende und der Alexanderroman* (Leipzig, 1913).
Frye, Richard. N., *The Heritage of Persia* (Cleveland, 1963).
——— 'The Sasanian system of walls for defense', in M. Rosen-Ayalon (ed.), *Studies in Memory of Gaston Wiet* (Jerusalem, 1977), pp. 7–15.
——— 'Two Iranian notes', *Papers in Honour of Professor Mary Boyce* (Leiden, 1985), vol. I, pp. 185–8.
——— (trans.), *Ibn Fadlan's Journey to Russia: A Tenth-Century Traveler from Baghdad to the Volga River* (Princeton, 2005).
Gad, El-Sayed M., 'Al-Ṭabari's tales of Alexander: history and romance', in Richard Stoneman, Kyle Erickson and Ian Netton (eds), *The Alexander Romance in Persia and the East* (Groningen, 2012), pp. 219–31.
Gagé, J., *Basiléia, les Césars, les Rois d' Orient et les Mages* (Paris, 1968).
Gaillard, Marina, 'Hero or anti-hero: the Alexander figure in the *Dārāb-nāma* of Ṭarsūsī', *Oriente Moderno* lxxxix/2, Studies on Islamic Legends (2009), pp. 319–31.
García Gual, C (trans.), *Pseudo-Calístenes: vida y hazañas de Alejandro de Macedonia* (Madrid, 1988).
Gero, S., 'The legend of Alexander the Great in the Christian Orient', *Bulletin of the John Rylands University Library of Manchester* lxxv (1993), pp. 3–9.
Ghazālī, Abū Ḥāmid Muḥammad, *Ghazali's Book of Counsel for Kings (Nasihat al-muluk)*, trans. F. R. C. Bagley (London, 1964).
——— *Naṣīḥat al-mulūk*, ed. J. Humā'ī (Tehran, 1351/1972).
——— *Iḥyā 'ulūm al-Dīn*, Vol. III: *Rub' mahlakāt*, trans. M. Muḥammad Khwarazmī, 3rd edn (Tehran, 1368/1989).
Ghīyāth al-Dīn, Muḥammad, *Ghīyāth al-lughāṭ*, ed. M. Dabīr-Siyāqī (Tehran, 1336/1958).
Gignoux, Ph., 'L'apocalyptique iranienne est-elle vraiment la source d'autres apocalypses?', *Acta Antiqua Academiae Scientiarum Hungaricae* xxxi (1985–8), pp. 67–78.

Gimaret, D., *Le livre de Bilawhar et Būḏāsf selon la version arabe ismaélienne* (Paris, 1971).
Gleixner, H. J., *Das Alexanderbild der Byzantiner* (Munich, 1961).
Golden, P. B., 'The conversion of the Khazars to Judaism', in P. B. Golden, H. Ben-Shammai and A. Róna-Tas (eds), *The World of the Khazars: New Perspectives* (Leiden, 2007), pp. 123–62.
Gow, Andrew Colin, *The Red Jews: Antisemitism in an Apocalyptic Age, 1200–1600* (Leiden, 1995).
Grafton, A., *The Classical Tradition*, ed. G. Most and S. Settis (Harvard, 2010).
Greatrex, Geoffrey and Samuel N. C. Lieu, *The Roman Eastern Frontier and the Persian Wars*, Part II: AD *363–630* (London/New York, 2002).
Green, T. M., *The City of the Moon God: Religious Traditions of Harran* (Leiden, 1992).
Grenet, Frantz, 'Regional interaction in Central Asia and northwest India in the Kidarite and Hephthalite periods', in N. Sims-Williams (ed.), *Indo-Iranian Languages and Peoples*, Proceedings of the British Academy 116 (London, 2002), pp. 203–24.
Grignaschi, 'Les *Rasā'il d'Arisṭūṭālīsa ilā-l-Iskandar* de Sālim Abū-l-'Alā' et l'activité culturelle à l'époque omeyyade', *Bulletin d'études orientales* xix (1965–6), pp. 7–83.
——— 'La *Nihāyatu-l-'arab fī akhbāri-l-Furs wa-l-'arab*', *Bulletin d'études orientales* xxii (1969), pp. 15–67.
——— 'La *Nihāyatu-l-'arab fī akhbāri-l-Furs wa-l-'arab* et les *Siyaru mulūki-l-'ağam* du Ps. Ibn-al-Muqaffa'', *Bulletin d'études orientales* xxvi (1973), pp. 83–184.
Guidi, Ignacio, 'Chronicon anonymum', *Chronica Minora* (Paris, 1903).
Gurgānī, Fakhr al-Dīn, *Vis u Rāmin*, ed. M. Maḥjūb (Tehran, 1337/1958).
Gutas, Dimitri, *Greek Wisdom Literature in Arabic Translation: A Study of the Graeco-Arabic Gnomologia* (New Haven, 1975).
——— 'Classical Arabic wisdom literature: nature and scope', *Journal of the American Oriental Society* ci (1981), pp. 49–86.
——— 'Paul the Persian on the classification of the parts of Aristotle's philosophy: a milestone between Alexandria and Baġdād', *Der Islam* lx (1983), pp. 231–67.
——— *Greek Thought, Arabic Culture: The Graeco-Arabic Translation Movement in Baghdad and Early 'Abbāsid Society (2nd–4th/8th–10th Centuries)* (London/New York, 1998).
——— 'The "Alexandria to Baghdad" complex of narratives: a contribution to the study of philosophical and medical historiography among the Arabs', *Documenti e Studi sulla Tradizione Filosofica Medievale* x (1999), pp. 155–93.
Hadot, Pierre, *What is Ancient Philosophy?* (Cambridge, 2002).
Ḥāfiẓ, *Dīvān*, ed. Parvīz Nātil Khānlarī (Tehran, 1359/1980).
——— *Dīvān*, ed. S. Ṣ. Sajjādī, 'A. Bahrāmīyān and K. Bargnīsī (Tehran, 1379/2001).
——— *Dīvān: bih taṣḥīḥ-i Muḥammad Qudsī bā maqābala-i chahār nuskha-i chāpī mu'tabar: Qazwīnāi, Khānlarī, Sāyih va Naysārī*, ed. Ḥasan Dhū'l-Faqār and Abū'l-Faḍl 'Alī Muḥammadī (Tehran, 1381/2002).
Hägg, Tomas and Bo Utas, *The Virgin and her Lover: Fragments of an Ancient Greek Novel and a Persian Epic Poem* (Leiden/Boston, 2003).
Hamadānī, Ibn al-Faqīh, *Mukhtaṣar Kitāb al-Buldān*, *Bibliotheca Geographorum Arabicorum*, Vol. V: *Compendium Libri Kitab al-boldan*, ed. M. J. de Goeje (Leiden, 1885; repr. 1967).

Hamori, Andreas, 'An allegory from the Arabian Nights: the city of brass', *On the Art of Medieval Arabic Literature* (Princeton, 1974), pp. 145–63.
Hanaway, William L., 'Persian popular romances before the Safavid period' (PhD thesis, Columbia University, 1970; published 1972).
——— 'Formal elements in the Persian popular romances', *Review of National Literatures* ii (1971), pp. 139–61.
——— 'Anāhitā and Alexander', *Journal of American Oriental Society* cii/2 (1982), pp. 285–95.
——— 'Eskandar-Nāma', *EIr* viii/6, pp. 609–12.
——— '*Dārābnāma*', *EIr* vii/1, pp. 8–9.
Henning, W.B., 'An astronomical chapter of the Bundahishn', *The Journal of the Royal Asiatic Society* lxxiv/3–4 (1942), pp. 229–48.
Higgins, Reynold A., *Greek and Roman Jewellery*, 2nd edn (San Francisco, 1980).
Hoffman, Herbert and Patricia F. Davidson, *Greek Gold: Jewelry from the Age of Alexander* (Mainz, 1965).
Honigmann, E. [C.E. Bosworth], 'al-Mawṣil', *EI* [2] vi, pp. 899–901.
Howard-Johnson, James, *Witnesses to a World Crisis: Historians and Histories of the Middle East in the Seventh Century* (Oxford, 2010).
Huyse, 'Parthian inscriptions', in Ronald E. Emmerick and M. Macuch (eds), *The Literature of Pre-Islamic Iran*: Companion Volume I to *A History of Persian Literature* (London/New York, 2009).
Ibn al-Bitrīq, Yuḥanna, *Sirr al-asrār, Al-uṣūl al-Yūnāniyya li naẓariyyat al-siyāsiyya fī'l-Islām*, ed. A. Badawī (Cairo, 1954).
Ibn al-Faqīh al-Hamadānī, *Bibliotheca Geographorum Arabicorum*, Vol. V: *Compendium Libri Kitab al-boldan*, ed. M. J. de Goeje (Leiden, 1885; repr. 1967).
Ibn Isfandīyār, *Tārīkh-i Ṭabaristān*, ed. 'A. Iqbāl (Tehran, 1320/1941).
Ibn Khalaf Tabrīzī, M. Ḥussayn, *Burhān-i Qāṭi'*, ed. M. Mu'īn (Tehran, 1330/1951).
Ibn Nadīm, *al-Fihrist*, trans. M. R. Tajaddud (Tehran, 1343/1964).
Irānshāh Ibn abī al-Khayr, Bahmannāma, ed. Raḥīm 'Afīfī (Tehran, 1370/1991).
——— *Kūshnāma*, ed. Jalāl Matīnī (Tehran, 1377/1998).
Iṣfahānī, Ḥamza, *Tārīkh sinī mulūk al-arḍ wa-l-anbīyā* (Beirut, 1961).
Ismailpūr, *Barrisī taṭbīqī shakhsīyat-i Āshīl va Isfandīyār* (Teheran, 1388/2009).
Jamzadeh, Parivash, *Alexander Histories and Iranian Reflections: Remnants of Propaganda and Resistance* (Leiden/Boston, 2012).
Kappler, Claude-Claire, 'Alexandre dans le *Shāh Nāma* de Firdousi: De la conquête du monde à la dé couverte de soi', in M. Bridges and J. Ch. Bürgel (eds), *The Problematics of Power: Eastern and Western Representations of Alexander the Great* (Bern, 1996), 165–90.
——— 'Alexandre le Grand en littérature persane classique: est-il devenu un mythe?' *Luqmān* xiv/2 (1998), pp. 17–31.
Karttunen, K., *India and the Hellenistic World* (Helsinki, 1997).
Kayvānī, Majd al-Dīn, 'Iskandar dar adabīyāt-i Irān' and 'Iskandar-nāmahā', in Ismā'īl Sa'ādat (ed.), *Dānishnāma-yi zabān va adabīyāt-i fārsī* (Tehran, 1384/2005), vol. I, pp. 402–10.
Kee, Howard Clark, *The Beginnings of Christianity: An Introduction to the New Testament* (New York/London, 2005).
Kennedy, E. S. and D. Pingree, *The Astrological History of Māshā'allāh* (Cambridge, 1971).
Kettenhofen, Erich, 'Darband', *EIr* vii/1, pp. 13–19.

Khaleghi-Motlagh, Jalāl, 'Farāmarznāma', *Irānnāma* i/1 (1361/1982), pp. 22–45.
——— 'Babr-i Bayān', *Irānnāma* vi/1 (1988), pp. 200–27 and *Irānnāma* vi/2 (1988), pp. 382–416.
——— 'Bahman', *EIr* iii/5 (1989), pp. 489–90.
——— 'Pīrāmūn-i vazn-i Shāhnāma', *Irānshināsī* v (1369/1990), pp. 48–63.
——— 'Kay Khusraw va Kūrush', *Irānshināsī* i/7 (1374/1995), pp. 158–70.
——— 'Tan kāma-sarāyī dar adab-i fārsī', *Majāla-yi Irānshināsī* viii/1 (1375/1996), pp. 20–2.
——— 'Dar pīrāmūn-i manābi'-i Firdawsī', *Irānshināsī* iii (1377/1998), pp. 512–13.
——— 'Az *Shāhnāma* tā *Khudāynāma*', *Nāma-yi Irān-i Bāstān, The International Journal of Ancient Iranian Studies* vii/1–2 (2007–8), pp. 3–119.
——— 'Jā-yi Rustam, Arash, Isfandīyār, Gushtāsp, Jāmāsp va Iskandar dar Khudāynāma', *Nāma-yi Irān-i Bāstān, The International Journal of Ancient Iranian Studies* ix/1–2 (2009–10), pp. 3–24.
——— *Yāddāsht-hā-yi Shāhnāma*, 3 vols (Tehran, 1389/2010).
——— 'Aždahā: ii. In Persian literature', *EIr* iii/2, pp. 195–201.
——— 'Babr-e Bayān', *EIr* iii/3, pp. 324–5
——— 'Bahman', *EIr* iii/5, pp. 489–90.
——— 'Amīrak Bal'amī', *EIr* i/9, pp. 971–2.
Khāqānī Shirvānī, *Dīvān*, ed. Sajjādī (Tehran, 1338/1959).
Khaṭībī, A., 'Yikī nāma būd az gah-i bāstān: justārī dar shinākht-i manba'-i *Shāhnāma*-yi Firdawsī', *Nāma-yi Farhangistān* iii/5 (1381/2002), pp. 54–73.
Khurramshāhī, Bahā' al-Dīn (ed.), *Dānishnāma-yi Qur'ān*, 2nd edn (Tehran, 1381/2002).
Kieckhefer, R., *Magic in the Middle Ages* (Cambridge, 1989).
Kitābī, A., 'Qiṣṣa-yi mirī kardan-i rūmīyān va chīnīyān dar 'ilm-i naqqāshī va ṣūratgarī', *Āyīna-yi Mīrāth* xxxvi–xxxvii (1386/2007), pp. 258–71.
Kleczar, A., 'The kingship of Alexander the Great in the Jewish versions of the Alexander narrative', in Richard Stoneman, Kyle Erickson and Ian Netton (eds), *The Alexander Romance in Persia and the East* (Groningen, 2012), pp. 339–48.
Kroll, W., *Historia Alexandri Magni* (Berlin, 1926).
Lakhnavi, Gh. and A. Bilgrami, *The Adventures of Amir Hamza*, trans. Musharraf Ali Farooqi (New York, 2007).
Lambton, A. K. S., '*Quis custodiet custodes?* Some reflections on the Persian theory of government (Part 1)', *Studia Islamica* v (1955), pp. 125–48.
——— '*Quis custodiet custodes?* Some reflections on the Persian theory of government (Part 2)', *Studia Islamica* vi (1956), pp. 125–46.
——— 'Justice in the medieval Persian theory of kingship', *Studia Islamica* xvii (1962), pp. 91–119.
——— 'Islamic mirrors for princes', *Atti del convegno internazionale sul tema, La Persia nel medioevo* (Rome, 1970), pp. 419–42.
——— 'Islamic mirrors for princes', *Quaderno dell'Accademia Nazionale dei Lincei* clx (1971), pp. 424–38.
——— *State and Government in Medieval Islam: An Introduction to the Study of Islamic Political Theory: The Jurists* (New York, 1981).
——— 'Changing concepts of justice and injustice from the fifth/eleventh century to the eighth/fourteenth century in Persia: the Saljuq Empire and the Ilkhanate', *Studia Islamica* lxviii (1988), pp. 27–60.

——— 'Sufis and the state in medieval Persia', in C. van Dijk and A.H. de Groot (eds), *State and Islam* (Leiden, 1995), p. 23.
Lewicki, T., 'al-Ḳazwīnī', *EI* ² iv, pp. 865–7.
Lewis, I., 'Berberā' *EI* ² i, pp. 1172–3.
Lewisohn, L., 'From the Moses of reason to the Khidr of the resurrection', in O. Alí-de-Unzaga (ed.), *Fortresses of the Intellect, Ismaili and Other Islamic Studies in Honour of Farhad Daftary* (London, 2011), pp. 407–33.
Lings, M., *Muhammad: His Life Based on the Earliest Sources* (New York, 1983).
MacDonald, D. B. [T. Fahd], 'Sīmiyā'', *EI* ² ix, pp. 612–13.
MacKenzie, D. N., 'Zoroastrian astrology in the *Bundahišn*', *Bulletin School of Oriental and African Studies* xxvii (1964), pp. 511–29.
Macuch, Maria, 'Pahlavi literature', in Ronald E. Emmerick and M. Macuch (eds), *The Literature of Pre-Islamic Iran*: Companion Volume I to *A History of Persian Literature* (London/New York, 2009), pp. 116–96.
Maróth, M., *The Correspondence between Aristotle and Alexander the Great: An Anonymous Greek Novel in Letters in Arabic Translation* (Piliscsaba, 2006).
Martínez, F. J., *Eastern Christian Apocalyptic in the Early Muslim Period: Pseudo-Methodius and Pseudo-Athanasius* (Ann Arbor, 1996).
Marzolph, U., 'The creative reception of the *Alexander Romance* in Iran', in Dominque Jullien (ed.), *Foundational Texts of World Literature* (New York, 2012), pp. 69–83.
Mas'ūdī, *Murūj al-dhahab wa ma'ādin al-jawhar* [*Meadows of Gold and Mines of Gems*], ed. Ch. Pellat, 3 vols (Beirut, 1966–79).
Matīnī, Jalāl, 'Kūsh yā gūsh?', *Irānnāma* xxi (1366/1987), pp. 13–14.
Maybudī, *Kashf al-asrār wa 'uddat al-abrār*, ed. 'A. A. Ḥikmat (Tehran, 1357/1978).
Meisami, Julie Scott, 'The past in service of the present: two views of history in medieval Persia', *Poetics Today* xiv/2 (1993), pp. 252–72.
——— (trans.), *The Haft Paykar: A Medieval Persian Romance* (Oxford, 1995).
——— *Persian Historiography to the End of the Twelfth Century* (Edinburgh, 1999).
——— 'Genre of court literature', in J. T. P. de Bruijn (ed.), *General Introduction to Persian Literature* (New York, 2009), pp. 233–69.
——— 'History as Literature', in Ch. Melville (ed.), *A History of Persian Literature*, Vol. X: *Persian Historiography* (London/New York, 2012), pp. 1–55.
——— *Medieval Persian Court Poetry* (Princeton, 2014).
Meisami, Julie Scott and Starkey, P. (eds), *Encyclopaedia of Arabic Literature* (London/New York, 1998).
Merkelbach, R., *Die Quellen des griechischen Alexanderromans*, 2nd edn (Munich, 1954, 1977).
Mīnavī, M (ed.), *Nāma-yi Tansar*, 2nd edn (Tehran, 1354/1975).
Minorsky, V., 'Vis u Ramin, a Parthian romance', *Bulletin of the School of Oriental and African Studies* xi (1946), pp. 741–64.
——— [C. E. Bosworth], 'al-Kurdj', *EI* ² v, pp. 487–98.
——— 'Khāqānī and Andronicus Comenus', *Bulletin of the School of Oriental and African Studies* ix (1943–6), pp. 550–78.
——— 'Vis u Ramin, a Parthian romance', *Bulletin of the School of Oriental and African Studies* xii (1947), pp. 20–35.
——— 'Caucasica II', *Bulletin of the School of Oriental and African Studies* xiii/4 (1951), pp. 868–77.

——— 'The older preface to the *Shāhnāma*', *Studi Orientalistici in Onore di Giorgio Levi Della Vida* ii (1956), pp. 159–79.

——— *History of Sharvān and Darband in the 10th–11th Centuries* (Cambridge, 1958).

Mitchell, Lynette, 'Alexander the Great: divinity and the rule of law', in L. Mitchell and Ch. Melville (eds), *Every Inch a King: Comparative Studies on Kings and Kingship in the Ancient and Medieval Worlds* (Leiden/Boston, 2013), pp. 91–107.

——— *The Heroic Rulers of Archaic and Classical Greece* (London/New York, 2013).

——— 'Remembering Cyrus the Persian: exploring monarchy and freedom in classical Greece', in E. Ben Zvi and D. Edelman (eds), *Remembering Biblical Figures in the Late Persian and Early Hellenistic Periods: Social Memory and Imagination* (Oxford, 2013), pp. 283–92.

Monferrer-Sala, Juan Pedro, 'Alexandri magni de anima dictum fictitum apud philosophos enuntiavit', *Hikma* v (2006), pp. 155–69.

——— 'Alexander the Great in the Syriac literary tradition', in Z. David Zuwiyya (ed.), *A Companion to Alexander Literature in the Middle Ages* (Leiden/Boston, 2011), pp. 40–72.

Mubashshir Ibn Fātiq, *Los Bocados de Oro (Mukhtār al-ḥikām wa maḥāsin al-kalam)*, ed. 'Abd al-Raḥmān Badawī (Madrid, 1958).

Mu'īn, *Farhang-i Fārsī*, 10th edn (Tehran, 1375/1996).

Murray, O., *Early Greece*, 2nd edn (Cambridge, MA, 1993).

Murtaḍavī, M., *Maktab-i Ḥāfiz, Muqaddama bar Ḥāfiz-shināsī* (Tabriz, 1383/2004).

Nafīsī, Sa'īd, 'Vazn-i Shāhnāma-yi Firdawsī', *Dānishnāma* ii (1326/1947), pp. 133–48.

——— *Tārīkh-i Naẓm va nathr dar Irān* (Tehran, 1344/1965).

Naṣr, S.Ḥ., *An Introduction to Islamic Cosmological Doctrines* (Cambridge, 1964).

——— *The Islamic Intellectual Tradition in Persia*, ed. Mehdi Amin Razavi (London, 1996).

Nautin, Pierre, 'L'auteur de la *Chronique Anonyme de Guidi*: Élie de Merw', *Revue de l'Histoire des Religions* cxcix/3 (1982), pp. 303–14.

Navia, Luis E., *Classical Cynicism: A Critical Study* (Greenwood, 1996).

Neugebauer, O. and H. B. Van Hoesen, *Greek Horoscopes* (Philadelphia, 1987).

Niẓām al-Mulk, *Siyar al-Mulūk or Sīyasatnāma*, ed. Hubert Darke, 3rd edn (Tehran, 2535 Shāhanshāhī/1976).

Niẓāmī Ganjavī, *Iskandarnāma*, trans. K. Lipskerov (Baku, 1953).

——— *Iskandarnāma*, trans. Y. E. Bertel and A. K. Arends (Baku, 1983).

——— *Das Alexanderbuch*, trans. J. Christoph Bürgel (Zurich, 1991).

——— *Iqbālnāma*, ed. V. Dastgirdī, re-ed. S. Ḥamīdiyān (Tehran, 1376/1997).

——— *Sharafnāma*, ed. V. Dastgirdī, re-ed. Sa'īd Ḥamīdīyān, 3rd edn (Tehran, 1378/1999).

Nöldeke, Theodor, *Beiträge zur Geschichte des Alexanderromans* (Wien, 1890).

——— 'Die von Guidi herausgegebene syrische Chronik übersetzt und commentiert', *Sitzungsberichte der kaiserlichen Akademie der Wissenschaften, Phil.–Hist. Classe* cxxviii (1893), pp. 1–48.

——— *Das iranische Nationalepos* (Berlin/Leipzig, 1920).

——— 'Ein Beitrag zur Schahname-Forschung', *Hizāra-yi Firdawsī*, 2nd edn (Tehran, 1362/1983), pp. 58–63.

Ogden, Daniel, *Greek and Roman Necromancy* (Princeton/Oxford, 2001).

——— *Magic, Witchcraft, and Ghosts in the Greek and Roman Worlds* (Oxford, 2002).

——— *Alexander the Great: Myth, Genesis and Sexuality* (Exeter, 2011).
——— 'Sekandar, dragon-slayer', in Richard Stoneman, Kyle Erickson and Ian Netton (eds), *The Alexander Romance in Persia and the East* (Groningen, 2012), pp. 277–94.
Omīdsālār, Maḥmūd, 'Babr-i Bayān', *Irānnāma* iii (1362/1983), pp. 447–58.
——— 'Could al-Tha'alibi have used the *Shāhnāma* as a source?', *Der Islam* lxxv/2 (1998), pp. 338–46.
——— 'Isfandīyār va Ashīl', *Irānshināsī* iv (1377/1998), pp. 734–44.
Palagia, Olga, 'The impact of Alexander the Great in the art of Central Asia', in Richard Stoneman, Kyle Erickson and Ian Netton (eds), *The Alexander Romance in Persia and the East* (Groningen, 2012), 369–82.
Panaino, Antonio, 'L'influsso greco nella letteratura e nella cultura medio-persiana', *Autori classici in lingue del Medio e Vicino Oriente* (Rome, 2001), pp. 29–45.
Parīsh-rūy, 'A., *Barābar-nahād-i Shāhnāma-yi Firdawsī wa Ghurar al-sayr Tha'ālibī* (Tehran, 1390/2011).
Perlman, S., 'The coins of Philip II and Alexander the Great and their Pan-Hellenic propaganda', *The Numismatic Chronicle and Journal of the Royal Numismatic Society*, 7th Series v (1965), pp. 57–67.
Peters, F. E., *Aristoteles Arabus: The Oriental Translations and Commentaries of the Aristotelian Corpus* (Leiden, 1961).
Philostratus, Flavius, *The Life of Apollonius of Tyana*, trans. C. P. Jones (London, 1970).
Pingree, David, 'Historical horoscopes', *Journal of the American Oriental Society* lxxxii/4 (1962), pp. 487–502.
——— *The Thousands of Abū Ma'shar* (London, 1968).
——— 'Mashā'allāh: some Sassanian and Syriac sources', in George F. Hourani (ed.), *Essays on Islamic Philosophy and Science* (Albany, 1975), pp. 5–14.
——— (ed.), *Picatrix: The Latin Version of the Ghayat al-hakim* (London, 1986).
Pinski, D., *Aleksander un Dyogenes* (Vilne, 1930).
Plessner, M., 'Balīnūs', *EI*^{2} i, pp. 994–5.
Pourshariati, Parvāna, 'The Parthians and the production of the canonical shāhnāmas: of Pahlavī, Pahlavānī and the Pahlav', in Henning Börm and Josef Wiesehöfer (eds), *Commutatio et Contentio: Studies in the Late Roman, Sasanian, and Early Islamic Near East in Memory of Zeev Rubin* (Düsseldorf, 2010), pp. 347–92.
Price, Martin, *The Coinage in the Name of Alexander the Great and Philip Arrhidaeus* (London, 1991).
Qābūs ibn Vūshmgīr 'Unṣur al-Ma'ālī Kaykāvūs Ibn Iskandar Ibn, *Qābūsnāma*, ed. Gh. Yūsifī, 2nd edn (Tehran, 1352/1973).
Qamber, 'The mirror symbol in the teachings and writings of some Sufi masters', *Temenos* xi (1990), pp. 163–79.
Qazwīnī, *Kitāb 'ajāyib al-Makhlūqāt*, ed. F. Wüstenfeld (Göttingen, 1849), vol. II.
——— *Kitāb 'Ajāyib al-makhlūqāt wa gharāyib al-mawjūdāt*, ed. N. Sabūḥī (Tehran, 1340/1961).
Qazwīnī, M., 'Muqaddama-yi qadīm-i *Shāhnāma*', *Bīst Maqāla* ii (1313/1934), pp. 5–29.
Rastigār Fasāyī, M., *Azhdahā dar asāṭīr-i Irān* (Tehran, 1379/2000).
Redford, Donald B., 'The literary motif of the exposed child', *Numen* xiv/3 (1967), pp. 209–28.

Reinink, G. J., *Das Alexanderlied: Die drei Rezensionen* (Louvain, 1983), vol. II, pp. 1–15.

——— 'Die Entstehung der syrischen Alexanderlegende als politisch–religiöse Propagandaschrift für Herakleios' Kirchenpolitik', in C. Laga, J. A. Munitiz and L. van Rompay (eds), *After Chalcedon: Studies in Theology and Church History, Offered to Professor Albert van Roey for His Seventieth Birthday* (Louvain, 1985), pp. 263–81.

——— 'Alexander the Great in seventh-century Syriac "apocalyptic" texts', *Byzantinorossica* ii (2003), pp. 150–78.

Renard, J., *Islam and the Heroic Image: Themes in Literature and the Visual Arts* (Columbia, 1993).

Ritter, H. and M. Plessner, *'Picatrix': Das Ziel des Weisen von Pseudo-Majrīṭī*, Studies of the Warburg Institute 27 (London, 1962).

Rohde, C. Erwin, *Der griechische Roman und sein Vorläufer*, 4th edn (Darmstadt, 1960).

Romm, J., *The Edges of the World in Ancient Thought* (Princeton, 1992).

——— 'Travel', in Tim Whitmarsh (ed.), *The Cambridge Companion to the Greek and Roman Novel* (Cambridge, 2008), pp. 109–26.

Rosenthal, Franz, *The Classical Heritage in Islam*, trans. Emile and Jenny Marmorstein (London/New York, 1975; repr. 1994).

Ross, David J. A., *Alexander Historiatus: A Guide to Medieval Illustrated Alexander Literature* (Frankfurt am Main, 1988).

Rūmī, J. M., *Mathnavī, Book One*, ed. and trans. R. A. Nicholson (Tehran, 1356/1977).

Rundgren, 'Arabische Literatur und orientalische Antike', *Orientalia Suecana* xix–xx (1970–1), pp. 81–124.

Ruska, J., *Tabula Smaragdina: Ein Beitrag Zur Geschichte Der Hermetischen Literatur* (Heidelberg, 1926).

Rypka, 'Poets and prose writers of the late Saljuq and Mongol periods', in J.A. Boyle (ed.), *Cambridge History of Iran*, V: *The Saljuq and Mongol Periods* (Cambridge, 1968), pp. 582–3.

Saccone, Carlo, 'The wasteland and Alexander, the righteous king, in Niẓāmī's *Iqbālnāma*', in J. Christoph Bürgel and Christine van Ruymbeke (eds), *A Key to the Treasure of the Hakīm* (Leiden, 2011), pp. 165–79.

Ṣafā, Dh., *Ḥamāsa-sarāyī dar Irān* (Tehran, 1363/1984).

——— *Tārīkh-i Adabīyāt dar Irān*, 12th edn (Tehran, 1371/1992), vol. I.

——— *Tārīkh-i adabīyāt dar Irān*, 13th edn (Tehran, 1373/1994), vol. II.

Ṣafavī, Sayyid Ḥasan, *Iskandar va adabīyāt-i Irān va shakhsīyat-i madhhabī-yi Iskandar* (Tehran, 1364/1985).

Ṣā'ib Tabrīzī, *Dīvān*, ed., Muḥammad Qahrimān (Tehran, 1370/1991).

Sanā'ī, *Kitāb Ḥadīqat al-ḥaqīqa wa sharī'at al-ṭarīqa*, ed. Muḥammad Rawshan (Tehran, 1377/1998).

Sattārī, Jalāl, *Usṭūra-yi Gīlgamish va afsāna-yi Iskandar* (Tehran, 1384/2005).

Schippmann, K., 'Azerbaijan: iii. Pre-Islamic history', *EIr* iii/2, p. 224.

Schmidt, T. S., 'Barbarians in Plutarch's political thought', in L. de Blois, J. Bons, T. Kessels and D. M. Schenkeveld (eds), *The Statesman in Plutarch's Works, Vol. I: Plutarch's Statesman and his Aftermath: Political, Philosophical, and Literary Aspects* (Leiden, 2004), pp. 227–35.

Schwarzbaum, H., *Biblical and Extra-Biblical Legends in Islamic Folk Literature* (Walldorf-Hessen, 1982).

Sellwood, D., Introduction to the Coinage of Parthia, 2nd edn (London, 1980).
——— 'Parthian coins', Cambridge History of Iran, ed. E. Yarshater (Cambridge, 1983), vol. III/1, pp. 279–98.
Seyed-Gohrab, Asghar, F. C. Wilhelmina and F. Doufikar-Aerts, *Gog and Magog: The Clans of Chaos in World Literature* (Rozenberg, 2007).
Shahbazi, Shapur, 'On the Xwadāy-Nāmag', *Iranica Varia: Papers in Honor of Professor Ehsan Yarshater* (Leiden, 1990), pp. 218–23.
——— 'Haft sīn', *EIr* xi/5, p. 525.
——— 'Arsacids: vi. Arsacid Chronology in Traditional History', *EIr* ii, p. 542.
——— 'Historiography II: Pre-Islamic period', *EIr* xii/3, pp. 325–30.
——— 'Early Sasanians' claim to Achaemenid heritage', *Nāma-yi Irān-i Bāstān. The International Journal of Ancient Iranian Studies* i/1 (2001), p. 69.
Shaked, Shaul, 'From Iran to Islam: notes on some themes in transmission', *Jerusalem Studies in Arabic and Islam* iv (1984), pp. 31–67.
——— '*Paymān*: an Iranian idea in contact with Greek thought and Islam', *Transition Periods in Iranian History: Actes du Symposium de Fribourg-en-Brisgau (22–24 mai 1985)*, *Studia Iranica* v (Paris, 1987), pp. 217–40.
Shākī, M., 'Dād nask', *EIr* vi/5, pp. 546–9.
Shapira, Dan D. Y., 'Iranian sources on the Khazars', in P. B. Golden, H. Ben-Shammai and A. Róna-Tas (eds), *The World of the Khazars* (Leiden, 2007), pp. 298–305.
Shayegan, M. Rahim, *Arsacids and Sasanians: Political Ideology in Post-Hellenic and Late Antique Persia* (Cambridge, 2011).
Sheikh, M. Saeed, *A Dictionary of Muslim Philosophy*, 2nd edn (Lahore, 1981).
Shi'ār, J (ed.), *Qiṣṣa-yi Amīr Ḥamza* (Tehran, 1347/1968).
Sims-Williams, N., 'Christian literature in Middle Iranian languages', in Ronald E. Emmerick and Maria Macuch (eds), *The Literature of Pre-Islamic Iran* (London/New York, 2009), pp. 266–70.
Soudavar, A., *The Aura of Kings: Legitimacy and Divine Sanction in Iranian Kingship* (Costa Mesa, 2003).
Southgate, M.S., 'Portrait of Alexander the Great in Persian *Alexander Romances* of the Islamic era', *Journal of the American Oriental Society* xcvii (1977), pp. 278–84.
——— (trans.), *Iskandarnamah: A Persian Medieval Alexander-Romance* (New York, 1978).
Standish, W. F., 'The Caspian Gates', *Greece & Rome* xvii (1970), pp. 12–24.
Stark, Freya, *Alexander's Path* (New York, 1988).
Steingass, Francis Joseph, *A Comprehensive Persian–English Dictionary* (London, 1963).
Stephen, H. Rapp Jr, *The Sasanian World through Georgian Eyes: Caucasia and the Iranian Commonwealth in Late Antique Georgian Literature* (Farnham, 2014).
Stone, C. and P. Lunde, *Ibn Faḍlān and the Land of Darkness: Arab Travellers in the Far North* (London, 2012).
Stoneman, Richard (trans.), *The Greek Alexander Romance* (London/New York, 1991).
——— 'Romantic ethnography: Central Asia and India in the *Alexander Romance*', *Ancient World* xxv (1994), pp. 93–107.
——— 'Who are the Brahmans? Indian lore and Cynic doctrine in Palladius' *De Brahmanibus* and its models', *Classical Quarterly* xliv/2 (1994), p. 507.
——— 'Naked philosophers: the Brahmans in the Alexander historians and the *Alexander Romance*', *Journal of Hellenic Studies* cxv (1995), pp. 99–114.

——— 'The Latin Alexander', *Latin Fiction*, ed. H. Hofmann (London, 1999), pp. 167–8.

——— 'The legacy of Alexander in ancient philosophy', *Brill's Companion to Alexander the Great*, ed. J. Roisman (Leiden, 2003), pp. 325–46.

——— *Il Romanzo di Alessandro*, trans. T. Gargiulo (Milan, 2007).

——— *Alexander the Great: A Life in Legend* (New Haven, 2008).

——— 'Tales of Utopia: Alexander, Cynics and Christian ascetics', Paper given at *ICAN IV: International Conference on the Ancient Novel: Crossroads in the Ancient Novel: Spaces, Frontiers, Intersections*, Lisbon, 21–6 July 2008.

——— 'The author of the *Alexander Romance*', *Readers and Writers in the Ancient Novel*, eds M. Paschalis, S. Panayotakis and G. Schmeling (Groningen, 2009), pp. 142–54.

——— 'Primary sources from the classical and early medieval periods', *A Companion to Alexander Literature in the Middle Ages*, ed. Z. David Zuwiyya (Leiden/Boston, 2011), pp. 1–9.

——— 'Persian aspects of the romance tradition', in R. Stoneman, K. Erickson, I. Netton (eds), *The Alexander Romance in Persia and the East* (Groningen, 2012), pp. 14–17.

——— 'The origins of Quintus Curtius' concept of fortuna', Paper given at the conference *Curtius Rufus The Roman Historian on Alexander Narrative Technique, Rhetoric, Psychology of Characters*, Wien, 4 October 2014.

——— *Xerxes: A Persian Life* (London, 2015).

——— 'Alexander's mirror', in *Temenos Academy Review* xix (2016), pp. 46–65.

Storey, Ch. Ambrose, *Persian Literature: Poetry to ca.* AD *1100* (London, 1997).

Sundermann, Werner, 'Mani', *EIr*, Online edition. Available at http://www.iranicaonline.org/articles/mani-founder-manicheism.

Sutūda, M (ed.), *Ḥudūd al-'ālam min al-mashriq ilā maghrib* (Tehran, 1362/1983).

Swain, Simon, *Themistius, Julian and Greek Political Theory under Rome: Texts, Translations and Studies of Four Key Works* (Cambridge, 2013).

Szalc, A., 'In search of Water of Life: the *Alexander Romance* and Indian mythology', in Richard Stoneman, Kyle Erickson and Ian Netton (eds), *The Alexander Romance in Persia and the East* (Groningen, 2012), pp. 327–38.

Ṭabarī, *Tārīkh al-rusul va al-mulūk*, ed. Dodge (Leiden, 1879–81).

——— *The History of al-Ṭabarī (Tārīkh al-rusul wa'l-mulūk), Vol. IV: The Ancient Kingdoms*, ed. E. Yarshater, trans. and annotated Moshe Perlmann and Shaul Shaked (New York, 1987).

Tafaḍḍulī, A., *Tārīkh-i adabīyāt-i Irān pīsh az Islam*, ed. Zh. Āmūzgār (Tehran, 1376/1997).

——— 'Dehqān i: in the Sasanian period', *EIr* vii/2, pp. 223–4.

——— 'Dehqān', *EIr* vii/2, pp. 223–4 and vii/3, pp. 225–6.

Ṭarsūsī, *Dārābnāma*, ed. Dh. Ṣafā, 2 vols (Tehran, 1344/1965–1346/1968).

——— *Alexandre le Grand en Iran: Le Dārāb Nāmeh d'Abū Ṭāhir Ṭarsūsī*, trans. and annotated Marina Gaillard (Paris, 2005).

Tatum, James, *Xenophon's Imperial Fiction: On the Education of Cyrus* (Princeton, 1989).

Tha'ālibī Nīshābūrī, *Tārīkh ghurar al-sayr*, ed. H. Zotenberg (Paris, 1900; repr. Tehran, 1342/1963).

Thorndike, Lynn, 'The Latin pseudo-Aristotle and medieval occult science', *Journal of English and Germanic Philology* xxi/2 (1922), pp. 229–58.

——— 'The Latin translations of astrological works by Messahala', *Osiris* xii (1956), pp. 49–72.

Troxell, H. A., *Studies in the Macedonian Coinage of Alexander the Great* (New York, 1997).

Trumpf, J., *Vita Alexandri regis Macedonum* (Stuttgart, 1974).

Ṭūsī, Aḥmad, *'Ajāyib al-makhlūqāt va gharāyib al-mawjūdāt*, ed. M. Sutūda (Tehran, 1345/1966).

'Unṣūrī Balkhī, *Dīvān*, ed. Muḥammad Dabīr Siyāqī (Tehran, 1363/1984).

Vaḥīd Dastgirdī, Ḥ., *Ganjīna-yi Ganjayī*, ed. S. Ḥamīdīyān (Tehran, 1376/1997).

Valerius, Julius, *Res gestae Alexandri Macedonis translatae ex Aesopo Graeco*, ed. M. Rossellini, 2nd edn (Munich, 2004).

Van Bekkum, W. Jac., 'Alexander the Great in medieval Hebrew literature', *Journal of the Warburg and Courtauld Institutes* xlix (1986), pp. 218–26.

——— *A Hebrew Alexander Romance according to MS Héb. 671.5 Paris, Bibliothèque nationale*, Hebrew Language and Literature Series 1 (Groningen, 1994).

——— 'Medieval Hebrew versions of the *Alexander Romance*', in A. Welkenhuysen, H. Braet, W. Verbeke (eds), *Medieval Antiquity* (Leuven, 1995), p. 296.

——— (ed. and trans.), *A Hebrew Alexander Romance according to MS London, Jews' College no. 145*, Orientalia Lovaniensia analecta 47 (Leuven, 1992).

Van Bladel, Kevin, 'The Syriac sources of the early Arabic narratives of Alexander', in H. Prabha Ray and D. T. Potts (eds), *Memory as History: The Legacy of Alexander in South Asia* (New Delhi, 2007), pp. 54–75.

——— *The Arabic Hermes: From Pagan Sage to Prophet of Science* (Oxford, 2009).

——— 'Hermes and Hermetica', in Kate Fleet, Gudrun Krämer, Denis Matringe, John Nawas and Everett Rowson (eds), *Encyclopaedia of Islam*, 3rd edn Brill Online.

Van Donzel, E. and A. Schmidt, *Gog and Magog in Early Eastern Christian and Islamic Sources: Sallam's Quest for Alexander's Wall* (Leiden, 2002).

Van Ruymbeke, Christine, *Science and Poetry in Medieval Persia: The Botany of Nizami's Khamsa* (Cambridge, 2007).

——— 'Hellenistic influences in classical Persian literature', in J. T. P. de Bruijn (ed.), *General Introduction to Persian Literature* (New York, 2009), pp. 345–68.

Van Thiel, H., *Die Rezension Lambda des Pseudo-Kallisthenes* (Bonn, 1959).

——— *Leben und Täten Alexanders von Makedonien: Der griechische Alexanderroman nach der Handschrift L* (Darmstadt, 1983).

Venetis, E., 'The Iskandarnama: an analysis of an anonymous medieval Persian prose romance' (PhD thesis, University of Edinburgh, 2006).

Vernet, J., 'al-Madjrīṭī', *EI* [2], Brill online.

Warner, Arthur George and Edmond Warner (trans.), *Shahnama of Firdausi* (London, 1912), vol. VI.

Watt, W. Montgomery, 'Ḥanīf', *EI* [2] iii, pp. 165–6.

Weinfield, Paul, 'The Islamic Alexander: a religious and political theme in Arabic and Persian literature' (PhD thesis, Columbia University, 2008).

Wensinck, A. J., 'Hadjdj', *EI* [2] iii, pp. 31–3.

——— 'al-Khaḍir', *EI* [2] iv, pp. 902–5.

——— 'Isrāfīl', *EI* [2] iv, p. 211.

Wheeler, Brannon M., *Moses in the Quran and Islamic Exegesis* (London/New York, 2002).

Wiesehöfer, Josef, 'The "accursed" and the "adventurer": Alexander the Great in Iranian tradition', in Z. David Zuwiyya (ed.), *A Companion to Alexander Literature in the Middle Ages* (Leiden/Boston, 2011), pp. 113–32.

Wilberforce Clarke, H., *The Sikandar Nāma e Bará* (London, 1881).

Williams, D (ed.), *The Art of the Greek Goldsmith* (London, 1998).

Wolohojian, A., *The Romance of Alexander the Great by Pseudo-Callisthenes* (New York, 1969).

Yamamoto, Keiji, 'Abū Ma'shar al-Balkhī', in Thomas Hockey et al. (ed.), *The Biographical Encyclopaedia of Astronomers* (New York, 2007), p. 11.

Yamanaka, Yuriko, 'From evil destroyer to Islamic hero: the transformation of Alexander the Great's image in Iran', *Annals of Japan Association for Middle East Studies* viii (1993), pp. 55–87.

——— 'The philosopher and the wise king: Aristotle and Alexander the Great in Arabic and Persian literature', in A. Etman (ed.), *Proceedings of the International Congress on Comparative Literature in the Arab World* (Cairo, 1998), pp. 73–88.

——— 'Ambiguité de l'image d'Alexandre chez Firdawsi: les traces des traditions sassanides dans le *Livre des Rois*', in Laurence Harf-Lancner, Claire Kappler and François Suard (eds), *Alexandre le Grand dans les littératures occidentales et proche-orientales* (Paris, 1999), pp. 341–53.

——— 'Alexander in the Thousand and One Nights and the Ghazālī connection', in Y. Yamanaka and T. Nishio (eds), *The Arabian Nights and Orientalism: Perspectives from East and West* (New York/London, 2006), pp. 93–115.

——— *Arekusandā-henso: kodai kara chusei isurāmu e* {*The Allegoresis of Alexander the Great: From Antiquity to Medieval Islam*} (Nagoya, 2009).

Ya'qūbī, *Tārīkh al-Ya'qūbī* (Beirut, 1960).

Yarshater, E., 'Were the Sasanians heirs to the Achaemenids?', *Academia Nazionale dei Lincei: Problemi attuali de scienza e cultura: Atti congegno internazionale sul themo La Persia nel medioevo* (Rome, 1971), pp. 517–31.

——— 'Chirā dar *Shāhnāma* az pādishāhān-i mād va hakhāmanishī dhikrī nīst?', *Shāhnāma-Shināsī* i (1357/1978), pp. 268–301.

——— 'Iranian national history', in E. Yarshater (ed.), *Cambridge History of Iran* (Cambridge, 1983), vol. III/1, pp. 359–481.

——— 'Iran: iii. Traditional history', *EIr* xiii/3, pp. 299–307.

Yoshida, Y., 'Buddhist literature in Sogdian', in Ronald E. Emmerick and M. Macuch (eds), *The Literature of Pre-Islamic Iran: Companion Volume I to A History of Persian Literature* (London/New York, 2009), pp. 288–329.

Zaehner, *The Dawn and Twilight of Zoroastrianism* (London, 1961).

——— *Zurvan: A Zoroastrian Dilemma* (New York, 1972).

Ẓahīrī Samarqandī, *Sindbādnāma*, ed. A. Qawīm (Tehran, 1333/1954).

Zarrīnkūb, *Tārīkh dar tarāzū* (Tehran, 1354/1975).

——— 'Niẓāmī, a life-long quest for a Utopia', *Colloquio sul poeta Persiano Niẓāmī e la leggenda Iranica di Alessandro Magno (Roma, 25–26 marzo 1975)* (Roma, 1977), pp. 5–10.

——— 'Falsafa-yi yūnān dar bazm-i Iskandar: Naẓarī bi *Iskandarnāma*-yi Niẓāmī', *Irānshināsī*, xi (1370/1991), pp. 482–98.

Zeimal, E. V., 'The Kidarite Kingdom and Central Asia', in B. A. Litvinsky (ed.), *History of Civilizations in Central Asia* (Paris, 1996), vol. III, pp. 119–33.

Ziai, H., 'Dreams and dream interpretation: ii. In the Persian tradition', *EIr* vii/5, pp. 549–51.

Zuwiyya, *Islamic Legends Concerning Alexander the Great* (New York, 2001).

——— 'The riddles of kings and philosophers in 'Umāra ibn Zayd's *Qiṣṣat al-Iskandar*', in Raif Georges Khoury, Juan Pedro Monferrer-Sala and María Jesus Viguera Molins (eds), *Legendaria medievalia: en honor de Concepción Castillo Castillo* (Cordoba, 2011), pp. 285–94.

INDEX

'Abbāsid, 2, 27, 201n.10
Abraham, 50, 95, 108, 110, 208n.111
Abū Manṣūr, 9, 26, 47, 62, 70, 164, 200n.169, 206n.79
Achaemenid, 25–7, 43, 135, 161, 163, 183n.27, 183n.28
Adab, 8
Adam (and Eve), 150
Afrāsīyāb, 16, 51, 65, 66, 214n.240
Africa, 95–7, 170
Afrīdhūn/Frīdūn (king), 36
Afshār, Īraj, 6, 176n.7, 176n.10, 198n.136, 217n.302, 219n.8
Agathias, 24, 182n.17, 188n.142, 230n.10
Ahl al-Kahf (Sura), 124, 150
Ahrīman, 29, 30, 64, 185n.66
Ā'īna-yi Iskandarī (Amīr Khusraw), 8, 13, 71, 178n.19, 212n.191, 225n.97
'Ajam, 45
Alexander Severus, 30
Alexander Poem, 14, 179n.34
Alexander Romance (AR)/Pseudo-Callisthenes
 AR (Arabic), 3, 8, 9, 11, 13, 15, 17–19, 22, 28, 42
 AR (Armenian), 11, 79
 AR (Ethiopic), 17, 19, 159, 227n.137
 AR (Greek), 1–5, 8, 9, 11, 17, 18, 20, 31, 32, 33, 34, 38, 39, 40, 50, 55, 65, 66, 67, 68, 69, 72, 89, 97, 98, 99, 101, 102, 103, 106, 112, 121, 126, 141, 146, 148, 153, 158, 159, 163
 AR (Hebrew), 32, 186n.89, 186n.90, 186n.91
 AR (Latin), 11
 AR (Middle Persian), 3, 8, 16, 17, 18, 21, 22, 23, 32, 42, 43, 44, 55, 70, 159, 160–4, 176n.9, 189n.148
 AR (Syriac), 3, 5, 11, 13, 14, 17, 18–19, 31, 32, 38, 42–5, 52, 55, 62–3, 70, 93, 99–102, 114, 159, 163, 176n.9
Alexandria (city of), 4, 11, 16, 20, 43, 44, 45, 51, 97, 98, 102, 120, 133, 140–2, 154, 158, 161, 170, 174, 175n.5, 179n.29, 225n.97
Alī Shīr Navā'ī, 8
Amazons, 37, 173, 192n.39
Amid (city), 14
Amīr Khusraw (of Delhi), 8, 13, 212n.191, 225n.97
Ammon, 93, 167, 168, 170

Anāhītā (goddess), 7, 30, 185n.72
Andalusia/Andalus, 50, 52–4, 80, 112, 140, 212n.213
Anderson, A. R., 204n.52, 213n.230
Angel (Isrāfīl), 50, 62, 68, 86, 199n.155
angel *(surūsh)*, 139
Antigonus, 173
Anūshīrvān (Khusraw I), 24, 43, 96, 114, 161, 163, 188n.126, 201n.9
Apocalypse (Pseudo-Methodius), 12, 178n.21
apocalypse/apocalyptic, 14, 65–6, 164, 198n.140
Apollo (temple of), 102, 171
Apollonius of Tyana (Balīnās), 109, 113, 129, 130, 134, 135, 148, 153, 212n.191, 221n.42, 230n.176
Arabian Nights see Thousand and One Nights
Arbela, 39, 104, 186n.93
Archpriest Leo, 11
Ardawān II, 27, 161
Aristotle, 16, 38, 41, 42, 48, 51, 62, 77, 94, 96, 109, 127, 129–31, 135, 140, 152, 156, 168–70, 173, 179n.29, 190n.14, 203n.39, 208n.109, 209n.129, 217n.292, 219n.6, 229n.175
Aristotle Letter, 37, 63, 65, 141, 145, 148, 173, 192n.36, 197n.127
Arrian, 10, 79, 114, 187n.107, 223n.67
Ashkānīyān/Arsacids, 22, 26, 27, 161
assassins/murderer (of Darius), 33, 41, 172, 187n.102, 191n.21
Āthār al-bāqīya (*Chronology of Ancient Nations*), 23, 29, 87, 156
Avesta/Avestan, 25, 35, 63, 64, 95, 107, 108, 125, 197n.125, 226n.130
Bāb al-abwāb, 79
Babylon/Babylonian, 16, 38, 50, 51, 61, 65, 69, 108, 110, 123, 130, 131, 152, 173, 174, 192n.48
Bāgniqyā (city), 16, 38
Bahman/Bahman Ardaxshīr (King), 28, 29, 63, 95, 161, 185n.64
Bahrām V Gōr/Bahrām Gūr, 4, 24, 165, 203n.35
Balīnās *see* Apollonius of Tyana
Balkh, 115, 174
Bertels, Y. E., 8, 204n.50
Bible/biblical, 14, 90, 120, 122, 124, 125, 217n.303
birds (speak Greek), 50, 67, 68
Bīrūnī, Abū Rayḥān, 23, 29, 156
Bladel, K. van, 18, 19
Bocados de Oro (Mubashshir ibn Fatik), 132, 220n.22
Book of Nahmuṭān on the Nativities (Abū Sahl ibn Nawbakht), 35
Book of Nativities (*Kitāb al-Mawālīd*), 35
Boyce, M., 26, 42, 45, 55, 70, 163
Brahmans, 12, 37, 39, 50, 56, 60, 62, 66, 67, 136, 152, 173, 196n.103
Bucephalus, 168
Budge, Wallis, 13, 14, 43, 163
Bukhāra, 42, 147

Candace/Qaidāfa, 37, 50–1, 54, 80, 89, 111, 173
Candaules, 173
cannibals, 171
Caracalla, 30
Carthage, 169
Chaucer (*Canterbury Tales*), 175n.1
chawgān/polo/*ṣawlajān*, 32, 100, 101, 210n.142
China, 14, 37, 39, 50, 74, 89, 111, 115, 116, 130, 147, 149, 173
Christian Syriac Alexander Legend, 13, 14, 22, 52, 120, 137, 150
Ciancaglini, C. A., 17–19, 163, 180n.53
City of Brass, 143

Constantinople (city), 142
Copts/Coptic, 36, 219n.6
Ctesiphon, 24
Curtius, 10, 157

Ḍaḥḥāk, 16
Dandamis/Dindimus, 56, 136, 196n.103
Daniel (Book of), 87
Dārā/Dārāb/Darius, 17, 19, 21, 23, 24, 28–36, 41, 43, 44, 46, 48–9, 51, 54, 55, 70, 82, 85, 87–91, 95, 98–106, 108, 109, 115, 156, 162, 164, 169–72
Dārābnāma (of Ṭarsūsī), 6, 7, 8, 142, 161, 162
Darband, 79, 82, 85, 88, 110, 113–15, 204n.51, 204n.53, 204n.54, 214n.235
Darius *see* Dārā
Darkness (Land of), 14, 21, 37, 50, 76, 85, 111, 118, 121–3, 146, 216n.279, 216n.284
Daryaee, T., 25–7, 30, 36, 43, 161
Davis, D., 30, 47, 165
Dhū'l-Qarnayn/Bicornous/Two-Horned One, 7, 8, 23, 53, 61, 66, 124, 129, 130, 137–8, 142, 145, 148, 150, 152, 154, 156, 166, 182n.10
Dīnawarī, 5, 23, 27, 28, 32, 33, 37, 38, 44, 53, 62, 110, 162, 163
Diodorus, 10
Diogenes (the Cynic), 133, 134, 221n.37
Dionysus (Temple of), 37, 168
diving bell, 11, 13
Doufikar-Aerts, F. C. W., 8, 9, 18, 19, 22, 56, 132, 137

ears (giant), 51, 52, 65, 138, 139, 198n.136
Edessa, 14
Egypt/Egyptian, 13, 14, 16, 20, 36, 43, 50, 51, 93, 96–8, 102, 141, 154, 158, 167, 168
Epistola Alexandri ad Aristotelem (Alexander's Letter to Aristotle) *see* Aristotle Letter
Epistolary Romance, 98
Estalraglos (river), 170
Euphrates, 16, 33, 48, 104
Eutychius (of Alexandria), 15

Farrukhī Sīstānī, 1, 10, 162
Firdawsī, (Abu 'l-Qāsim), 4–9, 15, 17, 20, 22–7, 29–35, 37, 38, 42, 45–7, 49, 51–5, 57–70, 71, 75, 76, 86, 88, 89, 91, 99, 103, 104, 106, 109, 111, 122, 125, 126, 149, 160, 162–5
flying machine, 11, 68
Fountain of Life, 14, 15, 68, 69, 76, 121–4
Frye, R. N., 17, 163
Fūr *see* Porus

Gaillard, M., 7
garlic, 29–30
geographical (works), 18, 22, 23
Georgia/Georgian, 79, 110, 111
Ghurar akhbār (Tha'ālibī), 27, 32, 55, 62, 164
gnomic (literature), 132 *see also* wisdom literature
Gog and Magog, 14, 15, 50, 52, 65, 66, 70, 79, 114, 115, 120, 124, 130, 137, 150, 164, 178n.21
golden eggs, 28, 31, 41, 48, 52, 169, 190n.13
Gōsāns (court minstrel), 27
Grignaschi, M., 29
Guidi, I., 15, 16
gujastak/cursed one, 16
Gushtāsp, 35

Ḥāfiz (of Shīrāz), 21
Haft Paykar (Niẓāmī Ganjavī), 4, 165, 200n.2, 203n.32, 204n.56, 206n.95
Hamadān (city of), 33, 41
Hamadānī, Ibn al-Faqīh, 23, 33
Ḥamza Iṣfahānī, 23, 36
Heraclius (Emperor), 14, 120
Hercules, 168, 197n.133
Hermes/Hermetism, 129, 130, 135, 219n.6
al-Ḥikma al-Khālida (Miskawayh), 209n.121
Hirāt, 38
Historia de Proeliis, 11, 87
Homer/Homeric, 46, 171, 190n.12
horns (Alexander's), 7, 23, 53, 93, 124, 129, 138, 139, 167, 218n.303
Ḥunayn ibn Isḥāq, 132, 220n.20
Huns, 120

Ibn al-Muqaffaʿ (ʿAbd Allāh), 29, 42, 44, 45
Ibn Nadīm, 144, 145, 162
Ilyās (Prophet), 122, 123
India/Indian, 15, 37, 42, 44, 49, 52, 54, 55, 58–67, 69, 71, 73, 74, 82, 85, 89, 93, 95, 111, 115, 123, 129, 130, 136, 141, 145, 147, 152, 164, 172
Iqbālnāma (Niẓāmī Ganjavī), 4, 5, 72, 73, 74, 114, 124, 128–33, 135–7, 140, 141, 144–6, 148, 149, 152, 154–7
Īraj, 36
Irānshar, 16
Isfandīyār, 29, 35, 52, 63, 88, 95, 162, 166
Iskandarnāma (of Niẓāmī Ganjavī), 4, 7, 8, 60, 70–4, 76–81, 114, 116, 127, 132–4, 138, 154, 155, 156, 162, 165–6, 200n.2
Iskandarnāma-yi manthūr (the anonymous), 6
Iskandarūs, 29, 39
Ismael, 50
Iṣṭakhr/Persepolis, 35, 48, 109

Jacob of Serūgh, 14, 124, 179n.35
Jahrum (city), 33, 48
Jāmī, 8, 71, 155
Jamshīd, 85
Jānūspār/Jānūshyār, 33, 49
Jazīra (city), 33, 104, 186n.93
Jerusalem, 11, 12, 40, 86, 87, 110, 140, 141, 156
Jew/Jewish, 79, 80, 87, 90, 93, 110, 120, 122, 124, 125, 127, 145, 156, 165
Josephus (Flavius), 87, 120
Julius Valerius, 11
Justin, 10
Justinian, 43, 162

Kand/Kayhan/Kayd/Kind/Qaydar, 49, 52, 54, 55–6, 58–62, 164 *see also* Dandamis
Kārēn, 26
Kayānids/Kayānīyān, 5, 19, 22–7, 29, 33, 41, 44, 63, 70, 103, 107, 161–3
Kayvānī, M., 7
Khaleghi-Motlagh, J., 9, 23, 33, 42, 45, 47, 59, 62, 64, 164
Khāqānī, 1, 111, 121
Khiḍr, 75, 76, 77, 122, 123, 158
Khudāynāmag (*Book of Sovereigns*)/ *Xwadāy-nāmag*, 3–7, 9, 23–30, 32, 37, 41–7, 52, 53, 55, 62, 70, 162–4
Khurāsān, 4, 38, 45, 47, 56, 70, 115, 162, 165
Khusraw I (Anūshīrvān), 24, 43, 96, 114, 161, 163
Khusraw II (Khusraw Parviz), 4, 14, 15, 120, 163, 165
Khusraw o Shīrīn (Niẓāmī Ganjavī), 4, 80, 165

Khuzistān Chronicle, 13, 15, 38
Kitāb al-Akhbār al-ṭawāl (Dīnawarī), 28, 32, 110
Kitāb al-Buldān, 23
Kitāb al-Mawālīd/*Book of Nativities*, 35

Laments/*Laments of Philosophers at Alexander's Funeral*, 13, 15, 52
Land of the Blessed, 151
Land of Darkness, 14, 21, 37, 50, 76, 85, 111, 118, 121–3, 146, 216n.284
Letter of Consolation, 51, 130, 152, 153, 220n.25
lighthouse/Pharos, 141, 142, 225n.97
Los Buenos Proverbios (Hunayn ibn Ishaq), 132
Luhrāsp, 35

Macedon/Macedonia, 29, 30, 54, 64, 77, 81, 86, 90, 97, 101, 140, 166, 167, 171, 172, 174
Macuch, M., 26
Māhyār, 33, 49
Mas'ūdī, 15, 55, 59, 62, 90
Mecca, 37, 50, 52, 53, 89, 109, 110, 162
Medes, 25
Merv (city of), 16, 38, 42, 115, 174, 180n.46
Mesopotamia, 14
Middle Persian, 2, 3, 8, 9, 16–19, 21, 22–4, 27, 28, 30–3, 35, 36, 38, 41–5, 55, 65, 70, 107, 109, 159–64
Mihrigān, 35
mirabilia, 4, 50, 129, 140, 141, 154, 159
Mirror for Princes, 4, 70, 72, 95, 96, 127, 128, 132, 140, 154, 159
Monferrer-Sala, J. P., 18, 19
monster, 37, 142, 155
Moses/Mūsā, 57, 87, 123, 124
Mosul/Mawsul, 104, 108
Mount Alburz, 88, 103, 113–15
Mujamal al-tavārīkh, 44
mulūk al-ṭawā'if/*kadag-xwādāy*, 38, 42

Nāhīd/Ānāhītā, 7, 48, 54, 55
Nawbakht (Abū Sahl ibn), 35
Nawrūz, 35, 108
Nectanebo, 14, 44, 167, 168, 170
Nihāya (Pseudo-Asma'i), 23, 27, 29, 32, 33, 37, 38, 44, 45, 62, 101, 162, 163
Nöldeke, Th., 6, 9, 15, 17–19, 42, 43, 56, 159, 163, 164

ocean, 65, 92, 95, 98, 142, 148, 149
Olympias, 13, 141, 167, 168, 169, 173, 174

Pahlavi *see* Middle Persian
pahlawān, 26
Paradise, 143, 144
Parthians, 25–7, 43, 70, 114, 161, 165
Pella, 168, 169
Pharos *see* lighthouse
Philip II (of Macedon)/Fīlifūs, 16, 28, 29, 31, 41, 48, 54, 86, 90–2, 94, 142, 161, 168, 169
philosopher-king, 153, 203n.42
philosophy/philosopher, 35, 77, 82, 133–7, 140, 153, 168
Pīshdādīyān, 22
Plutarch, 10, 93, 94, 152, 157
Porus/Fūr, 37, 42, 49, 66, 69, 89, 172, 173
prophecy, 71, 82, 103
Ptolemy, 110, 142, 174, 192

Quintus Curtius, 157
Qur'ān, 7, 8, 14, 23, 66, 110, 123–5, 137, 141, 150, 152, 156, 166

Rome, 90, 135, 169
Roxane/Rawshanak, 35, 41, 42, 44, 49, 89, 106, 109, 172

Salm, 36
Samarqand, 38, 42, 73, 82, 85, 115, 174
sandar (herb), 28–30, 41
Sasanian, 2–4, 6, 7, 9, 13–17, 19, 21, 22, 24–7, 31, 35, 36–8, 42–4, 47, 53, 56, 62, 70, 72, 91, 93, 96, 110, 114, 120, 122, 125, 156, 160–5
Saturn, 93
Sayr al-mulūk, 24, 44, 45 *see also Khudāynāmag*
Secretum Secretorum/Sirr al-Asrar, 132
Serāfīl/Isrāfīl, 50, 68
Shahbazi, Sh., 24, 25
Shāhnāma (Firdawsī), 4–9, 15, 20, 22–7, 29, 30–5, 37, 38, 42, 45–7, 51–6, 58, 60, 61–70, 75, 86, 88, 89, 91, 98, 101, 106, 109, 112, 122, 125, 160, 162–5
Shāpūr II, 25, 43
Sharafnāma (Niẓāmī Ganjavī), 4, 5, 32, 72–4, 76, 85, 86, 88–90, 93–100, 102, 104, 106–11, 114, 115, 119, 121, 122, 124–8, 134, 149, 155, 156, 165
Sīrat al-Iskandar, 162
Sirr al-Asrār, 132
snakes and scorpions, 64
Southgate, M. S., 6
statue (talismanic), 148, 149, 155
Stoneman, R., 29, 43, 85, 104, 144, 153
Strangas (River), 39, 172

Ṭabarī, 5, 16, 17, 23, 27–33, 35–8, 44, 53, 62, 101, 162, 163
Ṭabarīstān, 121
Tacitus, 27, 161
Tafaḍḍulī, 26, 37, 42, 45, 55, 70, 163
talisman/talismanic, 94, 148, 149, 155, 156, 229n.175
talking heads, 145
talking trees, 37, 50, 66, 69
Talmud, 87, 123, 143
tanīn (dragon), 53
tārīkh al-mulūk see Khudāynāmag
Tārīkh-i Sīstān (*The Sīstān Chronicle*), 44
Ṭarsūsī/Ṭarṭūsī (Abū Ṭāhir) *see Dārābnāma*
testament (of Alexander), 152, 154
Tha'ālibī Nīshābūrī, 23, 27, 32, 38, 55, 59, 60, 62
Thebes, 171
Thousand and One Nights/Arabian Nights, 146
Tūr, 36
Turkish/Turks, 66, 71, 115, 117
Turkistān, 36

Valerius, Juluis, 11
Valley of Diamonds, 50, 123, 145–6

Wall of Gog and Magog, 50, 79, 83, 85, 114, 115, 120, 130, 137, 149, 150
Wallis Budge, E. A., 13, 14, 43, 163
wisdom literature, 4, 8, 125, 130–2, 137, 154, 159

Xerxes, 43, 103, 172, 190n.13

Ya'qūbī, 15
Yarshater, E., 23, 25
Yazdgird III, 15
Yazdīn (Christian minister), 15
Yemen, 50, 109

Zanj, 95, 98
Zoroastrianism/Zoroastrian, 2, 25, 27, 30, 33, 35, 36, 47, 49, 63–5, 91, 93, 107–10, 123, 125, 156, 160, 161, 165
Zuwiyya, Z. D., 61